CW00945498

PHP : The Complete Reference

About the Author

Steven Holzner is the award-winning author of more than 100 computer books, including three bestsellers on PHP. He's been a contributing editor for *PC Magazine*, teaches programming classes at Fortune 500 companies, and has been on the faculty at Cornell University and MIT.

About the Technical Editor

Chris Cornutt has been involved in the PHP community for about eight or nine years now. Soon after discovering the language, he started up his news site, PHPDeveloper.org, to share the latest happenings and opinions from other PHPers around the world. Chris has written for PHP publications such as *php | architect* and the *International PHP Magazine* on topics ranging from geocoding to trackbacks. He was also a coauthor of the *PHP String Handling Handbook* (Wrox Press, 2003).

Chris lives in Dallas, Texas, with his wife and son and works for a large natural gas distributor, maintaining its Web site and developing PHP-based applications.

PHP : The Complete Reference

Steven Holzner

New York   Chicago   San Francisco
Lisbon   London   Madrid   Mexico City
Milan   New Delhi   San Juan
Seoul   Singapore   Sydney   Toronto

The McGraw·Hill Companies

Library of Congress Cataloging-in-Publication Data

Holzner, Steven.
  PHP: the complete reference/Steven Holzner.
    p. cm.
  ISBN 0-07-150854-6 (alk. paper)
  1. PHP (Computer program language)   I. Title.
  QA76.73.P224H64 2007
  005.2'762—dc22

                          2007044733

McGraw-Hill books are available at special quantity discounts to use as premiums and sales promotions, or for use in corporate training programs. For more information, please write to the Director of Special Sales, Professional Publishing, McGraw-Hill, Two Penn Plaza, New York, NY 10121-2298. Or contact your local bookstore.

PHP: The Complete Reference

Copyright © 2008 by The McGraw-Hill Companies. All rights reserved. Printed in the United States of America. Except as permitted under the Copyright Act of 1976, no part of this publication may be reproduced or distributed in any form or by any means, or stored in a database or retrieval system, without the prior written permission of publisher.

1234567890 FGR FGR 01987

ISBN   978-0-07-150854-4
MHID   0-07-150854-6

Sponsoring Editor Wendy Rinaldi	**Technical Editor** Chris Cornutt	**Composition** International Typesetting and Composition
Editorial Supervisor Patty Mon	**Copy Editor** Robert Campbell	**Illustration** International Typesetting and Composition
Project Manager Aparna Shukla, International Typesetting and Composition	**Proofreader** Ragini Pandey **Indexer** Kevin Broccoli	**Art Director, Cover** Jeff Weeks **Cover Designer** Pattie Lee
Acquisitions Coordinator Mandy Canales	**Production Supervisor** Jean Bodeaux	

Information has been obtained by McGraw-Hill from sources believed to be reliable. However, because of the possibility of human or mechanical error by our sources, McGraw-Hill, or others, McGraw-Hill does not guarantee the accuracy, adequacy, or completeness of any information and is not responsible for any errors or omissions or the results obtained from the use of such information.

To Nancy

Contents at a Glance

1   Essential PHP 1
2   Operators and Flow Control 41
3   Strings and Arrays 81
4   Creating Functions 123
5   Reading Data in Web Pages 161
6   PHP Browser-Handling Power 203
7   Object-Oriented Programming 245
8   Advanced Object-Oriented Programming 281
9   File Handling 319
10 Working with Databases 361
11 Sessions, Cookies, and FTP 395
12 Ajax 433
13 Advanced Ajax 467
14 Drawing Images on the Server 501
15 XML and RSS 537

    Index 575

Contents

Introduction xvii

1 Essential PHP 1

Enter PHP 1

Getting PHP 3

  PHP on the Internet 4

  PHP on Your Local Machine 5

Creating Your Development Environment 6

Creating a First PHP Page 8

Running Your First PHP Page 9

  Some Troubleshooting 9

Mixing HTML and PHP 10

Printing Some Text 14

Printing Some HTML 16

More Echo Power 17

Using PHP "Here" Documents 19

Command-Line PHP 20

Adding Comments to PHP Code 24

Working with Variables 26

Storing Data in Variables 27

Interpolating Strings 31

Creating Variable Variables 33

Creating Constants 35

Understanding PHP's Internal Data Types 37

2 Operators and Flow Control 41

PHP's Math Operators 41

Working with the Assignment Operators 46

Incrementing and Decrementing Values 48

The PHP String Operators 50

The Bitwise Operators 51

The Execution Operator 52

PHP Operator Precedence 53

Using the if Statement 55

The PHP Comparison Operators 59

The PHP Logical Operators 61

The else Statement 63

The elseif Statement 65

The ternary Operator 66

The switch Statement 67

Using for Loops 69

Using while Loops 72

Using do...while Loops 74

Using the foreach Loop 76

Terminating Loops Early 77

Skipping Iterations 78

PHP Alternate Syntax 80

3   Strings and Arrays **81**

The String Functions 81

Converting to and from Strings 87

Formatting Text Strings 88

Building Yourself Some Arrays 92

Modifying the Data in Arrays 95

Deleting Array Elements 97

Handling Arrays with Loops 99

    The for Loop 99

    The print_r Function 100

    The foreach Loop 101

    The while Loop 103

The PHP Array Functions 104

Converting Between Strings and Arrays Using implode and explode 106

Extracting Data from Arrays 107

Sorting Arrays 109

Using PHP's Array Operators 110

Comparing Arrays to Each Other 112

Handling Multidimensional Arrays 112

Using Multidimensional Arrays in Loops 114

Moving Through Arrays 116

Splitting and Merging Arrays 117

Other Array Functions 119

4   Creating Functions **123**

Creating Functions in PHP 123

Passing Functions Some Data 125

Passing Arrays to Functions 127

Passing by Reference 130

Using Default Arguments 132

Passing Variable Numbers of Arguments 133

Returning Data from Functions 135
Returning Arrays 137
Returning Lists 139
Returning References 141
Introducing Variable Scope in PHP 143
Accessing Global Data 145
Working with Static Variables 147
PHP Conditional Functions 150
PHP Variable Functions 153
Nesting Functions 156
Creating Include Files 157
Returning Errors from Functions 158

5   **Reading Data in Web Pages** **161**
Setting Up Web Pages to Communicate with PHP 161
Handling Text Fields 164
Handling Text Areas 167
Handling Check Boxes 170
Handling Radio Buttons 173
Handling List Boxes 175
Handling Password Controls 179
Handling Hidden Controls 182
Handling Image Maps 184
Handling File Uploads 187
Handling Buttons 191
    Making Button Data Persist 192
    Using Submit Buttons as HTML Buttons 195

6   **PHP Browser-Handling Power** **203**
Using PHP's Server Variables 203
Using HTTP Headers 205
Getting the User's Browser Type 206
Redirecting Browsers with HTTP Headers 209
Dumping a Form's Data All at Once 212
Handling Form Data with Custom Arrays 215
Putting It All in One Page 218
Performing Data Validation 221
Checking if the User Entered Required Data 223
Requiring Numbers 227
Requiring Text 230
Persisting User Data 234
Client-Side Data Validation 237
Handling HTML Tags in User Input 241

7   Object-Oriented Programming **245**
   Creating Classes 246
   Creating Objects 250
   Setting Access to Properties and Methods 253
      Public Access 253
      Private Access 254
   Using Constructors to Initialize Objects 257
   Using Destructors to Clean Up after Objects 260
   Basing One Class on Another with Inheritance 262
      Protected Access 264
      Constructors and Inheritance 266
      Calling Base Class Methods 267
   Overriding Methods 271
   Overloading Methods 273
   Autoloading Classes 277

8   Advanced Object-Oriented Programming **281**
   Creating Static Methods 281
      Creating a Static Method 283
      Passing Data to a Static Method 285
      Using Properties in Static Methods 286
   Static Members and Inheritance 291
   Creating Abstract Classes 294
   Creating Interfaces 297
   Supporting Object Iteration 301
   Comparing Objects 304
   Creating Class Constants 306
   Using the final Keyword 308
   Cloning Objects 312
   Reflection 315

9   File Handling **319**
   Opening Files Using fopen 319
   Looping over a File's Contents with feof 322
   Reading Text from a File Using fgets 322
   Closing a File 323
   Reading from a File Character by Character with fgetc 325
   Reading a Whole File at Once with file_get_contents 328
   Reading a File into an Array with file 330
   Checking if a File Exists with file_exists 332
   Getting File Size with filesize 334
   Reading Binary Reads with fread 335

Parsing Files with fscanf 338
Parsing ini Files with parse_ini_file 339
Getting File Info with stat 341
Setting the File Pointer's Location with fseek 343
Copying Files with copy 343
Deleting Files with unlink 345
Writing to a File with fwrite 346
Reading and Writing Binary Files 348
Appending to Files with fwrite 352
Writing a File All at Once with file_put_contents 355
Locking Files 357

10   **Working with Databases** **361**
What Is a Database? 362
Some Essential SQL 362
Creating a MySQL Database 364
Creating a New Table 367
Putting Data into the New Database 368
Accessing the Database in PHP 370
Connecting to the Database Server 371
Connecting to the Database 372
Reading the Table 372
Displaying the Table Data 374
Closing the Connection 376
Updating Databases 377
Inserting New Data Items into a Database 380
Deleting Records 383
Creating New Tables 385
Creating a New Database 389
Sorting Your Data 393

11   **Sessions, Cookies, and FTP** **395**
Setting a Cookie 395
Reading a Cookie 397
Setting Cookies' Expiration 399
Deleting Cookies 400
Working with FTP 402
Downloading Files with FTP 406
Uploading Files with FTP 408
Deleting a File with FTP 411
Creating and Removing Directories with FTP 414
Sending E-mail 416

Sending Advanced E-mail 418
Adding Attachments to E-mail 421
Storing Data in Sessions 425
Writing a Hit Counter Using Sessions 429

12   Ajax 433
Getting Started with Ajax 433
Writing Ajax 435
Creating the XMLHttpRequest Object 436
Opening the XMLHttpRequest Object 440
Handling Downloaded Data 441
Starting the Download 445
Creating XMLHttpRequest Objects 446
Ajax with Some PHP 448
Passing Data to the Server with GET 449
Passing Data to the Server with POST 453
Handling XML 456
Handling XML with PHP 464

13   Advanced Ajax 467
Handling Concurrent Ajax Requests
   with Multiple XMLHttpRequest Objects 467
Handling Concurrent Ajax Requests with an XMLHttpRequest Array 472
Handling Concurrent Ajax Requests with JavaScript Inner Functions 475
Downloading Images Using Ajax 479
Downloading JavaScript with Ajax 481
Connecting to Google Suggest 484
Connecting to Other Domains Using Ajax 494
Logging in with Ajax and PHP 495
Getting Data with Head Requests and Ajax 497

14   Drawing Images on the Server 501
Creating an Image 504
Displaying Images in HTML Pages 506
Drawing Lines 507
Setting Line Thickness 510
Drawing Rectangles 511
Drawing Ellipses 513
Drawing Arcs 514
Drawing Polygons 516
Filling in Figures 518
Drawing Individual Pixels 520
Drawing Text 522

Drawing Vertical Text 525
Working with Image Files 528
Tiling Images 531
Copying Images 535

15 XML and RSS **537**
Creating XML 537
Creating RSS 540
Using the SimpleXML Functions 544
Extracting Attributes 550
Using XPath 552
Modifying XML Elements and Attributes 555
Adding New Elements and Attributes 557
Sending XML to the Browser 560
Interacting with Other PHP XML Packages 561
Parsing with the XML Parser Functions 563

Index **575**

Introduction

This book is your guide to PHP, and it was written to be as complete and comprehensive as possible. It puts the power of PHP to work for you, emphasizing seeing example after example. We push the PHP envelope here, in more than a hundred examples, ready to run.

PHP is a hot topic—it's become the most popular server-side language by far. A Google search for "PHP" results in a hefty 2,890,000,000 hits. That's two billion, eight hundred and ninety million hits, far more than any other server-side language can boast.

What's behind this incredible popularity? PHP is fast and easy to use, fast and easy to develop in. You can mingle it with HTML in your Web pages. You can write it easier than other languages—PHP has learned from their mistakes. You don't need to compile it, as you do with other languages, before running it. But more than all that, developing with PHP is just plain fun. It's just a terrific language that people who write server-side code really enjoy. And this book is all about bringing you that experience.

People who have Web sites are requiring more and more power these days, and increasingly, they're finding their answer in PHP. No longer content to be limited to working with JavaScript in the browser, they want to have the power of writing code to be executed on the server. Guest books, interactive calendars, databases, autoresponder e-mailers, blogs, chat rooms—the things you can do with PHP are unlimited. Using PHP, you have total control over your Web applications—and the good part is that they're not much harder to write than the typical Web page. You can do a lot with a little.

You're getting into PHP at the right time. Excitement is soaring, and PHP is flying high. This book tries to stay as true to the spirit of that excitement as possible, giving you the full PHP experience. You're going to find more PHP in this book than in any similar book as you get the complete details on the PHP story.

This Book Is for You

This is your book if you want to develop all the power that PHP is capable of, and you want to see examples at every step along the way. You might, for example, want to start putting cookies on other people's computers rather than just accepting them on your computer. You might want to read the data the users enter into text fields, list boxes, check boxes, or radio buttons on your Web page. You might want to keep data for your online store in a database on the server. You might want to track users with sessions, gaining the capability to create multipage Web applications.

Whatever your online need, this book is for you.

And this book was written so that you don't need a lot of background to use it. In fact, the only thing you need to know before reading through and working with this book is a knowledge of HTML. You won't need to be an HTML wizard, but you'll need to know some HTML in this book. If you don't have any clue when it comes to HTML, now's the time to look up an online tutorial on the subject.

We use PHP 5.2 in this book—and you may already have it on your server. If not, you'll see where to get it for free in this book, and how to install it. In fact, you won't even need a Internet server that supports PHP to read this book—if you wish, you can develop and test your PHP pages all on the same computer. On the other hand, if you want to put your PHP code on the Internet, you'll need to use an ISP that supports PHP. Check with your ISP to find if they support PHP—more and more ISPs are doing so every day.

This book has been written to be as complete as possible, and to be at the top of its field. If you have questions or comments, please drop me a line—I'd love to hear from you.

Where Can You Get the Code?

All the code for the examples in this book is available online, so you don't have to type it in yourself. You should be able to unzip those examples to your server; they're ready to run (with the exception of examples that need passwords for your database system or to connect to another ISP).

You can get the code for the examples in this book at www.mhprofessional.com. All you have to do is to download the Zip file and unzip it—everything's in there.

Alright, that gives us the start we need. PHP is your gateway to server-side power, and you're going to get a guided tour of PHP in this book. All the PHP that can fit into a single book has been packed in here. All that remains is to get started, by turning to Chapter 1.

Essential PHP

T ake a look at Figure 1-1. That's the Ohio State University home page. Pretty snazzy,
eh? Now take a closer look at the URL in the address bar: http://www.osu.edu/
index.php. That's a PHP page you're looking at, index.php.

Here's another page for you: http://www1.umn.edu/twincities/index.php, the home
page for the University of Minnesota, which appears in Figure 1-2. Also a PHP page, as you
can see from the URL. Not bad.

And here's another one: the Yahoo Maps page you see in Figure 1-3, http://maps.yahoo
.com/index.php. Want driving directions? Just enter your start and end locations into that
page and click Go. PHP will do the rest.

Enter PHP

Welcome to the world of PHP. Officially, PHP stands for "PHP: Hypertext Preprocessor,"
but it's also still known around the world by its original name, Personal Home Page. It's the
server-side programming language that's taken the Web world by storm—PHP is far and
away the most popular programming language for use on Web servers. That's the idea
behind PHP: being able to do some easy programming on the Web server, creating
everything from online databases to guest books, from customer schedulers to chat rooms,
from file uploading tools to shopping carts. It's all possible with PHP.

Where did PHP come from? PHP users are sometimes startled to learn that PHP has been
around for quite some time; it was created by Rasmus Lerdorf in 1994 (Rasmus wanted a
way of logging who was looking at his online résumé). PHP got such a good reputation that
by 1995 it was available for use by other people, and the PHP revolution was underway.

PHP at that time was called Personal Home Page, or Personal Home Page Tools. At that
time, as you might expect, PHP was very simple, and could be used to create Web page hit
counters, guest books, and the like. The 1995 version of PHP was called PHP/FI Version 2
(FI was an HTML form reader package, also written by Rasmus).

In time, Rasmus added support for interfacing with Mini SQL (mSQL), and PHP/FI
started growing at an astonishing rate as more people contributed code to it. There was a
real need for an easy Web server programming language then, and the number of PHP
pages just kept growing. In 1996, PHP/FI was already being used by about 15,000 Web
pages. In 1997, that number grew to more than 50,000.

FIGURE 1-1   The Ohio State Home page

Things started happening fast at that point. In 1997, PHP/FI became just PHP, and more people got involved as PHP teams started appearing. Much core work was redone by Zeev Suraski and Andi Gutmans, and PHP Version 3 appeared—much of it totally rewritten.

Today, PHP is everywhere you look on the Web, with an estimated 100 million PHP pages (it's hard to get accurate statistics—if you do a search on Google for PHP, for example, you get an astounding estimated 2,740,000,000 hits). PHP is still true to its original name: Personal Home Page, because it gives you the easiest way to make your Web pages come alive on the server. But PHP has also become a very professional language, suitable for top-notch sites.

You're going to see it all in this book. This is where your Web pages and applications come alive.

The lid is off the box when you start to work with PHP now. Just about anything you can do on the Web, you can do with PHP. No longer do Web pages have to be static, unchanging things—you're going to be able to interact with users in a safe and secure way, sending them back Web pages tailored to their input. And it all happens in real time.

You can handle button clicks, radio button selections, and list box choices with ease using PHP. You can code simple Web applications such as guest books, or do anything advanced that's possible on the Web: create database applications, client/server applications, and multilayer data processors; create graphics interactively on the server and send them back to the browser; register students for your online school; create Web-based classrooms; and more.

FIGURE 1-2   The University of Minnesota Home page

Static Web pages are, well, static. They can display data just fine, as well as text and images. But there's nothing really going on there—the user can't interact with anything. PHP changes all that by making those Web pages come alive—things start happening on the server side. Unlike languages like JavaScript, which work in the browser and don't create any lasting effects (JavaScript can't write files, and it can't work with data on the server), languages that execute on the server can be used as the basis of true Web applications. Users will be able to open your pages, seeing everything they'd expect from a full-fledged application, including everything from text fields they can enter text in to tables full of data you create on the fly, from retrieving data from databases to fluidly creating graphics— everything you might see on the most professional interactive Web application is now within your grasp. That's the name of the PHP game—being able to respond to the user dynamically, on the fly.

Getting PHP

This book will use PHP 5.2.0, whose official Web site is www.php.net (PHP missed its chance for php.com—that's now the Parents Helping Parents Web site). You're going to need PHP to work with this book, and that's going to mean getting access to a Web server that runs it.

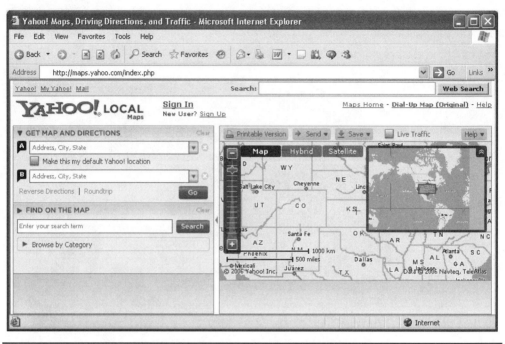

Figure 1-3   The Yahoo Maps page

As of this writing, PHP 6 is in the works. There are many minor changes coming up in PHP 6—none of which should stop your PHP 5 code from running—and a major change: support for Unicode. Unicode (www.unicode.org) is a character set that's designed to encompass many of the world's languages, unlike PHP today. As I'm writing this, support for Unicode in PHP 6 is transparent—that is, your PHP 5 code will run fine. At most, you'll be required to place a directive at the beginning of your scripts indicating whether you want Unicode support turned on or off. And then you'll have the full Unicode character set—everything from Arabic to Cherokee to Tibetan.

PHP on the Internet

In fact, your Internet service provider (ISP) quite probably already supports PHP—you can ask your support staff, or you can try to upload and run a PHP file of the kind we'll be developing shortly.

You can also open a command prompt for your server and check on PHP that way. You can open a command-prompt window connected to your server using various utilities—Telnet, SSH, or SSH2 (you won't need these applications in this book, so don't worry if you don't have them). Windows, for example, comes with a Telnet utility built in—just enter C:\>telnet followed by your ISP's name (e.g., phpbigserver.com), and press ENTER.

Once you have a command prompt open for your server, you can check if PHP is installed with the -v option, which gives the version of PHP if it can be reached (note that

I'm going to use % as a generic command prompt in this book, standing for the command prompt in Windows, Linux, and so forth):

```
%php -v
```

If PHP is installed and accessible, you'll see the PHP version and date displayed like this:

```
%php -v
PHP 5.2.0 (cli) (built: Nov  2 2006 11:57:36)
Copyright (c) 1997-2006 The PHP Group
Zend Engine v2.2.0, Copyright (c) 1998-2006 Zend Technologies
```

The other way to test if you have PHP installed is to upload a PHP script and see if it runs. To do that, check out the sample scripts you'll see in this chapter. Upload such a test script to your ISP, and see if you can access it in your browser.

Note that on Unix-based systems, you have to first explicitly set the permission of the script to *executable,* and most FTP utilities (File Transfer Protocol utilities, including the one built into Windows and accessible by typing **ftp** at a DOS command prompt) will let you set that permission. If you have a PHP script on a Unix-based server, you should set its permissions to Owner: Execute, Read, and Write; Group: Execute and Read; and Public: Execute and Read. Numerically, that works out to a permission setting of 755 for PHP scripts on Unix-based servers.

TIP *If you want a list of ISPs that already run PHP, take a look at www.php.net/links.php#hosts.*

PHP on Your Local Machine

It's a good idea to install PHP on your local machine if you want to do any substantial PHP development (and who doesn't?). That way, you can examine your PHP pages in your Web browser on your machine immediately after you edit them locally. That speeds things up tremendously, and it cuts the development cycle in half. But to do things this way, you'll need PHP installed locally.

Some operating systems, such as Linux, and some versions of Unix, come with PHP already installed. You can test that out with the php -v command, as described in the preceding section. If you get a response showing PHP's creation date, you're all set. In Windows, however, you're going to have to install PHP yourself.

There are prebuilt "binary" versions ready for download and immediate installation for a number of operating systems: Windows, Mac OS X, Novell NetWare, OS/2, RISC OS, SGI IRIX 6.5.x, AS/400. You can find the binary installation package for Windows at www.php .net/downloads.php, along with links to the binaries for the other operating systems mentioned.

You should be able to install PHP on your machine simply by using the appropriate binary file. For example, in Windows, you'll download a Windows installer (.msi) file, and double-click it. Answer the questions it asks, and you're in.

Before installation, you'll have to decide on the Web server you want to use. The installer will currently set up Microsoft Internet Information Server (IIS), Apache, Xitami, and Sambar Server; if you are using a different Web server you'll need to configure it manually using the directions you can find at www.php.net/download-docs.php (download the whole PHP documentation—it includes a section on installation).

The most popular Web server for use with local installations of PHP is the Apache Web server, which you can get at http://httpd.apache.org/. In Windows, however, it's even easier to use Microsoft Internet Information Server (IIS), which comes already built in to most versions of Windows. If you want to check if you've got IIS, look for the directory C:\inetpub—if you've got it, you've got IIS.

You'll also be asked what extensions you want to install (an extension is a PHP add-on, adding functionality). To handle the material this book is going to cover, select the MySQL, GD2, and SMTP extensions.

Tip *If you get stuck during the installation process, you can download the PHP documentation from www.php.net/download-docs.php—there's a special section for help with installation, and that section is extensive, covering an enormous array of issues.*

Downloading the PHP documentation is an excellent idea in any case—that's the official PHP manual, the one that can give you the answers you need if you want the official word on a PHP point.

Creating Your Development Environment

Okay, you've got access to PHP on a server at this point. To actually create PHP scripts, you're going to need to use a text editor of some kind—something that will let you write PHP and save it in files with the extension .php, which is the extension you need to give to PHP scripts (such as shoppingcart.php). There are plenty of editors available on many different operating systems that will work: vi, emacs, pico, Macintosh's BBEdit or SimpleText, Windows Notepad or WordPad.

Your text editor needs to be able to save files in plain text format—that is, text without any special formatting codes. Theoretically, you can even use word processors such as Microsoft Word, as long as you save your PHP pages in plain text format. On Windows, many people use Microsoft WordPad, which comes with Windows. If you are going to use WordPad, make sure you select the Save As Type option Text Document when you save your file, not the default RTF (Rich Text Format) type. WordPad also has the bad habit of appending the suffix .txt to any file whose extension it doesn't understand, and you need to fix that. So if you save a file as chatroom.php, for example, WordPad is going to save it as chatroom.php.txt, which is a problem. To get around that, enclose the name of the file you're saving in quotation marks, such as "chatroom.php". Doing so tells WordPad to keep its hands off the extension—which is good, because unless you use the extension .php for your files, your Web server isn't going to understand that your PHP is indeed a PHP file.

For example, you can see Windows WordPad editing a PHP page in Figure 1-4. That's a mix of HTML and PHP you see in that figure—PHP specializes in letting you insert HTML directly into your PHP pages. We're about to see this page, phphtml.php, in action in a few pages.

You can also use a PHP integrated development environment (IDE) to create your PHP pages. IDEs give you all kinds of tools that simple text editors don't, such as checking what you've written automatically to make sure it's valid PHP; automatic syntax highlighting

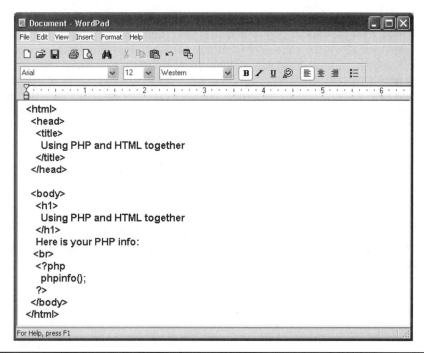

```
<html>
 <head>
  <title>
    Using PHP and HTML together
  </title>
 </head>

 <body>
  <h1>
    Using PHP and HTML together
  </h1>
  Here is your PHP info:
  <br>
  <?php
    phpinfo();
  ?>
 </body>
</html>
```

FIGURE 1-4   Windows WordPad

(which means that items like PHP keywords appear in various colors, making it easy to pick out what's going on at a glance); and automatic deployment, where the IDE can send your PHP pages up to your ISP when you click a button or select a menu item.

Here's a starter list of IDEs available online that can handle PHP. Note, however, that most of them are going to cost money, and although they have some features that are nice to have, we won't rely on those features in this book:

- **Komodo, www.activestate.com/Products/Komodo**   Runs on Linux and Windows.
- **Maguma, www.maguma.com**   Runs on Windows only.
- **PHPEdit, www.phpedit.com/products/PHPEdit**   Free, but runs on Windows only.
- **Zend Studio, www.zend.com/store/products/zend-studio.php**   Runs on Windows and Linux. This one is created by the same people who create the Zend software "engine" that actually runs at the core of PHP itself.

If you're running PHP on an ISP, you're also going to need some way of uploading your PHP to your Web server. You can use the same method you use to upload standard HTML pages to your ISP. For example, you can use a File Transfer Protocol (FTP) program to upload your PHP pages. If you're using a Unix-based server, don't forget to change the permission of your PHP page to executable, as mentioned earlier, under "PHP on the Internet." If you don't have an FTP program, ask your ISP technical staff for recommendations.

Creating a First PHP Page

Here's where the action starts—creating some PHP. This is where your Web applications—from guest books to professional database lookup applications, from interactive games to shopping carts—starts.

This first PHP page will be a very simple one. You can start this page with the special markup that indicates you're about to start using PHP, and that markup looks like this:

```
<?php
    .
    .
    .
```

That's how you start a PHP page—with the markup <?php. That starts a PHP section as far as the PHP engine on the server is concerned.

When the server sends a PHP page back to the browser, the PHP engine starts by opening that page. When it sees the markup <?php, it begins interpreting what follows as PHP. At the end of your PHP, you use the closing markup, which is ?>:

```
<?php
    .
    .
    .
?>
```

Okay, so far we've told the PHP engine on the server that we want to insert some PHP code into the page. Now let's do just that, by adding this line:

```
<?php
  phpinfo()
?>
```

This is a call to the PHP *function* phpinfo(). A function is a grouping of PHP code that is addressable using a single name, such as phpinfo(). PHP functions are coming up in Chapter 5; all that's necessary to know at this point is that when you use the name of the function, the code in that function is executed. In this case, the phpinfo() function creates a table of information about your PHP installation—what's installed, when it was built, and so on—and displays it in the Web page sent back to the browser.

So this first PHP page is just going to display information about the PHP installation itself. In fact, this first line of PHP code is not quite complete—you also have to end every PHP statement with a semicolon (;), so let's add that like this:

```
<?php
  phpinfo();
?>
```

Okay, that's our first PHP page. Save it as phpinfo.php, and load it into your server. As long as your Web server can handle and run PHP pages, you can place this page anywhere you'd place an HTML page. Then just use the URL of the page to view it, something like http://www.yourisp/youraccount/phpinfo.php.

If you're using a local Web server, such as Windows IIS, that means placing phpinfo.php in C;\Inetpub\wwwroot, or a subdirectory of wwwroot, and then opening your browser using an URL like http://localhost/phpinfo.php or http://localhost/*subdirname*/phpinfo .php if you've placed phpinfo.php in a subdirectory of wwwroot.

The code that accompanies this book is stored in the folders ch01 for Chapter 1, ch02 for Chapter 2, and so on. So you'll find phpinfo.php in the ch01 folder.

Running Your First PHP Page

Make sure the Web server is running (if you're using IIS in Windows, it's always running) and navigate to phpinfo.php in your browser, as shown in Figure 1-5. Congratulations, you're running your first PHP page.

You can see the results in that figure—the call to phpinfo() returned an HTML table containing information about your PHP installation. What actually happened is that the phpinfo() function returned the text holding the HTML table, and that table is inserted into the resulting page, which you see in Figure 1-5.

Some Troubleshooting

What if it doesn't work? What if you don't see the display in Figure 1-5? Unfortunately, there are many things that could go wrong, especially with a local installation of PHP. Don't panic—the problem can be fixed. It'll just take a little time.

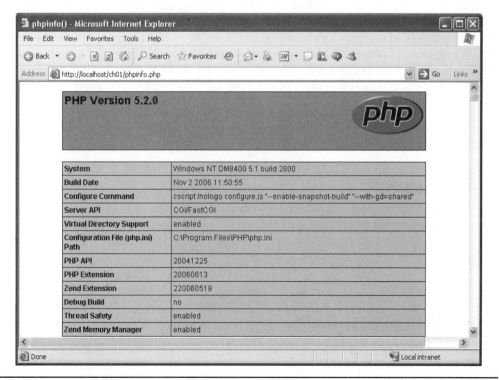

FIGURE 1-5   Calling phpinfo()

First, check if your PHP code was actually run by selecting View | Source in your browser. If you see your original PHP there, it wasn't run by the server. Make sure you did not open phpinfo.php directly in your browser, without running it through your Web server. Do not, for example, just double-click phpinfo.php directly or use your browser's File | Open menu item, because that would open it in your browser directly, without letting your PHP-enabled Web server run it. And your browser is not going to have any idea how to run a function like phpinfo(). So enter the actual URL for phpinfo.php in your browser, and run it that way.

Next, check if PHP is actually running. If you're running PHP locally, that's easy to check: open a command prompt window and try the php -v command. If you see PHP version information, PHP is running. If your PHP installation isn't local, use Telnet or SSH/ SSH2 to check the php -v command on your server. If you don't get version information, PHP might not be running, which would account for any problems with phpinfo.php.

The next most common trouble is that PHP may not have been installed correctly as far as your server is concerned. This is the problem if you get a blank page, and when you do a "view source" in the Web browser, you can see the source code of your PHP script. This means that the Web server did not pass the script to the PHP engine to be run. This can be a little finicky, which is why the instructions from www.php.net are so extensive. The best idea is to go through those directions again, line by line, to make sure you did everything just as it's listed.

Next, make sure that phpinfo.php is where your Web server expects to find it. In the Apache Web server, that's the htdocs directory in the directory where Apache has been installed. For IIS, it's inetpub/wwwroot. In Linux, it may be /var/www/html. The actual directory may be different on various servers; on one PHP server I use, the correct directory is /httpdocs/ROOT, so ask your ISP's tech support. If you've uploaded phpinfo.php to the usual directory on your ISP for your HTML pages and it's not working, ask your ISP's tech support; sometimes, they have to enable support on a directory-by-directory basis. For that matter, some ISPs even demand that you use a different extension for PHP 5 scripts, like .php5.

Finally, take a look at the "Problems?" section in the PHP manual for a troubleshooting guide. The PHP Frequently Asked Questions (FAQ), at www.php.net/FAQ.php, handles many such problems. So does PHP installation Frequently Asked Questions (FAQ) at www .php.net/manual/faq.installation, so take a look.

Mixing HTML and PHP

So far, you've just created a simple Web page that only included PHP code, specifically, a call to the phpinfo() function:

```
<?php
  phpinfo();
?>
```

But there's more to PHP pages than that. One of the charms of PHP is that you can intersperse your PHP code with HTML. That's very cool, because the HTML will be displayed by your browser, and the PHP will be run on your server—and if that PHP generates some HTML, that HTML will be displayed in your browser as well.

For example, take a look at a new page, phphtml.php. That page starts with a standard HTML <head> section, just as any HTML page might:

```
<html>
  <head>
    <title>
      Using PHP and HTML together
    </title>
  </head>
      .
      .
      .
```

And then it continues with a <body> section, which contains an <h1> header and some text:

```
<html>
  <head>
    <title>
      Using PHP and HTML together
    </title>
  </head>

  <body>
    <h1>
      Using PHP and HTML together
    </h1>
    Here is your PHP info:
    <br>

      .
      .
      .

  </body>
</html>
```

And now here're the key—you can insert PHP anywhere in this page and the PHP engine on the Web server will run it, as long as it's contained in the <?php...?> markup. When that PHP is run, any HTML it generates will be inserted into the page at the location of that PHP. So, for example, if you wanted to display the PHP configuration table returned by the phpinfo() function, you could call that function like this in the Web page:

```
<html>
  <head>
    <title>
      Using PHP and HTML together
    </title>
  </head>

  <body>
    <h1>
      Using PHP and HTML together
    </h1>
```

```
 Here is your PHP info:
 <br>
 <br>
  <?php
    phpinfo();
  ?>
 </body>
</html>
```

Now when this page is run by the PHP engine on the server, the HTML will be passed through to the browser unchanged—and the PHP part will be executed. Any HTML created by the PHP will be inserted into the page sent to the browser as well.

This page is called phphtml.php, and you can see it in Figure 1-6.

Note that the HTML in the page appears where it should—and so does the HTML generated by the PHP.

Want to give your pages a more professional appearance? You can use the PHP logos you can find at www.php.net/download-logos.php. These downloadable images can be used in your Web pages to give you that PHP look. For example, here's how you might use

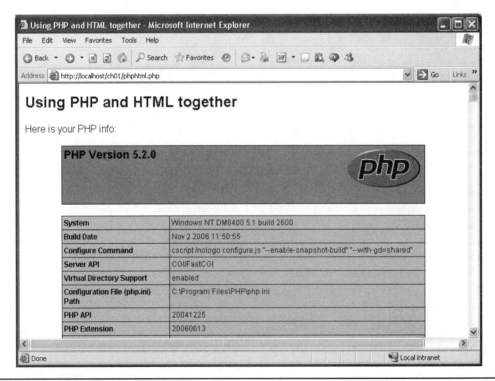

FIGURE 1-6   Mixing PHP and HTML

the image php-med-trans-light.gif in a page named phpimage.php (put the image file in the
same directory as phpimage.php on your server):

```
<html>
  <head>
    <title>
      Using PHP and HTML together
    </title>
  </head>

  <body>
    <h1>
      Using PHP and HTML together
    </h1>
    Here is your PHP info:
    <br>
    <br>
    <?php
      phpinfo();
    ?>
    <img src='php-med-trans-light.gif'>
  </body>
</html>
```

And you can see the results—the logo is at the lower right—in Figure 1-7.

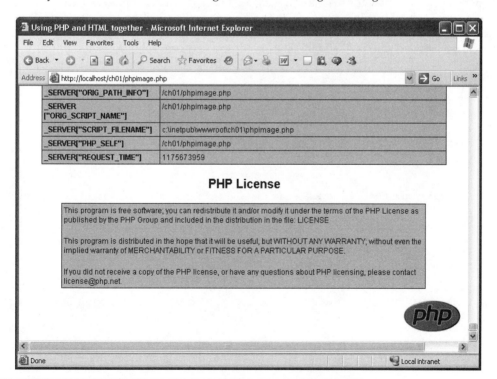

FIGURE 1-7   Using PHP logos

Printing Some Text

Alright, how about printing some text using PHP? You've already seen that you can put text into your PHP files much as you would an HTML page, as here, where you put an <h1> header and some text into a page:

```
<html>
  <head>
    <title>
      Using PHP and HTML together
    </title>
  </head>

  <body>
    <h1>
      Using PHP and HTML together
    </h1>
    Here is your PHP info:
        .
        .
        .
```

That's fine, but obviously, that's also static. The displayed text isn't going to change, no matter what's going on in the code part of your page, and that's clearly unacceptable. What if you wanted to display the results of a database lookup, or a ticket reservation?

You need to be able to insert text into the page using PHP as well, and you can do that using the PHP echo statement. For example, to echo the text "Welcome to PHP" to the Web page sent back to the browser, you could add this line of code to a new page, phpdisplaytext.php:

```
<html>
  <head>
    <title>
      Displaying text from PHP
    </title>
  </head>

  <body>
    <h1>
      Displaying text from PHP
    </h1>
    Here's what PHP has to say:
    <br>
    <br>
    <?php
      echo "Welcome to PHP.";
    ?>
  </body>
</html>
```

Take a look at this page, phpdisplaytext.php, in your browser now, as shown in Figure 1-8. You can see the text that PHP inserted into the page in the figure—not bad.

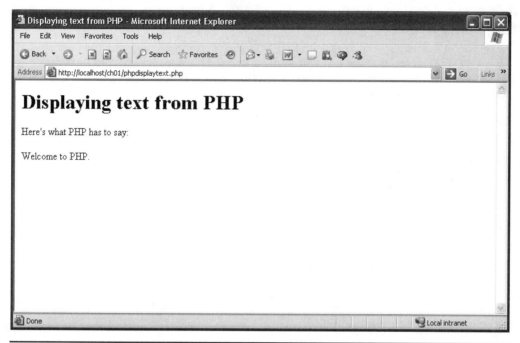

FIGURE 1-8   Displaying text from PHP

You can pass text to display to the echo statement using single or double quotes:

```
echo "Welcome to PHP.";
echo 'Welcome to PHP.';
```

There's a subtle difference between these two ways of passing text, which you'll see in the next chapter. You can also directly pass numbers to echo if you want, no quotation marks needed:

```
echo 1234.5678;
```

And you can pass text inside parentheses to echo as well:

```
echo ("Welcome to PHP.");
```

Passing data to functions also works like this: you place the data you want the function to operate on between parentheses. There are many functions built into PHP; however, echo, technically speaking, is not a function—it's a built-in PHP language construction.

Printing Some HTML

Never forget that when you work with PHP online, you're interacting with the user through a browser. That means that the text you send back to the browser will be interpreted as HTML, not just simple text. That also gives you the chance to make use of HTML to format your text, as shown here in a new sample, phpdisplayhtml.php:

```
<html>
  <head>
    <title>
      Displaying text from PHP
    </title>
  </head>

  <body>
    <h1>
      Displaying text from PHP
    </h1>
    Here's what PHP has to say:
    <br>
    <br>
    <?php
      echo "<i>Welcome</i><br>";
      echo "<u>to</u><br>";
      echo "<b>PHP</b>.";
    ?>
  </body>
</html>
```

You can see this page in Figure 1-9—including the HTML formatting.

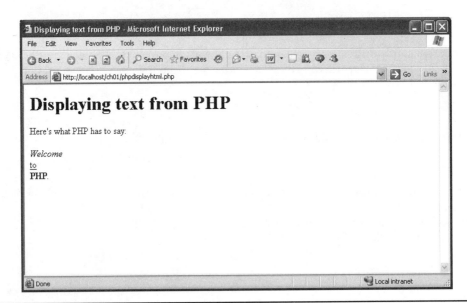

FIGURE 1-9   Displaying HTML from PHP

So if you want to skip to the next line in your displayed output, you have to insert the correct HTML, <br>, into your displayed text.

More Echo Power

You can also run PHP from the command line, in fact, simply by using the php command. Here's what you'd see if you ran phpdisplayhtml.php from the command line (remember that % stands for a generic command-line prompt in this book):

```
%php phpdisplayhtml.php
<html>
  <head>
    <title>
      Displaying text from PHP
    </title>
  </head>

  <body>
    <h1>
      Displaying text from PHP
    </h1>
    Here's what PHP has to say:
    <br>
    <br>
    <i>Welcome</i><br><u>to</u><br><b>PHP</b>.   </body>
</html>
%
```

Note that the HTML wasn't interpreted as HTML here; it was simply printed out as plain text. If you want to skip to the next line in this case, you should use the \n *control character,* which PHP will interpret as a newline character—this will display all three words on their own lines:

```
echo "Welcome\n";
echo "to\n";
echo "PHP.";
```

Here is a sampling of the control characters available in PHP:

- **\n** Newline character
- **\r** Carriage return
- **\t** Tab
- **** Displays a \
- **\$** Displays a $
- **\"** Displays a "
- **\0 to \777** Displays a character corresponding to a hexadecimal (base 8) code
- **\x0 to \xFF** Displays a character corresponding to a hexadecimal (base 16) code

You can print a sensitive character like a quotation mark (") without telling PHP that you're ending your text (which a " mark would otherwise do). To do this, use \" instead this way:

```
echo "He said, \"I like ice cream.\"";
```

This is called escaping the quotation mark so that PHP will display it instead of treating it as marking the end of a text string.

If you want to, you can break a long quoted string up across various lines in your script, and the line breaks will be preserved—if you're printing at the command line (if you're printing to a Web page, the line breaks will be ignored):

```
<?php
echo "This text
spans
multiple
lines
when
printed
at
the
command
line.";
?>
```

You can also separate the items you want to print with commas, like this:

```
echo "Welcome", "to", "PHP.";
```

All the items you want printed this way are printed, one right after another:

```
WelcometoPHP.
```

If you want to include spaces between the words, do something like this:

```
echo "Welcome ", "to ", "PHP.";
```

This would give you

```
Welcome to PHP.
```

You can also assemble text strings together into one string using a dot (.). Here's an example:

```
echo "Welcome " . "to " . "PHP.";
```

In this case, PHP takes your expression "Welcome " . "to " . "PHP." and assembles it together (this is called concatenation) into one single string, "Welcome to PHP."; it then passes that string on to the echo statement.

In addition, there's another way of displaying text: you can also use the PHP print statement using the same syntax, like this: print "Welcome to PHP.";. What's the difference between print and echo? Not much; print is more like a PHP function (see Chapter 5), so it returns a value, which is always set to 1. For most purposes, echo and print work the same way in PHP, so the one you use is up to you.

Using PHP "Here" Documents

In fact, there's another way of displaying text that you should be aware of, and that's using PHP "here" documents. A *here* document is just some text inserted directly in a PHP page, between two instances of the same token; that token is a word, such as END. Then you can display the text in a here document by using the syntax echo <<<*TOKEN*, where *TOKEN* is the word that begins and ends the here document.

Here's an example, phphere.php:

```
<html>
  <head>
    <title>
       Displaying text from PHP
    </title>
  </head>

  <body>
    <h1>
       Displaying text from PHP
    </h1>
    Here's what PHP has to say:
    <br>
    <br>
    <?php
echo <<<END
This example uses
"here document" syntax to display all
the text until the ending token is reached.
END;
    ?>
  </body>
</html>
```

And you can see what this produces in a browser in Figure 1-10. As the figure shows, the text in the here document was displayed in the browser.

Using the token END is by no means necessary; here's the same here document with the token FINISH:

```
echo <<<FINISH
This example uses
"here document" syntax to display all
the text until the ending token is reached.
FINISH;
```

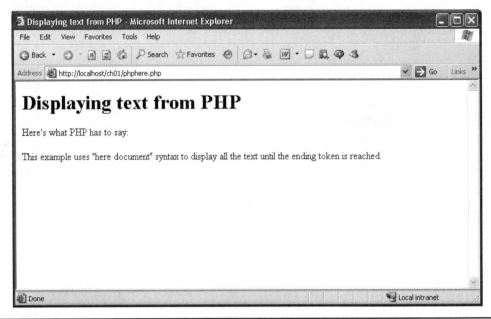

Figure 1-10   Displaying a here document in PHP

Command-Line PHP

This book concentrates on running PHP on Web servers, and seeing the results in Web browsers, but you can also run PHP on the command line. That can be great even if you're doing Web development—using PHP on the command line can pinpoint errors that cause Web servers to balk, and can also save you the time involved in uploading your PHP to the server. When you run Web-specific PHP on the command line, you'll see the HTML your page prints out, and you can debug that page more easily.

PHP is an interpreted language; the PHP engine just reads in the text of a PHP page and interprets it, executing that PHP immediately, line by line. The command-line version of PHP is called the command-line interpreter, or CLI, and is just given the name php. The online PHP engine is actually called php-cgi ("cgi" stands for Common Gateway Interface, a standard term for online programs that interface to Web servers). In fact, when you execute the command **php -v** on the command line, you can see that you're executing the CLI, because it tells you so:

```
%php -v
PHP 5.2.0 (cli) (built: Nov  2 2006 11:57:36)
Copyright (c) 1997-2006 The PHP Group
Zend Engine v2.2.0, Copyright (c) 1998-2006 Zend Technologies
```

It's easy to execute PHP files from the command line. For example, say you had a PHP file named echoer.php:

```
<?php
    echo "Hello, PHP here.";
?>
```

The <?php...?> is still mandatory, even though you're only using straight PHP here. You can run this file from the command line like this:

```
%php echoer.php
Hello, PHP here.";
%
```

And you see the result—the CLI printed out the message your file echoed. Any non-PHP text outside the <?php...?> section is interpreted as HTML and simply echoed to the output.

Executing PHP like this assumes that the CLI is in your computer's path, which it should be if you've installed PHP. If this doesn't work, you can specify the exact location of php. That might look like something this in Unix or Linux:

```
$/usr/local/bin/php echoer.php
```

And something like this in Windows:

```
C:\>C:\php\php echoer.php
```

The CLI has many command-line options, which you can use to customize its operation. In fact, php can tell you all about its options if you enter **php -h** to get this list:

```
%php -h
Usage: php [options] [-f] <file> [--] [args...]
       php [options] -r <code> [--] [args...]
       php [options] [-B <begin_code>] -R <code> [-E <end_code>] [--] [args...]
       php [options] [-B <begin_code>] -F <file> [-E <end_code>] [--] [args...]
       php [options] -- [args...]
       php [options] -a

  -a                 Run interactively
  -c <path>|<file> Look for php.ini file in this directory
  -n                 No php.ini file will be used
  -d foo[=bar]       Define INI entry foo with value 'bar'
  -e                 Generate extended information for debugger/profiler
  -f <file>          Parse and execute <file>.
  -h                 This help
  -i                 PHP information
  -l                 Syntax check only (lint)
  -m                 Show compiled in modules
  -r <code>          Run PHP <code> without using script tags <?..?>
  -B <begin_code>    Run PHP <begin_code> before processing input lines
  -R <code>          Run PHP <code> for every input line
  -F <file>          Parse and execute <file> for every input line
  -E <end_code>      Run PHP <end_code> after processing all input lines
```

```
-H                   Hide any passed arguments from external tools.
-s                   Display colour syntax highlighted source.
-v                   Version number
-w                   Display source with stripped comments and whitespace.
-z <file>            Load Zend extension <file>.

args...              Arguments passed to script. Use -- args when first argument
                     starts with - or script is read from stdin

--rf <name>          Show information about function <name>.
--rc <name>          Show information about class <name>.
--re <name>          Show information about extension <name>.
```

Many of these options are useful. For example, php -a lets you run the CLI in interactive mode, where you can execute PHP just by typing it. Here's an example—the CLI's response is in bold:

```
%php -a
Interactive mode enabled

<?php
echo "Hello from PHP.";
Hello from PHP.
```

And you can keep typing PHP and the CLI will execute it, as here:

```
%php -a
Interactive mode enabled

<?php
echo "Hello from PHP.";
Hello from PHP.
echo "Hello again.";
Hello again.
```

The php -i command gives you an enormous amount of information from phpinfo() about the way PHP was installed on the machine:

```
%php -i
phpinfo()
PHP Version => 5.2.0

System => Windows NT DM8400 5.1 build 2600
Build Date => Nov  2 2006 11:50:55
Configure Command => cscript /nologo configure.js  "--enable-snapshot-build" "--
with-gd=shared"
Server API => Command Line Interface
Virtual Directory Support => enabled
Configuration File (php.ini) Path => C:\Program Files\PHP\php.ini
PHP API => 20041225
PHP Extension => 20060613
Zend Extension => 220060519
Debug Build => no
```

```
Thread Safety => enabled
Zend Memory Manager => enabled
IPv6 Support => enabled
Registered PHP Streams => php, file, data, http, ftp, compress.zlib
Registered Stream Socket Transports => tcp, udp
Registered Stream Filters => convert.iconv.*, string.rot13, string.toupper, stri
ng.tolower, string.strip_tags, convert.*, consumed, zlib.*

This program makes use of the Zend Scripting Language Engine:
        .
        .
        .
```

Want to see the source code in your PHP file displayed using syntax highlighting, where PHP keywords are in green and data items in red? Just use php -s. For example, if you wanted to get a syntax-highlighted version of echoer.php and store it in an HTML document ready for viewing in your browser, echoer.html, you could execute this command:

```
%php -s echoer.php > echoer.html
```

Here's what echoer.html would end up containing:

```
<code><span style="color: #000000">
<span style="color: #0000BB">&lt;?php
<br /></span><span style="color: #007700">echo </span><span style="color:
#DD0000">"Hello, PHP here."</span><span style="color: #007700">;
<br /></span><span style="color: #0000BB">?&gt;
<br /></span>
</span>
</code>
```

You can also use the CLI to check the syntax of a PHP file to see if that file has any PHP errors in it. For example, say you omitted the opening quotation mark in this statement in echoer.php:

```
<?php
    echo Hello, PHP here.";
?>
```

Here's what you'd get when you tried to run this through the CLI using the -l option:

```
%php -l echoer.php
PHP Parse error:  parse error, unexpected T_STRING, expecting ',' or ';' in echo
er.php on line 2
Errors parsing echoer.php
```

That's the same error you'd get from PHP online (php-cgi).

You should know that the CLI output differs from the php-cgi output; for example, the CLI output does not include the standard HTTP headers that the php-cgi prints out when it sends output back to the browser. And error messages are printed out in plain text by the CLI, not the HTML that php-cgi will give you.

It's also worth noticing that in Linux and Unix, you can run PHP scripts simply by typing the name of the script on the command line, if you indicate where to find PHP with a line that begins with #!:

```
#! /usr/bin/php
<?php
    echo "Hello from PHP.";
?>
```

Adding Comments to PHP Code

Like virtually every other programming language, you can comment your PHP code. Comments are those human-readable annotations that you add to make your code more readable, and they're ignored by PHP. Comments are important to add to your PHP if that PHP code is extensive, because you—or someone else—may come back to that code years from now and have no idea what it does. You can laboriously reconstruct what's going on, but why not add comments to make it easy? That way, you can decipher your old code—or someone else's code—easily.

There are three types of comments in PHP. The first type of comment lets you create multiline comments, which start with /* and ends with */, this way:

```
<?php
/* Begin by displaying a
   message explaining what
   we are doing to the user */

    echo "Welcome to PHP.";
?>
```

That's great if you have a substantial comment that will take multiple lines to display. One thing that drives PHP crazy is nesting comments, however, so don't do something like this:

```
<?php
/* Begin by displaying an
   /* English */
   message explaining what
   we are doing to the user */

    echo "Welcome to PHP.";
?>
```

PHP looks for */ to mark the end of the comment, and if you nest comments, it'll find */ before the real end of the comment.

Both of the other types of comments are one-line comments. These types of comments only last for one line, not like the multiline /*...*/ type. The first type of single-line comment starts with //:

```
<?php
// Display a welcoming message.

    echo "Welcome to PHP.";
?>
```

And the second type of single-line comment works the same way, except that it starts with a # sign instead:

```php
<?php
// Display a welcoming message.
# Display a welcoming message.

    echo "Welcome to PHP.";
?>
```

In fact, PHP ignores everything after the // or # mark, so you can also put single-line comments at the end of lines, following valid PHP code like this:

```php
<?php
// Display a welcoming message.
# Display a welcoming message.

    echo "Welcome to PHP.";  // Display a welcoming message.
    echo "Welcome again!";   # Display another welcoming message.
?>
```

You can even use single-line comments to make comment blocks in your PHP code, which look something like multiline comments, like this:

```php
<?php
// Begin by displaying a
// message explaining what
// we are doing to the user

    echo "Welcome to PHP.";
?>
```

Want something that will really stand out, comment-wise? Try something like this:

```php
<?php
#############################
#  Begin by displaying a    #
#  message explaining what  #
#  we are doing to the user #
#############################

    echo "Welcome to PHP.";
?>
```

It's not necessarily pretty, but it does get your attention.

You're probably going to find that you use more single-line comments than multiline comments. Single-line comments are easier to write, because you don't have to keep track of the comment's end point. Multiline comments are useful too in PHP, however, and you'll often see them at the definition of PHP functions, explaining what data you pass to the function, and what data you'll get back.

Working with Variables

Up to this point, the text our scripts have produced has been static. In this case, for example, this script only displays the text "Welcome to PHP.":

```
<?php
    echo "Welcome to PHP.";
?>
```

That's pretty static text. You can do some addition with the PHP addition operator, +, to add numbers together like this:

```
<html>
 <head>
    <title>Here is the answer</title>
  </head>
  <body>
    <h1>
      The Answer
    </h1>
    <?php
      echo "Here is the answer: " , 1 + 5 + 8 , ".";
    ?>
  </body>
</html>
```

The first time you run this, it displays the message "Here is the answer: 14." And the second time you run it, it displays the message "Here is the answer: 14." again. So it's the same thing—you've got static text here once again.

That's fine as far as it goes, but that's not very far. If you just wanted static text, you might as well stick with HTML. That's where variables come in. As in any other programming language, PHP variables are named memory locations that hold data. Say for example that you wanted to keep track of the number of users of your site in three cities—Paris, London, and Boise—but the number of users in each location isn't known until your program runs. Variables to the rescue.

With variables, you could store the number of users in each city's variable at run time. In PHP, variable names begin with a $ sign, followed by a name—and that name must start with a letter or an underscore, not a number. For example, to store the number of users in Paris, you might have a variable named $paris; the number of users in London and Boise might be in variables $london and $boise. You could place data in those variables at run time, and add those three data items together, also at run time. Doing the addition might look like this:

```
<html>
 <head>
    <title>Here is the answer</title>
  </head>
  <body>
    <h1>
      The Answer
    </h1>
```

```php
<?php
  echo "Here is the answer: " , $paris + $london + $boise , ".";
?>
 </body>
</html>
```

At run time, the value inside each variable is substituted for that variable, so if $paris = 1, $london = 5, and $boise = 8, the preceding line of PHP code would look like this to PHP:

```php
<?php
  echo "Here is the answer: " , 1 + 5 + 8 , ".";
?>
```

And so you get "Here is the answer: 14."—the same answer as before. But now say that the three variables held 2, 4, and 6 at run time, you'd get

```php
<?php
  echo "Here is the answer: " , 2 + 4 + 6 , ".";
?>
```

So you'd get "Here is the answer: 12."—meaning our message is no longer static. That's why they're called variables—the data inside them can vary. That's the first step to working with data in PHP: using variables to store that data. So how exactly do you store data in variables?

Storing Data in Variables

In PHP, as in other languages, you can assign data to variables. PHP lets you store numbers and text to those variables, as in these examples:

```php
$pi = 3.1415926535;
$number_of_Jupiters = 1;
$name = "Egbert Stodge";
$fish = "haddock";
```

Unlike some other online languages, such as Java, PHP doesn't insist that you create different types of variables for different types of data. Here's how these variables might be created in Java:

```java
double pi = 3.1415926535;
int number_of_Jupiters = 1;
String name = "Egbert Stodge";
String fish = "haddock";
```

PHP can store all types of data in variables, and you don't have to create different variable types to store that data, which makes things a lot easier. On the other hand, due to the internal architecture of computers, your data is stored internally by PHP in different formats, and it's sometimes important to know what those internal formats are—more on that later.

Note the use of the = sign here, which you use to assign data to variables. The = sign is the *assignment operator* in PHP, letting you assign data to variables. (In fact, there are other assignment operators, as discussed in the next chapter, but the = sign is the primary one). For example, to set the number of cheeseburgers in your code to 1, you'd do this:

```php
<?php
    echo "Setting the number of cheeseburgers to 1.<br>";
    $cheeseburgers = 1;
        .
        .
        .
?>
```

Then you could echo the current number of cheeseburgers to the browser:

```php
<?php
    echo "Setting the number of cheeseburgers to 1.<br>";
    $cheeseburgers = 1;
    echo "Current number of cheeseburgers: ", $cheeseburgers, "<br>";
        .
        .
        .
?>
```

Now you might change the number stored in the variable $cheeseburgers as more cheeseburgers came online. If you got three more cheeseburgers, for example, you could use the PHP + operator to add them to the current number stored in $cheeseburgers like this:

```php
<?php
    echo "Setting the number of cheeseburgers to 1.<br>";
    $cheeseburgers = 1;
    echo "Current number of cheeseburgers: ", $cheeseburgers, "<br>";
    echo "Adding 3 more cheeseburgers.<br>";
    $cheeseburgers = $cheeseburgers + 3;
        .
        .
        .
?>
```

Now you can display the new number of cheeseburgers in this example, phpvariables. php, like this:

```html
<html>
    <head>
        <title>
            Storing data in variables
        </title>
    </head>
    <body>
        <h1>
            Storing data in variables
        </h1>
```

```
<?php
    echo "Setting the number of cheeseburgers to 1.<br>";
    $cheeseburgers = 1;
    echo "Current number of cheeseburgers: ", $cheeseburgers, "<br>";
    echo "Adding 3 more cheeseburgers.<br>";
    $cheeseburgers = $cheeseburgers + 3;
    echo "Number of cheeseburgers now: ", $cheeseburgers, "<br>";
?>
    </body>
</html>
```

You can see phpvariables.php in Figure 1-11, where, as you see, the value stored in $cheeseburgers was successfully changed.

In some languages, like Java, you have to declare variables, giving their type and name, before using them, such as

```
double pi;
int number_of_Jupiters = 1;
```

You don't have to declare variables in PHP before using them—another way that PHP saves you time and effort. All you have to do before using a variable in PHP is to assign a value to it—when you do, PHP will create that variable for you, and store your data in it.

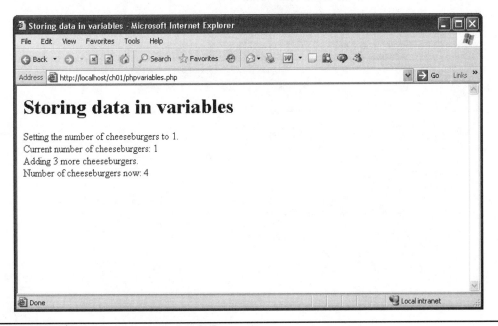

FIGURE 1-11   Putting variables to work in PHP

That means you have to assign data to a variable before attempting to read a variable's value, however. For example, if you tried to read the number of cheeseburgers without first setting them,

```php
<?php
    echo "Current number of cheeseburgers: ", $cheeseburgers, "<br>";
    echo "Adding 3 more cheeseburgers.<br>";
    $cheeseburgers = $cheeseburgers + 3;
    echo "Number of cheeseburgers now: ", $cheeseburgers, "<br>";
?>
```

you'd get the error you see in Figure 1-12.

Here's the error message:

```
PHP Notice: Undefined variable: cheeseburgers in C:\Inetpub\wwwroot\ch01\
phpvariables.php on line 14 PHP Notice: Undefined variable: cheeseburgers
in C:\Inetpub\wwwroot\ch01\phpvariables.php on line 16
```

Want to *un*create a variable? It's hard to think of occasions that you might no longer want a variable around, but you can indeed uncreate variables in PHP. Just use code like this:

```
unset($cheeseburgers);
```

After you execute this PHP statement, the $cheeseburgers will no longer exist, and you'd get an error if you tried to read the value in it.

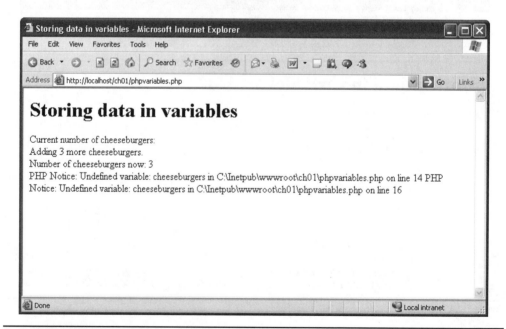

FIGURE 1-12   Forgetting to initialize a variable in PHP

Interpolating Strings

You can display the value in a variable like this, of course:

```php
<?php
    $cheeseburgers = 1;
    echo "Current number of cheeseburgers: ", $cheeseburgers, "<br>";
?>
```

In this case, you're explicitly put $cheeseburgers in the list of items whose values you want displayed. On the other hand, there's a shortcut way of doing this in PHP that you should be aware of, called *string interpolation.*

When you use interpolation, you only have to place the variable whose value you want to insert inside a double-quoted (not single-quoted) text string. For example, you could convert the earlier phpvariables.php example to use string interpolation in a new example named phpinterpolation.php like this:

```html
<html>
    <head>
        <title>
            Using string interpolation
        </title>
    </head>
    <body>
        <h1>
            Using string interpolation
        </h1>
        <?php
            echo "Setting the number of cheeseburgers to 1.<br>";
            $cheeseburgers = 1;
            echo "Current number of cheeseburgers: $cheeseburgers <br>";
            echo "Adding 3 more cheeseburgers.<br>";
            $cheeseburgers = $cheeseburgers + 3;
            echo "Number of cheeseburgers now: $cheeseburgers <br>";
        ?>
    </body>
</html>
```

Note how this works: PHP sees the name of a variable, $cheeseburgers, inside a double-quoted text string:

```php
echo "Current number of cheeseburgers: $cheeseburgers <br>";
```

That means that PHP will immediately place the value held in $cheeseburgers into the string, like this:

```php
echo "Current number of cheeseburgers: 1 <br>";
```

That's how string interpolation works; PHP will substitute the value of a variable for that variable in a double-quoted text string. You can see phpinterpolation.php at work in Figure 1-13.

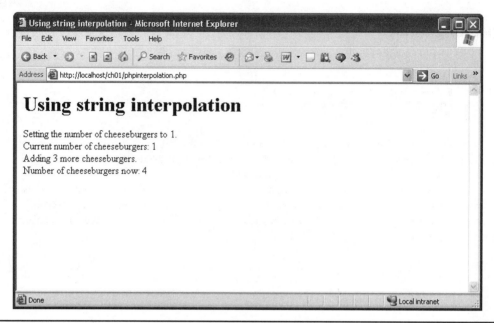

FIGURE 1-13   Using string interpolation in PHP

String interpolation is a quick shortcut, allowing you to pop the value of a variable into a double-quoted (not single-quoted) string, but there's something to know here: you need to surround the variable name with spaces or simple punctuation. If you put the variable name directly next to text, you could confuse PHP. For example, if the variable $type holds the text "basket" and you want to insert the text "basketball" into double-quoted text, you might be tempted to use the expression $typeball. And that's not going to work; you'll see

```
PHP Notice:  Undefined variable:  typeball in C:\php\wrong.php on line 8
```

The solution here is to enclose the name of the variable in curly braces like this: {$type}, making the expression ${type}ball, as you see in phpadjoininginterpolation.php:

```
<html>
    <head>
        <title>
            Using variable interpolation with adjoining words
        </title>
    </head>
    <body>
        <h1>
            Using variable interpolation with adjoining words
        </h1>
        <?php
            $type = "basket";
            echo "The name of the game is {$type}ball.<br>";
        ?>
    </body>
</html>
```

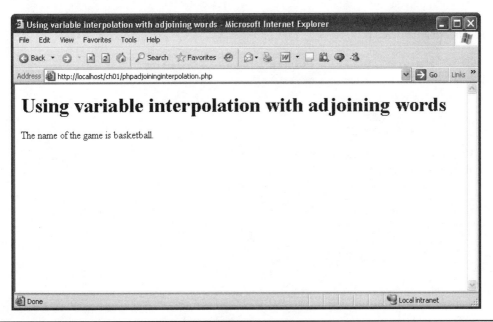

FIGURE 1-14   Using string interpolation with adjoining text in PHP

Now it works, as you can see in Figure 1-14.

String interpolation is useful, but you might not want to use it all the time. For example, what if you have the text string: "Got a great deal on lunch—it was $cheap even for Jessica."? As it stands, that's going to confuse PHP, which is going to try to find a variable named $cheap, and will give you an error when it can't find it.

There are two solutions to this problem; first, you could use single quotes instead of double quotes, like this: 'Got a great deal on lunch - it was $cheap even for Jessica.'. When you use single quotation marks, PHP does not apply string interpolation.

The second way to avoid interpolation when you don't want it—but you still want to use double quotation marks—is to escape the name of the variable by preceding the $ sign with a backslash (\), giving you: "Got a great deal on lunch—it was \$cheap even for Jessica." PHP will see the "\$" and convert it into a harmless $ sign, as it should be here, not the beginning of a variable name.

That's string interpolation—if you want to pop a variable's value into a double-quoted string, this is the tool for you.

Creating Variable Variables

While discussing variables, it's also worthwhile to discuss variable variables. No, that's no typo—PHP lets you create variable variables—which are variables that hold the *name* of another variable.

Here's how it works. You might have a variable named $cheeseburgers, which you might set to a value of 1:

```
<?php
  $cheeseburgers = 1;
     .
     .
     .
?>
```

Then you might create a new variable, $burgertype, that holds the name of the first variable, "cheeseburgers":

```
<?php
  $cheeseburgers = 1;
  $burgertype = "cheeseburgers";
     .
     .
     .
?>
```

You know that you can display the value in $cheeseburgers this way:

```
<?php
  $cheeseburgers = 1;
  $burgertype = "cheeseburgers";
  echo "Number of cheeseburgers: ", $cheeseburgers, "<br>";
     .
     .
     .
?>
```

It turns out that you can also access the value in $cheeseburgers using the variable variable, $burgertype, like this:

```
<?php
  $cheeseburgers = 1;
  $burgertype = "cheeseburgers";
  echo "Number of cheeseburgers: ", $cheeseburgers, "<br>";
  echo "That number again: ", $$burgertype, "<br>";
     .
     .
     .
?>
```

Note the syntax here—because $burgertype contains the text "cheeseburgers", the expression $$burgertype is the same as $cheeseburgers.

Want to use variable variables with string interpolation? PHP is going to have trouble with an expression like $$burgertype inside double quotes, so the way to fix that is to use the expression ${$burgertype}. You can see this at work in this example, phpvariablevariables.php:

```
<html>
    <head>
        <title>
            Using variable variables
        </title>
    </head>
    <body>
        <h1>
            Using variable variables
        </h1>
        <?php
          $cheeseburgers = 1;
          $burgertype = "cheeseburgers";
          echo "Number of cheeseburgers: ", $cheeseburgers, "<br>";
          echo "That number again: ", $$burgertype, "<br>";
          echo "Once again: ${$burgertype} <br>";
        ?>
    </body>
</html>
```

If you hadn't used the curly braces in this example, you would have gotten this output:

```
Number of cheeseburgers: 1
That number again: 1
Once again: $cheeseburgers
```

Variable variables might not look like much more than a curiosity right now, but they have their uses when you're working with loops and arrays, covered in Chapter 3.

Creating Constants

Sometimes, you don't want a data item to be a variable. For example, the value of pi, 3.1415926535, shouldn't change. If you created a variable named $pi, something in your code might assign a new value to $pi by mistake. The thing to do here is to create a *constant*, whose value can't be modified.

You create a constant in PHP with the define function, passing define the name of the constant you want to create and the value you want to give it, such as define ("PI", 3.1415926535). That creates a constant named PI—and that's case-sensitive: PI is not the same as pi (if you want to make a constant non-case-sensitive, you can pass a value of TRUE like this: define ("PI", 3.1415926535, TRUE)). Note that this just creates a constant named pi—you don't use a $ in front of the name because doing so would make it a variable.

Here's how creating a constant works in an example phpconstant.php:

```
<html>
    <head>
        <title>
            Defining constants
        </title>
    </head>
```

```
<body>
    <h1>
        Defining constants
    </h1>
    <?php
     define ("PI", 3.1415926535);
     echo "The value of pi is ", PI, "<br>";
    ?>
</body>
</html>
```

And you can see the results in Figure 1-15, where the constant was indeed created.

So that's the idea behind constants—if you try to alter the value of this constant, pi (like this pi = 3.14), PHP won't accept it and won't even start the script.

Here's one thing to note: because you don't prefix constants with a $, PHP can end up confused if you use a constant with the same name as one of the reserved keywords in PHP. These keywords appear in Table 1-1.

Also, there are a number of predefined constants available to your scripts. We'll use these constants as we need them; here's a sample:

- **__LINE__**   The current line number of the file
- **__FILE__**   The full path and filename of the file
- **__FUNCTION__**   The function name
- **__CLASS__**   The class name
- **__METHOD__**   The class method name
- **PHP_VERSION**   The PHP version

__CLASS__	__FILE__	__FUNCTION__	__LINE__
__METHOD__	and	array	as
break	case	cfunction	class
const	continue	declare	default
die	do	echo	else
elseif	empty	enddeclare	endfor
endforeach	endif	endswitch	endwhile
eval	exception	exit	extends
for	foreach	function	global
if	include	include_once	isset
list	new	old_function	or
php_user_filter	print	require	require_once
return	static	switch	unset
use	var	while	xor

TABLE 1-1   The PHP Keywords

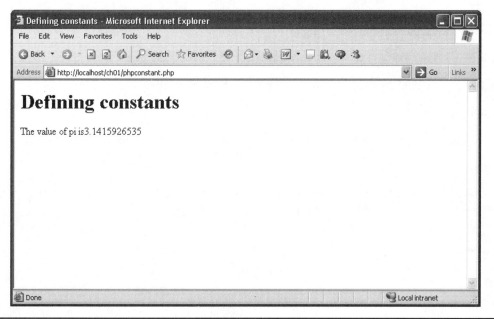

FIGURE 1-15   Defining constants

- **PHP_OS**   The operating system
- **DEFAULT_INCLUDE_PATH**   Where PHP will search for what it needs

For example, using echo __LINE__ at a specific location in a script will display the current line that's executing.

Understanding PHP's Internal Data Types

PHP does you a big favor by letting you store data without having to specify the data's type. In other languages, you need to specify the exact data format of each variable, but PHP handles that for you.

Sometimes, however, you have to know about the internal data types that PHP uses, as you're about to see. Here are those internal types:

- **boolean**   Holds true/false values
- **integer**   Holds numbers like -1, 0, 5 and so on
- **float**   Holds floating-point numbers ("doubles") like 3.14159 or 2.7128
- **string**   Holds text like "Welcome to PHP."
- **array**   Holds arrays of data items
- **object**   Holds programming objects
- **resource**   Holds a data resource
- **NULL**   Holds a value of NULL

PHP usually handles your data's types automatically. For example, this statement creates a variable that holds a string:

```
$data = "That is a lot of cheeseburgers you have there.";
```

This statement creates a variable that holds a float internally:

```
$data = 123.456;
```

Here's an example that creates a boolean (TRUE/FALSE) variable:

```
$data = TRUE;
```

That's all fine; the problem comes when you start mixing data types. For example, if you start with a simple variable set to "0",

```
<?php
  $variable = "0";              // $variable is a string set to "0"
       .
       .
       .
?>
```

then that creates a variable that contains the string "0". Now what if you add 1 to that variable's value:

```
<?php
  $variable = "0";              // $variable is a string set to "0"
  $variable = $variable + 1;    // $variable is now an integer set to 1
       .
       .
       .
?>
```

In this case, PHP does the best it can; adding the number 1 to the string "0" leaves $variable holding the integer 1. What if you add a floating-point value?

```
<?php
  $variable = "0";              // $variable is a string set to "0"
  $variable = $variable + 1;    // $variable is now an integer set to 1
  $variable = $variable + 1.2;  // $variable is now a float set to 2.2
       .
       .
       .
?>
```

Now $variable is left holding a float value of 2.2. What if you add 3 + "8 cheeseburgers"? PHP will again do its best, adding 3 + 8 and leaving the result, an integer value of 11, as the result:

```php
<?php
  $variable = "0";                   // $variable is a string set to "0"
  $variable = $variable + 1;         // $variable is now an integer set to 1
  $variable = $variable + 1.2;       // $variable is now a float set to 3.2
  $variable = 3 + "8 cheeseburgers"; // $variable is an integer set to 11
?>
```

You should avoid reliance on these rules. They're built into PHP, but relying on them could give you the wrong result. If you want to convert a value from one data type to another, you can explicitly use a data type *cast*. Casts are data types you put in parentheses; for example:

```php
$integer = (integer) $data;
```

explicitly converts the value in $data to an integer. This converts the value in $data to a $float:

```php
$float = (float) $data;
```

When you're converting to the boolean type, these values are considered FALSE:

- The boolean FALSE
- The integer 0
- The float 0.0
- The empty string, and the string "0"
- An array with zero elements
- An object with no member variables
- The special type NULL (including unset variables)

Every other value is considered TRUE.

When you're converting to the integer type, here are the rules:

- A boolean FALSE will yield 0 (zero), and boolean TRUE will yield 1 (one).
- Values of type float will be rounded toward zero.

When you're converting data to the float type, PHP first converts the data to an integer and then to a float. You can also convert from string to the numeric types, but that's a little involved—see Chapter 3 for the details.

PHP also includes special functions to let you check the internal format of data—is_int(), is_float(), is_array(), and so on—for example, if you pass a variable that PHP has stored as an integer internally to is_int(), that function will return a value of TRUE—more on this comes up in the next chapter.

Operators and Flow Control

C hapter 1 was an introduction to PHP, and this chapter gets down to nuts and bolts. Everything you see in this chapter is an essential skill for the rest of the book.

This chapter discusses the PHP *operators* that you use to manipulate your data; this is the most basic part of the PHP foundation you'll need. For example, the expression $variable + 8 adds 8 to the value in $variable. The expression $variable * 4 multiplies the value on $variable by 4. Even if you've seen operators in other languages, at least skim this material, because there's some PHP-specific material coming up.

You're also going to see all about *flow control* in this chapter. Flow control lets you make decisions in your code. Are you going to have a picnic? You can make that decision based on the current outside temperature in PHP code. Do you have enough inventory to handle customer orders? Again, a matter of flow control. In PHP, as in other languages, the primary flow control statement is the if statement, which allows you to make a decision and execute some code if that decision goes one way, and alternate code if the decision goes another.

Besides statements like the if statement, you're also going to see loops discussed here. Loops are fundamental to PHP, as they are to many programming languages, and they allow you to handle large sets of data by looping over those sets of data, one data item at a time. Computers were built for repetitive tasks like these, so loops get a prominent place in PHP.

PHP's Math Operators

We're going to start with the most basic of operators—the math operators. Here they are:

- + Adds two numbers
- - Subtracts one number from another
- * Multiplies two numbers together
- / Divides one number by another
- % Returns the remainder when one number is divided by another (modulus)

These operators work as you'd expect: to add two values, you use the + operator like this: a + b. To subtract b from a, it's a - b. Okay, it's time to get some code going. Here's an example, phpmathoperators.php, that puts the math operators to work:

```html
<html>
    <head>
        <title>
            Using the math operators
        </title>
    </head>
    <body>
        <h1>
            Using the math operators
        </h1>
        <?php
            echo "7 + 2 = ", 7 + 2;
            echo "7 - 2 = ", 7 - 2;
            echo "7 * 2 = ", 7 * 2;
            echo "7 / 2 = ", 7 / 2;
            echo "7 % 2 = ", 7 % 2;
        ?>
    </body>
</html>
```

You can see the results in Figure 2-1, where the math operators are doing their thing.

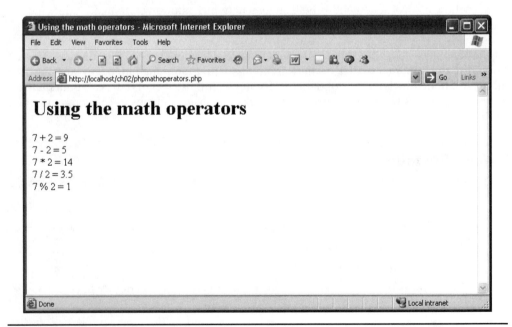

FIGURE 2-1   The PHP math operators at work

This example showed the use of the math operators with two numbers, 7 and 2, but of course you can use variables as well:

```
$result = $operand1 + $operand2;
$result = $operand1 - $operand2;
$result = $operand1 * $operand2;
$result = $operand1 / $operand2;
$result = $operand1 % $operand2;
```

Besides the built-in math operators, PHP also supports a number of math functions, and while discussing the math operators, it's worth taking a look at the math functions too. Here they are:

- **abs**   Absolute value
- **acos**   Arc cosine
- **acosh**   Inverse hyperbolic cosine
- **asin**   Arc sine
- **asinh**   Inverse hyperbolic sine
- **atan2**   Arc tangent of two variables
- **atan**   Arc tangent
- **atanh**   Inverse hyperbolic tangent
- **base_convert**   Converts a number between bases
- **bindec**   Converts binary to decimal
- **ceil**   Rounds fractions up
- **cos**   Cosine
- **cosh**   Hyperbolic cosine
- **decbin**   Converts decimal to binary
- **dechex**   Converts decimal to hexadecimal
- **decoct**   Converts decimal to octal
- **deg2rad**   Converts the number in degrees to the radian equivalent
- **exp**   Calculates the exponent of e
- **expm1**   Returns exp(number) − 1
- **floor**   Rounds fractions down
- **fmod**   Returns the floating-point remainder of the division of the arguments
- **getrandmax**   Shows the largest possible random value
- **hexdec**   Converts hexadecimal to decimal
- **hypot**   Returns sqrt(num1*num1 + num2*num2)
- **is_finite**   Determines whether a value is a legal finite number
- **is_infinite**   Determines whether a value is infinite
- **is_nan**   Determines whether a value is not a number
- **lcg_value**   Combined linear congruential generator

- **log10**   Base 10 logarithm
- **log1p**   Returns log(1 + number)
- **log**   Returns the natural logarithm
- **max**   Finds the highest value
- **min**   Finds the lowest value
- **mt_getrandmax**   Shows the largest possible random value
- **mt_rand**   Generates a better random value
- **mt_srand**   Seeds the better random number generator
- **octdec**   Converts octal to decimal
- **pi**   Gets the value of pi
- **pow**   Exponential expression
- **rad2deg**   Converts the radian number to the equivalent number in degrees
- **rand**   Generate a random integer
- **round**   Rounds a float
- **sin**   Sine
- **sinh**   Hyperbolic sine
- **sqrt**   Square root
- **srand**   Seed the random number generator
- **tan**   Tangent
- **tanh**   Hyperbolic tangent

Here's an example, phpmathfunctions.php, that puts some of these functions to work. For example, you might want to find the tangent of 45°, and you'd use the tan function for that. The tan function expects its operand to be in radians, so you first have to convert 45° into radians, which you can do with the deg2rad function:

```php
<?php
    echo "tan(deg2rad(45)) = ", tan(deg2rad(45)), "<br>";
    .
    .
    .
?>
```

How about calculating an exponent next? You can calculate 4 to the power 3, that is, 4^3, using the pow function:

```php
<?php
    echo "tan(deg2rad(45)) = ", tan(deg2rad(45)), "<br>";
    echo "pow(4, 3) = ", pow(4, 3), "<br>";
    .
    .
    .
?>
```

You can round numbers down using the floor function, or up using the ceil function. Here's an example, rounding pi downward:

```php
<?php
    echo "tan(deg2rad(45)) = ", tan(deg2rad(45)), "<br>";
    echo "pow(4, 3) = ", pow(4, 3), "<br>";
    echo "floor(3.14159) = ", floor(3.14159), "<br>";
    .
    .
    .
?>
```

How about a little hexadecimal math? The dechex function converts from decimal values to hexadecimal like this:

```php
<?php
    echo "tan(deg2rad(45)) = ", tan(deg2rad(45)), "<br>";
    echo "pow(4, 3) = ", pow(4, 3), "<br>";
    echo "floor(3.14159) = ", floor(3.14159), "<br>";
    echo "dechex(16) = ", dechex(16), "<br>";
    .
    .
    .
?>
```

And you can find the arc tangent of 1 with the atan function, converting the radians answer into degrees this way in phpmathfunctions.php:

```php
<html>
    <head>
        <title>
            Using the math functions
        </title>
    </head>
    <body>
        <h1>
            Using the math functions
        </h1>
        <?php
            echo "tan(deg2rad(45)) = ", tan(deg2rad(45)), "<br>";
            echo "pow(4, 3) = ", pow(4, 3), "<br>";
            echo "floor(3.14159) = ", floor(3.14159), "<br>";
            echo "dechex(16) = ", dechex(16), "<br>";
            echo "rad2deg(atan(1)) = ", rad2deg(atan(1)), "<br>";
        ?>
    </body>
</html>
```

You can see phpmathfunctions.php in Figure 2-2, where everything works as planned.

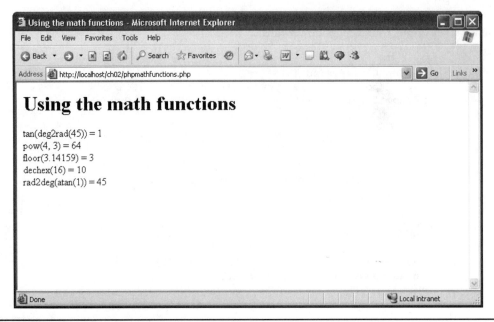

FIGURE 2-2   The PHP math functions at work

Working with the Assignment Operators

The main assignment operator is the = operator, which just assigns a value, like this, which stores the value 99 in $bottles_of_beer_on_the_wall:

```
$bottles_of_beer_on_the_wall = 99;
```

Here's something else you should know about the = assignment operator: you can make multiple assignments on the same line, like this:

```
<?php
  $a = $b = $c = $d = 3;
  .
  .
  .
?>
```

This line of code assigns the value 3 to each of the variables $a, $b, $c, and $d. Pretty handy.
    Now take a look at these lines of code:

```
<?php
  $a = 3;
  $a = $a + 6;
  .
  .
  .
?>
```

The idea here is we're assigning a value of 3 to the variable $a, and then adding 6 to that value to end up with 9 in $a. PHP gives you a set of combination assignment operators, so that if you want to collapse a line like $a = $a = 6, you can do it using the combination assignment operator +=. The += operator combines the + and = operators so that this line:

```
$a = $a + 6;
```

works the same way as this:

```
<?php
  $a = 3;
  $a += 6;
  .
  .
  .
?>
```

So the combination assignment operators give you a shortcut way of performing two operations, where one of them is an assignment; $a = $a + 6 becomes $a += 6;.

Similarly, the -= assignment operator combines subtraction with assignment; this code leaves 1 in $a:

```
<?php
  $a = 3;
  $a -= 2;
  .
  .
  .
?>
```

Here are the PHP combined assignment operators. Some of the operators here might not be familiar yet, but they're coming up in this chapter:

- +=
- -=
- *=
- /=
- .=
- %=
- &=
- |=
- ^=
- <<=
- >>=

Here's another example, using the PHP string concatenation operator (.) like this:

```php
<?php
  $a = "No ";
  $a .= "worries.";
  .
  .
  .
?>
```

This leaves the text "No worries." in $a.

Incrementing and Decrementing Values

Another thing you do frequently in PHP is to increment (add 1 to) or decrement (subtract 1 from) values. For example, you could use code like this to increment the value in $a:

```php
<?php
  $a = 1;
  $a = $a + 1;
  .
  .
  .
?>
```

In fact, you could even use the shortcut assignment operator += like this:

```php
<?php
  $a = 1;
  $a += 1;
  .
  .
  .
?>
```

But PHP has an easier operator specially for incrementing values: the ++ operator, which you use like this:

```php
<?php
  $a = 1;
  $a++;
  .
  .
  .
?>
```

After this code executes, $a is left with a value of 2. Similarly, the -- operator decrements values.

Here's something that's key to understand about ++ and --. If you use ++ or -- after a variable, as in $a++, the value in the variable is incremented after the rest of the statement is executed. So, for example, this line of code finds and displays the square root of 4, displaying a value of 2, and only then increments the value in $a:

```php
<?php
  $a = 4;
  echo sqrt($a++);
  .
  .
  .
?>
```

On the other hand, this code, where the ++ comes first, increments the value in $a first, and then displays the square root of 5:

```php
<?php
  $a = 4;
  echo sqrt(++$a);
  .
  .
  .
?>
```

That's important to keep in mind—if you put ++ or -- in front of a variable, the value in that variable is incremented or decremented *before* the rest of the statement is executed; if you put the ++ or -- after the variable, the value in that variable is incremented or decremented *after* the rest of the statement is executed.

Here's an example PHP page, showing how incrementing works in PHP, phpincrement. php:

```php
<html>
    <head>
        <title>
            Incrementing and Decrementing
        </title>
    </head>

    <body>
      <h1>
          Incrementing and Decrementing
      </h1>
      <?php
        $a = $b = $c = $d = 1;

        echo "\$a = \$b = \$c = \$d = 1 <br>";
        echo "\$a++ gives ", $a++, "<br>";
        echo "Now \$a = ", $a, "<br>";
        echo "++\$b gives ", ++$b, "<br>";
        echo "\$c-- gives ", $c--, "<br>";
        echo "Now \$c = ", $c, "<br>";
        echo "--\$d gives ", --$d, "<br>";
      ?>
    </body>
</html>
```

You can see this page, phpincrement.php, in Figure 2-3.

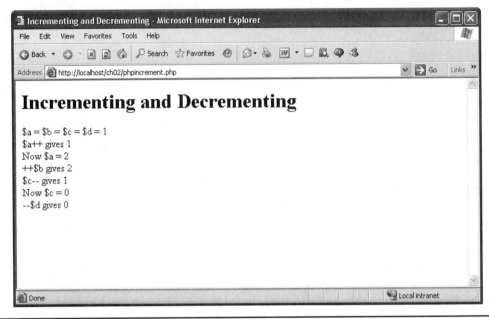

FIGURE 2-3   Incrementing and decrementing with PHP

The PHP String Operators

You may have heard that PHP excels at working with text strings, and that's true. So you may be surprised to learn that PHP only has two operators that work with strings: the concatenation operator, ., and the combined concatenation assignment operator, .=. The true string power in PHP is in its string functions, which you're going to see in Chapter 3.

Here's an example using the string operators, phpstringoperators.php:

```
<html>
  <head>
   <title>The string operators</title>
  </head>

  <body>
    <h1>The string operators</h1>
    <?php
      $a = "No ";
      echo "\$a = ", $a, "<br>";
      echo "\$b = \$a . \"worries \"<br>";
      $b = $a . "worries ";
      echo "Now \$b = ", $b, "<br>";
      echo "\$b .= \"at all.\"<br>";
      $b .= "at all.";
      echo "Now \$b = ", $b, "<br>";
    ?>
  </body>
</html>
```

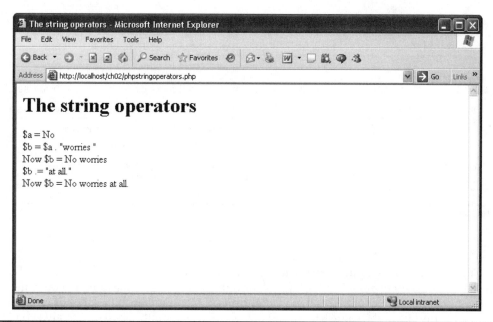

FIGURE 2-4   The string operators in PHP

You can see phpstringoperators.php in Figure 2-4.

The Bitwise Operators

PHP also provides you a set of bitwise operators that can work with the individual bits inside numbers. There's usually little call to use these operators unless you know what you're doing in detail. If you don't know about the bits in bytes, don't worry about this one. Although you normally use this one on integers and the like, you can in fact also use these operators on strings, in which case you'll be working with the numeric ASCII code of each character.

NOTE   *These operators are designed to work on the individual bits inside their operands; if you're looking for the boolean operators that work on TRUE/FALSE values, that's coming up later in this chapter.*

For example, the Or operator, |, works on two operands like this: $a | $b. In the result, bits that are set (that is, equal to 1, not 0) in either $a and $b are set in the result. So, for example, if $a equals 1 (which has the 0th bit set) and $b = 2 (which has the 1st bit set), then $a | $b will equal 1 | 2; both the 0th bit and the 1st bit set in the result, so it equals 3.

You can see the bitwise operators in Table 2-1.

Operator	Operation	Example	Result
$a & $b	And	$a & $b	Bits that are set in both $a and $b are set.
$a | $b	Or	$a | $b	Bits that are set in either $a or $b are set.
$a ^ $b	Xor	$a ^ $b	Bits that are set in $a or $b but not both are set.
~ $a	Not	~ $a	Bits that are set in $a are not set, and vice versa.
$a << $b	Shift left	$a << $b	Shift the bits of $a $b steps to the left (each step means "multiply by two").
$a >> $b	Shift right	$a >> $b	Shift the bits of $a $b steps to the right (each step means "divide by two").

TABLE 2-1   The Bitwise Operators

You might also notice the shift operators, << and >>, here. These operators let you shift the bits inside their operands to the left (<<) or right (>>). You give the number you want shifted, and the number of places you want the bits in that number shifted. For example, 8 << 1 shifts the bits of the value 8 to the left one place, which multiplies 8 by 2 to give you 16. Or, 8 >> 2 shifts the bits in the value 8 to the right two places, which is the same as dividing by 4, so 8 >> 2 = 2.

The Execution Operator

The PHP execution operator is cool—it allows you to execute system commands, such as the Windows date or dir (for directory) commands. All you have to do to execute a system command is to enclose it in backticks (`).

Here's an example. This code will run the Windows command "dir c:\Inetpub\ wwwroot\ch02" and display the results (note that the \ here is a sensitive character, so you have to escape it as \\):

```php
<?php
    $output = `dir c:\\Inetpub\\wwwroot\\ch02`;
    echo $output;
?>
```

Here's what you get when you execute this example, phpdir.php:

```
%php phpdir.php
 Volume in drive C has no label.

 Directory of c:\Inetpub\wwwroot\ch02

04/06/2007  03:06 PM    <DIR>          .
04/06/2007  03:06 PM    <DIR>          ..
```

```
04/06/2007  03:08 PM                  78 phpdir.php
04/06/2007  02:08 PM                 569 phpincrement.php
04/06/2007  12:45 PM                 539 phpmathfunctions.php
04/06/2007  12:17 PM                 457 phpmathoperators.php
04/06/2007  02:47 PM                 425 phpstringoperators.php
08/26/2004  11:55 AM                 464 phptext.html
07/11/2006  04:08 PM                 328 phptext.php
               7 File(s)          2,860 bytes
               2 Dir(s)  68,807,487,488 bytes free
```

Here's another example; this runs the date command:

```
<?php
$output =  `date`;
echo $output;
?>
```

Here's the kind of result you might see under Unix, using the bash shell:

```
-bash-2.05b$ php phpdate.php
Fri April 06 11:24:45 PDT 2007
```

Since date is also a command in DOS, here's what you might see in a DOS window:

```
C:\php>php phpdate.php
The current date is: Fri 04/06/2007
Enter the new date: (mm-dd-yy)
```

PHP Operator Precedence

Most of the additional PHP operators you'll see in this book are for use in if statements and loops, and they're coming up next. There's one thing to say about operators first, however, and that's about operator precedence—the order in which operators get executed.

For example, take a look at this expression:

```
4 + 3 * 9
```

What's going to happen here? Will the 4 + 3 be added and the result be multiplied by 9 to give you 63? Or will the 3 be multiplied by 9 to give you 27 and the 4 added to that to give you 31? It turns out that PHP processes multiplications before additions, so you'll get 31 here, as you can verify with this script, phpprecedence.php:

```
<?php
  echo 4 + 3 * 9;
?>
```

When you run this, you get

```
%php phpprecedence.php
31
```

How can you tell the precedence of the various operators? Take a look at Table 2-2, which lists precedence of the various operators, from high at the top of the table to low at the bottom.

Want to set the precedence yourself? Use parentheses. You can tell PHP what operations to execute first by enclosing them in parentheses. Here's an example, phpsettingprecedence.php:

```html
<html>
  <head>
    <title>Setting operator precedence</title>
  </head>

  <body>
    <h1>Setting operator precedence</h1>
    <?php
      echo "4 + 3 * 9 = ", 4 + 3 * 9, "<br>";
      echo "(4 + 3) * 9 = ", (4 + 3) * 9, "<br>";
    ?>
  </body>
</html>
```

TABLE 2-2 Operator Precedence

Operators
new
[
! ~ ++ – (int) (float) (string) (array) (object)
@
* / %
+ - .
<< >>
< <= > >=
== != === !==
&
^
|
&&
||
? :
= += -= *= /= .= %= &= |= ^= <<= >>=
print
and
xor
or
,

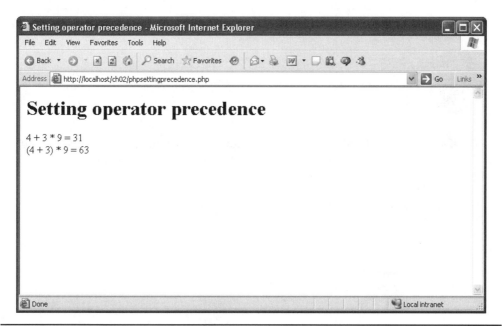

FIGURE 2-5 Setting precedence in PHP

You can see this page in a browser in Figure 2-5. As you can see, using parentheses sets the precedence of operator execution.

Using the if Statement

This is the point you start making decisions in your code, and executing other code depending on the results of that decision. This is the if statement, the primary decision-making statement in PHP. Here's what it looks like formally:

```
if(expression)
  statement
```

Here, *expression* is a PHP expression that evaluates to a TRUE or FALSE value. Just as in other languages you may have come across, if *expression* is TRUE, the *statement* that follows is executed; if it is FALSE, *statement* is not executed. You use conditional and logical operators, coming up next, to create expressions of the kind that can be evaluated by if statements. For example, you can use the greater-than operator, >, to form an expression such as 4 > 1, which is TRUE, because 4 is indeed greater than 1.

It's also worth noting that although statement can be a single line of code, it's also possible to use a compound PHP statement, which is made up of multiple single statements enclosed in curly braces, { and }. Here's a single statement:

```
echo "Here is the answer.";
```

Here is a compound statement:

```
{
  echo "Here";
  echo " is";
  echo " the";
  echo " answer.";
}
```

The if statement is a terrific one because it allows you to make choices on the fly, and have alternate code executed, depending on the results of that choice. For example, you could check the value of a password to make sure it's correct, or check the user's response to yes/no queries ("Do you want fries with that?").

For example, you might want to display some text if the outside temperature is above 65 degrees, which you could do like this:

```
<?php
  $temperature = 66;
  if ($temperature > 65)
    echo "It's nice outside.";
?>
```

Although this way of doing things, with a single statement following the if statement, works, it's more usual to put in the curly braces associated with compound statements like this:

```
<?php
  $temperature = 66;
  if ($temperature > 65) {
    echo "It's nice outside.";
  }
?>
```

Because this is the way you'll usually see things done—even with single statements—this is the way you'll see the if statement in this book—with the curly braces. You can, of course, use compound statements here as well:

```
<?php
  $temperature = 66;
  if ($temperature > 65) {
    echo "It's ";
    echo "nice ";
    echo "outside.";
  }
?>
```

Here's an example, phpif.php, that checks how many minutes someone has been in the pool—if it's more than 30 minutes, it's time to get out:

```
<html>
    <head>
        <title>Using the if statement</title>
    </head>
```

```
    <body>
        <h1>Using the if statement</h1>
        <?php
            $minutes = 31;
            if($minutes > 30) {
                .
                .
                .
            }
        ?>
    </body>
</html>
```

If it's time to get out, you can display a message:

```
<html>
    <head>
        <title>Using the if statement</title>
    </head>

    <body>
        <h1>Using the if statement</h1>
        <?php
            $minutes = 31;
            if($minutes > 30) {
                echo "Your time is up!<br>";
                echo "Please get out of the pool.";
            }
        ?>
    </body>
</html>
```

You can see phpif.php at work in Figure 2-6.

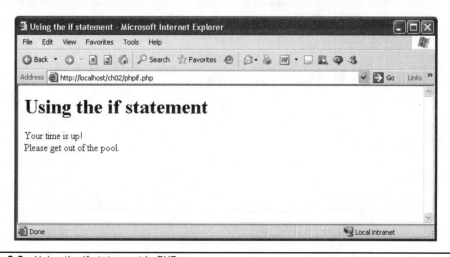

Figure 2-6   Using the if statement in PHP

Here's another example, phpisfloat.php. As mentioned in the preceding chapter, PHP includes special functions to let you determine the internal storage format that PHP has selected for variables—is_int, is_float, and so on. This example checks to make sure that a variable is stored as a floating-point number, then adds 4.5 to it, and uses the var_dump PHP function to "dump" (that is, display) the value of the variable to the browser:

```html
<html>
    <head>
        <title>Using the is_float function</title>
    </head>

    <body>
        <h1>Using the is_float function</h1>
        <?php
        $variable = 10.7;
        if (is_float($variable)) {
          $variable = $variable + 4.5;
          var_dump($variable);
        }
        ?>
    </body>
</html>
```

You can see phpisfloat.php at work in Figure 2-7. As you see there, the vardump function gives you the response float(15.2) here, indicating the variable's value and internal type.

There's more to the if statement, and that's coming up. For example, the greater-than operator (>) is just one of a set of PHP comparison operators, and they're coming up next.

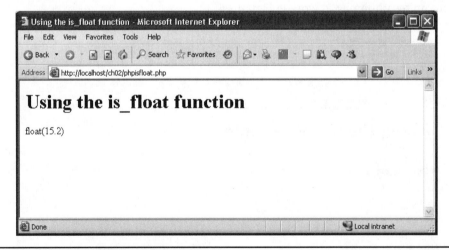

FIGURE 2-7   Using the is_float function in PHP

The PHP Comparison Operators

You've already seen one of the PHP comparison operators, the greater-than operator:

```php
<?php
  $temperature = 66;
  if ($temperature > 65) {
    echo "It's nice outside.";
  }
?>
```

There are plenty of other comparison operators, such as the less-than-or-equal-to operator (<=), which you see at work here:

```php
<?php
  $temperature = 66;
  if ($temperature <= 65) {
    echo "Pretty chilly outside.";
  }
?>
```

You can see all the PHP comparison operators in Table 2-3.

For example, you can see how to use the == equality operator in phpequality.php, which checks if someone has been in the pool for exactly 30 minutes:

```html
<html>
    <head>
        <title>Using the == operator</title>
    </head>
```

Operator	Operation	Example	Result
==	Equal	$a == $b	TRUE if $a is equal to $b
===	Identical	$a === $b	TRUE if $a is equal to $b, and they are of the same type
!=	Not equal	$a != $b	TRUE if $a is not equal to $b
<>	Not equal	$a <> $b	TRUE if $a is not equal to $b
!==	Not identical	$a !== $b	TRUE if $a is not equal to $b, or they are not of the same type
<	Less than	$a < $b	TRUE if $a is strictly less than $b
>	Greater than	$a > $b	TRUE if $a is strictly greater than $b
<=	Less than or equal to	$a <= $b	TRUE if $a is less than or equal to $b
>=	Greater than or equal to	$a >= $b	TRUE if $a is greater than or equal to $b

TABLE 2-3   The Comparison Operators

```
<body>
    <h1>Using the == operator</h1>
    <?php
        $minutes = 30;
        if($minutes == 30) {
            echo "Warning:<br>";
            echo "Your time in the pool is almost up.";
        }
    ?>
</body>
</html>
```

You can see phpequality.php in Figure 2-8; make sure you don't confuse the equality operator, ==, and the assignment operator, =.

Similarly, this example uses the not-equal operator, !=, to test if the temperature is not equal to 67 degrees:

```
<?php
  $temperature = 30;
  if($temperature != 67 {
    echo "The temperature is not 67 degrees.";
  }
?>
```

Here's what you get from this script:

```
The temperature is not 67 degrees.
```

Besides using comparison operators, there is also a set of logical operators you can use with decision-making statements like the if statement.

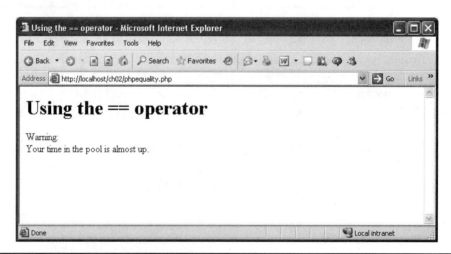

FIGURE 2-8   Using the equality operator in PHP

The PHP Logical Operators

You've already seen how to check if the outside temperature is greater than 65 degrees:

```php
<?php
  $temperature = 66;
  if ($temperature > 65) {
    echo "It's nice outside.";
  }
?>
```

But what if you wanted to check if the temperature is greater than 65 degrees *and* less than 75 degrees? In that case, you can use the and logical operator, &&, to connect two conditional clauses as shown in phplogical.php:

```html
<html>
    <head>
        <title>Using the logical operators</title>
    </head>

    <body>
        <h1>Using the logical operators</h1>
        <?php
          $temperature = 66;
          if ($temperature > 65 && $temperature < 75) {
            echo "It's between 65 and 75 outside.";
          }
        ?>
    </body>
</html>
```

Note the line

```php
        if ($temperature > 65 && $temperature < 75) {
            echo "It's between 65 and 75 outside.";
        }
```

You can see phplogical.php in Figure 2-9.

You use logical operators like && to connect clauses in an if statement—in this case, the if statement's conditional expression is true only if the value in $temperature is *both* greater than 65 and less than 75.

On the other hand, say that you wanted to check if the temperature was either less than 32 degrees *or* more than 100. You could do that with the or logical operator, | |, like this:

```html
<html>
    <head>
        <title>Using the logical operators</title>
    </head>

    <body>
        <h1>Using the logical operators</h1>
        <?php
```

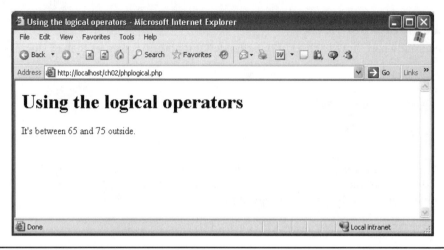

FIGURE 2-9   Using the and logical operator in PHP

```
    $temperature = 66;
    if ($temperature < 32 || $temperature > 100) {
      echo "Better stay inside today.";
    }
  ?>
  </body>
</html>
```

You can find all the PHP logical operators in Table 2-4.

You might wonder why there are two and logical operators ("and" and &&) and two or logical operators ("or" and ||). The answer is that the && and || operators have high precedence, and there are times when you might want low precedence logical operators so that you don't have to specifically use parentheses in your expressions to get things right.

Operator	Operation	Example	Result
and	And	$a and $b	TRUE if both $a and $b are TRUE
or	Or	$a or $b	TRUE if either $a or $b is TRUE
xor	Xor	$a xor $b	TRUE if either $a or $b is TRUE, but not both
!	Not	! $a	TRUE if $a is not TRUE
&&	And	$a && $b	TRUE if both $a and $b are TRUE
||	Or	$a || $b	TRUE if either $a or $b is TRUE

TABLE 2-4   The Logical Operators

The else Statement

There's more to the if statement. For example, what if the if statement's condition turns out to be false—is there still a way to execute code? Yes, there is; just use an else statement. Here's what the else statement looks like formally:

```
if expression
  statement1
else
  expression2
```

Here, if the *expression* is true, *statement1* will be executed. If *expression* is false, on the other hand, *expression2* will be executed.

Here's an example. phpelse.php. Say you want to print out one message if the outside temperature was outside the range 32 degrees to 100 degrees, and another message if the temperature is inside that range. You can start by determining if the temperature is outside that range and displaying a message if so:

```html
<html>
    <head>
        <title>Using the else statement</title>
    </head>

    <body>
        <h1>Using the else statement</h1>
        <?php
          $temperature = 66;
          if ($temperature < 32 || $temperature > 100) {
            echo "Better stay inside today.";
          }
          .
          .
          .
          ?>
    </body>
</html>
```

Otherwise, if the temperature is inside the range 32 to 100, you can display an alternate message, "Nice day outside.":

```html
<html>
    <head>
        <title>Using the else statement</title>
    </head>

    <body>
        <h1>Using the else statement</h1>
        <?php
          $temperature = 66;
          if ($temperature < 32 || $temperature > 100) {
            echo "Better stay inside today.";
          }
```

```
            else {
                echo "Nice day outside.";
            }
        ?>
    </body>
</html>
```

You can see the results in Figure 2-10—nice day outside.

Here's another example, testing whether or not your plane has enough gas to get to the airport:

```
<html>
    <head>
        <title>Using the else statement</title>
    </head>

    <body>
        <h1>Using the else statement</h1>
        <?php
            $gallons = 6;
            if ($gallons < 5) {
                echo "Got a parachute?";
            }
            else {
                echo "You'll be OK.";
            }
        ?>
    </body>
</html>
```

The output from this script:

```
You'll be OK.
```

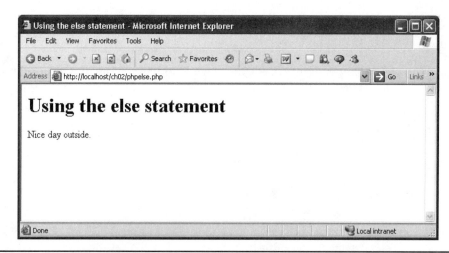

FIGURE 2-10   Using the else statement in PHP

The elseif Statement

PHP also has an elseif statement, which you can use to check alternate if conditions—if an if statement's conditional expression is false, you can make additional tests with elseif. Here's how the full if statement looks, including elseif statements:

```
if expression1
  statement1
elseif expression2
  expression2
elseif expression3
  expression3
elseif expression4
  expression4
elseif expression5
  expression5
      .
      .
      .
else
  expression6
```

And here's an example, phpelseif.php, which displays a variety of messages depending on the temperature. If the temperature is less than 32 degrees, this script displays the message "Too cold.". If the temperature is between 32 and 60, it displays "Pretty chilly." If the temperature is between 61 and 70, it displays "Pretty nice outside.", and so on:

```
<html>
    <head>
        <title>Using the elseif statement</title>
    </head>

    <body>
        <h1>Using the elseif statement</h1>
        <?php
          $temperature = 66;
          if ($temperature < 32) {
            echo "Too cold.";
          }
          elseif ($temperature < 60) {
            echo "Pretty chilly.";
          }
          elseif ($temperature < 70) {
            echo "Pretty nice outside.";
          }
          elseif ($temperature < 80) {
            echo "Pretty warm outside.";
          }
          else {
            echo "Too hot.";
          }
        ?>
    </body>
</html>
```

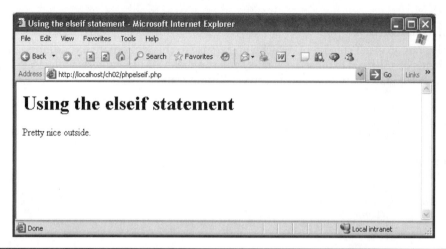

FIGURE 2-11   Using the elseif statement in PHP

You can see how this works. If the if statement's conditional expression is false, PHP checks the first elseif statement's conditional expression, and if that's true, the elseif statement's code is executed. If the first elseif statement's conditional expression is false, PHP moves on to the next elseif statement and so on. At the end of the whole chain is an else statement, whose code is executed if no other code has been executed in the if statement up to this point. The whole thing appears in Figure 2-11.

And with the addition of the elseif clauses, you've now mastered the if statement—you know all there is to know about it.

The ternary Operator

There's actually a built-in operator that acts like an if statement in PHP: the ternary operator, which PHP shares with several other languages. This operator has an unusual form, and here it is:

```
$result = condition ? expression1 : expression2;
```

Okay, what's going on here? If condition is true, the ternary operator—which is made up of the characters ?:—returns expression1. Otherwise, it returns expression2. So as you can see, this is an operator that lets you make real-time choices.

Here's an example. This code displays "Nice day outside." if the outside temperature is between 32 and 100 degrees, and "Better stay inside today." otherwise:

```php
<?php
  $temperature = 66;
  if ($temperature < 32 || $temperature > 100) {
    echo "Better stay inside today.";
  }
  else {
    echo "Nice day outside.";
  }
?>
```

Here's the same code using the ternary operator—note how compact this is:

```
<?php
    $temperature = 66;
    echo ($temperature < 32 || $temperature > 100) ? "Better stay inside
today." : "Nice day outside.";
    ?>
```

Here's another example that finds the absolute value of numbers—all it does is to use the negation operator, -, to change the sign of a value if that value if negative:

```
<?php
    $value = -3;
    $abs_value = $value < 0 ? -$value : $value;
    echo $abs_value;
?>
```

This example displays the value 3.

Here's another example—a slightly more involved one. This example converts decimal into hexadecimal digits (as long as the result is a single hexadecimal digit, 0–F). Here's the code:

```
<?php
    $value = 15;
    $hex = $value < 10 ? "0x" . $value : "0x" . chr($value - 10 + 65);
    echo "In hex, $value = $hex";
?>
```

This script will give you: In hex, 15 = 0xF (you preface hex values with 0x in PHP to tell PHP that it's a hex value). Pretty cool—the conversion is done in a single statement (of course, the PHP dechex function can do even better, converting multidigit values).

The switch Statement

The PHP switch statement lets you replace long if-elseif-else ladders of condition checking with an easy single statement. You pass the switch statement a single value and it tests that value against case statements that you list, executing the code in any case statement whose test value matches the value you're checking. Here's how the switch statement looks formally—note that values in square brackets [ ] are optional:

```
switch (testvalue) {
    case expression1:
        statement1
        [break;]
    case expression2:
        statement2
        [break;]
    case expression3:
        statement3
        [break;]
    case expression4:
        statement4
```

```
        [break;]
            .
            .
            .
    [default:
      default_statement]
  }
```

Here's how this works: You pass a value (integer or floating-point numbers or strings) to the switch statement, and the switch statement checks it against all the cases you've listed; if the value you're checking matches the value in a case statement, that case statement's code is executed. If no case matches the value you're checking, the code in the default statement, if there is a default statement, is executed. The break statement ends execution of the switch statement—if you omit the break statement, execution will continue with the code in the following case statement automatically.

And here's an example, phpswitch.php, which displays different messages, depending on the current outside temperature:

```html
<html>
    <head>
        <title>
            Using the switch statement
        </title>
    </head>

    <body>
        <h1>
            Using the switch statement
        </h1>
        <?php
            $temperature = 70;
            switch ($temperature) {
                case 70:
                case 71:
                case 72:
                    echo "Nice day outside.";
                    break;
                case 73:
                case 74:
                case 75:
                    echo "OK, but a little warm.";
                    break;
                case 76:
                case 77:
                case 78:
                    echo "A little warmer.";
                    break;
                default:
                  echo "Temperature outside the range this statement can handle.";
            }
        ?>
    </body>
</html>
```

You can see the results of phpswitch.php in Figure 2-12.

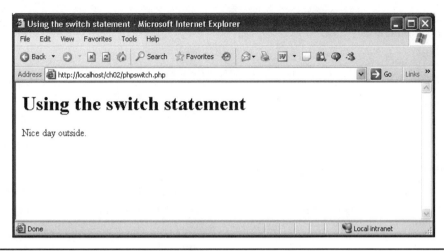

FIGURE 2-12   Using the switch statement in PHP

Using for Loops

Computers are great at repetitive tasks—that's their strong point. For that reason, PHP comes stocked with the standard loops that other programming languages, such as the for loop, which you're going to see now. Here's how it works formally:

```
for (expression1; expression2; expression3)
  statement
```

The for loop executes *expression1* before it starts; then it checks the value of *expression2*—if it's true, the loop executes *statement* once. Then the loop executes *expression3* (which often increments the value in a loop counter variable) and after that checks the value of *expression2* again (which might check the value in the loop counter variable). If *expression2* is still true, the loop executes *statement* once again. Then the loop executes *expression3* again, and the process keeps going until *expression2* evaluates to false, when the loop ends. Note that *expression2* is checked before the loop executes, and *expression3* is executed after every time the loop loops.

Here's an example, phpfor.php, which displays a message six times. You can start by initializing a loop counter variable to 0:

```
<?php
    for ($loop_counter = 0;...){
    .
    .
    .
    }
?>
```

Each time through the loop, you can check if the loop counter is greater than 6, in which case you should quit:

```php
<?php
    for ($loop_counter = 0; $loop_counter < 6;...){
        .
        .
        .
    }
?>
```

And after each time the loop is executed, you can increment the loop counter:

```php
<?php
    for ($loop_counter = 0; $loop_counter < 6; $loop_counter++){
        .
        .
        .
    }
?>
```

That sets up the loop, which will execute six times. All that's left is the body of the loop—the statement (which can be a compound statement) that you want to execute each time the loop loops. In this case, the example will just display another line of text, as you see in phpfor.php:

```html
<html>
    <head>
        <title>
            Using the for loop
        </title>
    </head>

    <body>
        <h1>
            Using the for loop
        </h1>
        <?php
            for ($loop_counter = 0; $loop_counter < 6; $loop_counter++){
                echo "You're going to see this message six times.<br>";
            }
        ?>
    </body>
</html>
```

You can see the results in Figure 2-13, where as you can see, the message appears six times, once for each iteration of the for loop. Very nice.

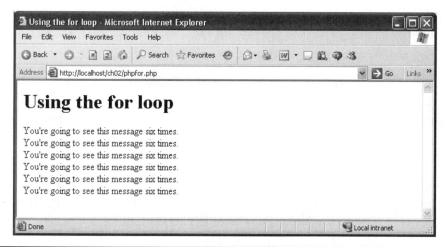

FIGURE 2-13   Using the for loop in PHP

There's more about for loops as well; for loops can handle multiple loop counters if you want, as long as you separate them with the comma operator. Here's an example that uses two loop counters:

```php
<?php
for ($loop1 = 2, $loop2 = 2; $loop1 < 6 && $loop2 < 6; $loop1++, $loop2++){
    echo "$loop1 x $loop2 = ", $loop1 * $loop2, "<br>";
}
?>
```

And here's what the result looks like in a browser:

```
2 x 2 = 4
3 x 3 = 9
4 x 4 = 16
5 x 5 = 25
```

In fact, you don't have to use loop counters at all in a for loop. Here's an example that starts by initializing a connection to a database, gets a new record each time through the loop, and processes the new record until the end of the data is reached, at which point the process_record function returns -1:

```php
for (initialize_connection(); process_record() != -1; get_next_record()){
}
```

You can also nest for loops, one inside another, as you'll see when we work with arrays. Here's a quick example:

```php
<?php
    for ($loop_counter1 = 0; $loop_counter1 < 6; $loop_counter1++){
        for ($loop_counter2 = 0; $loop_counter2 < 2; $loop_counter2++){
```

```
        echo "You're going to see this message twelve times.<br>";
      }
    }
  ?>
```

Using while Loops

PHP has another type of loop: the while loop. This one's real easy—here's what it looks like:

```
while (expression)
  statement
```

While *expression* is true, the loop executes *statement*. That's all there is to it. When *expression* is false, the loop ends (which means, please note, that it's possible that *statement* will never get executed). In other words, the while loop keeps executing while its test expression is true.

Here's an example, phpwhile.php, which keeps incrementing a variable until its value is greater than or equal to 10, at which point it quits:

```
<html>
    <head>
        <title>
            Using the while loop
        </title>
    </head>

    <body>
        <h1>
            Using the while loop
        </h1>
        <?php
            $variable = 1;

            while ($variable < 10){
                echo "Now \$variable holds: ", $variable, "<br>";
                $variable++;
            }
        ?>
    </body>
</html>
```

And you can see the results in Figure 2-14—the while loop kept looping while $variable held less than 10—and when that was no longer true, it quit.

You can even convert a while loop into a for loop if you use an explicit loop counter, as in this example:

```
<?php
    $loop_counter = 0;
    while ($loop_counter < 6){
        .
        .
        .
    }
?>
```

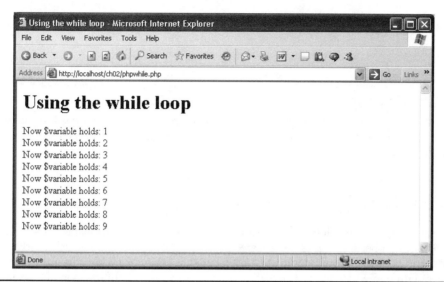

Using the while loop - Microsoft Internet Explorer

FIGURE 2-14   Using the while loop in PHP

Then you increment and use the loop counter in the body of the loop:

```php
<?php
    $loop_counter = 0;
    while ($loop_counter < 6){
        echo "You're going to see this message six times. <br>";
        $loop_counter++;
    }
?>
```

You often use the while loop when you have a looping situation where you don't actually need a loop counter. For example, while loops are often used to read data from files; you might open a file, and then use a while loop to check if you're at the end of the file:

```php
<?php
    open_file();
    while (not_at_end_of_file()){
        .
        .
        .
    }
?>
```

If you're not at the end of the file, you can read data from the file and echo it:

```php
<?php
    open_file();
    while (not_at_end_of_file()){
```

```
            $data = read_data_from_file();
            echo $data;
        }
    ?>
```

Using do...while Loops

There's another kind of while loop—the do...while loop. This kind of loop is just like the while loop with one exception: it checks its test expression at the end of the loop, not the beginning. Here's what the do...while loop looks like:

```
do
    statement
while (expression)
```

In this case, the do...while loop keeps executing *statement* while *expression* is true—and note in particular that because *expression* is tested at the end of the loop, *expression* could actually be false, and the loop's body would still be executed at least once. That's useful when you have a situation in which the test condition is set inside the body of the loop and so can't be tested until the end of the loop.

Here's an example, phpdowhile.php, that converts the previous while example into do...while form:

```
<html>
    <head>
        <title>
            Using the do...while loop
        </title>
    </head>

    <body>
        <h1>
            Using the do...while loop
        </h1>
        <?php
            $variable = 1;

            do {
                echo "Now \$variable holds: ", $variable, "<br>";
                $variable++;
            }
            while ($variable < 10)
        ?>
    </body>
</html>
```

You can see the results in Figure 2-15, where the do...while loop has done its thing.

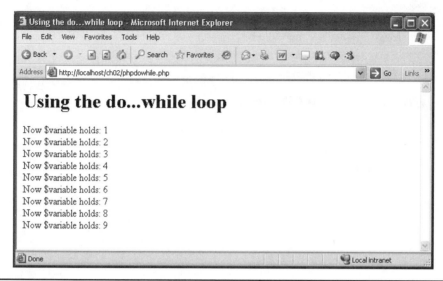

FIGURE 2-15   Using the do...while loop in PHP

Here's another example that points out the difference between the while loop and the do...while loop, phpdoornot.php. Here, even though its condition evaluates to false, you'll see that the do...while loop executes its body once—but the while loop does not:

```
<html>
    <head>
        <title>
            Using the do...while loop
        </title>
    </head>

    <body>
        <h1>
            Using the do...while loop
        </h1>
        <?php
            $variable = 20;

            do {
                echo "The do...while loop says \$variable = ", $variable, "<br>";
            }
            while ($variable < 10);

            while ($variable < 10){
                echo "The while loop says \$variable = ", $variable, "<br>";
            }
        ?>
    </body>
</html>
```

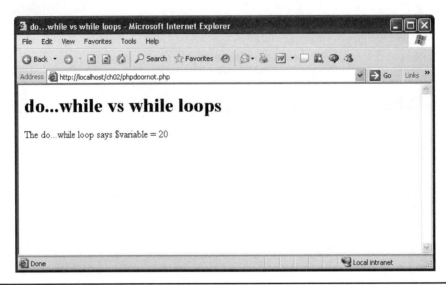

FIGURE 2-16   The do...while loop vs. the while loop in PHP

You can see the results in Figure 2-16—the do...while loop executed once, but the while loop didn't.

Using the foreach Loop

There's a special loop designed to work with PHP collections, such as the arrays you're going to see in the next chapter. Collections are made up of multiple items, and the foreach loop is designed to handle collections. It's useful to have a loop like foreach around, because it automatically loops over all the items in the collection—in particular, you don't have to worry about getting the loop counters just right. Here's what the foreach loop looks like:

```
foreach (collection_expression as $value) statement
foreach (collection_expression as $key => $value) statement
```

And here's an example, phpforeach.php, putting the foreach loop to work. This example loops over all the items in an array—types of sandwiches (see the next chapter for more on arrays)—and displays each item:

```
<html>
  <head>
    <title>
      Using the foreach loop
    </title>
  </head>
```

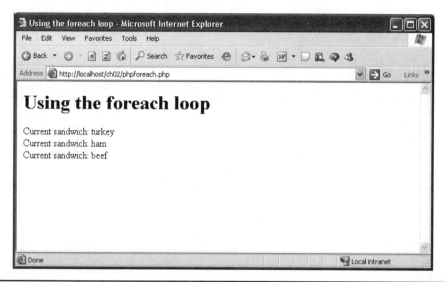

FIGURE 2-17   The foreach loop in PHP

```
<body>
   <h1>Using the foreach loop</h1>
     <?php
       $arr = array("turkey", "ham", "beef");
       foreach ($arr as $value) {
         echo "Current sandwich: $value<br>";
       }
     ?>
</body>
</html>
```

You can see the results in Figure 2-17, where the foreach loop has looped over the array. Nice.

Terminating Loops Early

You can stop a loop or switch statement at any time with the break statement. You've already seen the break statement in the switch statement:

```
switch ($temperature) {
    case 70:
    case 71:
    case 72:
        echo "Nice day outside.";
        break;
        .
        .
        .
```

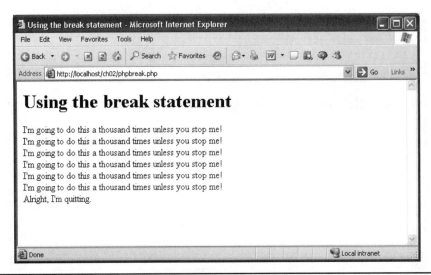

FIGURE 2-18   Using the break statement in PHP

But you can also use break in loops. Here's an example, phpbreak.php, that stops a loop when the loop counter reaches a value of 5:

```
<html>
  <head>
    <title>
      Using the break statement
    </title>
  </head>

  <body>
    <h1>Using the break statement</h1>
    <?php
      for ($loop_counter = 0; $loop_counter < 1000; $loop_counter++){
        echo "I'm going to do this a thousand times unless you stop me!<BR>";
        if ($loop_counter == 5) {
          echo "Alright, I'm quitting.<BR>";
          break;
        }
      }
    ?>
  </body>
</html>
```

And you can see this example at work in Figure 2-18.

Skipping Iterations

Sometimes, you might want to skip an iteration of a loop to avoid some kind of problem, such as a division by zero—and you can do that with the continue statement, which makes the loop move on to the next iteration.

Here's an example, phpcontinue.php, which finds the reciprocals (that is, 1 divided by the number) of various integers—note that it checks to see if it's being asked to divide by zero, and if so, it skips to the next iteration:

```
<html>
  <head>
    <title>
      Using the continue statement
    </title>
  </head>

  <body>
    <h1>Using the continue statement</h1>
    <?php
      $number =1;
      for ($number = -2; $number < 3; $number++){
        if($number == 0){
          continue;
        }
        echo "1/$number = ", 1 / $number, "<br>";
        $number++;
      }
    ?>
  </body>
</html>
```

And you can see the results in Figure 2-19, where, as you can see, the script skipped the step where it was supposed to divide by zero. Cool.

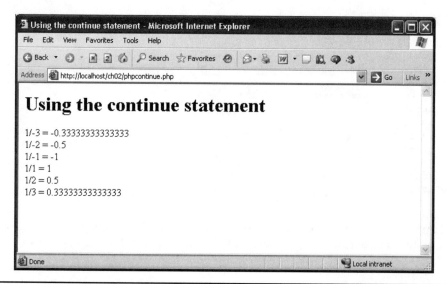

FIGURE 2-19 Using the continue statement in PHP

PHP Alternate Syntax

PHP also supports an alternative syntax for if, while, for, foreach, and switch. In each case, the form of the alternate syntax changes the opening curly brace to a colon (:) and the closing brace to endif;, endwhile;, endfor;, endforeach;, or endswitch;, respectively.

Here's an example showing an if statement using alternate syntax:

```
<?php
  $temperature = 61;
  if ($temperature == 60):
    echo "The temperature is 60";
  elseif ($temperature == 70):
    echo "The temperature is 70";
  else:
    echo "The temperature is not 60 or 70";
  endif;
?>
```

This example echoes: "The temperature is not 60 or 70".

Here's an example using a for loop and alternate syntax:

```
<?php
  for ($loop_counter = 0; $loop_counter < 6; $loop_counter++) :
      echo "You're going to see this message six times.<BR>";
  endfor;
?>
```

Here's a switch statement that uses alternate syntax:

```
<?php
  $temperature = 65;
  switch ($temperature) :
    case 60:
      echo "The temperature is 60.";
      break;
    case 70:
      echo "The temperature is 70.";
      break;
    case 80:
      echo "The temperature is 80.";
      break;
    default:
      echo "The temperature is not 60, 70, or 80.";
endswitch;
?>
```

Okay, you've gotten a good grounding in working with PHP operators and control structures like if statements and for loops. Coming up next: handling arrays and strings.

CHAPTER

Strings and Arrays

This chapter represents the next step up in handling your data in PHP: text strings and arrays. You've seen strings already to some extent, but there's a lot more to the story. Data on the Internet is usually in text format, and PHP excels in handling strings—there's a huge library of prebuilt string functions in PHP. From sorting strings to searching them, from trimming extra spaces to getting the length of a string, we'll master the PHP string functions in this chapter.

In addition to strings, you're also going to see how to work with arrays in PHP in this chapter. Arrays represent our first contact with collections in PHP—the storing of more than one data item under a single name. Arrays are an important part of PHP because, among other things, you use array notation to read data sent you from the user.

You've already seen simple variables, which hold simple data items like strings or numbers. Arrays store whole sets of data items in the same way, and you can access those individual data items with, for example, a numeric array index. That's great from a programming point of view, because you can use a loop to steadily increment that array index, letting you loop over, and handle, all the items in an array.

Say you have 12,000 numeric data items and want to find their average value. It would be a serious chore to write code to handle all those data items individually. But you can stash them all in a single array, and then loop over that array, handling the data items one by one, with a simple loop in a couple of lines. No problem.

Okay, we're ready to start. Let's begin by taking a look at the PHP built-in string functions.

The String Functions

PHP is string-oriented, and it comes packed with many string functions. PHP programs are often text-intensive—the data you get from the user is in text form, for example, and you might want to strip extra spaces from the beginning and end of such text. Or you might want to search that text for command words that the user can use. Or you might want to capitalize that text, or any of a hundred other things.

You can perform all those operations with the PHP string functions. To get us started with string functions, and to give you an indication of what's available, you can find all the string functions in Table 3-1.

Function	Does This
addcslashes	Quotes a string with slashes (in C style)
addslashes	Quotes a string with slashes
bin2hex	Converts binary data into hexadecimal representation
chop	Alias of the rtrim function
chr	Returns a specific character given its ASCII code
chunk_split	Splits a string into smaller chunks
convert_cyr_string	Converts from one Cyrillic character set to another
count_chars	Returns information about characters in a string
crc32	Calculates the crc32 polynomial of a string
crypt	Supports one-way string encryption (hashing)
echo	Displays one or more strings
explode	Splits a string on a substring
fprintf	Writes a formatted string to a stream
get_html_translation_table	Returns the translation table
hebrev	Converts Hebrew text to visual text
hebrevc	Converts logical Hebrew text to visual text
html_entity_decode	Converts all HTML entities to their applicable characters
htmlentities	Converts all applicable characters to HTML entities
htmlspecialchars	Converts special characters to HTML entities
implode	Joins array elements with a string
join	Alias of the implode function
levenshtein	Calculates the Levenshtein distance between two strings
localeconv	Gets the numeric formatting information
ltrim	Strips whitespace from the beginning of a string
md5_file	Calculates the md5 hash of a given filename
md5	Calculates the md5 hash of a string
metaphone	Calculates the metaphone key of a string
money_format	Formats a number as a currency string
nl_langinfo	Queries language and locale information
nl2br	Inserts HTML line breaks before all newlines in a string
number_format	Formats a number with grouped thousand separators
ord	Returns the ASCII value of a character

TABLE 3-1   The String Functions

Function	Does This
parse_str	Parses the string into variables
print	Displays a string
printf	Displays a formatted string
quoted_printable_decode	Converts a quoted-printable string to an 8-bit string
quotemeta	Quotes metacharacters
rtrim	Strips whitespace from the end of a string
setlocale	Sets locale information
sha1_file	Calculates the sha1 hash of a file
sha1	Calculates the sha1 hash of a string
similar_text	Calculates the similarity between two strings
soundex	Calculates the soundex key of a string
sprintf	Returns a formatted string
sscanf	Parses input from a string according to a format
str_ireplace	Case-insensitive version of the str_replace function
str_pad	Pads a string with another string
str_repeat	Repeats a string
str_replace	Replaces all occurrences of the search string with the replacement string
str_rot13	Performs the rot13 transform on a string
str_shuffle	Shuffles a string randomly
str_split	Converts a string to an array
str_word_count	Returns information about words used in a string
strcasecmp	Binary case-insensitive string comparison
strchr	Alias of the strstr function
strcmp	Binary-safe string comparison
strcoll	Locale-based string comparison
strcspn	Finds the length of the initial segment not matching a mask
strip_tags	Strips HTML and PHP tags from a string
stripcslashes	Un-quotes string quoted with addcslashes()
stripos	Finds position of first occurrence of a case-insensitive string
stripslashes	Un-quotes string quoted with addslashes()
stristr	Case-insensitive version of the strstr function
strlen	Gets a string's length

TABLE 3-1   The String Functions *(continued)*

Function	Does This
strnatcasecmp	Case insensitive string comparisons
strnatcmp	String comparisons using a "natural order" algorithm
strncasecmp	Binary case-insensitive string comparison of the first *n* characters
strncmp	Binary-safe string comparison of the first *n* characters
strpos	Finds position of first occurrence of a string
strrchr	Finds the last occurrence of a character in a string
strrev	Reverses a string
strripos	Finds the position of last occurrence of a case-insensitive string
strrpos	Finds the position of last occurrence of a char in a string
strspn	Finds the length of initial segment matching mask
strstr	Finds the first occurrence of a string
strtok	Tokenizes a string
strtolower	Converts a string to lowercase
strtoupper	Converts a string to uppercase
strtr	Translates certain characters
substr_compare	Binary-safe (optionally case-insensitive) comparison of two strings from an offset
substr_count	Counts the number of substring occurrences
substr_replace	Replaces text within part of a string
substr	Returns part of a string
trim	Strips whitespace from the beginning and end of a string
ucfirst	Makes a string's first character uppercase
ucwords	Uppercases the first character of each word in a string
vprintf	Outputs a formatted string
vsprintf	Returns a formatted string
wordwrap	Wraps a string to a given number of characters

TABLE 3-1   The String Functions *(continued)*

As you can see, there are plenty of string functions. Let's put some of them to work in an example called phpstrings.php. You might start with the string "No problem":

```
echo "The test string is 'No problem'.<br>";
```

You can use the strlen function to find the string's length:

```
echo "'No problem' is ", strlen("No problem"), " characters long<br>";
```

And you can extract substrings with substr:

```
echo "The substring substr('No problem', 3, 7) is '", substr("No problem",
  3, 7), "'<br>";
```

You can search strings with the strpos:

```
echo "The word 'problem' is at position ", strpos("No problem", "problem"),
  "<br>";
```

And you can replace substrings with substr_replace:

```
    echo "Replacing 'problem' with 'problems' gives: ", substr_replace(
      "No problem", "problems", 3, 9), "<br>";
```

The chr function converts ASCII numeric codes into their corresponding characters—here's ABC in ASCII:

```
    echo "Using ASCII codes: ", chr(65), chr(66), chr(67), "<br>";
```

You can uppercase the first letter of the string with ucfirst:

```
echo "Uppercasing the first letter gives you: ", ucfirst("no problem"),
  "<br>";
```

Or uppercase the whole string with strtoupper:

```
    echo "In upper case: ", strtoupper("No problem"), "<br>";
```

And you can lowercase the whole string with strtolower:

```
    echo "In lower case: ", strtolower("No problem"), "<br>";
```

You can trim excess spaces with the trim function (the   codes you see here are to create nonbreaking spaces in the browser so that the browser doesn't collapse the four spaces here into one space):

```
    echo "'    No problem' trimmed is: '", trim(
      "    No problem"), "'<br>";
```

You can reverse strings with strrev:

```
    echo "Reversed: ", strrev("No problem"), "<br>";
```

And you can count the number of occurrences of a substring with the substr_count function like this in phpstrings.php:

```
<html>
  <head>
    <title>
      Using string functions
    </title>
  </head>
```

```
<body>
  <h1>
    Using string functions
  </h1>
  <?php
    echo "The test string is 'No problem'.<br>";
    echo "'No problem' is ", strlen("No problem"), " characters long<br>";
    echo "The substring substr('No problem', 3, 7) is '", substr("No problem",
      3, 7), "'<br>";
    echo "The word 'problem' is at position ", strpos("No problem",
problem"),
      "<br>";
    echo "Replacing 'problem' with 'problems' gives: ", substr_replace(
      "No problem", "problems", 3, 9), "<br>";
    echo "Using ASCII codes: ", chr(65), chr(66), chr(67), "<br>";
    echo "Uppercasing the first letter gives you: ", ucfirst("no problem"),
      "<br>";
    echo "In upper case: ", strtoupper("No problem"), "<br>";
    echo "In lower case: ", strtolower("No problem"), "<br>";
    echo "'    No problem' trimmed is: '", trim(
    "   No problem"), "'<br>";
    echo "Reversed: ", strrev("No problem"), "<br>";
    echo "There are ", substr_count("No problem", "o"), " o's in 'No problem'.";
  ?>
  </body>
</html>
```

How will all this look in a browser? Take a look at Figure 3-1, where you can see the results. As you can see, there's plenty of string-handling power that comes with PHP.

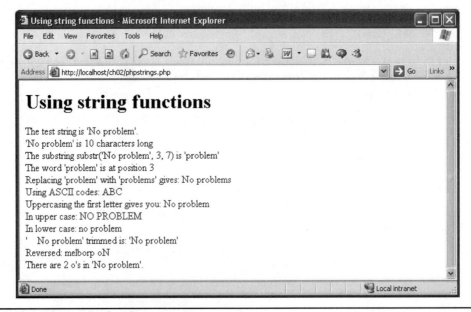

FIGURE 3-1   Using string functions

Converting to and from Strings

Because data is sent to you in string format, and because you'll have to display your data in string format in the user's browser, converting between strings and numbers is one of the most important interface tasks in PHP.

Here's an example, phpconvert.php. To convert to a string, you can use the *cast* (string) or the strval function, which returns the string value of the item you pass to it (using the cast and strval here isn't technically necessary, since echo converts numbers to strings itself):

```
<?php
    $float = 3.1415;
    echo (string) $float, "<br>";
    echo strval($float), "<br>";
?>
```

How do the (string) cast and the strval function work when converting other values? A boolean TRUE value is converted to the string "1"; the FALSE value is represented as "" (empty string). An integer or a floating-point number (float) is converted to a string representing the number with its digits (including the exponent part for floating-point numbers). The value NULL is always converted to an empty string.

You can also go the other way, and convert a string into a number. The string will be treated as a float if it contains any of the characters '.', 'e', or 'E'. Otherwise, it will be treated as an integer. The numeric value of a string is given by the *initial part* of the string. If the string starts with numeric data, that will be the value used. Otherwise, the value will be 0 (zero). Valid numeric data consists of an optional sign (+ or -), followed by one or more digits (including, if you use it, a decimal point), followed by an optional exponent (the exponent part is an 'e' or 'E' followed by one or more digits).

For example, you can add a number and a quoted number (that is, a number in a string) and PHP will do the right thing:

```
$value = 1 + "19.2";
echo "$value <br>";
```

Here's another example, showing a number with a power of 10:

```
$value = 1 + "2.5e4";
echo "$value <br>";
```

You can also explicitly convert text to floats with the (float) cast, for example:

```
$text = "3.0";
$value = (float) $text;
echo $value / 2.0, "<br>";
```

Here's what phpformat.php looks like, putting this all together:

```
<html>
  <head>
    <title>
      Converting from strings and numbers
    </title>
  </head>
```

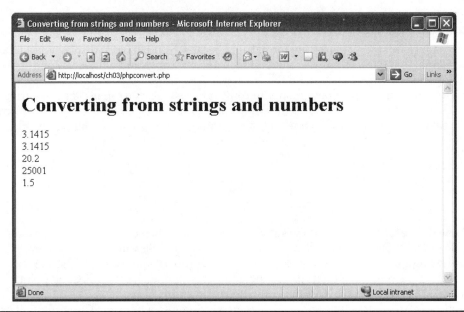

FIGURE 3-2 Converting between strings and numbers

```
<body>
  <h1>
    Converting from strings and numbers
  </h1>
  <?php
  $float = 3.1415;
  echo (string) $float, "<br>";
  echo strval($float), "<br>";
  $value = 1 + "19.2";
  echo "$value <br>";
  $value = 1 + "2.5e4";
  echo "$value <br>";
  $text = "3.0";
  $value = (float) $text;
  echo $value / 2.0, "<br>";
?>
  </body>
</html>
```

You can see phpconvert.php at work in Figure 3-2.

Formatting Text Strings

Because all the data sent to your PHP scripts and the data you send back to the browser is in text form, formatting that data is one of the most important things you'll be doing in PHP. For example, what if you want to make sure that price you're displaying has exactly two places after the decimal point? It turns out that there are two PHP functions that specifically handle formatting of text strings, and here they are—printf and sprintf:

```
printf (format [, args])
sprintf (format [, args])
```

The printf function prints a string (much like echo), and the sprintf function also "prints" its data, but in this case, the output is a string—that is, it returns a string.

The format string is a little complex here. It's made up of zero or more directives, which are characters copied to the result, and conversion specifiers, which are made up of a percent sign (%) followed by one or more of these items (in this order):

- An optional *padding specifier* that indicates which character should be used to pad the results to the correct string size. This may be a space character or a 0 (zero character). The default is to pad with spaces.

- An optional *alignment specifier* that indicates if the results should be left-justified or right-justified. The default is right-justified (a - character here will make it left-justified).

- An optional number, the *width specifier,* specifying how many characters (minimum) this conversion should result in.

- An optional *precision specifier* that indicates how many decimal digits should be displayed for floating-point numbers. (There is no effect for other types than float.)

- A *type specifier* that says what type the argument data should be treated as.

Here are the possible type specifiers:

- **%**   A literal percent character. No argument is required.
- **b**   The argument is treated as an integer and presented as a binary number.
- **c**   The argument is treated as an integer and presented as the character with that ASCII value.
- **d**   The argument is treated as an integer and presented as a (signed) decimal number.
- **u**   The argument is treated as an integer and presented as an unsigned decimal number.
- **f**   The argument is treated as a float and presented as a floating-point number.
- **-**   The argument is treated as an integer and presented as an octal number.
- **s**   The argument is treated as and presented as a string.
- **x**   The argument is treated as an integer and presented as a hexadecimal number (with lowercase letters).
- **X**   The argument is treated as an integer and presented as a hexadecimal number (with uppercase letters).

Getting formats to work can be tricky. Here's an example, phpformat.php. You might start with the %s format, which just inserts a string, with printf:

```
printf("I have %s pants and %s shirts.<br><br>", 4, 12);
```

This will display "I have 4 pants and 12 shirts.". That's the way it works—you put the format into a string template, and then the data to be formatted follows.

Here's how to use sprintf, which returns a string:

```
$string = sprintf("After the sale I have %s pants and %s shirts.<br>", 6,
   21);
echo $string, "<br>";
```

Here's a more involved use of formatting, using the format %01.2f, which results in two places after the decimal point:

```
$price = 2789.992;
echo "The price is ";
printf("\$%01.2f<br><br>", $price);
```

This will display "The price is 2789.99". Here are some more uses of format strings for formatting floating-point numbers:

```
echo "printf(\"%6.2f\", 3.1) gives you ";
printf("%6.2f<br>", 3.1);
echo "printf(\"%6.2f\", 30.1) gives you ";
printf("%6.2f<br>", 30.1);
echo "printf(\"%6.3f\", 300.1) gives you ";
printf("%6.2f<br><br>", 300.1);
```

Here's an example using the d format specifier, for formatting integers:

```
$year = 2007;
$month = 9;
$day = 2;
echo "The date is ";
printf("%04d-%02d-%02d<br>", $year, $month, $day);
```

Here's the whole thing in phpformat.php:

```
<html>
  <head>
    <title>
      Using string formatting
    </title>
  </head>
  <body>
    <h1>
      Using string formatting
    </h1>
    <?php
      printf("I have %s pants and %s shirts.<br><br>", 4, 12);

      $string = sprintf("After the sale I have %s pants and %s shirts.<br>", 6,
         21);
      echo $string, "<br>";
```

```
$price = 2789.992;
echo "The price is ";
printf("\$%01.2f<br><br>", $price);

echo "printf(\"%6.2f\", 3.1) gives you ";
printf("%6.2f<br>", 3.1);
echo "printf(\"%6.2f\", 30.1) gives you ";
printf("%6.2f<br>", 30.1);
echo "printf(\"%6.3f\", 300.1) gives you ";
printf("%6.2f<br><br>", 300.1);

$year = 2007;
$month = 9;
$day = 2;
echo "The date is ";
printf("%04d-%02d-%02d<br>", $year, $month, $day);

    ?>
  </body>
</html>
```

And you can see phpformat.php in Figure 3-3.

Tip *Incidentally, there's another function for formatting numbers in PHP: number_format().*

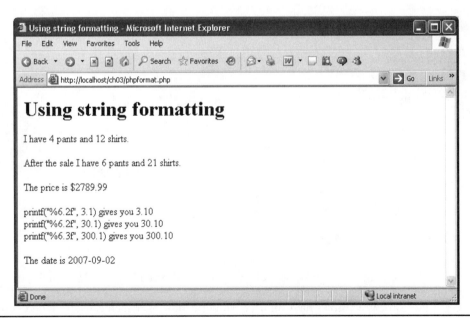

FIGURE 3-3   Formatting strings in PHP

Building Yourself Some Arrays

Now we're going to plunge into a new topic: arrays. Arrays are integral to PHP, more so than in other languages—for example, you communicate with the user of your Web application using arrays in PHP. You also use arrays when you have a set of data—multiple data items.

Arrays are collections of data items stored under a single name. You might be keeping track of the grades of 500 students in that PHP class you're teaching, for example, and arrays are perfect for that.

You can create arrays the same way you can create variables—just assign values to a variable name. For example, you might create an array named $actors and assign the name "Cary Grant" to the first place in that array, element 0:

```
$actors[0] = "Cary Grant";
```

This statement creates a new array named $actors, and stores "Cary Grant" in the first element, element 0. As in other programming languages, arrays start with element 0 in PHP. Now when you echo $actors like this:

```
echo $actors[0];
```

you'll see "Cary Grant".

You can also add other actors to the $actors array, like this in phpactors.php:

```
<html>
  <head>
    <title>
      Creating an array
    </title>
  </head>
  <body>
    <h1>
      Creating an array
    </h1>
    <?php
      $actors[0] = "Cary Grant";
      $actors[1] = "Myrna Loy";
      $actors[2] = "Lorne Green";

      echo "\$actors[0] = ", $actors[0], "<br>";
      echo "\$actors[1] = ", $actors[1], "<br>";
      echo "\$actors[2] = ", $actors[2], "<br>";
    ?>
  </body>
</html>
```

Now $actors[0] holds "Cary Grant", $actors[1] holds "Myrna Loy", and $actors[2] holds "Lorne Green", as you can see in Figure 3-4.

So far, these array examples have all used numeric indexes, which is useful when you want to loop over an array—coming up soon—because you can use the loop counter as the array index. However, PHP also lets you use a string array index, and that can be useful too,

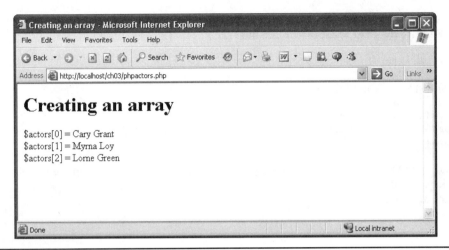

FIGURE 3-4   Creating arrays in PHP

because you might forget that the amount cousin Jill owes you is stored in $debts[342], but you won't forget $debts["Jill"]:

```
$debts["Jill"] = 2493.77;
```

Now $debts["Jill"] holds 2493.77. And you can store other debts in that array as well:

```
$debts["Jill"] = 2493.77;
$debts["Bob"] = 4930.33;
$debts["Sam"] = 5493.22;
```

In fact, even though you are using string indexes for these array elements, it turns out that you can loop over this array using PHP—more on that later.

There's a shortcut for creating arrays—you can simply use the array name followed by empty square brackets like this, and PHP will fill in the numbers:

```
$actors[] = "Cary Grant";
$actors[] = "Myrna Loy";
$actors[] = "Lorne Green";
```

After you execute this code, $actors[0] will hold "Cary Grant", $actors[1] will hold "Myrna Loy", and $actors[2] will hold "Lorne Green".

In fact, there's even a shorter shortcut in PHP for creating an array: you can use the array function, which returns an array. That looks like this:

```
$actors = array("Cary Grant", "Myrna Loy", "Lorne Green");
```

This also creates an array such that $actors[0] will hold "Cary Grant", $actors[1] will hold "Myrna Loy", and $actors[2] will hold "Lorne Green".

By default, arrays start with index 0. What if you wanted to start with index 1 instead? You could use the PHP => operator like this:

```
$actors = array(1 => "Cary Grant", "Myrna Loy", "Lorne Green");
```

This would leave you with

```
$actors[1] = "Cary Grant";
$actors[2] = "Myrna Loy";
$actors[3] = "Lorne Green";
```

The => operator lets you create key/value pairs in arrays—the item on the left of the => is the key, and the item on the right is the value. For example, you could do this in phparrayfunction.php:

```
<html>
  <head>
    <title>
      Using the array function
    </title>
  </head>
  <body>
    <h1>
      Using the array function
    </h1>
    <?php
      $debts = array("Jill" => 2493.77, "Bob" => 4930.33, "Sam" => 5493.22);

      echo "\$debts['Jill'] = ", $debts["Jill"], "<br>";
      echo "\$debts['Bob'] = ", $debts["Bob"], "<br>";
      echo "\$debts['Sam'] = ", $debts["Sam"], "<br>";
    ?>
  </body>
</html>
```

As you can see in Figure 3-5, this leaves you with

```
$debts["Jill"] = 2493.77;
$debts["Bob"] = 4930.33;
$debts["Sam"] = 5493.22;
```

As you can see, the => operator is a useful one. For example, you can put it to work in case you don't want to fill consecutive values, like this:

```
$actors = array(1 => "Cary Grant", 5 => "Myrna Loy", 7 => "Lorne Green");
```

This would leave you with

```
$actors[1] = "Cary Grant";
$actors[5] = "Myrna Loy";
$actors[7] = "Lorne Green";
```

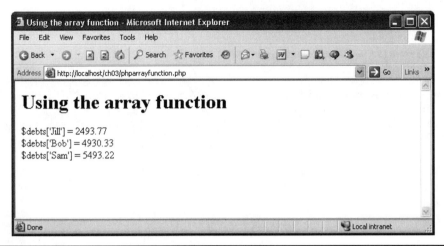

FIGURE 3-5   Creating arrays using the array function in PHP

Here's one more shortcut: if you have a specific range of data, such as the numbers 1 to 10 or the characters a to z, you can use the PHP range function to create arrays. Here's an example:

```
$data = range(1, 4);
```

This gives you

```
$data[0] = 1
$data[1] = 2
$data[2] = 3
$data[3] = 4
```

Modifying the Data in Arrays

Now that you've seen how to create arrays, how about modifying the data in those arrays? No worries here—you can modify the values inside an array as easily as you can modify the value held by a variable.

For example, say that you've created this array:

```
<?php
    $actors[0] = "Cary Grant";
    $actors[1] = "Myrna Loy";
    $actors[2] = "Lorne Green";
?>
```

Now say that you wanted to change $actors[2] from "Lorne Green" to "Jimmy Stewart". No trouble, just do this:

```
<?php
    $actors[0] = "Cary Grant";
```

```
        $actors[1]  =  "Myrna Loy";
        $actors[2]  =  "Lorne Green";

        $actors[2]  =  "Jimmy Stewart";
    ?>
```

Now say you wanted to add a new actor, "Julie Andrews" to this list. No problem, you could just do this in phpmodify.php:

```
<html>
  <head>
    <title>
      Modifying arrays
    </title>
  </head>
  <body>
    <h1>
      Modifying arrays
    </h1>
    <?php
        $actors[0]  =  "Cary Grant";
        $actors[1]  =  "Myrna Loy";
        $actors[2]  =  "Lorne Green";

        $actors[2]  =  "Jimmy Stewart";

        $actors[]  =  "Julie Andrews";

        echo "\$actors[0]  =  ", $actors[0], "<br>";
        echo "\$actors[1]  =  ", $actors[1], "<br>";
        echo "\$actors[2]  =  ", $actors[2], "<br>";
        echo "\$actors[3]  =  ", $actors[3], "<br>";
    ?>
  </body>
</html>
```

You can see the results in Figure 3-6, where you've been able to successfully modify the values in the array.

You can copy entire arrays with a single assignment statement—for example, you might copy the array $actors over to a new array named $creative_staff like this—note that you refer to the array with its name alone, no square brackets needed:

```
    <?php
        $actors[0]  =  "Cary Grant";
        $actors[1]  =  "Myrna Loy";
        $actors[2]  =  "Lorne Green";

        $actors[2]  =  "Jimmy Stewart";

        $actors[]  =  "Julie Andrews";
```

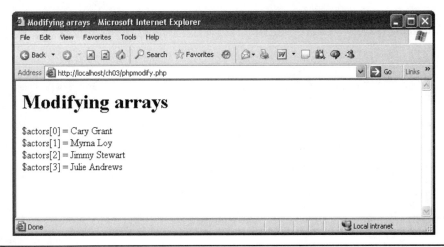

FIGURE 3-6   Modifying arrays in PHP

```
  echo "\$actors[0]  =  ",  $actors[0],  "<br>";
  echo "\$actors[1]  =  ",  $actors[1],  "<br>";
  echo "\$actors[2]  =  ",  $actors[2],  "<br>";
  echo "\$actors[3]  =  ",  $actors[3],  "<br>";

  $creative_staff = $actors;

  echo $creative_staff[1];
?>
```

At the end of this script, then, the statement echo $creative_staff[1]; will display "Myrna Loy". Not bad.

Deleting Array Elements

You can delete the elements in arrays if you do it right. You might be tempted to do something like this, just setting an array element to an empty string:

```
<?php
  $actors[0]  =  "Cary Grant";
  $actors[1]  =  "Myrna Loy";
  $actors[2]  =  "Lorne Green";

  $actors[1]  =  "";
?>
```

But that doesn't delete the element—it just sets it to an empty string, so if you display the array elements:

```php
<?php
    $actors[0] = "Cary Grant";
    $actors[1] = "Myrna Loy";
    $actors[2] = "Lorne Green";

    $actors[1] = "";

    echo "\$actors[0] = ", $actors[0], "<br>";
    echo "\$actors[1] = ", $actors[1], "<br>";
    echo "\$actors[2] = ", $actors[2], "<br>";
?>
```

you'll get this display:

```
$actors[0] = Cary Grant
$actors[1] =
$actors[2] = Lorne Green
```

So how do you actually remove an element from an array? You use the unset function like this in phpunset.php:

```php
<html>
  <head>
    <title>
      Deleting an array element
    </title>
  </head>
  <body>
    <h1>
      Deleting an array element
    </h1>
    <?php
        $actors[0] = "Cary Grant";
        $actors[1] = "Myrna Loy";
        $actors[2] = "Lorne Green";

        unset($actors[1]);

        echo "\$actors[0] = ", $actors[0], "<br>";
        echo "\$actors[1] = ", $actors[1], "<br>";
        echo "\$actors[2] = ", $actors[2], "<br>";
    ?>
  </body>
</html>
```

You can see the results in Figure 3-7.
Note in particular that you get a warning here because $actors[1] is undefined:

```
PHP Notice: Undefined offset: 1 in C:\Inetpub\wwwroot\ch03\phpunset.php on line 19
```

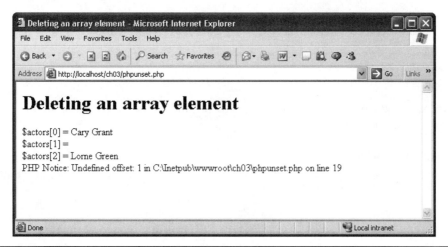

Figure 3-7   Deleting an array element in PHP

Handling Arrays with Loops

As already mentioned, arrays and loops are a natural combination—arrays are indexed using an array index, and loops use a loop counter—by using the loop counter as the array index, you can increment through an entire array in a few lines. For example, you might store student scores in an array and want to find the average score—and loops provide a great way of looping over the entire array, letting you add all the scores together and then dividing by the total number of elements to find the average score.

The for Loop

A handy function that you can use when using loops with arrays is the count function. This function returns the number of elements in an array, and that's useful when you want to set, say, the number of times to loop in a for loop like this, in phparrayfor.php:

```
<html>
  <head>
    <title>
      Using a for loop to loop over an array
    </title>
  </head>
  <body>
    <h1>
      Using a for loop to loop over an array
    </h1>
  <?php
    $actors[0] = "Cary Grant";
    $actors[1] = "Myrna Loy";
    $actors[2] = "Lorne Green";
```

```
   for ($loop_index = 0; $loop_index < count($actors); $loop_index++){
     echo "\$actors[$loop_index] = ", $actors[$loop_index], "<br>";
   }
 ?>
</body>
</html>
```

You can see the results in Figure 3-8. As you see, the for loop looped over all the elements in the array. Beautiful.

The print_r Function

In fact, there's a simple function for displaying the contents of an array—the print_r function:

```
print_r ($array [, bool return])
```

For example, if you wanted to print out the $actors array, you could use print_r like this:

```
<?php
   $actors[0] = "Cary Grant";
   $actors[1] = "Myrna Loy";
   $actors[2] = "Lorne Green";

   print_r($actors);
 ?>
```

This function uses newlines to print, not HTML <br> elements, so run this at the command line to give

```
%php phpprint_r.php
   Array
(
   [0] => Cary Grant
   [1] => Myrna Loy
   [2] => Lorne Green
)
```

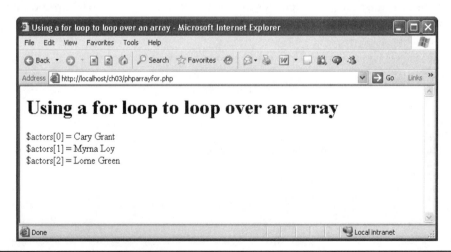

FIGURE 3-8   Looping over an array element in PHP

Note that this gives you the result in key => value form. Try this one:

```
<?php
  $debts["Jill"] = 2493.77;
  $debts["Bob"] = 4930.33;
  $debts["Sam"] = 5493.22;

  print_r($debts);
?>
```

Running this new version shows how print_r gives you key/value pairs:

```
%php phpprint_r.php
  Array
(
    [Jill] => 2493.77
    [Bob] => 4930.33
    [Sam] => 5493.22
)
```

You can also pass a value of true to the print_r function to make it return its text as a string, which you can assign to a variable:

```
$output = print_r($debts, true);
```

The foreach Loop

The foreach loop is designed to work with collections such as arrays, and it's a handy one because you don't have to set up initialization and termination conditions, as you do with for loops. Here's how to use the foreach loop formally:

```
foreach (array as $value) statement
foreach (array as $key => $value) statement
```

This next example, phpforeach1.php, puts the foreach loop to work, looping over the $actors array like this:

```
<html>
  <head>
    <title>
      Using a foreach loop to loop over an array
    </title>
  </head>
  <body>
    <h1>
      Using a foreach loop to loop over an array
    </h1>
    <?php
      $actors[0] = "Cary Grant";
      $actors[1] = "Myrna Loy";
      $actors[2] = "Lorne Green";
```

```
            foreach ($actors as $value) {
                echo "Value: $value <br>";
            }      ?>
       </body>
    </html>
```

The foreach loop here fills the variable $value with a new element from the $actors array each time through. You can see the results in Figure 3-9.

You can use the second form of the foreach loop—the version that lets you work with keys as well as values—in an example named phpforeach2.php. That looks like this:

```
<html>
  <head>
    <title>
      Using a foreach loop with keys and values in an array
    </title>
  </head>
  <body>
    <h1>
      Using a foreach loop with keys and values in an array
    </h1>
    <?php
      $debts["Jill"] = 2493.77;
      $debts["Bob"] = 4930.33;
      $debts["Sam"] = 5493.22;

      foreach ($debts as $key => $value) {
        echo "Key: $key; Value: $value <br>";
      }
    ?>
  </body>
</html>
```

You can see the results in Figure 3-10.

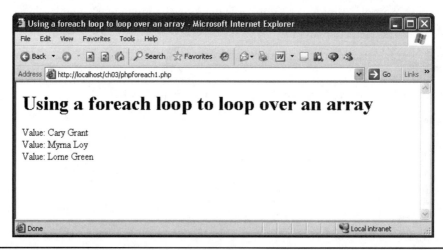

FIGURE 3-9   Using the foreach loop on an arrays in PHP

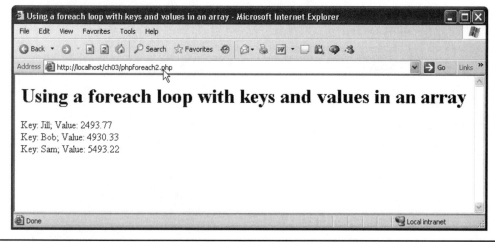

FIGURE 3-10   Using the foreach loop with keys and values on an array in PHP

The while Loop

You can use a while loop to iterate over an array in PHP as well, if you use a new function, *each*. The each function is meant to be used in loops over collections like arrays; each time through the array, it returns the current element's key *and* value. To handle a multiple-item return value from the each function, you can use the PHP *list* function, which will assign the two return values from each to separate variables. Here's what it looks like in phparraywhile.php:

```
<html>
  <head>
    <title>
      Using a while loop with keys and values in an array
    </title>
  </head>
  <body>
    <h1>
      Using a while loop with keys and values in an array
    </h1>
    <?php
      $debts["Jill"] = 2493.77;
      $debts["Bob"] = 4930.33;
      $debts["Sam"] = 5493.22;

      while (list($key, $value) = each ($debts)) {
        echo "Key: $key; Value: $value <br>";
      }
    ?>
  </body>
</html>
```

The results appear in Figure 3-11.

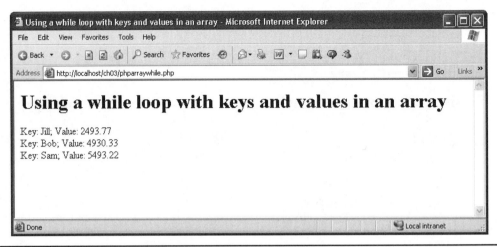

Using a while loop with keys and values in an array - Microsoft Internet Explorer

File   Edit   View   Favorites   Tools   Help

Back   Search   Favorites

Address   http://localhost/ch03/phparraywhile.php   Go   Links

Using a while loop with keys and values in an array

Key: Jill; Value: 2493.77
Key: Bob; Value: 4930.33
Key: Sam; Value: 5493.22

FIGURE 3-11   Using the while loop with keys and values on an array in PHP

The PHP Array Functions

PHP has a great deal of support for working with arrays built in. There are many string functions built into PHP—and there are plenty of array functions as well. You can see them in Table 3-2.

Function	Does This
array_change_key_case	Returns an array with all string keys converted to lowercase or uppercase
array_chunk	Splits an array into chunks
array_combine	Creates an array by using one array for the keys and another for the values
array_count_values	Counts the values in an array
array_diff_assoc	Computes the difference of two arrays with additional index check
array_diff_uassoc	Computes the difference of two arrays with additional index check, performed by a user-supplied callback function
array_diff	Computes the difference of arrays
array_fill	Fills an array with values
array_filter	Filters elements of an array using a callback function
array_flip	Exchanges all keys with their associated values in an array
array_intersect_assoc	Computes the intersection of arrays with additional index check
array_intersect	Computes the intersection of arrays

TABLE 3-2   The Array Functions

Function	Does This
array_key_exists	Checks if the given key or index exists in the array
array_keys	Returns the keys in an array
array_map	Applies the callback to the elements of the given arrays
array_merge_recursive	Merges two or more arrays recursively
array_merge	Merges two or more arrays
array_multisort	Sorts multiple or multidimensional arrays
array_pad	Pads array to the specified length with a value
array_pop	Pops the element off the end of array
array_push	Pushes one or more elements onto the end of array
array_rand	Picks one or more random elements out of an array
array_reduce	Reduces the array to a single value with a callback function
array_reverse	Returns an array with elements in reverse order
array_search	Searches the array for a given value and returns the corresponding key
array_shift	Shifts an element off the beginning of an array
array_slice	Extracts a slice of the array
array_splice	Removes part of the array and replaces it with something else
array_sum	Calculates the sum of values in an array
array_udiff_assoc	Computes the difference of arrays with an additional index check. Here, the data is compared by using a callback function
array_udiff_uassoc	Computes the difference of arrays with an index check. Here, the data is compared by using a callback function, and the index check is also performed by callback function
array_udiff	Computes the difference between arrays by using a callback function
array_unique	Removes duplicate elements from an array
array_unshift	Adds one or more elements to the beginning of an array
array_values	Returns all the values of an array
array_walk	Calls a user-supplied function on every member of an array
array	Creates an array
arsort	Sorts an array in reverse order, preserving index association
asort	Sorts an array and maintains index association
compact	Creates array containing variables and their values
count	Counts the elements in an array
current	Returns the current element in an array

TABLE 3-2   The Array Functions *(continued)*

Function	Does This
each	Returns the current key and value pair from an array and advance the array cursor
end	Sets the array pointer to the last element
extract	Imports variables into the current symbol table from an array
in_array	Checks if a value exists in an array
key	Gets a key from an associative array
krsort	Sorts an array by key in reverse order
ksort	Sorts an array by key
list	Assigns variables as if they were an array
natcasesort	Sorts an array using a case-insensitive "natural order" algorithm
natsort	Sorts an array using a "natural order" algorithm
next	Advances the array pointer of an array
pos	Alias of the current function
prev	Moves the array pointer back on element
range	Creates an array containing a range of elements
reset	Sets the pointer of an array to its first element
rsort	Sorts an array in reverse order
shuffle	Shuffles an array's elements
sizeof	Alias of the count function
sort	Sorts an array
uasort	Sorts an array with a user-defined comparison function, maintaining indexes
uksort	Sorts an array by keys; uses a user-defined comparison function
usort	Sorts an array by values; uses a user-defined comparison function

TABLE 3-2   The Array Functions *(continued)*

There are many array functions here—a great deal of array power. The rest of the chapter shows you the kinds of things these functions can do, such as "imploding" and "exploding" arrays.

Converting Between Strings and Arrays Using implode and explode

The implode function implodes an array into a string, and the explode function explodes a string into an array. That's useful if you've stored your data in strings in files and want to convert those strings into array elements when your Web application runs.

Here's an example in which an array is "imploded" into a text string and displayed:

Chapter 3: Strings and Arrays 107

```php
<?php
    $ice_cream[0] = "chocolate";
    $ice_cream[1] = "pecan";
    $ice_cream[2] = "strawberry";

    $text = implode(", ", $ice_cream);
    echo $text;
?>
```

This gives you

```
chocolate, pecan, strawberry
```

As you can see, you specify the string that separates the array items yourself—in this case, that's ", ".

How about exploding a string into an array? To do that, you indicate which text you want to split the string on, such as ", ", and pass that to explode. Here's an example:

```php
<?php
    $text = "chocolate, pecan, strawberry";
    $ice_cream = explode(", ", $text);
    print_r($ice_cream);
?>
```

And here are the results—you exploded the string into an array:

```
Array
(
    [0] => chocolate
    [1] => pecan
    [2] => strawberry
)
```

Extracting Data from Arrays

You can use the extract function to extract data from arrays and store it in variables. Say you have this array:

```php
<?php
    $ice_cream["good"] = "orange";
    $ice_cream["better"] = "vanilla";
    $ice_cream["best"] = "rum raisin";
?>
```

Now you can use extract to create variables whose names will be taken from the keys in the array, and those variables will be assigned the values in the array. Here's how that works in phpextract.php:

```html
<html>
  <head>
    <title>
      Extracting variables from arrays
    </title>
  </head>
```

```
<body>
  <h1>Extracting variables from arrays</h1>
  <?php
    $ice_cream["good"] = "orange";
    $ice_cream["better"] = "vanilla";
    $ice_cream["best"] = "rum raisin";

    extract($ice_cream);

    echo "\$good = $good<BR>";
    echo "\$better = $better<BR>";
    echo "\$best = $best<BR>";
  ?>
</body>
</html>
```

You can see this page at work in Figure 3-12.

In fact, you can also use the list function to extract variables from an array, and you can name those variables as you like; here's an example:

```
<?php
    $ice_cream[0] = "chocolate";
    $ice_cream[1] = "pecan";
    $ice_cream[2] = "strawberry";
    list($one, $two) = $ice_cream;
    echo $one, "<br>";
    echo $two;
?>
```

Here's what you get:

```
chocolate
pecan
```

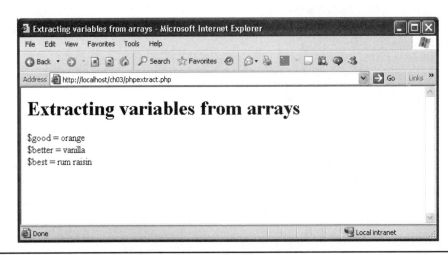

FIGURE 3-12   Using the extract function with arrays in PHP

Sorting Arrays

There's a bunch of array sorting power built into PHP, starting with the sort function, which sorts arrays in ascending order. Here's an example, phpsortarray.php:

```php
<?php
    $ice_cream[0] = "orange";
    $ice_cream[1] = "vanilla";
    $ice_cream[2] = "rum raisin";

    print_r($ice_cream);

    sort($ice_cream);

    print_r($ice_cream);
?>
```

Here is the result of phpsortarray.php:

```
%php phpsortarray.php
Array
(
    [0] => orange
    [1] => vanilla
    [2] => rum raisin
)
Array
(
    [0] => orange
    [1] => rum raisin
    [2] => vanilla
)
```

How about a reverse sort? You can do that with rsort:

```php
<?php
    $ice_cream[0] = "orange";
    $ice_cream[1] = "vanilla";
    $ice_cream[2] = "rum raisin";

    print_r($ice_cream);

    rsort($ice_cream);

    print_r($ice_cream);
?>
```

which gives you

```
Array
(
    [0] => orange
    [1] => vanilla
    [2] => rum raisin
)
```

```
Array
(
    [0] => vanilla
    [1] => rum raisin
    [2] => orange
)
```

This doesn't work so well if you're using text string keys in your arrays instead of numeric index values—the text string keys will just be replaced with numbers. Use asort instead, as in phpasortarray.php:

```
<?php
  $ice_cream["good"] = "orange";
  $ice_cream["better"] = "vanilla";
  $ice_cream["best"] = "rum raisin";

  print_r($ice_cream);

  asort($ice_cream);

  print_r($ice_cream);
?>
```

Here's what you get:

```
%php phpasortarray.php
Array
(
    [good] => orange
    [better] => vanilla
    [best] => rum raisin
)
Array
(
    [good] => orange
    [best] => rum raisin
    [better] => vanilla
)
```

And you can use arsort to sort arrays in reverse order.

You might ask: what if you wanted to sort an array based on keys, not values? Use ksort instead. To sort by reverse by keys, use krsort. You can even define your own sorting operations with a custom sorting function you use with PHP's usort. And natsort performs "natural" sorts on mixed string/number data. For example, natsort would sort "option1", "option2", "option15" as "option1", "option2", "option15" (not "option1", "option15", "option2" which is what you'd get with sort).

Using PHP's Array Operators

PHP also lets you operate on arrays with operators, which can be very handy. Here are the array-handling operators:

- $a + $b yields the union of $a and $b.
- $a == $b yields TRUE if $a and $b have the same elements.
- $a === $b yields TRUE if $a and $b have the same elements in the same order.
- $a != $b yields TRUE if $a is not equal to $b.
- $a <> $b yields TRUE if $a is not equal to $b.
- $a !== $b yields TRUE if $a is not identical to $b.

Here's an example, phparrayoperators.php, which puts the addition and equality operators to work:

```php
<?php
  $pudding["raspberry"] = 333;
  $pudding["peach"] = 222;
  $ice_cream["pecan"] = 111;
  $ice_cream["chocolate"] = 999;
  echo "\$ice_cream: ";
  print_r($ice_cream);
  echo "\n";
  echo "\$pudding: ";
  print_r($pudding);
  echo "\n";
  $desserts = $pudding + $ice_cream;
  echo "\$desserts: ";
  print_r($desserts);
  echo "\n";
  if ($pudding == $ice_cream){
    echo "\$pudding has the same elements as \$ice_cream";
  }
  else {
    echo "\$pudding does not have the same elements as \$ice_cream";
  }
?>
```

Here's what you get when you run this code:

```
%php phparrayoperators.php
  $ice_cream: Array
(
    [pecan] => 111
    [chocolate] => 999
)

$pudding: Array
(
    [raspberry] => 333
    [peach] => 222
)
```

```
$desserts: Array
(
    [raspberry] => 333
    [peach] => 222
    [pecan] => 111
    [chocolate] => 999
)

$pudding does not have the same elements as $ice_cream
```

Comparing Arrays to Each Other

You can find the difference between two arrays using the array_diff function; here's an example, phparraydiff.php:

```php
<?php
  $ice_cream = array("vanilla", "chocolate", "strawberry");
  $ice_cream2 = array("vanilla", "chocolate", "papaya");

  $difference = array_diff($ice_cream, $tice_cream2);

  foreach ($difference as $key => $value) {
      echo "Key: $key; Value: $value\n";
  }
?>
```

This example compares two arrays and displays the elements that are different. Here's what you get in this case:

```
%php phparraydiff.php
Key: 2; Value: strawberry
```

If you're using text string keys, use the array_diff_assoc function (arrays with text string keys are also called associative arrays). If you want to find all the elements that two arrays have in common, just use array_intersect or array_intersect_assoc.

Handling Multidimensional Arrays

PHP can also work with multidimensional arrays. For example, say that you're keeping track of student scores on an exam:

```
$scores["Sam"] = 79;
$scores["Ellen"] = 69;
```

Now say that you gave a second exam. You could just add another index—for exam number—to each student:

```php
<?php
    $scores["Sam"][1] = 79;
    $scores["Sam"][2] = 74;
```

```
    $scores["Ellen"][1] = 69;
    $scores["Ellen"][2] = 84;
    print_r($scores);
?>
```

At this point, $scores["Sam"][1] is Sam's test score on the first test, $scores["Sam"][2] is his score on the second test, and so on. This script displays the new, multidimensional array with print_r, giving you this:

```
[Sam] => Array
    (
        [1] => 79
        [2] => 74
    )

[Ellen] => Array
    (
        [1] => 69
        [2] => 84
    )
```

In addition, you can access elements using both indexes, like this:

```
echo "Sam's first test score was ", $scores["Sam"][1], "\n";
```

If you want to interpolate an array item in double quotes, it takes a little more work—you have to enclose it in curly braces:

```
echo "Sam's first test score was {$scores['Sam'][1]}\n";
```

As you might expect, you can also create multidimensional arrays this way (note that this will start the arrays off at an index value of 0):

```
<?php
    $scores["Sam"][] = 79;
    $scores["Sam"][] = 74;
    $scores["Ellen"][] = 69;
    $scores["Ellen"][] = 84;
    print_r($scores);
?>
```

You can also think of multidimensional arrays as arrays of arrays. For instance, you can think of a two-dimensional array as a one-dimensional array (the rows of the two-dimensional array) of one-dimensional arrays (the columns of the two-dimensional array). That means that this syntax is legal:

```
<?php
    $scores = array("Sam" => array(79, 74), "Ellen" => array(69, 84));
    print_r($scores);
?>
```

Here's what you get from this code:

```
[Sam] => Array
    (
        [0] => 79
        [1] => 74
    )

[Ellen] => Array
    (
        [0] => 69
        [1] => 84
    )
```

You could even start the array indexes at 1 instead of 0 like this:

```
<?php
    $scores = array("Sam" => array(1 => 79, 2 => 74),
        "Ellen" => array(1 => 69, 2 => 84));
    print_r($scores);
?>
```

And here's what you get:

```
[Sam] => Array
    (
        [1] => 79
        [2] => 74
    )

[Ellen] => Array
    (
        [1] => 69
        [2] => 84
    )
```

Using Multidimensional Arrays in Loops

Working with multidimensional arrays in loops takes a little extra thought. For example, say that you have a two-dimensional array called $scores, and you want to loop over that array, displaying each element in it. You could start with a loop over the outer index, which goes from 0 to 1:

```
<?php
    $scores[0][] = 79;
    $scores[0][] = 74;
    $scores[1][] = 69;
    $scores[1][] = 84;
    for ($outer = 0; $outer < count($scores); $outer++){

        .
        .
        .
    }
?>
```

Now you can loop over the inner index like this in phpmultiloop.php:

```
<html>
  <head>
    <title>
      Looping over multidimensional arrays
    </title>
  </head>

  <body>
    <h1>
      Looping over multidimensional arrays
    </h1>
    <?php
      $scores[0][] = 79;
      $scores[0][] = 74;
      $scores[1][] = 69;
      $scores[1][] = 84;
      for ($outer = 0; $outer < count($scores); $outer++){
        for($inner = 0; $inner < count($scores[$outer]); $inner++){
          echo "\$scores[$outer][$inner] = ",
            $scores[$outer][$inner], "<br>";
        }
      }
    ?>
  </body>
</html>
```

You can see the results, where the two-dimensional array has indeed been looped over, in Figure 3-13.

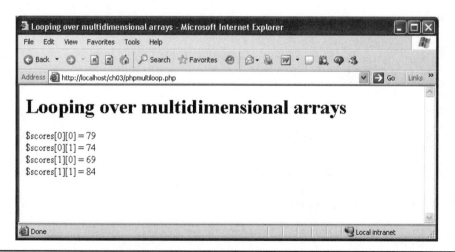

FIGURE 3-13   Looping over a multidimensional array in PHP

Moving Through Arrays

PHP supports a number of functions that you can use to move through arrays. Such navigation is done with an *array pointer,* which keeps track of your location in the array between calls to the navigation functions. Say you have this array:

```
$ice_cream[0] = "chocolate";
$ice_cream[1] = "pecan";
$ice_cream[2] = "strawberry";
```

You can access the current element in the array with the current function:

```
echo "Current: ", current($ice_cream), "<BR>";
```

You can move the array pointer to the next element with the next function:

```
echo "Next: ", next($ice_cream), "<BR>";
```

The prev function moves the pointer back to the previous element:

```
echo "Prev: ", prev($ice_cream), "<BR>";
```

The end function moves the pointer to the last element in the array:

```
echo "End: ", end($ice_cream), "<BR>";
```

If you want to move back to the beginning of the array, use the reset function:

```
reset($ice_cream);
```

Here's an example, phpnavigatearray.php, putting these functions to work:

```
<html>
  <head>
        <title>
            Navigating through arrays
        </title>
  </head>

  <body>
    <h1>
      Navigating through arrays
    </h1>
    <?php
      $ice_cream[0] = "chocolate";
      $ice_cream[1] = "pecan";
      $ice_cream[2] = "strawberry";

      echo "Current element: ", current($ice_cream), "<br>";
      echo "Next element: ", next($ice_cream), "<br>";
      echo "Previous element: ", prev($ice_cream), "<br>";
      echo "End element: ", end($ice_cream), "<br>";
      echo "Resetting the array...<br>";
```

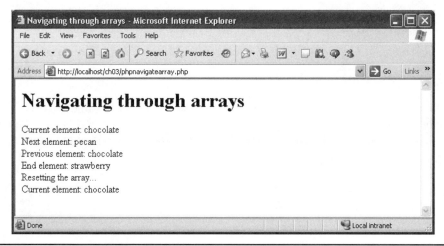

FIGURE 3-14   Navigating through an array in PHP

```
      reset($ice_cream);
      echo "Current element: ", current($ice_cream), "<br>";
   ?>
  </body>
</html>
```

You can see the results, where you've navigated through the array, in Figure 3-14.

Splitting and Merging Arrays

You can get sections of arrays with the array_slice function, passing it the array you want to get a section of, the offset at which to start, and the length of the array you want to create. Here's an example, phparraysplit.php:

```
<html>
  <head>
    <title>
      Splitting arrays
    </title>
  </head>

  <body>
    <h1>
      Splitting arrays
    </h1>
    <?php
      $ice_cream["good"] = "orange";
      $ice_cream["better"] = "vanilla";
      $ice_cream["best"] = "rum raisin";
      $ice_cream["bestest"] = "lime";
      $subarray = array_slice($ice_cream, 1, 2);
```

```
    foreach ($subarray as $value) {
      echo "$value <br>";
    }
    ?>
  </body>
</html>
```

And you can see what this gives you in Figure 3-15—you've been able to extract a section of an array.

You can also merge arrays with the array_merge function, like this in phpmergearrays.php:

```
<html>
  <head>
    <title>
      Merging arrays
    </title>
  </head>

  <body>
    <h1>
      Merging arrays
    </h1>
    <?php
      $pudding = array("vanilla", "rum raisin", "orange");
      $ice_cream = array("chocolate", "pecan", "strawberry");

      $desserts = array_merge($pudding, $ice_cream);

      foreach ($desserts as $value) {
        echo "$value <br>";
      }
```

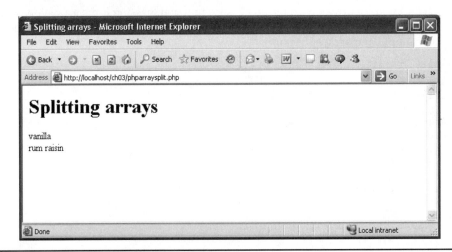

FIGURE 3-15   Getting a section of an array in PHP

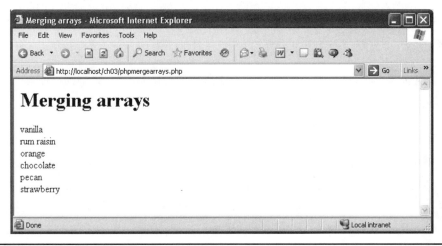

FIGURE 3-16   Merging arrays in PHP

```
    ?>
  </body>
</html>
```

You can see the result in Figure 3-16, where the two arrays have been merged.

Other Array Functions

There are a couple of other array functions we'll take a look at as well, such as the array_ sum function, which sums the numeric elements in an array. For example, here's how to find the average score of a set of students:

```
<?php
    $scores = array(65, 61, 70, 64, 65);

    echo "The average score is ", array_sum($scores) / count($scores);
?>
```

Here's what you see:

```
The average score is 65
```

In addition, the array_flip function will flip an array's keys and values. You can see that at work in phparrayflip.php:

```
<html>
  <head>
    <title>
      Flipping keys and values in arrays
    </title>
  </head>
```

```
<body>
  <h1>
    Flipping keys and values in arrays
  </h1>
  <?php
    $ice_cream = array("flavor_1" => "vanilla", "flavor_2" => "rum raisin",
      "flavor_3" => "orange");

    foreach ($ice_cream as $key => $value) {
      echo "Key: $key; Value: $value<br>";
    }
    echo "<br>";

    $ice_cream = array_flip($ice_cream);

    foreach ($ice_cream as $key => $value) {
      echo "Key: $key; Value: $value<br>";
    }
  ?>
  </body>
</html>
```

You can see the results in Figure 3-17.

Finally, the array_unique function will eliminate duplicates from an array. Take a look at this example, phparrayunique.php:

```
<?php
  $scores = array(65, 61, 70, 64, 65);
  print_r($scores);
  $scores = array_unique($scores);
  print_r($scores);
?>
```

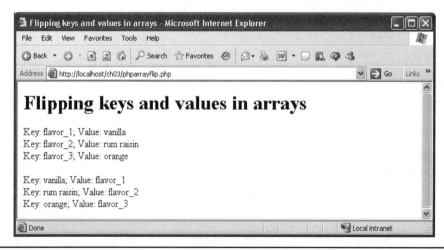

FIGURE 3-17   Flipping arrays in PHP

Here's what you get when you run this script:

```
%php phparrayunique.php
Array
(
    [0] => 65
    [1] => 61
    [2] => 70
    [3] => 64
    [4] => 65
)
Array
(
    [0] => 65
    [1] => 61
    [2] => 70
    [3] => 64
)
```

As you can see, the duplicate array element has been removed.

Creating Functions

I t's time to take the next step in programming power, and that means creating your own functions. You've seen many built-in PHP functions already—functions are those callable sections of code that you can pass data to, and that can return data to you.

Functions let you break your code up, following that old programming dictum: Divide and Conquer. Got some code that needs to be run multiple times in your application? Put it into a function. Got some code that shouldn't be run automatically when the page loads (as all the code up to now has)? Put it into a function. Got code that's just getting too long to effectively debug and maintain? Put it in a function.

By putting code into a function, you get it out of the way—out of sight, out of mind is the idea. You pass data to that function, and the function can pass data back to you. You may have seen functions in other languages, but as you're going to see, PHP functions support many unique features.

Restricting code to functions breaks up your code in an especially useful way: the variables you use inside a function are, by default, not visible outside that function. That means you don't have to worry about conflicts with variables names; using a $account variable in two different parts of your code may conflict, but not if you wrap code inside a function.

Using functions is only the beginning of dividing up your code—using object-oriented programming is going to let you wrap both functions and data into classes and objects. That is, functions were vital to letting programmers section their code, but in time, developers' needs outgrew simple functions, and combining functions and data into objects was the next step. It all starts with functions, however, and that's coming up now.

Creating Functions in PHP

How do you build functions in PHP? That's easy enough—here's how you do that, formally speaking:

```
function function_name([argument_list...])
{
    [statements]
    [return return_value;]
}
```

Time for an example. You might create a function named display that displays some text in the browser in an example named phpdisplay.php. You might have phpdisplay.php display some text indicating it's about to call the function:

```php
<?php
   echo "About to call the function...<br>";
   echo "Calling the function...<br>";
   .
   .
   .
?>
```

Next, add the code for the display function; that looks like this:

```php
<?php
   echo "About to call the function...<br>";
   echo "Calling the function...<br>";

   function display()
   {
       echo "This text was displayed by the function.";
   }
?>
```

There are a couple of things to note here. First, the code inside a PHP function isn't executed until that function is called. That's different from the scripts you've seen up to now—if you simply place code in a script, outside a function, that code is executed when the page loads.

Note also the syntax of the function definition; that definition starts with the keyword function, followed by the name of the function, which is followed by parentheses (empty at this point, because you're not passing any data to the function). The body of the function—that is, the statements that will be executed when the function is called—are enclosed in curly braces.

Alright, that creates the function; how do you call it? You can call the display function as you'd call it in any other programming language—by using its name as a statement, followed by parentheses (empty parentheses in this example, because you're not passing any data to the display function):

```html
<html>
  <head>
    <title>
      Creating functions
    </title>
  </head>
  <body>
    <h1>
      Creating functions
    </h1>
    <?php
      echo "About to call the function...<br>";
      echo "Calling the function...<br>";
      display();
```

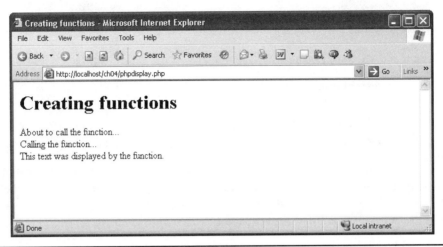

FIGURE 4-1   Calling the display function

```
    function display()
    {
        echo "This text was displayed by the function.";
    }
  ?>

  </body>
</html>
```

You can see this example at work in Figure 4-1—note that the display function was called and did its thing, displaying text. Not bad.

Passing Functions Some Data

How do you pass data to functions so those functions can operate on that data? As in other languages, that's what the argument_list part of the function syntax is about:

```
function function_name([argument_list...])
{
    [statements]
    [return return_value;]
}
```

Here's an example, phppassdata.php. Say you wanted to pass the text data to the display function that the function should display. You can do that by adding a function argument to the argument list, like this in the display function:

```
    function display($greeting)
    {
        .
        .
        .
    }
```

Now you can refer to the passed data by name, $greeting, like this in the display function's code:

```
function display($greeting)
{
    echo $greeting;
}
```

That's how to let a function accept passed data—you list the name you want to give to the passed data in the function's argument list, and then you can refer to that data in the code for the function.

You pass data to a function by placing that data inside the parentheses that follow the function's name when you call that function. For example, if you wanted to pass the text "Hello!" to the display function to make that function display that text, you could do so like this:

```
display("Hello!");
        .
        .
        .
function display($greeting)
{
    echo $greeting;
}
```

Now when the display function is called like this, the $greeting argument—also called a parameter—is assigned the value "Hello!", when the line echo $greeting is executed, "Hello!" will appear in the browser.

What if you wanted to pass two data items to a function? You can list them in the argument list of the function, separated by commas. For example, to make the display function accept two arguments, you simply list them by name, say $greeting and $message:

```
function display($greeting, $message)
{
    echo $greeting;
}
```

Now you can refer to $greeting and $message by name in your function's code:

```
function display($greeting, $message)
{
    echo $greeting;
    echo $message;
}
```

When you call the display function, you list the arguments you want to pass to that function, separated by commas like this in phppassdata.php:

```
<html>
  <head>
    <title>
```

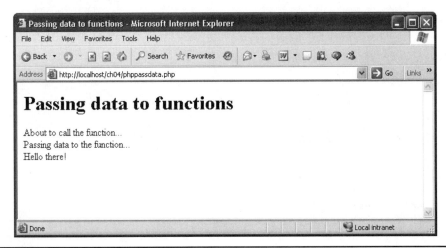

FIGURE 4-2   Passing data to functions

```
    Passing data to functions
  </title>
 </head>
 <body>
  <h1>
    Passing data to functions
  </h1>
  <?php
    echo "About to call the function...<br>";
    echo "Passing data to the function...<br>";
    display("Hello", " there!");

    function display($greeting, $message)
    {
        echo $greeting;
        echo $message;
    }
  ?>
 </body>
</html>
```

You can see the results in Figure 4-2, where the data has indeed been passed to the display function.

Passing Arrays to Functions

You can also pass arrays to functions as easily as simple data items like strings or numbers. For example, you might want a function that averages a set of students' test scores and displays that average, called averager. And you might want to pass an array to the averager function.

Here's what the test scores array might look like:

```php
<?php
  $scores = array(65, 32, 78, 98, 66);
       .
       .
       .

?>
```

And here's how you might pass the $scores array to the averager function:

```php
<?php
  $scores = array(65, 32, 78, 98, 66);

  averager($scores);
       .
       .
       .

?>
```

In the averager function, you specify the name of the array, which we'll call simply $array here:

```php
<?php
  $scores = array(65, 32, 78, 98, 66);

  averager($scores);
       .
       .
       .

  function averager($array)
  {

  }
?>
```

In the averager function, you can use a foreach statement to loop over the array:

```php
<?php
  $scores = array(65, 32, 78, 98, 66);

  averager($scores);
       .
       .
       .

  function averager($array)
  {
    foreach ($array as $value) {
       .
       .
       .

    }
  }
?>
```

Then you might add up all the elements in the array in a variable named $total:

```php
<?php
  $scores = array(65, 32, 78, 98, 66);

  averager($scores);
      .
      .
      .
  function averager($array)
  {
    $total = 0;
    foreach ($array as $value) {
      $total += $value;
    }
  }
?>
```

And finally, you can determine the average value of the array elements and display it in phppassarray.php:

```php
<html>
  <head>
    <title>
      Passing arrays to functions
    </title>
  </head>
  <body>
    <h1>
      Passing arrays to functions
    </h1>
    <?php
      $scores = array(65, 32, 78, 98, 66);
      averager($scores);

      function averager($array)
      {
        $total = 0;
        foreach ($array as $value) {
          $total += $value;
        }

        if(count($array) > 0){
          echo "The average was ", $total/count($array);
        } else {
          echo "No elements to average!";
        }
      }
    ?>
  </body>
</html>
```

And you can see the result—the average was 67.8, as you see in Figure 4-3.

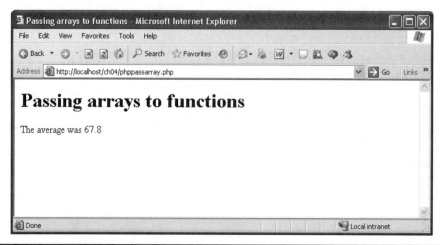

FIGURE 4-3   Passing arrays to functions

Passing by Reference

When you pass data to a function, what's really passed is a *copy* of that data. So, for example, if you pass a variable, a copy is made of that variable, and that copy is actually passed to the function.

What if you wanted to actually pass the real thing to the function? Say for example that you wanted a function to alter the value in a variable? For example, say that you had a variable $value:

```
<?php
  $value = 4;
      .
      .
      .

?>
```

and you wanted a function to square the value in $value. You might try that by passing $value to a function named, say, squarer, which squares the number passed to it:

```
function squarer($number)
{
    $number *= $number;
}
```

However, that's not going to work, because the arguments passed to the squarer function are passed by value. You can change that by prefacing the argument you want passed by reference with an ampersand (&)—which will make PHP pass that argument by reference. When you pass an argument by reference, that gives the code in the function direct access to that argument back in the calling code, so to square the value in $value, all you have to do is to preface the argument with & in the argument list like this in phpreference.php:

```html
<html>
  <head>
    <title>
      Passing data to functions by reference
    </title>
  </head>
  <body>
    <h1>
      Passing data to functions by reference
    </h1>
    <?php
      $value = 4;

      echo "Before the call, \$value holds $value <br>";
      squarer($value);
      echo "After the call, \$value holds $value <br>";

      function squarer(&$number)
      {
          $number *= $number;
      }
    ?>
  </body>
</html>
```

And you can see the results in Figure 4-4, where, as you can see, the data in $value back in the calling code was squared. Very cool.

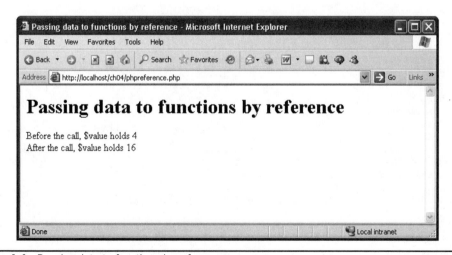

FIGURE 4-4   Passing data to functions by reference

Using Default Arguments

What happens if you have a function named display that takes two arguments like this:

```
function display($greeting, $message)
{
    echo $greeting;
    echo $message;
}
```

and call it like this, with one argument:

```
display("No worries");
```

PHP isn't going to like that; here's the kind of warning you get:

```
PHP Warning:  Missing argument 2 for display() in phpdisplay.php on line 5
```

On the other hand, you can fix this problem by supplying a *default* argument here.

Here's the way it works: you add the default argument in the argument list, using an equal sign, as you see here:

```
function display($greeting, $message = "Hello there!")
{
    echo $greeting;
    echo $message;
}
```

Now if you don't pass anything for the second argument to the display function, the default argument is automatically used. Here's the way you might call the display function in an example, phpdefaultarguments.php

```
<html>
  <head>
    <title>
      Using default function arguments
    </title>
  </head>
  <body>
    <h1>
      Using default function arguments
    </h1>
    <?php
      echo "About to call the function...<br>";
      echo "Passing data to the function...<br>";
      display("The default argument is: ");

      function display($greeting, $message = "Hello there!")
      {
          echo $greeting;
          echo $message;
      }
    ?>
  </body>
</html>
```

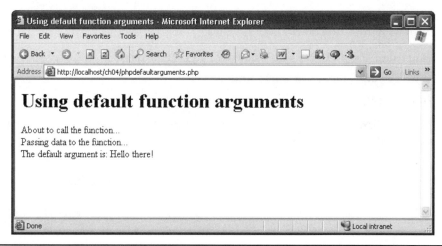

FIGURE 4-5   Using default arguments

And you can see the result in Figure 4-5, where the default argument was indeed used. Want to provide multiple default arguments? No problem:

```
function display($greeting, $message = "Hello there!", $message2 = "No worries.")
{
  echo $greeting;
  echo $message;
  echo $message2;
}
```

You can give default values to more than one argument, but once you start assigning default values, you have to give them to all arguments that follow as well so that PHP won't get confused if more than one argument is missing.

Passing Variable Numbers of Arguments

While discussing passing arguments to functions, it's worth noting that you can set up functions so that they can take a variable number of arguments. In other words, say you have a function named connector, which connects words into a text string. You could call it like this:

```
connector("Hello");
```

or like this:

```
connector("Hello", "there");
```

or like this:

```
connector("Hello", "there", "again");
```

How do you handle variable number of arguments like this in a function? You can handle them with these functions:

- **func_num_args**   Returns the number of arguments passed
- **func_get_arg**   Returns a single argument
- **func_get_args**   Returns all arguments in an array

For example, here's how you start the connector function—by getting an array of the arguments passed to the function:

```
function connector()
{
    $arguments = func_get_args();
       .
       .
       .
}
```

Then you can loop over the arguments like this—note that you can get the number of arguments from the func_num_args function:

```
function connector()
{
    $data = "";
    $arguments = func_get_args();

    for ($loop_index = 0; $loop_index < func_num_args(); $loop_index++) {
        $data .= $arguments[$loop_index] . " ";
    }
    echo $data;
}
```

Note that the final, resulting string is echoed. Here's how you might put the connector function to work in an example, phpvariableargs.php:

```
<html>
  <head>
    <title>
      Passing variable arguments to functions
    </title>
  </head>
  <body>
    <h1>
      Passing variable arguments to functions
    </h1>
    <?php
      echo "Passing 'How' 'are' 'things?' to connector...<br>";
      echo "Getting this result: ";
      connector("How", "are", "things?");
```

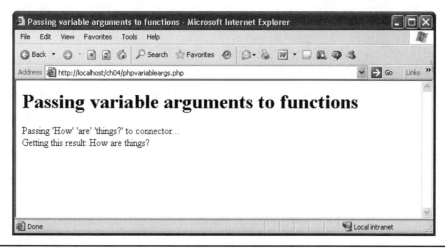

FIGURE 4-6   Passing a variable number of arguments to functions

```
function connector()
{
  $data = "";
  $arguments = func_get_args();

  for ($loop_index = 0; $loop_index < func_num_args(); $loop_index++) {
    $data .= $arguments[$loop_index] . " ";
  }
  echo $data;
}
?>
</body>
</html>
```

You can see the results in Figure 4-6, where the connector function was able to handle the arguments passed to it.

Now say that you didn't want the connector function to display the connected string, but wanted to have that string returned to your code so that you could put it to work yourself. That's a very common thing for functions to do—return values that give you their results. And it's coming up next.

Returning Data from Functions

Say you've got a simple function named adder that returns the sum of the two numbers passed to it. You might start writing adder like this:

```
<?php
  function adder(operand_1, operand_2)
  {
    $sum = $operand_1 + $operand_2;
```

```
        .
        .
        .
    }
  ?>
```

Now that you've got the sum in the variable named $sum, how do you return that value to the calling code? You can use the PHP return statement:

```
<?php
  function adder(operand_1, operand_2)
  {
    $sum = $operand_1 + $operand_2;

    return $sum;
  }
?>
```

This returns the value in $sum to the calling code. Here's how you can put adder to work—the expression adder($value_1, $value_2) here is replaced by the value returned by the adder function, which is 5:

```
<?php
  $value_1 = 2;
  $value_2 = 3;

  echo "The sum of $value_1 + $value_2 is ", adder($value_1, $value_2);

  function adder(operand_1, operand_2)
  {
    $sum = $operand_1 + $operand_2;

    return $sum;
  }
?>
```

This script produces

```
The sum of 2 + 3 is 5
```

Here's another example using the connector function from the preceding topic. You just have to modify the connector function to return its data like this in phpreturndata.php:

```
<html>
  <head>
    <title>
      Returning values from functions
    </title>
  </head>
  <body>
    <h1>
      Returning values from functions
    </h1>
```

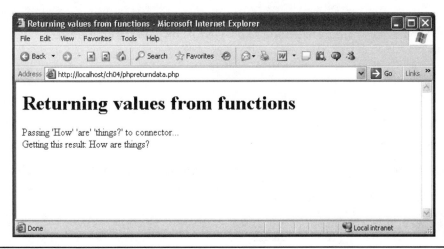

FIGURE 4-7   Returning data from functions

```php
<?php
  echo "Passing 'How' 'are' 'things?' to connector...<br>";
  echo "Getting this result: ", connector("How", "are", "things?");

  function connector()
  {
    $data = "";
    $arguments = func_get_args();

    for ($loop_index = 0; $loop_index < func_num_args(); $loop_index++) {
      $data .= $arguments[$loop_index] . " ";
    }
    return $data;
  }
?>
</body>
</html>
```

You can see the results in Figure 4-7, where the connector function returned its result string, which was then displayed by the calling code.

That's how to return simple values like strings from functions. How about arrays? Coming up next.

Returning Arrays

You can return arrays from functions as easily as you return simple values. Say you have a function, create_array, that creates arrays of the length you specify by passing a number to the create_array function. This function stores 0 in the zeroth element, 1 in the first element, 2 in the second element, and so on.

So if you passed a 3 to create_array, you should get the array [0, 1, 2] back. If you passed a 4, you should get [0, 1, 2, 3] back, and so on. Here's how you start the create_array function:

```
function create_array($number)
{
    .
    .
    .
}
```

Here's how you can create the array, $array, to return from this function:

```
function create_array($number)
{
    for ($loop_counter = 0; $loop_counter < $number; $loop_counter++){
     $array[] = $loop_counter;
    }
    .
    .
    .
}
```

That creates the array named $array. Now you can return it from the create_array function just as you would return any simple value—with the return statement:

```
function create_array($number)
{
    for ($loop_counter = 0; $loop_counter < $number; $loop_counter++){
     $array[] = $loop_counter;
    }

    return $array;
}
```

Here's how you can put the create_array function to work in an example named phpreturnarray.php:

```
<html>
  <head>
    <title>
      Returning arrays from functions
    </title>
  </head>
  <body>
    <h1>
      Returning arrays from functions
    </h1>
```

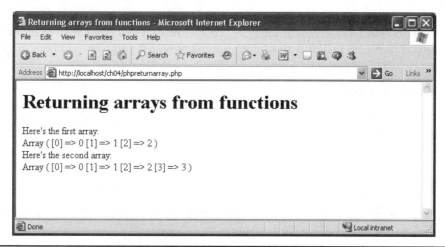

FIGURE 4-8   Returning arrays from functions

```php
<?php
  $data = create_array(3);
  echo "Here's the first array:<br>";
  print_r($data);
  echo "<br>";

  $data_2 = create_array(4);
  echo "Here's the second array:<br>";
  print_r($data_2);

  function create_array($number)
  {
    for ($loop_counter = 0; $loop_counter < $number; $loop_counter++){
     $array[] = $loop_counter;
    }

    return $array;
  }
?>
  </body>
</html>
```

You can see the results in Figure 4-8, where the create_array function created the array it was asked to create and returned it. Very nice.

Returning Lists

You may recall the list function from Chapter 3, which converted arrays into lists of variables. That's the key to letting your functions return multiple values as well.

Normally, functions can only return single values, but if you return an array and handle that array as a list in the calling code, you'll find that you can return as many values as you like from PHP functions. For example, say that you wanted to convert the create_array function from the preceding topic into a function create_list:

```php
function create_list($number)
{
  for ($loop_counter = 0; $loop_counter < $number; $loop_counter++) {
   $array[] = $loop_counter;
  }

  return $array;
}
```

Now you can handle the returned array as a list in the calling code in phpreturnlist.php like this:

```html
<html>
  <head>
    <title>
      Returning lists from functions
    </title>
  </head>
  <body>
    <h1>
      Returning lists from functions
    </h1>
    <?php
      list($first, $second, $third) = create_list(3);
      echo "Here's the first list:<br>";
      echo "$first, $second, $third<br>";

      list($first, $second, $third, $fourth) = create_list(4);
      echo "Here's the second list:<br>";
      echo "$first, $second, $third, $fourth<br>";

      function create_list($number)
      {
        for ($loop_counter = 0; $loop_counter < $number; $loop_counter++) {
         $array[] = $loop_counter;
        }

        return $array;
      }
    ?>
  </body>
</html>
```

You can see the results in Figure 4-9, where the create_list function returned an array that was properly handled as a list. Cool.

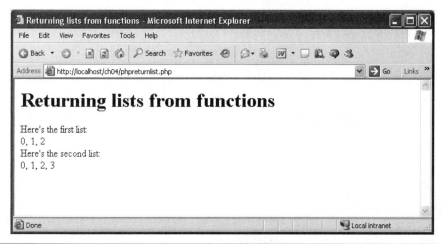

FIGURE 4-9   Returning lists from functions

Returning References

Functions can also return references in PHP. That's not something you're going to do all the time, so feel free to move on to the next topic if you want. But if you want the complete story, keep reading.

References are interesting items in PHP. For example, say that you had a variable named $value; you could get a reference to that variable with the reference operator, &:

```
$value = 4;
$ref = & $value;
```

Now $ref is a reference to $value, and it will point to the same data in memory as $value—changing one changes the other:

```
$value = 4;
$ref = & $value;
$ref = 6;
```

Now $value will hold 6.

Let's take a look at passing and returning a reference to and from a function, return_ reference. First, let's create the function return_reference:

```
function &return_reference(& $ref)
{
    return $ref;
}
```

Note that this function takes a reference as its argument, as the & in the argument list indicates. And it also returns a reference, as is indicated by the & in front of the function's name.

So you pass the return_reference function a reference to a variable, and it returns the same reference. Now let's pass a reference to a variable to the return_reference function, and get that reference back:

```php
<?php
  $value = 4;
  echo "Current value: ", $value, "\n";

  $ref = &return_reference($value);
      .
      .
      .
```

Then you might increment the reference $ref:

```php
<?php
  $value = 4;
  echo "Current value: ", $value, "\n";

  $ref = &return_reference($value);

  $ref++;
      .
      .
      .
```

And you can confirm that the original variable was incremented like this in phpreturnreference.php:

```html
<html>
  <head>
    <title>
      Returning references from functions
    </title>
  </head>
  <body>
    <h1>
      Returning references from functions
    </h1>
    <?php
      $value = 4;
      echo "Current value: ", $value, "\n";

      $ref = &return_reference($value);

      $ref++;

      echo "New value: ", $value, "\n";

      function &return_reference(& $ref)
      {
        return $ref;
      }
    ?>
  </body>
</html>
```

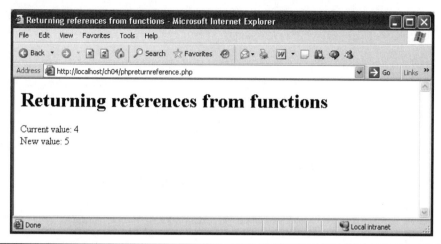

FIGURE 4-10   Returning references from functions

You can see the results in Figure 4-10, where the reference was created and passed to the return_reference function, which returned the same reference. And then that reference was used to increment the variable it points to.

Introducing Variable Scope in PHP

Part of the whole idea behind using functions is that you can wrap your variables up in a function, hiding them from the rest of your code. Doing so makes your whole application easier to write, because you don't need to worry about conflict between variables.

Here's an example showing how variables of the same name don't conflict with each other inside functions and out. This example uses two variables named $value, one outside any function, and the other inside a function named scoper. As you're going to see, those variables are independent of each other.

This example starts by creating $value and setting it to 4, and then echoing that value in the browser:

```php
<?php
  $value = 4;

  echo "In the calling code, \$value = ", $value, "<br>";
      .
      .
      .
?>
```

Next, it calls the scoper function, which also has a variable named $value, which is set to 8000000, and echoes that variable from inside the function. Then it goes back to script scope again and echoes the script-level $value again—which is still 4. You can see it all in phpscope.php:

```html
<html>
  <head>
    <title>
      Handling scope in functions
    </title>
  </head>
  <body>
    <h1>
      Handling scope in functions
    </h1>
    <?php
      $value = 4;

      echo "In the calling code, \$value = ", $value, "<br>";

      scoper();

      echo "In the calling code again, \$value still = ", $value, "<br>";

      function scoper()
      {
        $value = 8000000;
        echo "In the function, \$value = ", $value, "<br>";
      }
    ?>
  </body>
</html>
```

You can see the results in Figure 4-11, where you can see the scope of the $value variable both inside and outside the scoper function.

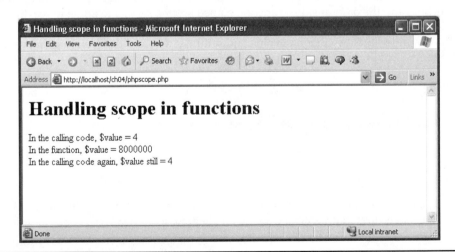

FIGURE 4-11   Function scope

Accessing Global Data

What if you actually wanted to access data outside a function from code inside a function? For example, say that in the function scoper, you really did want to access the script-level variable named $value, not just the local version of that variable:

```php
<?php
  $value = 4;
      .
      .
      .
  function scoper()
  {
    $value = 8000000;
    echo "In the function, \$value = ", $value, "<br>";
  }
?>
```

How would you do that? In PHP, script-level data is called *global* data, and you can access that data from inside a function with the global keyword. You can see how this works in a new example, phpglobalscope.php, which modifies the preceding example to also call a function named global_scoper:

```php
<?php
  $value = 4;

  echo "In the calling code, \$value = ", $value, "<br>";

  scoper();
  global_scoper();

  echo "In the calling code again, \$value still = ", $value, "<br>";

  function scoper()
  {
    $value = 8000000;
    echo "In the scoper function, \$value = ", $value, "<br>";
  }

  function global_scoper()
  {
      .
      .
      .
  }
?>
```

To access the global variable $value from inside global_scoper, you can declare that variable using the global keyword:

```php
<?php
  $value = 4;
```

```
      echo "In the calling code, \$value = ", $value, "<br>";

      scoper();
      global_scoper();

      echo "In the calling code again, \$value still = ", $value, "<br>";

      function scoper()
      {
        $value = 8000000;
        echo "In the scoper function, \$value = ", $value, "<br>";
      }

      function global_scoper()
      {
        global $value;

          .
          .
          .
      }
    ?>
```

Now you can echo the $value variable inside the global_scoper function to verify that you're really dealing with the global $value variable like this in phpglobaldata.php:

```
<html>
  <head>
    <title>
      Handling local and global scope in functions
    </title>
  </head>
  <body>
    <h1>
      Handling local and global scope in functions
    </h1>
    <?php
      $value = 4;

      echo "In the calling code, \$value = ", $value, "<br>";

      scoper();
      global_scoper();

      echo "In the calling code again, \$value still = ", $value, "<br>";

      function scoper()
      {
        $value = 8000000;
        echo "In the scoper function, \$value = ", $value, "<br>";
      }
```

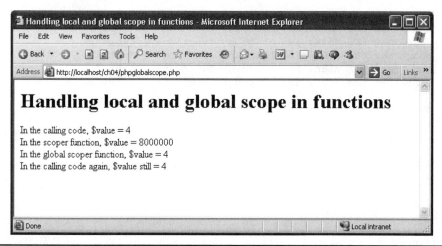

FIGURE 4-12 Local and global scope

```
function global_scoper()
{
  global $value;
  echo "In the global scoper function, \$value = ", $value, "<br>";
}
?>
</body>
</html>
```

You can see the results in Figure 4-12, where you can see you can indeed access global data from inside a function if you use the global keyword.

Working with Static Variables

One issue with functions is that the variables inside them are reset every time you call them—that is, those variables' values aren't preserved between function calls. That's a problem if you *want* those variables to retain their values.

For example, say that you wanted to keep track of the number of times a function has been called with a variable named $counter. You might try that something like this in phpcounter.php:

```
<html>
  <head>
    <title>
      Keeping a count of function calls
    </title>
  </head>
  <body>
    <h1>
      Keeping a count of function calls
    </h1>
```

```php
<?php
  echo "Now the count is: ", count_function(), "<br>";
  echo "Now the count is: ", count_function(), "<br>";
  echo "Now the count is: ", count_function(), "<br>";
  echo "Now the count is: ", count_function(), "<br>";
  echo "Now the count is: ", count_function(), "<br>";

  function count_function()
  {
    $counter = 0;
    $counter++;
    return $counter;
  }
?>
</body>
</html>
```

But you get the results shown in Figure 4-13, where the count is always 1. That's because $counter is reset to 0 every time you call the count_function.

How do you fix this?

There are two easy ways to fix this issue. First, you can make $counter a global variable, and access it as such in the count_function like this:

```php
<?php
  $counter = 0;
  echo "Now the count is: ", count_function(), "<br>";
  echo "Now the count is: ", count_function(), "<br>";
  echo "Now the count is: ", count_function(), "<br>";
  echo "Now the count is: ", count_function(), "<br>";
  echo "Now the count is: ", count_function(), "<br>";
```

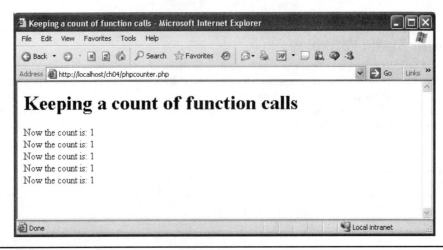

Figure 4-13   Problems with function variables

```
function count_function()
{
   global $counter;
   $counter++;
   return $counter;
}
?>
```

That works, and you get:

```
Now the count is: 1
Now the count is: 2
Now the count is: 3
Now the count is: 4
Now the count is: 5
```

There's another way as well, and it doesn't compromise by insisting you use global variables. You can also declare the $counter variable in the counter_function as *static*, which means that it will preserve its value between function calls. Here's how you do that with the static keyword:

```
<html>
  <head>
    <title>
      Keeping a count of function calls
    </title>
  </head>
  <body>
    <h1>
      Keeping a count of function calls
    </h1>
    <?php
      echo "Now the count is: ", count_function(), "<br>";
      echo "Now the count is: ", count_function(), "<br>";
      echo "Now the count is: ", count_function(), "<br>";
      echo "Now the count is: ", count_function(), "<br>";
      echo "Now the count is: ", count_function(), "<br>";

      function count_function()
      {
         static $counter = 0;
         $counter++;
         return $counter;
      }
    ?>
  </body>
</html>
```

Now you can see the results in Figure 4-14—as you see there, the static keyword did the trick, because the number of times the function was called is indeed reported correctly.

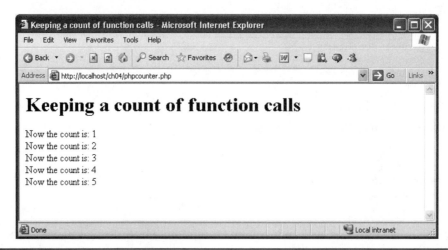

FIGURE 4-14   Keeping count of function calls

PHP Conditional Functions

PHP is an interpreted language, which means that code isn't accessible until it's actually handled by the interpreter. That's not a problem with normal functions, but you can define functions in conditional statements like if statements—and your function doesn't exist, as far as PHP is concerned, until the code defining it is executed.

Here's an example. You might have a normal function like this:

```php
<?php
  echo "normal_function() is ready to go as soon as the script starts.<br>";

  normal_function();
      .
      .
      .
  function normal_function()
  {
    echo "Hello from the normal function.<br>";
  }
?>
```

This code will call and execute normal_function as soon as the page loads, and there's no problem with that. However, now say that you have another function, conditional_ function, whose code is inside an if statement. That function isn't available until the code inside the if statement is executed, so you're going to have problems calling conditional_ function before the if statement is run, as here:

```php
<?php
  echo "normal_function() is ready to go as soon as the script starts.<br>";

  normal_function();
```

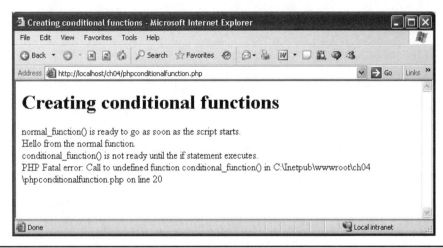

Figure 4-15 Trying to call a function before it exists

```
$create_function = TRUE;

echo "conditional_function() is not ready until the if statement ";
echo "executes.<br>";

conditional_function();

if ($create_function) {
  function conditional_function()
  {
    echo "Hello from the conditional function.<br>";
  }
}

function normal_function()
{
  echo "Hello from the normal function.<br>";
}
?>
```

You can see the results in Figure 4-15—as you see, the conditional_function doesn't exist before the if statement containing it executes, and you get a fatal error.

So let's change this to make sure that conditional_function is called only after it exists, which you can keep track of with a variable named $function_created:

```
<?php
  echo "normal_function() is ready to go as soon as the script starts.<br>";

  normal_function();
```

```
      $create_function = TRUE;

      echo "conditional_function() is not ready until the if statement ";
      echo "executes.<br>";

      $function_created = FALSE;

      if ($create_function) {
        function conditional_function()
        {
          echo "Hello from the conditional function.<br>";
        }
        $function_created = TRUE;
      }

      function normal_function()
      {
        echo "Hello from the normal function.<br>";
      }
    ?>
```

And you can call conditional_function after it has been created, like this in phpconditionalfunction.php:

```
<html>
  <head>
    <title>
      Creating conditional functions
    </title>
  </head>
  <body>
    <h1>
      Creating conditional functions
    </h1>
    <?php
      echo "normal_function() is ready to go as soon as the script starts.<br>";

      normal_function();

      $create_function = TRUE;

      echo "conditional_function() is not ready until the if statement ";
      echo "executes.<br>";

      $function_created = FALSE;

      if ($create_function) {
        function conditional_function()
        {
          echo "Hello from the conditional function.<br>";
        }
        $function_created = TRUE;
      }
```

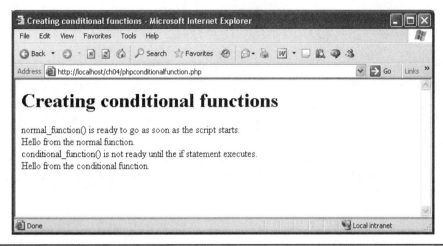

Figure 4-16 Executing a conditional function

```
  if ($function_created){
    conditional_function();
  }

  function normal_function()
  {
    echo "Hello from the normal function.<br>";
  }
?>
</body>
</html>
```

Now you can see the results in Figure 4-16—as you see there, the conditional function was accessible after the if statement was executed. Cool.

PHP Variable Functions

You may recall that in PHP variable variables, you only had to load the name of a variable into another variable to be able to access the first variable. Well, you can do the same thing with functions in PHP—assign a variable the name of a function, and then treat that variable as though it's the name of a function.

Here's an example, phpvariablefunctions.php. This example starts with three functions, red, white, and blue:

```
<?php
  function red()
  {
    echo "In red() now.<br>";
  }
```

```
function white($argument)
{
  echo "$argument <br>";
}

function blue($argument)
{
  echo "$argument <br>";
}
?>
```

Now you can assign the name of the red function to a variable that we'll call $function_variable in this example—and then you can treat $function_variable as though it is the name of a function, and call it like this:

```
<?php
$function_variable = "red";
$function_variable();
    .
    .
    .
function red()
{
  echo "In red() now.<br>";
}

function white($argument)
{
  echo "$argument <br>";
}

function blue($argument)
{
  echo "$argument <br>";
}
?>
```

Similarly, you can use the same technique to call the white and blue functions (note that the functions called this way can have different argument lists):

```
<html>
  <head>
    <title>
      Creating variable functions
    </title>
  </head>
  <body>
    <h1>
      Creating variable functions
    </h1>
    <?php
      $function_variable = "red";
      $function_variable();
```

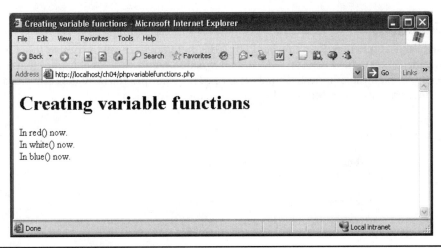

FIGURE 4-17   Executing variable functions

```
      $function_variable = "white";
      $function_variable("In white() now.");

      $function_variable = "blue";
      $function_variable("In blue() now.");

      function red()
      {
        echo "In red() now.<br>";
      }

      function white($argument)
      {
        echo "$argument <br>";
      }

      function blue($argument)
      {
        echo "$argument <br>";
      }
    ?>
  </body>
</html>
```

The results appear in Figure 4-17.

Being able to assign functions to variables this way is a powerful technique. You can write extensive code and tailor it at the last minute to call the functions you want—depending on run-time conditions—without having to edit that code.

Nesting Functions

You can also nest function definitions in PHP. Note that you can't call the nested function until its enclosing function has been run—the nested function won't be accessible until that time.

Here's an example, phpnestedfunctions.php. This example starts by defining a function, outer_function, which encloses another function, inner_function:

```php
<?php
  function outer_function()
  {
    echo "In the outer function.<br>";
    function inner_function()
    {
      echo "In the inner function.<br>";
    }
  }
?>
```

Now you can call outer_function and inner_function—but only in that order, because calling outer_function makes PHP define inner_function—like this in phpnestedfunctions.php:

```html
<html>
  <head>
    <title>
      Nesting functions
    </title>
  </head>
  <body>
    <h1>
      Nesting functions
    </h1>
    <?php
      outer_function();
      inner_function();

      function outer_function()
      {
        echo "In the outer function.<br>";
        function inner_function()
        {
          echo "In the inner function.<br>";
        }
      }
    ?>
  </body>
</html>
```

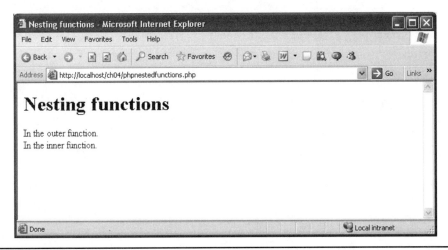

FIGURE **4-18**   Nesting functions

The results appear in Figure 4-18, where you can see the calls to both outer_function and inner_function were successful.

Creating Include Files

PHP also lets you create *include files* whose contents will be inserted into you code file. For example, say that you want to keep track of some constants, such as your health insurance premium. You could do that by defining a constant in a file named, say, premium.inc:

```php
<?php
    define("premium", 176.53);
?>
```

Now you can include premium.inc in your code with the PHP include statement this way:

```php
<?php
  echo "Including constants.inc....<br>";
  include("premium.inc");
    .
    .
    .
?>
```

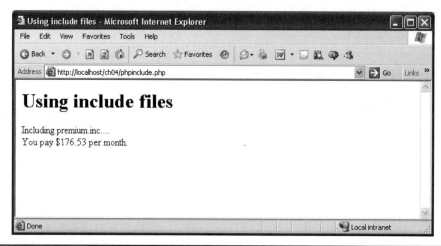

FIGURE 4-19   Using include files

After you include premium.inc, the contents of that file are available to your code. In this case, that means the constant named premium is now accessible to your code, so you can make use of that constant like this:

```
<html>
  <head>
    <title>
      Using include files
    </title>
  </head>
  <body>
    <h1>
      Using include files
    </h1>
    <?php
      echo "Including premium.inc....<br>";
      include("premium.inc");

      echo "You pay \$", premium, " per month.<br>";
    ?>
  </body>
</html>
```

The results appear in Figure 4-19, where you can see that the constant from the include file has indeed been included.

Returning Errors from Functions

It's common for the built-in PHP functions to return FALSE if there's been an error, and you can use the same technique in your own functions. When a function returns FALSE, you can use the die function in PHP to print an error message.

Here's an example—say you have a function named reciprocal that calculates reciprocals (one divided by a number). But you don't want to try to calculate one divided by zero, so return FALSE if you're asked to like this in the reciprocal function, and TRUE if things worked out okay:

```
<?php
  function reciprocal($value)
  {
    if ($value != 0) {
      echo 1 / $value, "<br>";
      return TRUE;
    }
    else {
      return FALSE;
    }
  }
?>
```

Now you can call the reciprocal function and add the clause "or die (*message*)", where *message* is a message that will be displayed if the reciprocal function returned a value of FALSE. It looks like this in code—when you call the die function, the application quits:

```
<html>
  <head>
    <title>
      Handling errors from functions
    </title>
  </head>
  <body>
    <h1>
      Handling errors from functions
    </h1>
    <?php
      echo "The reciprocal of 2 is: ";
      reciprocal(2) or die ("Cannot take the reciprocal of zero.");
      echo "The reciprocal of 0 is: ";
      reciprocal(0) or die ("Cannot take the reciprocal of zero.");

      function reciprocal($value)
      {
        if ($value != 0) {
          echo 1 / $value, "<br>";
          return TRUE;
        }
        else {
          return FALSE;
        }
      }
    ?>
  </body>
</html>
```

The results appear in Figure 4-20, where you can see that the reciprocal of 2 appears fine, but then when you ask the reciprocal function to calculate the reciprocal of zero, it choked and returned FALSE, which ended the application.

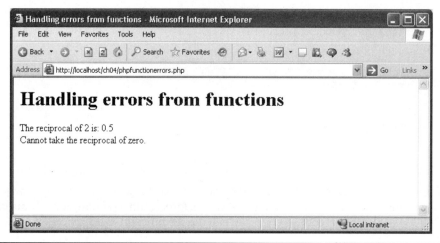

FIGURE 4-20   Handling error results from functions

Reading Data in Web Pages

This is the chapter a lot of developers have been waiting for—the chapter that covers connecting HTML controls in Web pages like text fields, radio buttons, check boxes and so on, to PHP back on the server.

You have the basics of PHP down at this point, which means you can handle the code necessary to work with PHP and HTML controls. So we're going to get connected to HTML in this chapter, seeing how to read data that the user has entered into HTML controls in Web pages.

Setting Up Web Pages to Communicate with PHP

To connect to PHP on the server, or any code on the server, you've got to set up your Web pages a particular way. You have to enclose all your HTML controls in an HTML form, and you have to indicate in that form where the data in those controls will be sent. For example, the user might enter their name in a text field, and you have to let the browser know where to send that name when the user clicks the Submit button.

Here's what an HTML form might look like:

```
<form>
        .
        .
        .
</form>
```

You need to specify the method with which your data will be sent—the two most common methods are "get" and "post" (more on the difference between them later—both methods will get your data to your PHP script), and you might choose the get method here:

```
<form method="get">
        .
        .
        .
</form>
```

Alright, this tells the browser how it's supposed to send the data in the Web page—and you also have to tell the browser where to send that data with an URL. You assign that URL to the <form> element's action attribute, like this:

```
<form method="get" action="http://www.phpisgreat.com/phpreader.php">
    .
    .
    .
</form>
```

This <form> element will send its data to the URL http://www.phpisgreat.com/phpreader. php when the Submit button (coming up in a moment) is clicked.

You can also assign relative URLs to the action attribute. If, for example, this HTML page resided on the server in a specific directory, and the PHP script phpreader.php resided in the *same* directory on the server, you could shorten the URL to this:

```
<form method="get" action="phpreader.php">
    .
    .
    .
</form>
```

This version of the <form> element assumes that the HTML page currently in the browser came from the same directory as the PHP script is in. For example, if this HTML page was http://www.phpisgreat.com/input.html, then the PHP script specified by simply assigning "phpreader.php" to the action attribute would send the data in the HTML page to the PHP script at http://www.phpisgreat.com/phpreader.php.

There's even another version—you can omit the action element altogether:

```
<form method="get">
    .
    .
    .
</form>
```

In this case, the form's data is sent back to the same URL that the current document is at. For example, if you have a PHP script that can display HTML controls, phpcomplete.php, then when you navigate to that script in your browser, you'll see those HTML controls. If there's no action attribute, the data in the form will be sent back to the exact same script when the user clicks the Submit button.

That's a common thing to do—have a PHP script handle both the display of the HTML controls, and then read the data in those HTML controls when the user clicks the Submit button. You'll see how this works in this book.

Besides the HTML controls like text fields and check boxes, you'll also need a submit button in your form, because the data in the form is sent to your PHP script when that submit button is clicked. The submit button need not have the caption "Submit"—you can set its caption to anything you like by assigning that caption to the submit button's value attribute.

Here's how to create a submit button—note it has to be inside the HTML <form> element—with the caption Send, and that you use an <input> element with the type attribute set to "submit" to create a submit button:

```
<html>
  <head>
    <title>
      Connecting to PHP
    </title>
  </head>
  <body>
    <h1>
      Connecting to PHP
    </h1>
    <form method="get" action="phpreader.php">
         .
         .
         .
      <input type="submit" value="Send">
      <input type="reset" value="Reset">
    </form>
  </body>
</html>
```

Note that there's also a (optional) reset button here; when clicked, this button resets the data in all the HTML controls in the form back to their default values.

Say you wanted to use a text field (that is, a <input type = "text"> HTML control) to ask for the user's name; you could do that like this in the HTML form:

```
<html>
  <head>
    <title>
      Connecting to PHP
    </title>
  </head>
  <body>
    <h1>
      Connecting to PHP
    </h1>
    <form method="get" action="phpreader.php">
      What's your name?

      <input name="data" type="text">                  .
         .
         .
      <input type="submit" value="Send">
      <input type="reset" value="Reset">
    </form>
  </body>
</html>
```

Note that this HTML gives the name "data" to the text field. How can you access the name entered into this text field on the server, in your PHP script?

If you've used the POST method, you can find that data in the $_POST array, as we're going to start seeing in the next chunk on retrieving data from text fields. If you've used the GET method, you use the $_GET array. These arrays are "superglobal" arrays, which means that they're available to you without having to use the global keyword. Also, the $_REQUEST array holds data from both $_GET and $_POST.

That means that to recover the name the user entered into the text field named "data", you can use the expression $_REQUEST["data"] in your PHP script.

Let's put all this into practice with real text fields, coming up next.

Handling Text Fields

Say you've put together a Web page, phptext.html, that has a text field and a submit button in a form, as you see here:

```html
<html>
  <head>
    <title>
      Entering data into text fields
    </title>
  </head>
  <body>
    <h1>
      Entering data into text fields
    </h1>
    <form method="get" action="phptext.php">
      What's your name?

      <input name="data" type="text">        .

      <input type="submit" value="Send">
    </form>
  </body>
</html>
```

You can see this HTML page in Figure 5-1, waiting for you to enter your name.

Okay, so how do you read the data the user entered in this Web page—that is, their name in a text field we've named "data"—from PHP on the server?

This HTML page is set up to send its data to the PHP script phptext.php (note that because you've assigned a relative URL to the action attribute—just the name of the PHP script—that PHP script must be stored in the same directory on the server as phptext.html):

```html
<form method="get" action="phptext.php">
  What's your name?

  <input name="data" type="text">        .

  <input type="submit" value="Send">
</form>
```

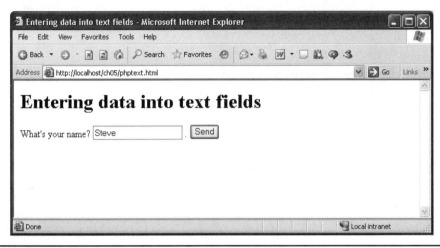

FIGURE 5-1   Using a text field in an HTML page

In phptext.php, you can access the text in the text field named "data" as $_REQUEST["data"]. So here's phptext.php:

```
<html>
  <head>
    <title>
      Reading data from text fields
    </title>
  </head>
  <body>
    <h1>
      Reading data from text fields
    </h1>
    Thanks for answering,
    <?php
      echo $_REQUEST["data"];
    ?>
  </body>
</html>
```

All this PHP script, phptext.php, does is to echo the name the user entered into the data text field. Make sure that phptext.php goes in the same directory as phptext.html on your server, and give this example a try. When you click the submit button in phptext.html, you see the results, something like what you see in Figure 5-2, where the user's name appears.

Note the URL in Figure 5-2: http://localhost/ch05/phptext.php?data=Steve. That URL includes the data the user entered into the text field, placed there following a question mark (?). The data sent with the "get" method is always URL-encoded (spaces are replaced with + signs, different controls name/data pairs are separated with an &), and placed into the URL.

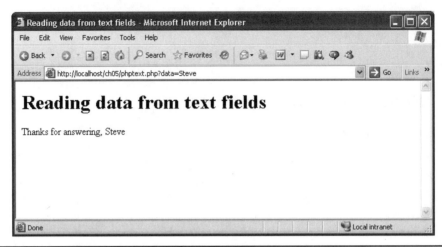

FIGURE 5-2 Reading text from a text field in PHP

The get method works, but as you can see, it can create less-than-professional results. If you don't want the user's data to appear in the URL they access the server with, use the "post" method instead, like this in phptext.html:

```
<html>
  <head>
    <title>
      Entering data into text fields
    </title>
  </head>
  <body>
    <h1>
      Entering data into text fields
    </h1>
    <form method="post" action="phptext.php">
      What's your name?

      <input name="data" type="text">               .

      <input type="submit" value="Send">
    </form>
  </body>
</html>
```

When you use this new version of phptext.html, the user's data is sent in the HTTP headers that the browser sends to the server, instead of the URL. That results in a cleaner URL, as you can see in the URL text area in the browser in Figure 5-3. Because posted data is sent in HTTP headers and not in the URL, data that you send with the post method is slightly more secure.

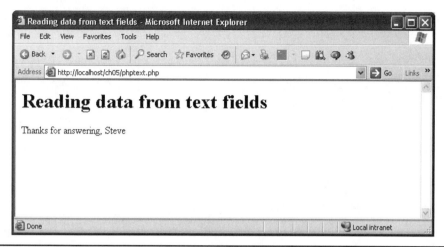

FIGURE 5-3   Reading text from a text field without visible URL-encoding

Excellent, you've been able to read data from a text field. A similar HTML control, text areas, is coming up next.

Handling Text Areas

Text fields are fine if you only want a single line of text, but if you want multiline text input, you have to go with text areas.

Here's an example, phptextarea.html, that presents the user with a text area, and asks what pizza toppings they want. It starts like this:

```html
<html>
  <head>
    <title>
      Entering data into text areas
    </title>
  </head>
  <body>
    <h1>
      Entering data into text areas
    </h1>
    <form method="post" action="phptextarea.php">
      Enter the pizza toppings you want: <br>
        .
        .
        .
      <br>
      <input type="submit" value="Send">
    </form>
  </body>
</html>
```

Then it adds a text area like this, where the numbers 1–4 will appear in the text area:

```
<html>
  <head>
    <title>
      Entering data into text areas
    </title>
  </head>
  <body>
    <h1>
      Entering data into text areas
    </h1>
    <form method="post" action="phptextarea.php">
      Enter the pizza toppings you want: <br>
      <textarea name="data" cols="50" rows="5">
1.
2.
3.
4.
      </textarea>
      <br>
      <input type="submit" value="Send">
    </form>
  </body>
</html>
```

You can see this page in Figure 5-4, waiting for you to enter your pizza toppings.

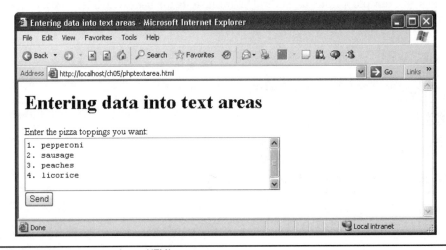

FIGURE 5-4   Using a text area in an HTML page

So how do you read the data the user entered in this Web page—in the text area named "data"—from PHP on the server? The data the user entered will be sent to phptextarea.php on the server, and you can access the text from the text area as $_REQUEST["data"] in that script:

```
<html>
  <head>
    <title>
      Reading data from text areas
    </title>
  </head>
  <body>
    <h1>
      Reading data from text areas
    </h1>
    You ordered a pizza with: <br>
    <?php
      $text = $_REQUEST["data"];
            .
            .
            .

    ?>
  </body>
</html>
```

Note that because you're dealing with a text area, multiline text will be filled with newline characters, \n. When you display that text, the browser is going to ignore the newlines, so you might replace them with <br> elements instead, like this, where we display the user's pizza toppings in phptextarea.php:

```
<html>
  <head>
    <title>
      Reading data from text areas
    </title>
  </head>
  <body>
    <h1>
      Reading data from text areas
    </h1>
    You ordered a pizza with: <br>
    <?php
      $text = $_REQUEST["data"];
      echo str_replace("\n", "<br>", $text);
    ?>
  </body>
</html>
```

And you can see the results in Figure 5-5, where the application has not only echoed the text the user entered, but also preserved the multiline nature of that text. Nice.

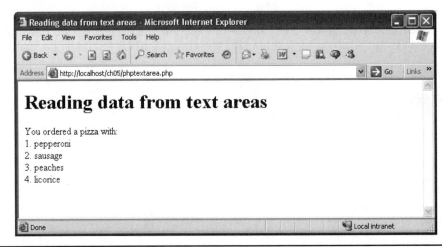

FIGURE 5-5   Reading text from a text area in PHP

Handling Check Boxes

The next step up in controls are check boxes—those square controls that you can select or de-select with the mouse.

You create check boxes with the <input> element like this in a Web page, where you're asking the user if they want fries in phpcheckbox.html:

```
<html>
  <head>
    <title>
      Entering data into check boxes
    </title>
  </head>
  <body>
    <h1>
      Entering data into check boxes
    </h1>
    <form method="post" action="phpcheckbox.php">
      Do you want fries with that?
      <input name="check1" type="checkbox" value="yes">
      Yes
      <input name="check2" type="checkbox" value="no">
      No
      <br>
      <br>
      <input type="submit" value="Send">
    </form>
  </body>
</html>
```

Note that the value of the first check box is "yes" and the value of the second is "no"—those are the values that will be sent to your script on the server.

And you can see the results in Figure 5-6, where the application is asking the user if they want fries.

How do you read the data from the check boxes, check1 and check2? You might think you could do that simply like this, where you simply use expressions like $_REQUEST["check1"]:

```
<html>
  <head>
    <title>
      Reading data from check boxes
    </title>
  </head>
  <body>
    <h1>
    You selected:
    <?php
      echo $_REQUEST["check1"], "<br>";
      echo $_REQUEST["check2"], "<br>";
    ?>
  </body>
</html>
```

Unfortunately, that's not right—the user may not have checked a check box, so attempting to display the data from that check box would give you an error in PHP. For example, if the user has not check check1, then echo $_REQUEST["check1"] will give you an error (because the array $_REQUEST doesn't have an element with the index "check1").

In this case, you have to first check if there is any data waiting for you from a particular check box before you attempt to display that data. You can check if an array has an element with a certain index with the isset function, so before echoing $_REQUEST["check1"], check

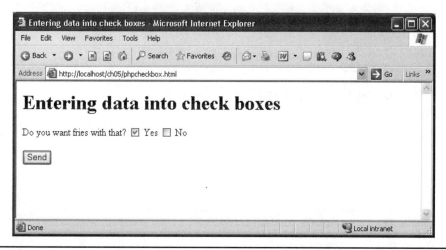

FIGURE 5-6   Setting check boxes

if that array element exists with isset($_REQUEST["check1"]). Here's how that works in phpcheckbox.php:

```
<html>
  <head>
    <title>
      Reading data from text fields
    </title>
  </head>
  <body>
    <h1>
      Reading data from check boxes
    </h1>
    You selected:
    <?php
      if (isset($_REQUEST["check1"])) {
        echo $_REQUEST["check1"], "<br>";
      }
      if (isset($_REQUEST["check2"])) {
        echo $_REQUEST["check2"], "<br>";
      }
    ?>
  </body>
</html>
```

And you can see the results in Figure 5-7, where you're reading what check boxes the user selected.

Note that the user could click both check boxes here—which would mean that they both wanted fries and didn't want fries. A better choice for the controls here are radio buttons, where only one can be selected at a time, and they're coming up next.

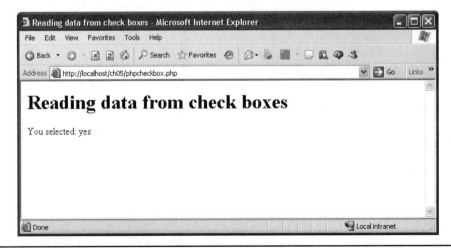

FIGURE 5-7   Reading check box data in PHP

Handling Radio Buttons

Check boxes are good if you want the user to be able to select multiple items from a number of choices. But if you want to let the user select only one item from a number of choices, you should use radio buttons instead, because they only allow the user to make one selection at a time.

Here's an example, phpradiobutton.html, that, like the preceding example, asks the user if they want fries—but unlike the previous example, this time, the user can only select yes or no, not both (note that we're giving both radiobuttons the same name here, "radios"):

```html
<html>
  <head>
    <title>
      Entering data with radio buttons
    </title>
  </head>
  <body>
    <h1>
      Entering data with radio buttons
    </h1>
    <form method="post" action="phpradiobutton.php">
      Do you want fries with that?
      <input name="radios" type="radio" value="yes">
      Yes
      <input name="radios" type="radio" value="no">
      No
      <br>
      <br>
      <input type="submit" value="Send">
    </form>
  </body>
</html>
```

You can see this page in Figure 5-8, waiting for your answer.

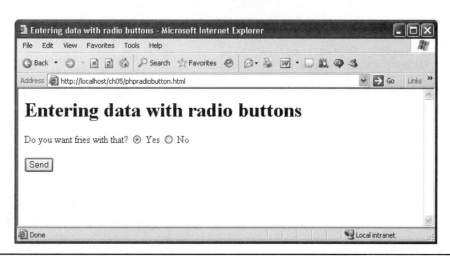

FIGURE 5-8   Using radio buttons in an HTML page

How do you read data from radio buttons? You can use $_REQUEST like this in phpradiobutton.php:

```
<html>
  <head>
    <title>
      Reading data from radio buttons
    </title>
  </head>
  <body>
    <h1>
      Reading data from radio buttons
    </h1>
    You selected
    <?php
      echo $_REQUEST["radios"];
    ?>
  </body>
</html>
```

But you'd run into the same problem as with the check boxes—the user may not have selected either radio button. On the other hand, there will only be one entry in the $_REQUEST array under the index "radios", so you only need one statement like this in phpradiobutton.php:

```
<html>
  <head>
    <title>
      Reading data from radio buttons
    </title>
  </head>
  <body>
    <h1>
      Reading data from radio buttons
    </h1>
    You selected
    <?php
      if (isset($_REQUEST["radios"])) {
        echo $_REQUEST["radios"];
      }
    ?>
  </body>
</html>
```

In fact, you can indicate that no radio button was selected if that was the case:

```
<head>
  <title>
    Reading data from radio buttons
  </title>
</head>
```

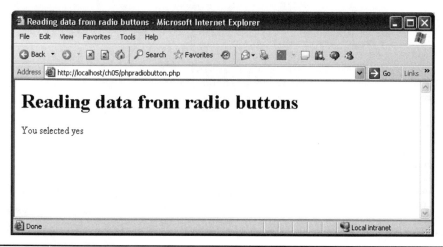

FIGURE 5-9   Reading radio buttons in PHP

```
<body>
  <h1>
    Reading data from radio buttons
  </h1>
  You selected
  <?php
    if (isset($_REQUEST["radios"])) {
      echo $_REQUEST["radios"];
    }
    else {
      echo "No radio button was selected. <br>";
    }
  ?>
</body>
</html>
```

You can see the results in Figure 5-9, where the application has accurately determined which radio button was clicked.

Handling List Boxes

List boxes are also a common HTML control, and they take a little special handling. Say that you wanted to let the user select their favorite flavors of ice cream; you might start like this in phplistbox.html, where you're creating the list box with a <select> HTML control:

```
<html>
  <head>
    <title>
      Entering data with list boxes
    </title>
  </head>
```

```
<body>
  <h1>
    Entering data with list boxes
  </h1>
  Select your favorite ice cream flavors:
  <form method="post" action="phplistbox.php">
    <select>
       .
       .
       .
    </select>
    <br>
    <br>
    <input type="submit" value="Send">
  </form>
</body>
</html>
```

To let the user select multiple ice cream flavors, we're going to make this a multiple select control, which you do in HTML with the stand-alone attribute multiple in the <select> element. And here's the trick that will let this multiple-selection control work with PHP—you give the control the name of an array, not just a name. For example, if this control were a single-selection control, you might call it "ice_cream"—but because it's a multiple-selection control, you call it "ice_cream[]", which tips PHP off that this is a control that allows multiple selections:

```
<html>
  <head>
    <title>
      Entering data with list boxes
    </title>
  </head>
  <body>
    <h1>
      Entering data with list boxes
    </h1>
    Select your favorite ice cream flavors:
    <form method="post" action="phplistbox.php">
      <select name="ice_cream[]" multiple>
         .
         .
         .
      </select>
      <br>
      <br>
      <input type="submit" value="Send">
    </form>
  </body>
</html>
```

Now you're free to add the ice cream flavors as <option> elements inside the <select> control (the items in <select> controls are given as <option> elements in HTML):

```
<html>
  <head>
    <title>
      Entering data with list boxes
    </title>
  </head>
  <body>
    <h1>
      Entering data with list boxes
    </h1>
    Select your favorite ice cream flavors:
    <form method="post" action="phplistbox.php">
      <select name="ice_cream[]" multiple>
        <option>vanilla</option>
        <option>strawberry</option>
        <option>chocolate</option>
        <option>herring</option>
      </select>
      <br>
      <br>
      <input type="submit" value="Send">
    </form>
  </body>
</html>
```

You can see this page in Figure 5-10, waiting for your ice cream selections.

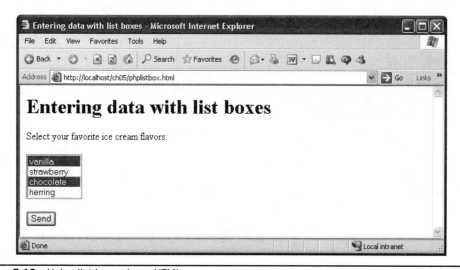

FIGURE 5-10   Using list boxes in an HTML page

Alright, what about reading the selections the user made? Up until now, you would have handled their selections like this, simply echoing $_REQUEST["ice_cream"] to the browser:

```
<head>
  <title>
    Reading data from list boxes
  </title>
</head>
<body>
  <h1>
    Reading data from list boxes
  </h1>
  Your ice cream flavors:
  <BR>
  <?php
    echo $_REQUEST["ice_cream"];
  ?>
</body>
</html>
```

But that won't work here, because ice_cream is an array, not a single variable. So you might use a foreach loop to display the user's ice cream selections like this in phplistbox.php:

```
<head>
  <title>
    Reading data from list boxes
  </title>
</head>
<body>
  <h1>
    Reading data from list boxes
  </h1>
  Your ice cream flavors:
  <BR>
  <?php
    foreach($_REQUEST["ice_cream"] as $flavor){
      echo $flavor, "<br>";
    }
  ?>
</body>
</html>
```

You can see the results in Figure 5-11, where the PHP page has accurately reported the user's ice cream selections.

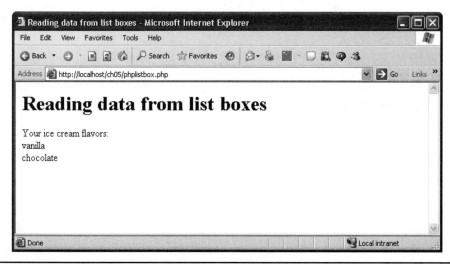

Figure 5-11   Reading list boxes in an HTML page

Handling Password Controls

A common use of PHP is to check passwords on the server, giving the user access to a resource if they have the right password, and you can use password controls for that.

Here's an example that asks the user for their password, phppassword.html:

```
<html>
  <head>
    <title>
      Entering data with password controls
    </title>
  </head>
  <body>
    <h1>
      Entering data with password controls
    </h1>
    <form method="post" action="phppassword.php">
    Enter your password:

    <input name="password" type="password">

    <br>
    <br>
    <input type="submit" value="Send">
    </form>
  </body>
</html>
```

You can see this page in Figure 5-12, where the user has entered their password.

FIGURE 5-12   Using password controls in an HTML page

You can store the password on the server—which is the charm of using PHP for password verification. In this case, you check $_REQUEST["password"] against the password, which is "letmein" in this case, and if it matches, display a welcome page to the user in phppassword.php:

```
<head>
  <title>
    Reading data from password controls
  </title>
</head>
<body>
  <h1>
    Reading data from password controls
  </h1>
  <?php
    if ($_REQUEST["password"] == "letmein"){
  ?>
    <h2>
     Password accepted
    </h2>
    OK, you're in.<br>
    Please act responsibly.

        .
        .
        .

    ?>
  </body>
</html>
```

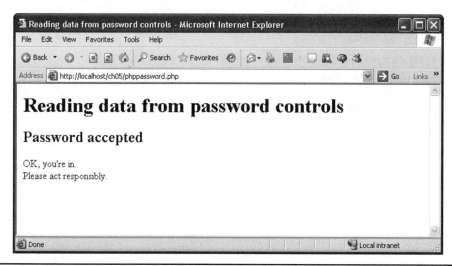

FIGURE 5-13   Gaining access with a password

You can see this result in Figure 5-13.

On the other hand, if the password the user entered is not right, you can display an error page—note how this page mixes HTML and PHP:

```
<head>
  <title>
    Reading data from password controls
  </title>
</head>
<body>
  <h1>
    Reading data from password controls
  </h1>
  <?php
    if ($_REQUEST["password"] == "letmein"){
  ?>
    <h2>
     Password accepted
    </h2>
    OK, you're in.<br>
    Please act responsibly.
  <?php
    }
    else {
  ?>
    <h2>
     Password denied
    </h2>
```

FIGURE 5-14   Denying access for the wrong password

```
      You did not enter the correct password.<br>
      What are you, some kind of hacker?
   <?php
      }
   ?>
   </body>
</html>
```

And you can see the error result in Figure 5-14.

Handling Hidden Controls

HTML hidden controls are a good match for PHP scripts, because they let you store data in Web pages that the user doesn't usually see, and that you can make use of on the server (the user can see hidden data if they look at a Web page's source).

Here's an example that uses a hidden control named customer_type to store what we think of the customer, behind the scenes. In this case, phphidden.php, customer_type is set to "good":

```
<html>
  <head>
    <title>
      Storing data with hidden controls
    </title>
  </head>
  <body>
    <h1>
      Storing data with hidden controls
    </h1>
```

```
What kind of customer do we think you are? <br>
Click the button to find out. <br>
<form method="post" action="phphidden.php">
   <input name="customer_type" type="hidden" value="good">
   <br>
   <br>
   <input type="submit" value="Send">
</form>
</body>
</html>
```

The customer type is not apparent by just looking at the Web page, however, as you can see in Figure 5-15.

However, you can read the data in the customer_type hidden control in PHP on the server. That looks like this:

```
<head>
   <title>
      Reading data from password controls
   </title>
</head>
<body>
   <h1>
      Reading data from password controls
   </h1>
   We think you are a
   <?php
      echo $_REQUEST["customer_type"];
   ?>
   customer.
</body>
</html>
```

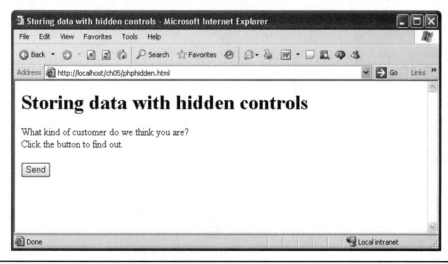

FIGURE 5-15   Using hidden controls in an HTML page

FIGURE 5-16   Reading hidden controls in an HTML page

And you can see the result in Figure 5-16—the customer is a good customer.

Hidden controls like this are popular for storing information about the user for use with PHP—another popular way of storing information about the user is to use cookies, also coming up in this book.

Handling Image Maps

You can also handle image maps—those clickable images you see in browsers—with PHP, although doing so takes a little extra effort.

You can see an image map example in phpimagemap.html, which uses an <input type="image"> element to display an image map:

```
<html>
  <head>
    <title>
      Entering data with image maps
    </title>
  </head>
  <body>
    <h1>
      Entering data with image maps
    </h1>
    <form method="post" action="phpimagemap.php">
      Click the image:
      <br>

      <input name="imap" type="image" src="map.jpg">
    </form>
  </body>
</html>
```

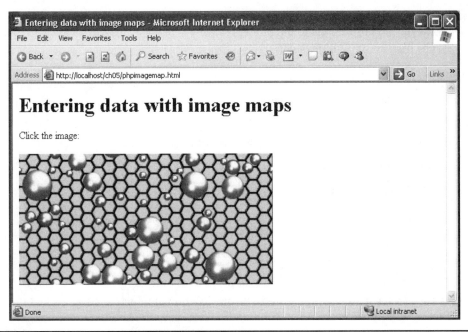

Figure 5-17   Using hidden controls in an HTML page

And you can see the image map in Figure 5-17. Note that no Submit button is needed here—clicking the image itself sends that location of that click in the image to the server.

So how do you handle image clicks in PHP? You might try something like this in phpimagemap.php—the image map was given the name imap, so you might make a first attempt by simply using $_REQUEST["imap"]:

```
<head>
  <title>
    Reading data from image maps
  </title>
</head>
<body>
  <h1>
    Reading data from image maps
  </h1>
    You clicked the image map at
    <?php
      echo $_REQUEST["imap"];
    ?>
</body>
</html>
```

However, that's not going to work, because the mouse location in the image map consists of two coordinates, an x coordinate and a y coordinate. In PHP, those coordinates are stored under the name of the image map with _x and _y appended. That means you can display the location at which the user clicked the image (in image coordinates, (0, 0) is the upper-left corner of the image, positive x is to the right, positive y is downward, and all measurements are in pixels) like this in phpimagemap.php:

```
<head>
  <title>
    Reading data from image maps
  </title>
</head>
<body>
  <h1>
    Reading data from image maps
  </h1>
    You clicked the image map at location (
    <?php
      echo $_REQUEST["imap_x"], ", ", $_REQUEST["imap_y"];
    ?>
    ).
</body>
</html>
```

And you can see the result in Figure 5-18—the location at which the user clicked the image map is displayed.

Tɪᴘ *Image maps are good for all kinds of things in PHP—with them, you can let the user make selections or jump to other URLs.*

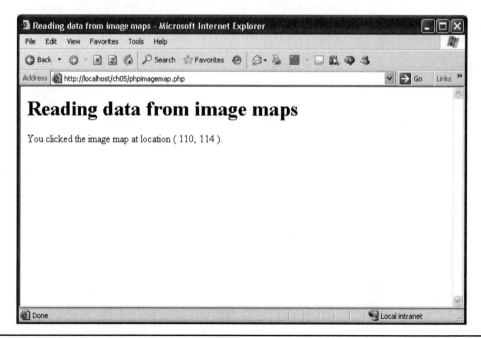

Figure 5-18   Reading hidden controls in an HTML page

Handling File Uploads

You can also use Web pages to upload files, not an infrequent thing to see on the Web. Very few PHP books cover this topic, however—but we will.

You have to set up the form as a multipart form if you want to use file upload controls. In this example, that means you set the <form> element's enctype (encoding type) attribute to "multipart/form-data". You can also set the action attribute to the URL where you want the file data to be sent—that's phpfile.php here—and the method to "post":

```
<html>
  <head>
    <title>
      Entering data with file uploads
    </title>
  </head>
  <body>
    <h1>
      Entering data with file uploads
    </h1>
    <form method="post" action="phpimagemap.php"

        enctype="multipart/form-data"
        action="phpfile.php" method="post">
        .
        .
        .
        <input type="submit" value="Send File" />
    </form>
  </body>
</html>
```

To actually upload the file, you use a file upload control, <input type="file">. In this case, you might give the upload control the name userfile like this in phpfile.html:

```
<html>
  <head>
    <title>
      Entering data with file uploads
    </title>
  </head>
  <body>
    <h1>
      Entering data with file uploads
    </h1>
    <form method="post" action="phpimagemap.php"

        enctype="multipart/form-data"
        action="phpfile.php" method="post">
        Upload file: <input name="userfile" type="file" />
        <br>
        <br>
        <input type="submit" value="Send File" />
    </form>
  </body>
</html>
```

Here's the file we're going to test uploading: file.text:

```
Here
are
the
file's
contents.
```

You can see what this looks like in Figure 5-19, where the user has browsed to the file to upload.

Okay, that takes care of the HTML side of things—how about the PHP side? You use the $_FILES array in PHP to handle uploaded files; here are the array elements that are available:

- **$_FILES['userfile']['name']**   The name of the file on the user's machine.

- **$_FILES['userfile']['type']**   The MIME type of the file. For example, this could be "image/jpeg" or "text/plain".

- **$_FILES['userfile']['size']**   The size of the uploaded file (in bytes).

- **$_FILES['userfile']['tmp_name']**   The temporary filename of the file in which the uploaded file was stored on the server.

- **$_FILES['userfile']['error']**   The error code associated with this file upload.

As you can see, there's a lot of power here. To actually read the uploaded file, we're going to use come techniques that will be introduced later in this book, under the topic of file handling.

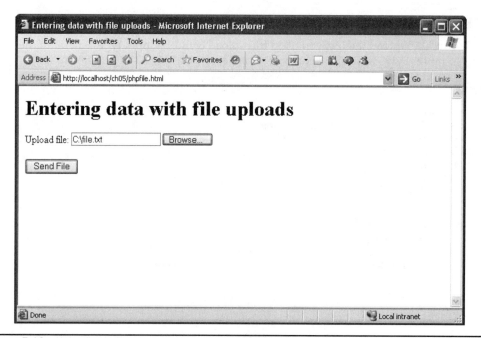

Figure 5-19   Uploading a file

You start by getting a *file handle* corresponding to the file. This value corresponds to the file as far as PHP is concerned, and you get a file handle when you open a file. The file-handling functions in PHP often start with "f," and opening a file is no exception—you open a file with the fopen function. Opening a file gives you access to the data in that file; the name of the file to open, as you see in the preceding list, is $_FILES['userfile']['tmp_name'], so here's how you open the uploaded file—note the final "r" argument, which opens the file for reading (as opposed to opening it for writing, which would allow you to overwrite the data in the file):

```html
<html>
  <head>
    <title>Reading file data</title>
  </head>
  <body>
    <h1>Reading file data</h1>
    <br>
    The file contained:
    <br>
    <?php
      $handle = fopen($_FILES['userfile']['tmp_name'], "r");
        .
        .
        .

    ?>
  </body>
</html>
```

Okay, that's great—now you have opened the uploaded file and have a file handle corresponding to it. You can now read the data from the file. This example assumes that the data in the file is text data, and we're going to read strings of text from the file repeatedly until we've reached the end of the file. You can check when you've reached the end of the file with the feof function, which returns true when you're at the end of a file and there's no more data to read.

The way the file-reading process usually works is to use a while loop that keeps looping while you're not at the end of the file. That looks like this:

```html
<html>
  <head>
    <title>Reading file data</title>
  </head>
  <body>
    <h1>Reading file data</h1>
    <br>
    The file contained:
    <br>
    <?php
      $handle = fopen($_FILES['userfile']['tmp_name'], "r");
      while (!feof($handle)){
        .
        .
        .

      }
    ?>
  </body>
</html>
```

Each time through the loop, we can read another line of text from the file using the fgets function, which reads a string from the file:

```
<html>
  <head>
    <title>Reading file data</title>
  </head>
  <body>
    <h1>Reading file data</h1>
    <br>
    The file contained:
    <br>
    <?php
      $handle = fopen($_FILES['userfile']['tmp_name'], "r");
      while (!feof($handle)){
        $text = fgets($handle);
          .
          .
          .

      }
    ?>
  </body>
</html>
```

This code reads a line of text from the file and stores it in the variable $text. Now you can display that line of text in the browser:

```
<html>
  <head>
    <title>Reading file data</title>
  </head>
  <body>
    <h1>Reading file data</h1>
    <br>
    The file contained:
    <br>
    <?php
      $handle = fopen($_FILES['userfile']['tmp_name'], "r");
      while (!feof($handle)){
        $text = fgets($handle);
        echo $text, "<br>";
      }
    ?>
  </body>
</html>
```

Okay, that loops over the file's contents, echoing it line by line to the browser. When you're done with a file, you should close it, and that works like this, where you pass the file handle to the fclose function:

```
<html>
  <head>
    <title>Reading file data</title>
  </head>
```

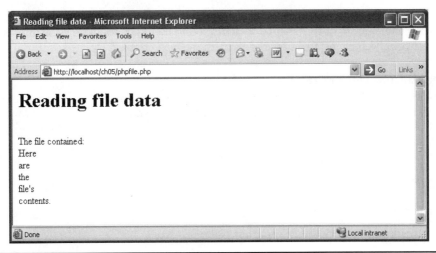

FIGURE 5-20   Displaying an uploaded file's contents

```
<body>
  <h1>Reading file data</h1>
  <br>
  The file contained:
  <br>
  <?php
    $handle = fopen($_FILES['userfile']['tmp_name'], "r");
    while (!feof($handle)){
      $text = fgets($handle);
      echo $text, "<br>";
    }
    fclose($handle);
  ?>
</body>
</html>
```

You can see all this at work in Figure 5-20, where the uploaded file's contents are displayed.

Although this example worked with a text file, you can also upload binary files, of course. All you have to do is to use the techniques for handling binary files coming up in the general discussion of file-handling in this book.

So now you've been able to upload files that the user passes to you. Cool.

Handling Buttons

There's still one popular HTML control that we haven't covered—buttons. Although you often see buttons in Web pages, they are more difficult to work with using server-side scripts for one reason—they pop back. That is, there's no data that's stored that will be sent to the server when a Submit button is clicked.

So how do you handle buttons in Web pages with PHP? There are a couple of solutions here, and the remainder of this chapter is dedicated to them—if you have little interest in buttons in your Web pages, feel free to skip on to the next chapter.

Making Button Data Persist

One obvious solution to the fleeting nature of button data is to make that data persist. You might do that by storing text data in a hidden control, for example:

```
<html>
  <head>
    <title>Handling buttons</title>
  </head>
  <body>
    <h1>Handling buttons</H1>
    <form name="form1" action="phpbuttons.php" method="post">
      <input type="hidden" name="button">
         .
         .
         .

    </form>
  </body>
</html>
```

Then you can add, say, three standard HTML buttons to the page:

```
<html>
  <head>
    <title>Handling buttons</title>
  </head>
  <body>
    <h1>Handling buttons</H1>
    <form name="form1" action="phpbuttons.php" method="post">
      <input type="hidden" name="button">
      <input type="button" value="Button 1" onclick="setbutton1()">
      <input type="button" value="Button 2" onclick="setbutton2()">
      <input type="button" value="Button 3" onclick="setbutton3()">
    </form>
  </body>
</html>
```

So how do you store data in the hidden control when the user clicks a button? Since these are standard HTML buttons, all the action has to take place in the browser—so that means using a browser-side scripting language like JavaScript; there's no other choice. Here's how you can store the name of the button that was clicked in the hidden control:

```
<html>
  <head>
    <title>Handling buttons</title>
    <script language="JavaScript">
      function setbutton1()
```

```
      {
        document.form1.button.value = "button 1"
        .
        .
        .
      }

      function setbutton2()
      {
        document.form1.button.value = "button 2"
        .
        .
        .
      }

      function setbutton3()
      {
        document.form1.button.value = "button 3"
        .
        .
        .
      }
    </script>
  </head>
  <body>
    <h1>Handling buttons</H1>
    <form name="form1" action="phpbuttons.php" method="post">
      <input type="hidden" name="button">
      <input type="button" value="Button 1" onclick="setbutton1()">
      <input type="button" value="Button 2" onclick="setbutton2()">
      <input type="button" value="Button 3" onclick="setbutton3()">
    </form>
  </body>
</html>
```

After the name of the button has been stored in the hidden field, you can complete the process by submitting the form from JavaScript:

```
<html>
  <head>
    <title>Handling buttons</title>
    <script language="JavaScript">
      function setbutton1()
      {
        document.form1.button.value = "button 1"
        form1.submit()
      }

      function setbutton2()
      {
        document.form1.button.value = "button 2"
        form1.submit()
      }
```

```
      function setbutton3()
      {
        document.form1.button.value = "button 3"
        form1.submit()
      }
    </script>
  </head>
  <body>
    <h1>Handling buttons</H1>
    <form name="form1" action="phpbuttons.php" method="post">
      <input type="hidden" name="button">
      <input type="button" value="Button 1" onclick="setbutton1()">
      <input type="button" value="Button 2" onclick="setbutton2()">
      <input type="button" value="Button 3" onclick="setbutton3()">
    </form>
  </body>
</html>
```

You can see this page, phpbuttons.php, in Figure 5-21.

Reading the data now that you've stored it in a hidden field is easy using PHP. Here's what the script that reads the button you've clicked, phpbuttons.php, looks like:

```
<html>
  <head>
    <title>
      Reading buttons
    </title>
  </head>
  <body>
    <h1>Reading buttons</h1>
```

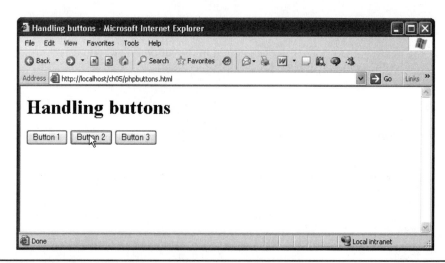

Figure 5-21   Buttons in a Web page

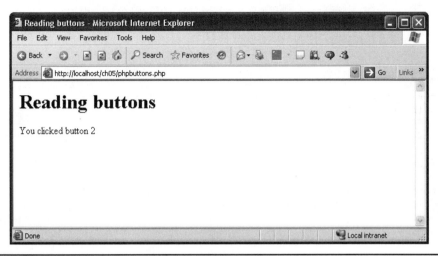

FIGURE 5-22   Displaying the clicked button

```
    You clicked
    <?php
      if (isset($_REQUEST["button"])) {
        echo $_REQUEST["button"], "<br>";
      }
    ?>
  </body>
</html>
```

You can see the result in Figure 5-22, where the PHP script has correctly identified the clicked button.

However, this is a book on PHP, not on JavaScript. Isn't there a better way to handle buttons in Web pages?

Using Submit Buttons as HTML Buttons

Since the action in PHP takes place on the server, you can also use submit buttons in place of standard HTML buttons. Submit buttons look the same as HTML buttons, so the user won't be any wiser.

Here's a way you might use Submit buttons to mimic HTML buttons—create three forms for three buttons:

```
<html>
  <head>
    <title>Reading submit buttons</title>
  </head>

  <body>
    <h1>Reading submit buttons</h1>
    <form name="form1" action="phpsubmit.php" method="post">
```

```
          <input type="submit" value="Button 1">
            .
            .
            .
       </form>

       <form name="form2" action="phpsubmit.php" method="post">
          <input type="submit" value="Button 2">
            .
            .
            .
       </form>

       <form name="form3" action="phpsubmit.php" method="post">
          <input type="submit" value="Button 3">
            .
            .
            .
       </form>
    </body>
</html>
```

Then give each form its own hidden control with the button's name like this in phpsubmit.html:

```
<html>
   <head>
     <title>Reading submit buttons</title>
   </head>

   <body>
     <h1>Reading submit buttons</h1>
     <form name="form1" action="phpsubmit.php" method="post">
       <input type="hidden" name="button" value="button 1">
       <input type="submit" value="Button 1">
     </form>

     <form name="form2" action="phpsubmit.php" method="post">
       <input type="hidden" name="button" value="button 2">
       <input type="submit" value="Button 2">
     </form>

     <form name="form3" action="phpsubmit.php" method="post">
       <input type="hidden" name="button" value="button 3">
       <input type="submit" value="Button 3">
     </form>
   </body>
</html>
```

You can see the result in Figure 5-23, where the three apparent "buttons" are really Submit buttons.

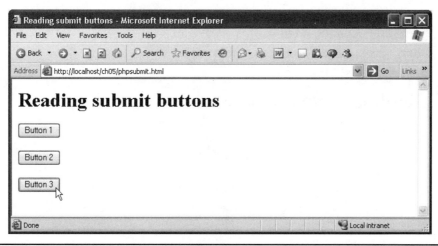

FIGURE 5-23   Using Submit buttons as HTML buttons

Now all you need to do is to read the value stored in the hidden control in your PHP script to determine which button was clicked, like this in phpsubmit.php:

```
<html>
  <head>
    <title>
      Reading submit buttons
    </title>
  </head>
  <body>
    <h1>
      Reading submit buttons
    </h1>
    You clicked
    <?php
      if (isset($_REQUEST["button"])) {
        echo $_REQUEST["button"], "<br>";
      }
    ?>
  </body>
</html>
```

You can see the result in Figure 5-24, where the PHP script has correctly identified the clicked button. Not bad.

In fact, there's an easier way to use Submit buttons as standard HTML buttons—you can actually read the values (that is, the captions) of Submit buttons in PHP. So you don't need any hidden controls to hold the name of each button, like this in phpsubmit2.html:

```
<html>
  <head>
    <title>
      Using submit buttons with values
    </title>
  </head>
```

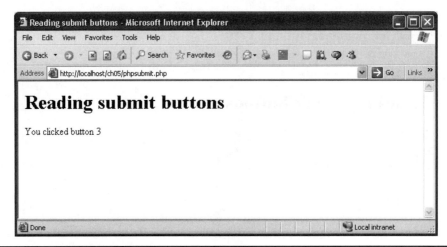

FIGURE 5-24 Identifying a clicked button

```
    <body>
      <h1>
        Using submit buttons with values
      </h1>
      <form name="form1" action="phpsubmit2.php" method="post">
        <input type="submit" name="button" value="button 1">
      </form>

      <form name="form2" action="phpbuttons2.php" method="post">
        <input type="submit" name="button" value="button 2">
      </form>

      <form name="form3" action="phpbuttons2.php" method="post">
        <input type="submit" name="button" value="button 3">
      </form>
    </body>
</html>
```

You can see this page, phpsubmit2.html, in Figure 5-25.

Now you can simply read the value of each Submit button in phpsubmit2.php:

```
<html>
  <head>
    <title>
      Reading submit buttons
    </title>
  </head>
  <body>
    <h1>
      Reading submit buttons
    </h1>
```

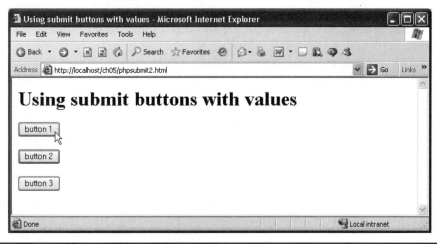

FIGURE 5-25   Using Submit buttons with values

```
You clicked
<?php
  if (isset($_REQUEST["button"])) {
    echo $_REQUEST["button"], "<br>";
  }
?>
</body>
</html>
```

And you can see the results from phpsubmit2.php in Figure 5-26, where the correct button was identified.

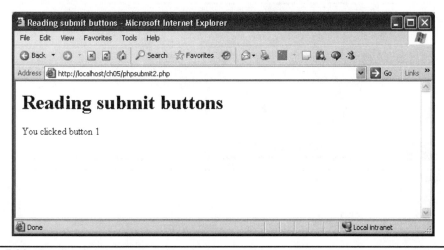

FIGURE 5-26   Reading Submit buttons with values

In fact, you can make this even simpler—you don't need three separate forms here; you can use three different Submit buttons in the same form. That looks like this in phpsubmit3.html:

```
<html>
  <head>
    <title>
      Using submit buttons in the same form
    </title>
  </head>

  <body>
    <h1>
      Using submit buttons in the same form
    </h1>
    <form name="form1" action="phpsubmit3.php" method="post">
      <input type="submit" name="button" value="button 1">

      <input type="submit" name="button" value="button 2">

      <input type="submit" name="button" value="button 3">
    </form>
  </body>
</html>
```

You can see this page in Figure 5-27.

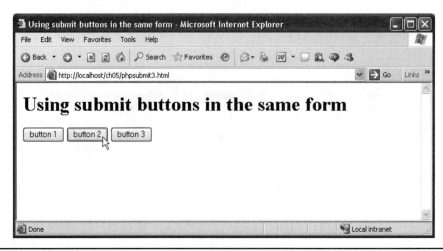

FIGURE 5-27   Multiple Submit buttons in the same form

Then you can simply read the value of the clicked Submit button in phpsubmit3.php:

```
<html>
  <head>
    <title>
      Reading submit buttons
    </title>
  </head>
  <body>
    <h1>
      Reading submit buttons
    </h1>
    You clicked
    <?php
      if (isset($_REQUEST["button"])) {
        echo $_REQUEST["button"], "<br>";
      }
    ?>
  </body>
</html>
```

And you can see the result in Figure 5-28, where phpsubmit3.php did its thing correctly—determined which button was clicked.

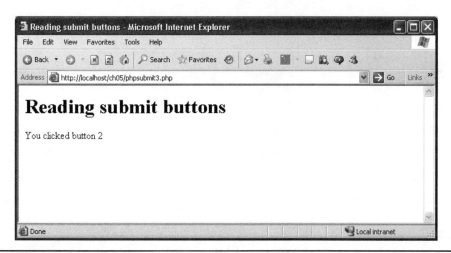

FIGURE 5-28   Reading multiple Submit buttons in the same form

PHP Browser-Handling Power

This chapter gets us into the power of PHP when it comes to working with browsers—using server variables to gain control of the browser, determining browser type, reading Web page data using custom arrays, and so on. The preceding chapter got us started on handling the browser/server connection in PHP, and this chapter takes it from there, introducing many new and powerful tools.

Also, you're going to see a discussion of how to validate user-supplied data in this chapter. Knowing how to check and validate data—has the user entered data in a required field? has the user entered a number where a number is required?—is a big part of creating Web applications. And how to implement data validation is coming up in this chapter.

Using PHP's Server Variables

It turns out that there's a superglobal (that is, accessible from anywhere) array, $_SERVER, that contains a great deal of information about what's going on with your Web application. You can use $_SERVER['PHP_SELF'] to get the name of the current script, for example; $_SERVER['REQUEST_METHOD'] holds the request method that was used ("GET", "POST", and so on), $_SERVER['HTTP_USER_AGENT'] holds the type of the user's browser, and so on. You can see a sampling of the most useful server variables available in $_SERVER in Table 6-1.

Here's an example—this script, phpserver.php, displays the script name and the port used to access it on the server:

```
<html>
  <head>
    <title>
      Welcome to my script
    </title>
  </head>

  <body>
    <h1>Welcome to my script</h1>
    <?php
      echo "You have accessed ", $_SERVER["PHP_SELF"], " on port ",
      $_SERVER["SERVER_PORT"];
    ?>
  </body>
</html>
```

Server Variable	Description
'AUTH_TYPE'	When running under Apache as module doing HTTP authenticated, this variable holds the authentication type.
'DOCUMENT_ROOT'	The document root directory under which the script is executing, as defined in the server's configuration file.
'GATEWAY_INTERFACE'	What revision of the CGI specification the server is using; such as 'CGI/1.1'.
'PATH_TRANSLATED'	File system-based path to the current script.
'PHP_AUTH_PW'	When running under Apache as module doing HTTP authentication, this variable holds the password provided by the user.
'PHP_AUTH_USER'	When running under Apache as module doing HTTP authentication this variable holds the username provided by the user.
'PHP_SELF'	The filename of the currently executing script, relative to the document root.
'QUERY_STRING'	The query string, if there was any, with which the page was accessed.
'REMOTE_ADDR'	The IP address from which the user is viewing the current page.
'REMOTE_HOST'	The Host name from which the user is viewing the current page.
'REMOTE_PORT'	The port being used on the user's machine to communicate with the Web server.
'REQUEST_METHOD'	Specifies which request method was used to access the page; such as 'GET', 'HEAD', 'POST', 'PUT'.
'REQUEST_URI'	The URI which was given in order to access this page, such as '/index.html'.
'SCRIPT_FILENAME'	The absolute pathname of the currently executing script.
'SCRIPT_NAME'	Contains the current script's path. This is useful for pages that need to point to themselves.
'SERVER_ADMIN'	The value given to the SERVER_ADMIN (for Apache) directive in the Web server configuration file.
'SERVER_NAME'	The name of the server host under which the script is executing.
'SERVER_PORT'	The port on the server machine being used by the Web server for communication. By default setup, this is '80'.
'SERVER_PROTOCOL'	Name and revision of the information protocol via which the page was requested; such as 'HTTP/1.0'.
'SERVER_SIGNATURE'	String containing the server version and virtual host name, which are added to server-generated pages.
'SERVER_SOFTWARE'	The server identification string.

TABLE 6-1   The PHP Server Variables

You can see the results of this script in Figure 6-1, where the script has correctly identified itself.

FIGURE 6-1   A self-identifying PHP script

Using HTTP Headers

In addition to the server variables you see in Table 6-1, you also have access to some good HTTP headers in the $_SERVER array as well. These headers are sent by the browser and contain information about the browser.

One useful HTTP header is HTTP_USER_AGENT, which refers to the user's browser type: that is, $_SERVER['HTTP_USER_AGENT'] holds the user's type of browser. Because you have to connect to the user through their browser in Web applications, knowing their browser type can be invaluable in some cases.

You can see the HTTP headers accessible to you in Table 6-2.

HTTP Variable	Description
'HTTP_ACCEPT'	Text in the Accept: header from the current request, if there is one.
'HTTP_ACCEPT_CHARSET'	Text in the Accept-Charset: header from the current request, if there is one, such as: '*, utf-8'.
'HTTP_ACCEPT_ENCODING'	Text in the Accept-Encoding: header from the current request, if there is one, such as: 'zip'.
'HTTP_ACCEPT_LANGUAGE'	Text in the Accept-Language: header from the current request, if there is one, such as 'en' for English.
'HTTP_CONNECTION'	Text in the Connection: header from the current request, if there is one, such as: 'Keep-Alive'.
'HTTP_HOST'	Text in the Host: header from the current request, if there is one.
'HTTP_REFERER'	The address of the page (if any) that referred the user agent to the current page. This is set by the browser.
'HTTP_USER_AGENT'	Text in the User-Agent: header from the current request, if there is one. This is a string denoting the browser that is accessing the page.

TABLE 6-2   The HTTP Server Variables

One of the most popular HTTP headers for use with PHP is HTTP_USER_AGENT, and that's coming up next.

Getting the User's Browser Type

Sometimes, it's important to know the user's browser type. For example, you might want to use a scrolling <marquee> element—only available in the Internet Explorer. Checking if the user has the Internet Explorer is crucial in such cases.

You can use the HTTP header HTTP_USER_AGENT to determine the type of browser the user has. Here's an example, phpbrowser.html, that connects to a PHP page, phpbrowser .php, that will tell you what type of browser you're using:

```html
<html>
  <head>
    <title>
      Getting the user's browser type
    </title>
  </head>

  <body>
    <h1>Getting the user's browser type</h1>

    <form method="post" action="phpbrowser.php">
      Click the button to determine your browser type....
      <input type="submit" value="Submit">
    </form>

  </body>
</html>
```

You can see this page in Figure 6-2.

FIGURE 6-2 First page in the browser-checking application

When the user clicks the button in Figure 6-2, the browser contacts phpbrowser.php on the server, sending all the usual HTTP headers—including HTTP_USER_AGENT. The string returned by $_SERVER["HTTP_USER_AGENT"] will include the text "MSIE" if the user has Microsoft Internet Explorer, and you can acknowledge that fact with a <marquee> element:

```
<html>
  <head>
      <title>Determining Browser Type</title>
  </head>

  <body>
    <h1>Determining Browser Type</h1>
    <br>
    <?php
      if(strpos($_SERVER["HTTP_USER_AGENT"], "MSIE")){
        echo("<marquee><h1>You're using the Internet Explorer</h1></marquee>");
      }
        .
        .
        .

    ?>
  </body>
</html>
```

On the other hand, you can check if the user has Firefox by searching $_SERVER["HTTP_USER_AGENT"] for "Firefox" this way:

```
<html>
  <head>
      <title>Determining Browser Type</title>
  </head>

  <body>
    <h1>Determining Browser Type</h1>
    <br>
    <?php
      if(strpos($_SERVER["HTTP_USER_AGENT"], "MSIE")){
        echo("<marquee><h1>You're using the Internet Explorer</h1></marquee>");
      }
      elseif (strpos($_SERVER["HTTP_USER_AGENT"], "Firefox")) {
        echo("<h1>You are using Firefox</h1>");
      }
        .
        .
        .

    ?>
  </body>
</html>
```

If the user has neither of these two browsers, you can also indicate that fact:

```html
<html>
  <head>
      <title>Determining Browser Type</title>
  </head>

  <body>
    <h1>Determining Browser Type</h1>
    <br>
    <?php
      if(strpos($_SERVER["HTTP_USER_AGENT"], "MSIE")){
        echo("<marquee><h1>You're using the Internet Explorer</h1></marquee>");
      }
      elseif (strpos($_SERVER["HTTP_USER_AGENT"], "Firefox")) {
        echo("<h1>You are using Firefox</h1>");
      }
      else {
        echo("<h1>You are not using Internet Explorer or Firefox</h1>");
      }
    ?>
  </body>
</html>
```

You can see the results in the Internet Explorer in Figure 6-3, in a scrolling marquee element.

And you can see the results in Firefox in Figure 6-4.

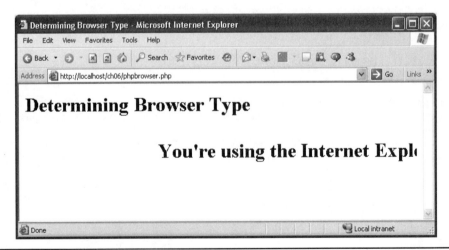

FIGURE 6-3   Identifying the Internet Explorer

FIGURE 6-4   Identifying Firefox

Redirecting Browsers with HTTP Headers

You can also create your own HTTP headers and send them back to the browser; you create your own HTTP headers in PHP with the header function. Probably the most common HTTP header to create and send back to the browser are redirection headers that redirect the browser to a new URL.

Here's an example; say that you have two HTML pages you want to redirect users to—welcome.html:

```
<html>
  <head>
    <title>Welcome</title>
  </head>

  <body>
    <h1>Welcome</h1>
    Welcome to this application.
  </body>
</html>
```

and hello.html:

```
<html>
  <head>
    <title>Hello</title>
  </head>
```

```
  <body>
    <h1>Hello</h1>
    Hello from this application.
  </body>
</html>
```

Here's phpredirect.html, which passes the name of the page to redirect to using the value—that is, the caption—of the Submit button in two forms, one for welcome.html, and the other for hello.html:

```
<html>
  <head>
    <title>Redirecting the browser</title>
  </head>

  <body>
    <h1>Redirecting the browser</h1>

    Which page would you like to see?

    <form name="form1" action="phpredirect.php" method="post">
      <input type="submit" name="button" value="welcome">
    </form>

    <form name="form2" action="phpredirect.php" method="post">
      <input type="submit" name="button" value="hello">
    </form>
  </body>
</html>
```

And you can see this page, phpredirect.html, in Figure 6-5.

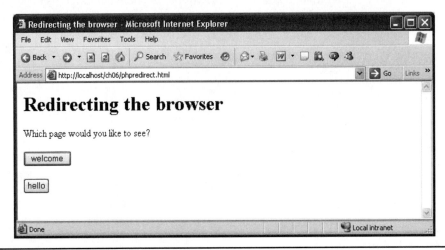

FIGURE 6-5 phpredirect.html

The redirection script, phpredirection.php, takes the name of the script to redirect to from the value of the Submit button that was clicked ($_REQUEST['button']) like this:

```php
<?php
    $redirect = "Location: " . $_REQUEST['button'] . ".html";
        .
        .
        .
?>
```

Now the $redirect variable holds the text for a new redirect header: "Location: welcome. html" or "Location: hello.html". You can create the actual HTTP header and send it back to the browser using the PHP header function like this:

```php
<?php
    $redirect = "Location: " . $_REQUEST['button'] . ".html";
    echo header($redirect);
?>
```

You can see this script, phpredirect.php, at work in Figure 6-6, where the person has clicked the welcome button and so was redirected to welcome.html.

As you can see, you can easily make the browser do what you want from your PHP code, making it navigate where you want.

Another use for redirection headers is with image maps, the clickable images discussed in the preceding chapter. For example, in PHP, you might check if the user clicked a particular "hotspot" in an image map:

```php
<?php
    if($REQUEST["map_x"] > 20 && $REQUEST["map_x"] < 80){
        if($REQUEST["map_y"] > 10 && $REQUEST["map_y"] < 40){
            .
            .
            .
        }
    }
?>
```

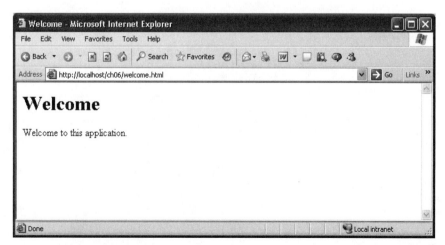

FIGURE 6-6   welcome.html

And, if the user did indeed click a hotspot, you can make their browser navigate to a new URL simply by redirecting it like this:

```php
<?php
    if($REQUEST["map_x"] > 20 && $REQUEST["map_x"] < 80){
        if($REQUEST["map_y"] > 10 && $REQUEST["map_y"] < 40){
            $redirect = "Location: www.php.net";
            echo header($redirect);
        }
    }
?>
```

Very cool.

Dumping a Form's Data All at Once

While on the topic of handling data sent your PHP scripts from the browser, it's useful to have a script around that will dump all the data from an HTML form. Such a script is useful for debugging your Web applications.

For example, take a look at phpform.html, which displays a form with several controls:

```html
<html>
  <head>
    <title>
      Dumping form data
    </title>
  </head>

  <body>
  <h1>Dumping form data</h1>

    <form method="post" action="phpform.php">
    How old are you?<input name="age" type="text">
    <br>
    <br>
    How many siblings do you have?<input name="number_siblings" type="text">
    <br>
    <br>
    Select your favorite ice cream flavor(s):
    <select name="ice_cream[]" multiple>
            <option>Vanilla</option>
            <option>Chocolate</option>
            <option>Strawberry</option>
            <option>Sardine</option>
    </select>
    <br>
    <br>
    <input type="submit" value="Submit">
    </form>
  </body>
</html>
```

You can see this page, phpform.html, at work in Figure 6-7, where the user has entered data into the form.

It's easy enough to create a script that will dump all the form data from phpform.html. You can start by looping over all the key/value pairs in the $_REQUEST array:

```
<html>
  <head>
    <title>
      Dumping form data
    </title>
  </head>

  <body>
    <h1>Dumping form data</h1>
    Here is the data from the form:
    <br>
    <?php
      foreach($_REQUEST as $key => $value){
        .
        .
        .
      }
    ?>
  </body>
</html>
```

If the form data item you're working with is an array—such as the array that holds ice cream flavors in phpform.html, you can loop over that array, displaying all the elements

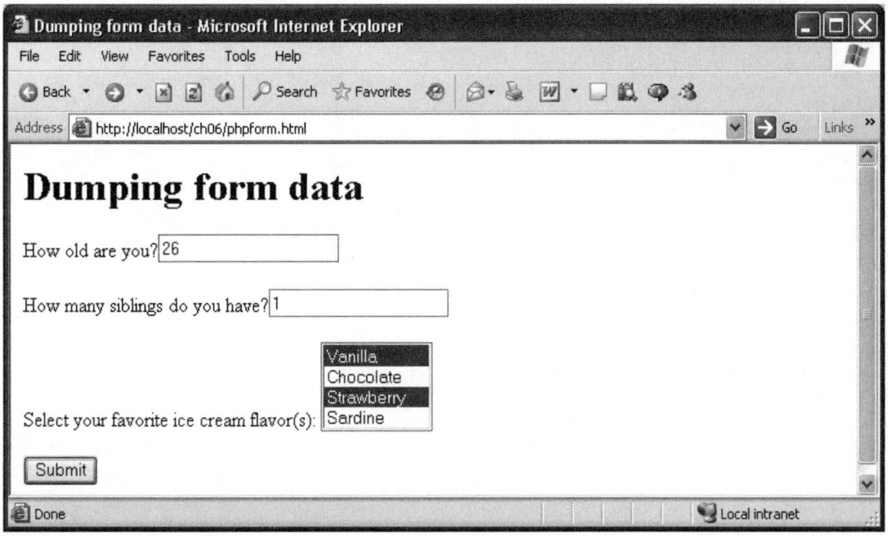

FIGURE 6-7   Entering data into a form

in it this way—note that we're checking if the data item is an array with the PHP is_array function:

```
<html>
  <head>
    <title>
      Dumping form data
    </title>
  </head>

  <body>
    <h1>Dumping form data</h1>
    Here is the data from the form:
    <br>
    <?php
      foreach($_REQUEST as $key => $value){
        if(is_array($value)){
          foreach($value as $item){
            echo $key, " => ", $item, "<br>";
          }
        }
        .
        .
        .
      }
    ?>
  </body>
</html>
```

If the data item from the form is not an array, it's a simple data item, and you can echo it to the browser like this:

```
<html>
  <head>
    <title>
      Dumping form data
    </title>
  </head>

  <body>
    <h1>Dumping form data</h1>
    Here is the data from the form:
    <br>
    <?php
      foreach($_REQUEST as $key => $value){
        if(is_array($value)){
          foreach($value as $item){
            echo $key, " => ", $item, "<br>";
          }
        }
```

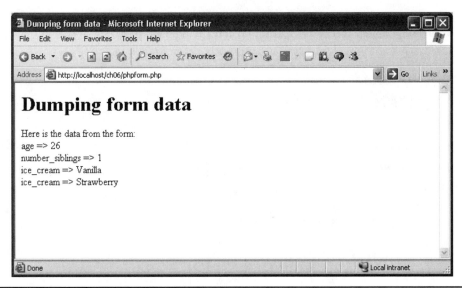

FIGURE 6-8   Dumping a form's data

```
        else {
          echo $key, " => ", $value, "<br>";
        }
      }
    ?>
  </body>
</html>
```

Okay, that's the script phpform.php, a general-purpose script for dumping form data. You can see this script at work, dumping the data passed to it from phpform.html, in Figure 6-8.

Handling Form Data with Custom Arrays

You may recall from the preceding chapter that PHP handles data from multiple-select controls like list boxes by using arrays. That looked like this:

```
Select your favorite ice cream flavors:
<form method="post" action="phplistbox.php">
  <select name="ice_cream[]" multiple>
    <option>vanilla</option>
    <option>strawberry</option>
    <option>chocolate</option>
    <option>herring</option>
  </select>
```

You can also tell PHP to group together data into custom arrays with similar syntax. For example, say that you wanted to group a form's data sent to you into an array named data.

You might have a text field that will take the user's name, and whose data you wanted to refer to as data['name']. You could set up that control in a Web page like this:

```html
<html>
  <head>
    <title>
      Using custom form arrays
    </title>
  </head>

  <body>
    <h1>Using custom form arrays</h1>

    <form method="post" action="phparray.php">
      What's your name?
      <input name="data[name]" type="text">
      <br>
      <br>

        .
        .
        .

      <input type="submit" value="Submit">
    </form>
  </body>
</html>
```

Similarly, you might ask the user their favorite ice cream flavor, storing that text in the array element data['flavor'] this way:

```html
<html>
  <head>
    <title>
      Using custom form arrays
    </title>
  </head>

  <body>
    <h1>Using custom form arrays</h1>

    <form method="post" action="phparray.php">
      What's your name?
      <input name="data[name]" type="text">
      <br>
      <br>
      What's your favorite ice cream flavor?
      <input name="data[flavor]" type="text">
      <br>
      <br>
      <input type="submit" value="Submit">
    </form>
  </body>
</html>
```

You can see this Web page, phparray.html, in Figure 6-9.

Now you can get an array holding your data from the $_REQUEST array, and refer to your data using the keys you've already specified. That looks like this in phparray.php:

```
<html>
  <head>
    <title>
      Using form arrays
    </title>
  </head>

  <body>
    <h1>Using form arrays</h1>
    Your name is
    <?php
      $data = $_REQUEST['data'];
      echo $data['name'], "<br>";
    ?>

    Your favorite flavor is
    <?php
      $data = $_REQUEST['data'];
      echo $data['flavor'], "<br>";
    ?>
  </body>
</html>
```

And you can see the results in Figure 6-10, where the application was successful in retrieving the data from a custom array.

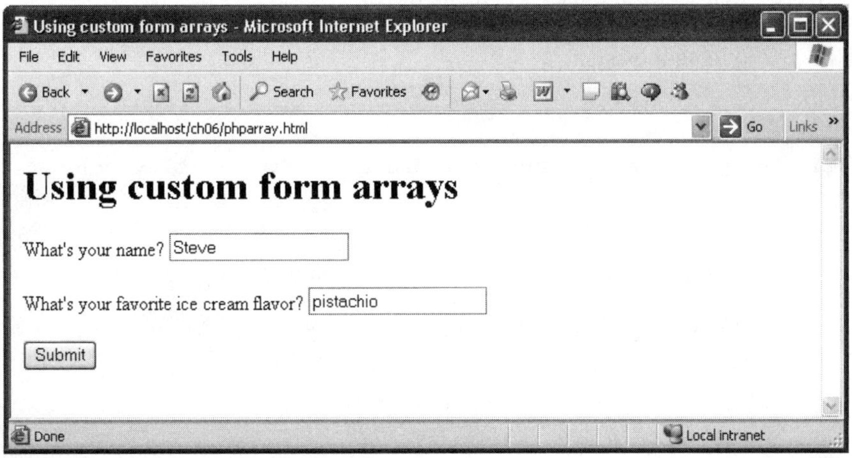

FIGURE 6-9   Storing a form's data in a custom array

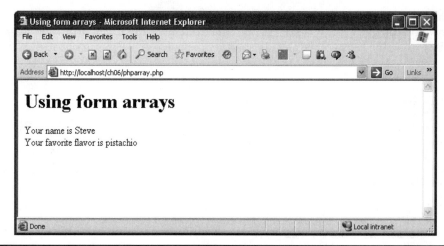

FIGURE 6-10   Getting form data from custom arrays

Putting It All in One Page

So far, the applications we've developed have relied on an HTML start page that connects to a PHP page. However, it's more usual to handle everything with one PHP page.

Here's an example, which asks the user their favorite ice cream flavor. Bear in mind that this example is meant to handle everything with one page; in this case, the data that the user enters—their ice cream flavor—will be stored in the $_REQUEST array under the name "flavor". That means that if data is waiting for you in the $_REQUEST array under the name "flavor", you should display that data. If data is not waiting for you, you should display the welcome page that asks for the user's favorite flavor.

You can check if data is waiting for you with the PHP isset function, which returns TRUE if an array element exists:

```
<html>
  <head>
    <title>Using one page to accept and process data</title>
  </head>

  <body>
    <h1>Using one page to accept and process data</h1>
    <?php
      if(isset($_REQUEST["flavor"])){
    ?>
          .
          .
          .
    <?php
      }
    ?>
  </body>
</html>
```

If there is data waiting for you, you can display that data like this:

```
<html>
  <head>
    <title>Using one page to accept and process data</title>
  </head>

  <body>
    <h1>Using one page to accept and process data</h1>
    <?php
      if(isset($_REQUEST["flavor"])){
    ?>
    Your favorite ice cream flavor is
    <?php
      echo $_REQUEST["flavor"];
      }
    ?>
        .
        .
        .
  </body>
</html>
```

If, on the other hand, there is no data waiting for you, the user hasn't entered anything yet, so it's time to ask them for their favorite flavor. That looks like this:

```
<html>
  <head>
    <title>Using one page to accept and process data</title>
  </head>

  <body>
    <h1>Using one page to accept and process data</h1>
    <?php
      if(isset($_REQUEST["flavor"])){
    ?>
    Your favorite ice cream flavor is
    <?php
      echo $_REQUEST["flavor"];
      }
      else {
    ?>
    <form method="post" action="phpone.php">
      What's your favorite ice cream flavor?
      <input name="flavor" type="text">
      <br>
      <br>
      <input type=submit value=Submit>
    </form>
    <?php
      }
    ?>
  </body>
</html>
```

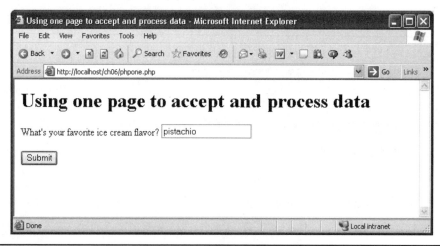

FIGURE 6-11   What is your favorite flavor?

You can see this example, phpone.php, in Figure 6-11—there's no data waiting for the application to display yet, so it displays the welcome page, asking for your favorite flavor.

After you enter a flavor and click the Submit button, the application displays your selection, as you see in Figure 6-12.

Not bad—you've handled this entire application with one PHP page, no HTML page needed. The whole application turned on one point: checking to see whether or not some data was ready for you to read. If that data was ready, it was processed; if not, the welcome page was displayed, and the data was entered by the user. In this way, you can create entire Web applications that use only a single PHP page.

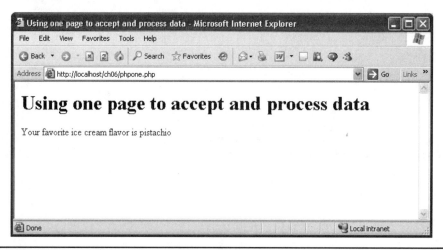

FIGURE 6-12   Your favorite flavor

Performing Data Validation

In the next couple of topics, we'll develop examples to show how to work with data validation in PHP. Did the user enter an integer for their age? If not, you can tell them so with a red error message, giving them another chance. Did they enter a text string for their name? If not, you can tell them about it.

In the preceding topic, you checked to see if data was waiting by checking the data stored for a particular data-entry control, but that's not a very general technique—you might not require the user to enter data into your controls, for example. For that reason, these examples will use a hidden field, welcome_already_seen, to determine if the welcome page has already been seen. If this item is present in $_REQUEST, the user has already seen the welcome page, and it's time to start processing the data they've entered; if that item is not present, we should display the welcome page. In code, that might look like this:

```
if(isset($_REQUEST["welcome_already_seen"])){
    .
    .
    .
}
else {
    show_welcome();
}
```

If the user has seen the welcome page, they've presumably entered their data (that's what we're about to check) and you should start processing that data. You can check whether the entered data is in the format you want with a function named, say, check_data, which will store any errors found in a global array named $errors_array:

```
$errors_array = array();

if(isset($_REQUEST["welcome_already_seen"])){

    check_data();
    .
    .
    .
}
else {
    show_welcome();
}
```

Now you can check if there were any errors—the $errors_array array will be empty if not, so you might check on errors this way— show the errors with a function named show_errors, and then show the welcome page again:

```
$errors_array = array();

if(isset($_REQUEST["welcome_already_seen"])){

    check_data();
    if(count($errors_array) != 0){
        show_errors();
```

```
            show_welcome();
        }
            .
            .
            .
    }
    else {
        show_welcome();
    }
```

If there were no errors, you can handle the data the user entered in another function, named, say, handle_data:

```
    $errors_array = array();

    if(isset($_REQUEST["welcome_already_seen"])){

        check_data();
        if(count($errors_array) != 0){
            show_errors();
            show_welcome();
        }
        else {
            handle_data();
        }
    }
    else {
        show_welcome();
    }
```

So the idea is to check the data the user entered in a function named check_data:

```
    function check_data()
    {
            .
            .
            .
    }
```

The array $errors_array will be filled with any errors by the check_data function, and the show_errors function will display those errors:

```
    function show_errors()
    {
        global $errors_array;
        foreach ($errors_array as $err){
            echo $err, "<br>";
        }
    }
```

The show_welcome function depends on what data you want to ask from the user, of course. This function displays the controls the user should use. One thing that will be the same in all cases is that we want to make sure to create the hidden field "welcome_already_seen" here:

```
function show_welcome()
{
    echo "<form method='post' action=phpvalidate.php'>";
        .
        .
        .
    echo "<input type='submit' value='Submit'>";
    echo "<input type='hidden' name='welcome_already_seen'
        value='already_seen'>";
    echo "</form>";                  }
```

That's how our example data-validation framework works. Now let's put it to work.

Checking if the User Entered Required Data

Alright, let's put our validation framework to work in an example that requires the user to enter some data. This next example will ask for the user's favorite ice cream flavor, and if the user doesn't enter any text, the application will complain.

We start this example, phprequireddata.php, with the code we've already developed for handling validation:

```
<html>
  <head>
    <title>
      Checking required data
    </title>
  </head>

  <body>
    <h1>Checking required data</h1>
    <?php
      $errors_array = array();

      if(isset($_REQUEST["welcome_already_seen"])){

        check_data();
        if(count($errors_array) != 0){
          show_errors();
          show_welcome();
        }
        else {
          handle_data();
        }
      }
      else {
        show_welcome();
      }
```

Now you've got to write the functions called by this code. You might start with the show_welcome page, which displays the welcome page that asks the user for their favorite flavor and sends it back to the same page under the key "flavor"—note that the form doesn't need an action attribute, because you want the browser to send its data back to the same PHP page:

```
function show_welcome()
{
  echo "<form method='post'>";
  echo "What's your favorite ice cream flavor?";
  echo "<br>";
  echo "<input name='flavor' type='text'>";
  echo "<br>";
  echo "<br>";
  echo "<input type='submit' value='Submit'>";
     .
     .
     .
  echo "</form>";
}
```

Also, don't forget to create the hidden field welcome_already_seen here—if this hidden field exists, the application knows that the user has already seen the welcome page:

```
function show_welcome()
{
  echo "<form method='post'>";
  echo "What's your favorite ice cream flavor?";
  echo "<br>";
  echo "<input name='flavor' type='text'>";
  echo "<br>";
  echo "<br>";
  echo "<input type='submit' value='Submit'>";
  echo "<input type='hidden' name='welcome_already_seen'
   value='already_seen'>";
  echo "</form>";
}
```

Next, the check_data function will check if the user has entered anything for their favorite ice cream flavor. That flavor will be stored in the $_REQUEST array with the key 'flavor', so you might check if the user has left the corresponding text field blank like this in check_data:

```
function check_data()
{
  if($_REQUEST["flavor"] == "") {
     .
     .
     .
  }
}
```

If the user has not entered any text, you can add an entry to the global $errors_array array like this—note that this error is going to display its message in red, "Please enter your flavor":

```
function check_data()
{
  global $errors_array;
  if($_REQUEST["flavor"] == "") {
    $errors_array[] = "<font color='red'>Please enter your flavor</font>";
  }
}
```

The show_errors function simply displays the errors in the browser, using the echo statement. All this function has to do is to loop over the $errors_array array and display each error:

```
function show_errors()
{
  global $errors_array;

  foreach ($errors_array as $err){
    echo $err, "<br>";
  }
}
```

If everything is okay—if there were no data validation errors—the application will call the handle_data function, and in this example, that function displays the user's favorite ice cream flavor:

```
function handle_data()
{
  echo "Your favorite ice cream flavor is ";
  echo $_REQUEST["flavor"];
}
```

You can see this application at work in Figure 6-13, where it's waiting for the user to enter their favorite ice cream flavor.

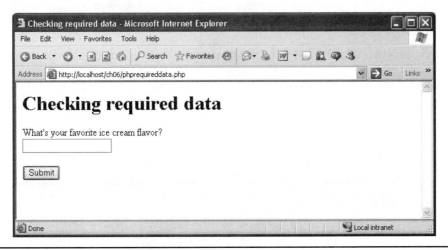

FIGURE 6-13   Not entering required data

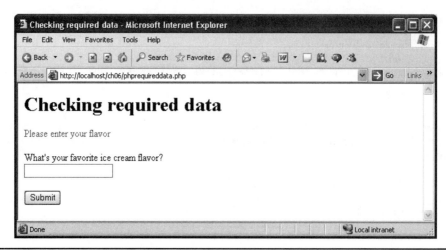

FIGURE 6-14   A required data error

If the user doesn't enter anything but just clicks the Submit button, they'll see the error that appears in Figure 6-14, asking them to enter their flavor.

If the user then enters a flavor and clicks Submit, that flavor is displayed by the application, as you see in Figure 6-15. Very nice.

Okay, that handles the case where you want to check that the user entered some data. But there are other things you can check for—for example, whether the user entered a text string.

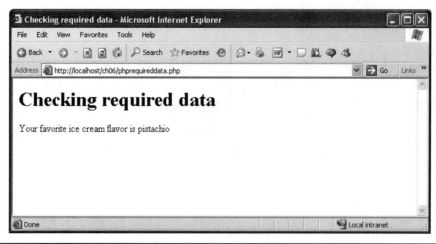

FIGURE 6-15   Fixing a required data error

Requiring Numbers

How about requiring that the user enter integer data? Here's an example, phprequirednumber .php, that does that. It starts off with the boilerplate code for validation checking:

```
<html>
  <head>
    <title>
      Requiring integer input
    </title>
  </head>

  <body>
    <h1>Requiring integer input</h1>
    <?php
      $errors_array = array();
        if(isset($_REQUEST["welcome_already_seen"])){
          check_data();
          if(count($errors_array) != 0){
            show_errors();
            show_welcome();
          }
          else {
            handle_data();
          }
        }
        else {
          show_welcome();
        }
```

Okay, now it's time to write the functions called by this code, starting with the show_ welcome function, which asks the user their age, passing that age under the key "number" back to the server:

```
function show_welcome()
{
  echo "<form method='post'>";
  echo "Please enter your age as an integer.";
  echo "<br>";
  echo "<input name='number' type='text'>";
  echo "<br>";
  echo "<br>";
  echo "<input type='submit' value='Submit'>";
  echo "<input type=hidden name='welcome_already_seen'
    value='already_seen'>";
  echo "</form>";
}
```

Next is the check_data function, where you're supposed to check if the age the user entered is in the correct form. So how do you check if the string $_REQUEST["number"] holds an integer in string format? One way of checking that is to convert the string into an integer using the PHP intval function, then convert it back to a string using the strval function—and then compare that to the original string. If the two strings are equal, the string represents an integer. Here's what that looks like in code:

```
function check_data()
{
  if(strcmp($_REQUEST["number"], strval(intval($_REQUEST["number"])))) {
    .
    .
    .
  }
}
```

If the strings are equal, strcmp returns 0, which is interpreted as FALSE. On the other hand, if the strings are not equal, strcmp will return a non-zero result, which is interpreted as TRUE. If the result is TRUE, you should add a new error to the global array $errors_array, indicating that the user should enter an integer:

```
function check_data()
{
  global $errors_array;

  if(strcmp($_REQUEST["number"], strval(intval($_REQUEST["number"])))) {
    $errors_array[] = "<font color='red'>Please enter an integer</font>";
  }
}
```

And in the show_errors function, you can display the errors, if there were any:

```
function show_errors()
{
  global $errors_array;

  foreach ($errors_array as $err){
    echo $err, "<br>";
  }
}
```

The handle_data function displays the user's age in case the user indeed entered an integer:

```
function handle_data()
{
  echo "Your age is ";
  echo $_REQUEST["number"];
}
```

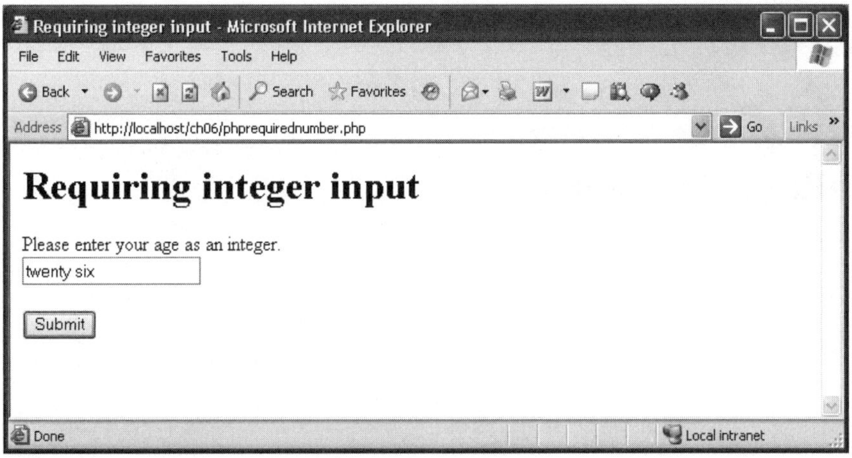

Figure 6-16 Spelling out the user's age

Okay, that's it. You can see this application, phprequirednumber.php, in Figure 6-16. The user has, unaccountably, decided to enter their age by spelling it out, rather than entering an integer.

And you can see the results in Figure 6-17—an error was indeed reported.

Fixing the error by actually entering a number gives you the result you see in Figure 6-18—everything's okay.

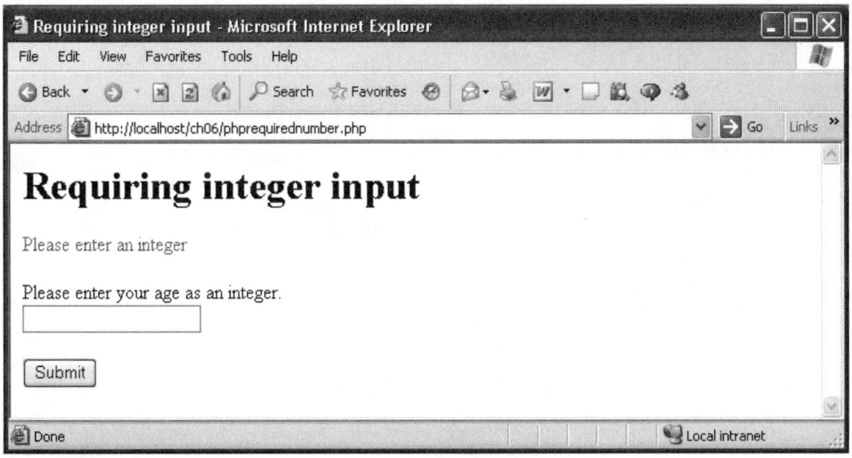

Figure 6-17 Fixing a required data error

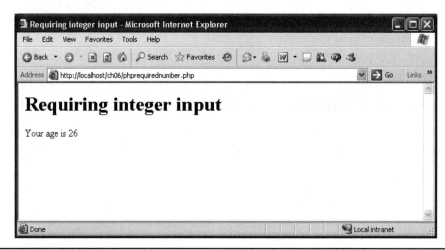

FIGURE 6-18 The corrected required data

Requiring Text

You can also write applications that require the user to enter text, or even specific text. For example, you may want to ask the user's favorite ice cream flavor—and then make sure they enter your own favorite flavor, pistachio. You can start this application, phprequiredtext.php, like this:

```
<html>
  <head>
    <title>
      Requiring text input
    </title>
  </head>

  <body>
    <h1>Requiring text input</h1>
    <?php
      $errors_array = array();
        if(isset($_REQUEST["welcome_already_seen"])){
          check_data();
          if(count($errors_array) != 0){
            show_errors();
            show_welcome();
          }
          else {
            handle_data();
          }
        }
        else {
          show_welcome();
      }
```

You can ask the user their favorite flavor this way in the show_welcome function:

```
function show_welcome()
{
  echo "<form method='post'>";
  echo "What is your favorite ice cream flavor?";
  echo "<br>";
    .
    .
    .
  echo "<input type='submit' value='Submit'>";
  echo "<input type=hidden name='welcome_already_seen'
    value='already_seen'>";
  echo "</form>";
}
```

And you can make sure the flavor gets sent to the server under the key 'flavor' like this in show_welcome:

```
function show_welcome()
{
  echo "<form method='post'>";
  echo "What is your favorite ice cream flavor?";
  echo "<br>";
  echo "<input name='flavor' type='text'>";
  echo "<br>";
  echo "<br>";
  echo "<input type='submit' value='Submit'>";
  echo "<input type='hidden' name='welcome_already_seen'
    value='already_seen'>";
  echo "</form>";
}
```

On the server, you can check the flavor the user entered in the check_data function. This function handles text using *regular expressions*. Regular expressions (the complete specification is at www.perldoc.com/perl5.6/pod/perlre.html) let you match text in your PHP code. For example, if you want to insist that the user's text entry includes the word "pistachio", you can use the PHP preg_match function like this (the "I" here makes the search case-insensitive):

```
function check_data()
{
  global $errors_array;

  if(!preg_match('/pistachio/i', $_REQUEST["flavor"])){
    .
    .
    .
  }
}
```

Although this regular expression check was to make sure a particular word appeared in the user's text entry, you can also use regular expressions to make sure their data entry is in a particular format--for example, you might want the person to enter a social security number, with the format xxx-xx-xxxx, where each "x" is a digit. You could do that by matching their text to the regular expression "\d\d\d-\d\d-\d\d\d\d", where "\d" is the regular-expression way of specifying a single digit. Or you might want the person to enter a social security number, with the format xxx-xx-xxxx, where each *x* is a digit.

If the user's response doesn't include the word "pistachio", you can complain with an error message like this:

```
function check_data()
{
  global $errors_array;

  if(!preg_match('/pistachio/i', $_REQUEST["flavor"])){
    $errors_array[] = "<font color='red'>Your favorite flavor should be
\"pistachio\".</font>";
  }
}
```

In the show_errors function, you can show any errors that have been placed into the global $errors_array array:

```
function show_errors()
{
  global $errors_array;

  foreach ($errors_array as $err){
    echo $err, "<br>";
  }
}
```

And in the handle_data function, you can display the person's favorite flavor (which better be pistachio):

```
function handle_data()
{
  echo "Your favorite flavor is ";
  echo $_REQUEST["flavor"];
}
```

You can see this application, phprequiredtext.php, in Figure 6-19. There, the user is attempting to indicate that their favorite ice cream flavor is strawberry.

You can see the results in Figure 6-20—an error was reported, because their flavor was not pistachio.

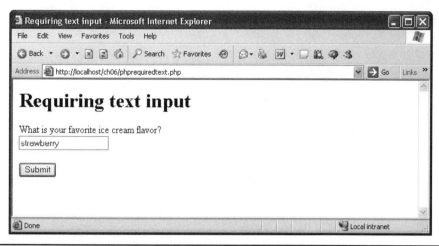

FIGURE 6-19   Entering incorrect data

Entering pistachio as the user's favorite flavor gives you the results you see in Figure 6-21—everything's okay now.

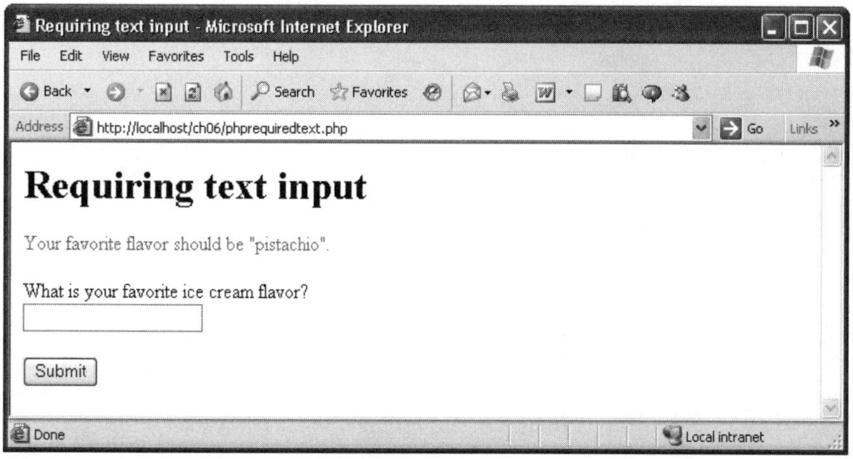

FIGURE 6-20   Fixing a required data error

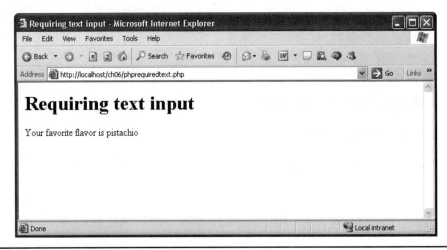

FIGURE 6-21 The corrected data

Persisting User Data

Sometimes, you might have multiple controls for the user to enter data in, and if they enter incorrect data in one control, you might want to still display the correct data they've entered in the other controls so that they don't have to start all over. That's what this next example, phppersist.php, is all about.

This example starts with our data validation framework:

```
<html>
  <head>
    <title>
      Persisting user data
    </title>
  </head>

  <body>
    <h1>Persisting user data</h1>
    <?php
      $errors_array = array();

      if(isset($_REQUEST["welcome_already_seen"])){
        check_data();
        if(count($errors_array) != 0){
          show_errors();
          show_welcome();
        } else {
          handle_data();
        }
      }
      else {
        show_welcome();
      }
```

The show_welcome function has to check if the user already entered data into any controls, and if so, you can display that data. Here's how that works—you fill the variables $first_name and $last_name with either what the user has already entered, or an empty string, "":

```
function show_welcome()
{
  $first_name = isset($_REQUEST["first"]) ? $_REQUEST["first"] : "";
  $last_name = isset($_REQUEST["last"]) ? $_REQUEST["last"] : "";
    .
    .
    .
}
```

Then when you display the text fields in the welcome page, you can use $first_name and $last_name as the values of those controls:

```
function show_welcome()
{
  $first_name = isset($_REQUEST["first"]) ? $_REQUEST["first"] : "";
  $last_name = isset($_REQUEST["last"]) ? $_REQUEST["last"] : "";
  echo "<form method='post'>";
  echo "Enter your first name: ";
  echo "<input name='first' type='text' value='", $first_name, "'>";
  echo "<br>";
  echo "<br>";
  echo "Enter your last name: ";
  echo "<input name='last' type='text' value='", $last_name, "'>";
  echo "<br>";
  echo "<br>";
  echo "<input type='submit' value='Submit'>";
  echo "<input type=hidden name='welcome_already_seen'
    value='already_seen'>";
  echo "</form>";
}
```

That'll make what the user has already entered reappear if they have to be notified of an error. The check_data function checks to see if the user has left any text field blank, and if so, it generates an error:

```
function check_data()
{
  global $errors_array;

  if($_REQUEST["first"] == "") {
  $errors_array[] = "<font color='red'>Enter your first name</font>";
  }
  if($_REQUEST["last"] == "") {
  $errors_array[] = "<font color='red'>Enter your last name</font>";
  }
}
```

The show_errors function displays any errors:

```
function show_errors()
{
  global $errors_array;

  foreach ($errors_array as $err){
    echo $err, "<br>";
  }
}
```

And the handle_data function displays the data the user entered:

```
function handle_data()
{
  echo "Here is your first name: ";
  echo $_REQUEST["first"];
  echo "<br>Here is your first name: ";
  echo $_REQUEST["last"];
}
```

You can see this application in Figure 6-22, where the user has only entered their first name.

When the user clicks the Submit button, the application indicates their error—and also redisplays the correctly entered data ("Edward"), saving the user the effort of retyping that as in Figure 6-23.

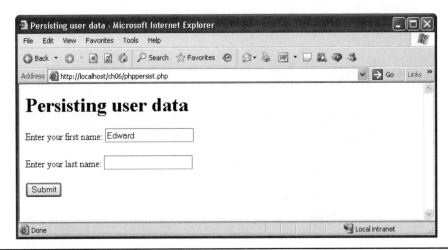

FIGURE 6-22   Entering only the first name

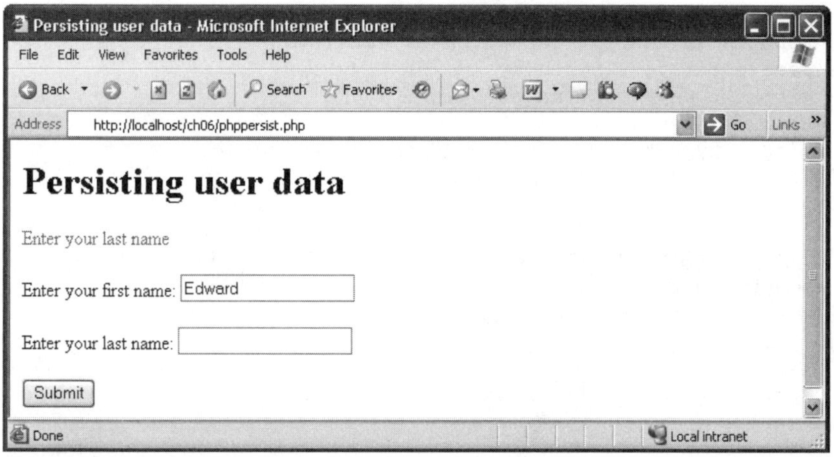

FIGURE 6-23   Catching the error

Client-Side Data Validation

Performing your data validation in PHP does have one drawback: you need a round trip to the server to check the data the user entered. There are some advantages to doing data validation in the browser, without sending anything to the server at all.

Here's a short example that performs client-side—that is, browser-side—validation using JavaScript. This example, phpclientside.html, asks the user for their birthday using a text field in an HTML form:

```
<body>
  <h1>
    Client-side data validation
  </h1>
  <form name="form1" action="script.php" method="post">
    Please enter your birthday (mm/dd/yyyy):
      <input type="text" name="date">
      <br>
      <input type="submit" value="Submit">
  </form>
</body>
```

Note that this example posts its data to a (non-existent) script named script.php. To check the user's data before submitting the form, you can connect the form's onsubmit attribute to a JavaScript function, check_data. If that function returns a value of false, the form won't be submitted:

```
<body>
  <h1>
    Client-side data validation
  </h1>
```

```
        <form name="form1" action="script.php" method="post"
          onsubmit="javascript:return check_data()">
          Please enter your birthday (mm/dd/yyyy):
            <input type="text" name="date">
            <br>
            <input type="submit" value="Submit">
        </form>
    </body>
```

You create the JavaScript function check_data like this in the page's <head> section, inside a <script> element:

```
<head>
  <title>
    Client-side data validation
  </title>

  <script language="javascript">

    function check_data()
    {
        .
        .
        .
    }
  </script>
</head>
```

JavaScript supports regular expressions, so you can create a regular expression to check for dates using the format dd/mm/yyyy like this:

```
<head>
  <title>
    Client-side data validation
  </title>

  <script language="javascript">

    function check_data()
    {
      var regexp = /^(\d{1,2})\/(\d{1,2})\/(\d{4})$/
        .
        .
        .
    }
  </script>
</head>
```

Then you can check the date the user entered against that regular expression like this:

```
<head>
  <title>
    Client-side data validation
  </title>
```

```
<script language="javascript">

  function check_data()
  {
    var regexp = /^(\d{1,2})\/(\d{1,2})\/(\d{4})$/
    var result = document.form1.date.value.match(regexp);
        .
        .
        .

  }
</script>
</head>
```

If the result of attempting to match the regular expression to what the user entered was null, the user did not enter the date in the format you want. You can display an error using a JavaScript alert box, and return false from the function, which means the form will not be submitted, giving the user a chance to fix the problem:

```
<head>
  <title>
    Client-side data validation
  </title>

  <script language="javascript">

    function check_data()
    {
      var regexp = /^(\d{1,2})\/(\d{1,2})\/(\d{4})$/
      var result = document.form1.date.value.match(regexp); .
      if (result == null) {
        alert("Please enter a date in dd/mm/yyyy format.");
        document.form1.date.value = "";
        return false;
          .
          .
          .

    }
  </script>
</head>
```

If the data is okay, you can submit the form from JavaScript with the JavaScript submit function:

```
<head>
  <title>
    Client-side data validation
  </title>

  <script language="javascript">

    function check_data()
    {
      var regexp = /^(\d{1,2})\/(\d{1,2})\/(\d{4})$/
      var result = document.form1.date.value.match(regexp);
```

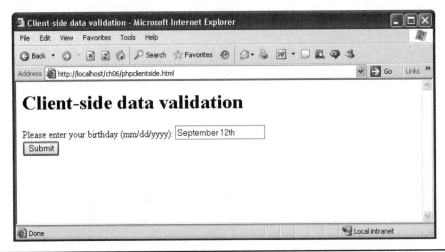

FIGURE 6-24 Entering a date in an incorrect format

```
      if (result == null) {
         alert("Please enter a date in dd/mm/yyyy format.");
         document.form1.date.value = "";
         return false;
      } else {
      document.form1.submit();
      return true;
      }
   }
   </script>
</head>
```

And you can see this application, phpclientside.html, in Figure 6-24. There, the user has entered their birth date in the wrong format.

You can see the results in Figure 6-25—the error is displayed in a JavaScript alert box. Cool.

FIGURE 6-25 Catching a date error in JavaScript

Handling HTML Tags in User Input

Sometimes, users may embed HTML elements in the text they send you, and it pays to watch out for that—if you display that text in a Web page, it could include malicious scripts to make your Web page close, or navigate to another page.

PHP includes functions to deactivate HTML that you don't want. Here's an example, phphtml.php, which lets the user enter HTML—but deactivates that HTML before it's displayed in a browser. The way this works is simply by applying the PHP function htmlentities to the user-supplied data, like this:

```
<html>
  <head>
    <title>Handling HTML in user input</title>
  </head>

  <body>
    <H1>Handling HTML in user input</H1>
    <?php
      $errors_array = array();

      if(isset($_REQUEST["welcome_already_seen"])){
              check_data();
              if(count($errors_array) != 0){
                  show_errors();
                  show_welcome();
              }
              else {
                  handle_data();
              }
         }
      else {
              show_welcome();
         }
      function check_data()
      {
        global $errors_array;
        if($_REQUEST["flavor"] == "") {
          $errors_array[] = "<font color='red'>Enter your favorite
flavor</font>";
        }
      }

      function show_errors()
      {
        global $errors_array;

        foreach ($errors_array as $err){
          echo $err, "<br>";
        }
      }
```

```
function handle_data()
{
  echo "Your favorite flavor is ";
  $ok_text = htmlentities($_REQUEST["flavor"]);
  echo $ok_text;
}

function show_welcome()
{
  echo "<form method='post'>";
  echo "What's your favorite ice cream flavor?<br>";
  echo "<input name='flavor' type='text'>";
  echo "<br><br>";
  echo "<input type='submit' value='Submit'>";
  echo "<input type='hidden' name='welcome_already_seen'
    VALUE='already_seen'>";
  echo "</form>";
}
?>
</body>
</html>
```

Now the user can enter HTML in their data, as you see in Figure 6-26.

Using the htmlentities function escapes any included HTML, so the text "strawberry" is converted to "<b>strawberry</b>", and that's what gets displayed, as you can see in Figure 6-27.

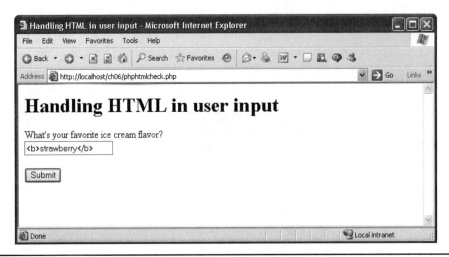

FIGURE 6-26 Including HTML in user data

FIGURE 6-27   Escaping HTML in user data

You can also use the strip_tags function like this:

```
function handle_data()
{
  echo "Your name is ";
  $ok_text = strip_tags($_REQUEST["flavor"]);
  echo $ok_text;
}
```

Using the strip_tags function strips any HTML tags from text—and the result appears in Figure 6-28.

FIGURE 6-28   Removing HTML in user data

CHAPTER

Object-Oriented Programming

Phas not designed to be an object-oriented language from start to finish, but it's
got an incredible number of object-oriented features built into it, including many
that were added in PHP 5. You're going to see those features in this chapter and
the next.

On the other hand, you don't need object-oriented programming (OOP) to create Web
applications in PHP, so don't feel you have to read this material if it doesn't apply to you.
OOP is targeted at larger applications. That's why OOP was created—to let you break up
bigger applications when simply packaging code in functions isn't going to help.

Programming started as a very linear affair—you just wrote your code, line after line.
Then functions were introduced, and that let you break up your code—the code in functions
wouldn't run until called. And that's fine up to a point. But when you get still bigger
applications, you need another solution.

That solution is to use objects. Object-oriented programming might sound daunting if
you've never used it before, but it shouldn't—the whole idea is to make life easier for you.
For example, say that in real life you have all the interconnected parts of a refrigerator in
your kitchen. To refrigerate food, you have to turn on pumps, start fans, circulate the
refrigeration fluid, run the compressor, and so on. That sounds like a lot of work—better to
wrap all that up into an easily conceptualized *object*—a refrigerator. Now all the internal
workings are hidden from view, and you can think—there's the refrigerator. It refrigerates
food. Easy.

That's the idea behind object-oriented programming. You break your code up into
objects—a database manager, for example, or a screen manager. That's the way
programmers can think of their applications: in terms of objects with specific duties and
responsibilities. All the functions necessary for the internal workings of the object are
wrapped up inside that object, and hidden from exterior view. The data used by the object
is also hidden inside the object, and that's one of the main ways that objects differ from
just using functions—you can wrap not only many functions together into an object, but
also the data those functions use.

So instead of the 200 functions and 500 variables needed to support printing in your
application, you can wrap everything up into an object, named, say, printer. All the
functions and variables are hidden inside that object, not accessible from outside it.
Functions in object-oriented programming are given a new name—methods. And the data
items stored in an object are called properties.

The printer object might hide nearly all its methods internally, but it will also intentionally *expose* some methods for public use, and those methods are the ones that you use to work with the printer object. For example, the printer object may have a method called print, and you can pass text to that method to print: printer("This is a test.");.

Okay, let's start getting to the details. To create an object, you first need to create a *class*. Classes are to objects what cookie cutters are to cookies—you create objects using classes. In fact, an object is called an *instance* of a class. All that's coming up next.

Creating Classes

Everything OOP starts with classes. Classes are the *type* of objects, in the same way that "integer" may be the type of a variable. You have to create the type before you can create specific objects of that type. That's important to realize—a class is an object's type. And because you can structure objects as you like, you have to specify their structure when you create classes. After you've created a class, you can then create objects of that class, as you're going to see.

The class is the type of the object, and the object is an instance of the class. You normally create objects using classes, and then use those objects in your code.

Here's an example, a class named Person. In a few pages, we're going to create people objects from the Person class; the class is the specification of what will be inside those objects. Here's how you create a class in PHP, with the class keyword:

```
class Person
{
        .
        .
        .
}
```

Okay, that creates a class named Person. In PHP, classes are usually given names that start with a capital letter, and objects are given names that start with a lowercase letter. As you know, classes can hold data items, called properties, so let's give the person a name, $name. In the class, you're declaring the properties and methods that will go into the objects of this class—and that means you use the var statement to declare properties in PHP. Here's how you add a property named $name to the Person class:

```
class Person
{
    var $name;
        .
        .
        .
}
```

You can also add methods (functions in non-OOP speak) to the Person class. For example, you'll need some way to set the person's name, so you might use a method named set_name to do that. Here's how you add that method to the Person class—note that it takes the person's name as an argument named $data:

```
class Person
{
    var $name;

    function set_name($data)
    {
        .
        .
        .
    }
}
```

Now you've got to store the name passed to the set_name function in the $name variable. You could do that, by accessing $name as a global variable:

```
class Person
{
    var $name;

    function set_name($data)
    {
        global $name;
        .
        .
        .
    }
}
```

Then you can assign the argument passed to set_name, $data, to the internally stored name, $name, like this:

```
class Person
{
    var $name;

    function set_name($data)
    {
        global $name;
        $name = $data;
    }
}
```

That stores the person's name. You'll also need some way to read the person's name, so you might add another method called get_name:

```
class Person
{
    var $name;

    function set_name($data)
    {
        global $name;
        $name = $data;
    }
```

```
        function get_name()
        {
                        .

                        .

                        .

        }
}
```

In the get_name method, you can access the internal name, $name, and return it like this:

```
class Person
{
    var $name;

    function set_name($data)
    {
        global $name;
        $name = $data;
    }

    function get_name()
    {
        global $name;
        return $name;
    }
}
```

That looks good, and it will work, but there's one change to make. You won't normally see OOP done using the global keyword. Instead, you usually refer to the properties of the class using the $this keyword. The $this keyword points to the current object. In PHP terms, this:

```
        global $name;
        $name = $data;
```

can be replaced by this:

```
        $this->name = $data;
```

Note the syntax here—you use $this, followed by the -> operator. In addition, you omit the $ in front of the property you're referring to, like this: $this->name.

Using this syntax, which is the normal syntax you'll see in PHP OOP programming, you can write the methods in the Person class like this:

```
class Person
{
    var $name;

    function set_name($data)
    {
        $this->name = $data;
    }
```

```
    function get_name()
    {
        return $this->name;
    }
}
```

Here's one thing to know when talking about creating properties: you can't assign a property a computed value inside a class. For example, this is okay; it assigns the name "Ralph" to $name:

```
class Person
{
    var $name = "Ralph";

    function set_name($data)
    {
        $this->name = $data;
    }

    function get_name()
    {
        return $this->name;
    }
}
```

This means that when you create objects of the Person class, $name will be assigned the name "Ralph". However, you can't assign anything but a constant value to a property in a class. For example, you can't even assign the expression "Ralph " . "Kramden", which concatenates "Ralph " and "Kramden", to the $name property. This won't work:

```
class Person
{
    var $name = "Ralph " . "Kramden";   //NO GOOD.

    function set_name($data)
    {
        $this->name = $data;
    }

    function get_name()
    {
        return $this->name;
    }
}
```

That's one thing to be careful about when creating properties. Are there similar restrictions on methods? Not really, except that you shouldn't begin the name of a method with a double underscore (__)—there are a number of built-in methods that start that way, and you might conflict with them.

Okay, you've now created a PHP class, the Person class. Now it's time to put it to work, creating some objects.

Creating Objects

To create a new object, you use the new operator in PHP. You just need to define your class, and then you can use the new operator to create an object of that class. Objects are stored as variables, so the object-creation process using the new operator looks like this:

```
class Person
{
  var $name;
  function set_name($data)
  {
      $this->name = $data;
  }

  function get_name()
  {
      return $this->name;
  }
}
```

```
$ralph = new Person;
```

Great, that's created a new Person object named $ralph. Easy.

All the methods and properties in the Person class are built into the $ralph object. So how can you call the set_name method, for example, to set the name stored in the object?

You can call the $ralph object's set_name method like this, using the -> operator again:

```
$ralph = new Person;
$ralph->set_name("Ralph");
```

That's how it works in PHP; you create an object, and then you can call the methods built into that object using the -> operator. Executing the statement $ralph->set_name("Ralph"); sets the name stored internally in $ralph to "Ralph".

And you can read that name from the object using the object's get_name method. That looks like this in phpobject.php, where you can display the object's internal name:

```
<html>
  <head>
    <title>
      Creating an object
    </title>
  </head>

  <body>
    <h1>Creating an object</h1>
    <?php
      class Person
      {
        var $name;
```

```
        function set_name($data)
        {
            $this->name = $data;
        }

        function get_name()
        {
            return $this->name;
        }
    }

    $ralph = new Person;
    $ralph->set_name("Ralph");

    echo "The name of your friend is ", $ralph->get_name(), ".";
    ?>
  </body>
</html>
```

You can see the results in Figure 7-1—this example created a class, then created an object of that class, configured that object by calling its set_name method—and then called get_name to get the stored name. Not bad.

You saw that, after you create an object, you can access the methods of that object like this:

```
    $ralph = new Person;
    $ralph->set_name("Ralph");
```

By default, you can also access the properties inside an object the same way. For example, you might want to read the name stored internally (as $name) in the $ralph

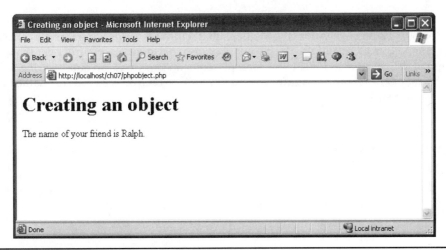

FIGURE 7-1   Creating an object

object, without having to call the get_name method. You can indeed access that property like this:

```php
<?php
  class Person
  {
    var $name;
    function set_name($data)
    {
        $this->name = $data;
    }

    function get_name()
    {
        return $this->name;
    }
  }

  $ralph = new Person;
  $ralph->set_name("Ralph");

  echo "The name of your friend is ", $ralph->name, ".";
?>
```

So you can recover the name stored in the using the get_name method:

```php
$ralph->get_name()
```

or this way, using just the property:

```php
$ralph->name
```

In OOP programming, you usually call a method to get data from an object, you don't access the object's properties directly. Methods that return the values of properties are called *accessor* methods in OOP, and they're popular because they give you control over the way the internal data in an object is set. For example, someone may pass an empty string to the set_name method, and in such a case, you may want to set the object's internal name to a default value instead:

```php
function set_name($data)
{
    if($data != ""){
      $this->name = $data;
    }
    else {
      $this->name = "Ralph";
    }
}
```

If you just let code outside the object set the value of the $name property directly, you wouldn't have this kind of control over the acceptable values of the $name property.

Okay, you might want to restrict access to an object's internal data and want code to have to call get_name instead of access the $name property directly. But how would you stop code from accessing that property directly? You can do it.

Setting Access to Properties and Methods

At this point, any code has access to the $name property in your object. That's because, by default, all the members (properties and methods) of a class or object are declared public. That means those members are accessible from everywhere in your code. That means that this code works, which accesses the $name property from outside the object:

```php
<?php
  class Person
  {
    var $name;

    function set_name($data)
    {
        $this->name = $data;
    }

    function get_name()
    {
        return $this->name;
    }
  }

  $ralph = new Person;
  $ralph->set_name("Ralph");

  echo "The name of your friend is ", $ralph->name, ".";
?>
```

You can restrict access to the members of a class or object with the PHP *access modifiers,* and here they are:

- **public**   Means "Accessible to all"
- **private**   Means "Accessible in the same class"
- **protected**   Means "Accessible in the same class and classes derived from that class"

Public Access

Public access is the most unrestricted access of all, and it's the default. You can explicitly declare properties and methods to be public with the public keyword:

```php
<?php
  class Person
  {
    public $name;
```

```
    public function set_name($data)
    {
        $this->name = $data;
    }

    public function get_name()
    {
        return $this->name;
    }
}

$ralph = new Person;
$ralph->set_name("Ralph");

echo "The name of your friend is ", $ralph->name, ".";
?>
```

This code works, echoing the name stored internally in the object, because that name has been stored with public access. Now let's restrict access to that name.

Private Access

You can make a class or object member private with the private keyword. When you make a member private, you can't access it outside the class or object. Here's an example, phpprivate .php, where the $name property has been made private to the Person class, and we're trying to access it from outside the $ralph object:

```
<html>
  <head>
    <title>
      Creating an object
    </title>
  </head>

  <body>
    <h1>Creating an object</h1>
    <?php
      class Person
      {
        private $name;

        function set_name($data)
        {
            $this->name = $data;
        }

        function get_name()
        {
            return $this->name;
        }
      }
```

```
      $ralph = new Person;
      $ralph->set_name("Ralph");

      echo "The name of your friend is ", $ralph->name, ".";
   ?>
  </body>
</html>
```

You can see this example at work in Figure 7-2—as you can see, you get an error because the property you're trying to access is private:

```
The name of your friend is PHP Fatal error: Cannot access private property
Person::$name in C:\Inetpub\wwwroot\ch07\phpprivate.php on line 29
```

That means you have forced code outside the object to access the name stored in the $ralph object using the get_name accessor method, instead of directly accessing the $name property:

```
<?php
  class Person
  {
    private $name;

    function set_name($data)
    {
        $this->name = $data;
    }

    function get_name()
    {
        return $this->name;
    }
  }
```

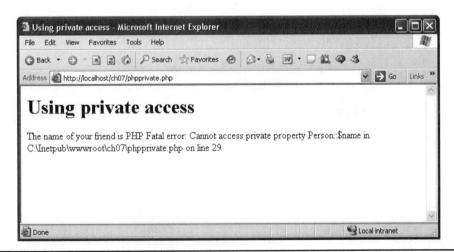

FIGURE 7-2   Attempting to access a private property

```
$ralph = new Person;
$ralph->set_name("Ralph");

echo "The name of your friend is ", $ralph->get_name(), ".";
?>
```

Now everything works okay, as you can see in Figure 7-3.

You can also make methods private, as you see here:

```
<html>
  <head>
    <title>
      Creating an object
    </title>
  </head>

  <body>
    <h1>Creating an object</h1>
    <?php
      class Person
      {
        var $name;

        function set_name($data)
        {
            $this->name = $data;
        }

        private function get_name()
        {
            return $this->name;
        }
      }
```

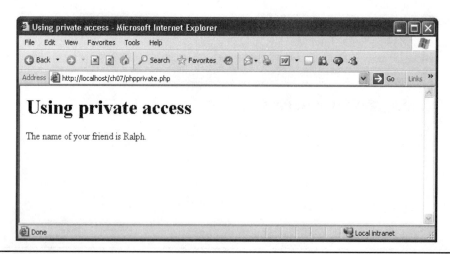

FIGURE 7-3   Accessing a private property

```
      $ralph = new Person;
      $ralph->set_name("Ralph");

      echo "The name of your friend is ", $ralph->get_name(), ".";
    ?>
  </body>
</html>
```

But now this code isn't going to work, because you're trying to call get_name outside the object—and the get_name method is private. That means that you can call it only from code inside the same object. For example, code like this is legal (although not very useful), because it calls the now-private method get_name from inside the object's own code:

```
<?php
  class Person
  {
    var $name;

    function set_name($data)
    {
        $this->name = get_name();
    }

    private function get_name()
    {
        return $this->name;
    }
  }

  $ralph = new Person;
  $ralph->set_name("Ralph");

  echo "The name of your friend is ", $ralph->get_name(), ".";
?>
```

We'll take a look at the other access modifier, the protected modifier, after talking about inheritance, coming up in this chapter.

Using Constructors to Initialize Objects

As you have seen, you can create objects with the new operator, and then use methods like set_name to set the internal data in that object:

```
function set_name($data)
{
  $this->name = $data;
}
```

In this way, you can initialize the data inside an object before you start working with that object.

Wouldn't it be convenient if you could both create and initialize an object at the same time? PHP allows you to do that with *constructors*, which, as in other languages that support OOP, are special methods automatically run when an object is created.

Constructors have a special name in PHP—__construct; that is, "construct" preceded by two underscores. Here's an example:

```
function __construct($data)
{
        .
        .
        .

}
```

As you see, this constructor takes an argument, $data. You can assign that data to the internal name stored in the object like this:

```
function __construct($data)
{
    $this->name = $data;
}
```

How do you use this constructor? You pass data to the constructor when you use the new operator to create new objects, and you pass data to the constructor by enclosing that data in parentheses following the class name. Here's an example, phpconstructor, that initializes an object with the name "Dan":

```
<html>
  <head>
    <title>
      Using a constructor
    </title>
  </head>

  <body>
    <h1>Using a constructor</h1>
    <?php
      class Person
      {
        var $name;

        function __construct($data)
        {
          $this->name = $data;
        }

        function set_name($data)
        {
            $this->name = $data;
        }
```

```
        function get_name()
        {
            return $this->name;
        }
    }

    $dan = new Person("Dan");

    echo "The name of your friend is ", $dan->get_name(), ".";
  ?>
 </body>
</html>
```

You can see the results in Figure 7-4, where the constructor did indeed initialize the object.

You can pass as many arguments to constructors as you need—as long as the constructor is set up to take those arguments:

```
    $dan = new Person("Dan", "brown hair", "blue eyes");
```

All PHP classes come with a default constructor that takes no arguments—it's the default constructor that gets called when you execute code like this:

```
    $ralph = new Person;
    $ralph->set_name("Ralph");
```

However, as soon as you create your own constructor, no matter how many arguments it takes, the default constructor is no longer accessible.

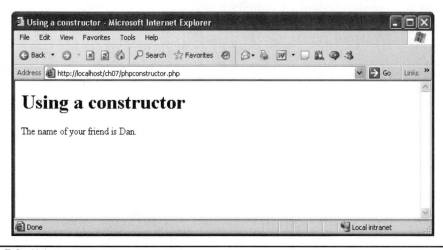

FIGURE 7-4   Using a constructor

You can also give the constructor the name of the class (as in other languages that support OOP) instead of __construct, like this for the Person class:

```
class Person
{
  var $name;

  function Person($data)
  {
    $this->name = $data;
  }
  .
  .
  .
}
```

Using Destructors to Clean Up after Objects

Besides constructors, PHP also supports *destructors,* which are called when you destroy an object. You use destructors to clean up after an object—terminating database or Internet connections, for example. In PHP, destructors are called when you explicitly destroy an object, or when all references to the object go out of scope.

Destructors are named __destruct in PHP, like this (you don't pass arguments to destructors):

```
function __destruct()
{
}
```

Here's an example, phpdestructor.php:

```
<html>
  <head>
    <title>
      Using a destructor
    </title>
  </head>

  <body>
    <h1>Using a destructor</h1>
    <?php
      class Person
      {
        var $name;

        function __construct($data)
        {
          echo "Constructing ", $data, "...<br>";
```

```
            $this->name = $data;
        }

        function set_name($data)
        {
            $this->name = $data;
        }

        function get_name()
        {
            return $this->name;
        }

        function __destruct()
        {
            echo "Destructing ", $this->name, "...<br>";
        }
    }

    $dan = new Person("Dan");

    echo "The name of your friend is ", $dan->get_name(), ".<br>";
    ?>
  </body>
</html>
```

You can see the results in Figure 7-5, where the destructor was run when the $dan object was destroyed when the script ended.

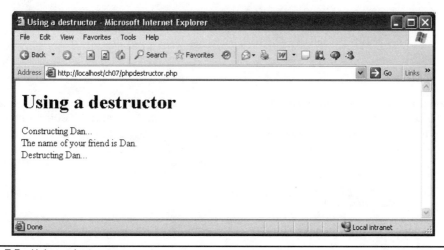

FIGURE 7-5   Using a destructor

Basing One Class on Another with Inheritance

The Person class is fine as far as it goes, but what if you wanted to customize it for your friends so that each friend could have their own saying? For example, Dan might say, "Hi, I'm Dan."; Ralph might say, "Ralph here.", and so on.

You can add functionality to your classes, like the Friend class, through *inheritance*. Inheritance in PHP works much the same as it does in other languages, like Java. Here's how it works; the Person class supports the set_name and get_name methods:

```
class Person
{
  var $name;

  function set_name($data)
  {
      $this->name = $data;
  }

  function get_name()
  {
      return $this->name;
  }
}
```

Now say that you want to create a new class, Friend, that has all the functionality of the Person class—that is, the set_name and get_name methods—but also supports some new methods. You can base the Friend class on the Person class with the *extends* keyword this way:

```
class Friend extends Person
{
  .
  .
  .
}
```

Now the Friend class supports the Person methods, set_name and get_name. You can also add your own methods to the Friend class. If you wanted each Friend object to have their own personalized messages, you might add a set_message method that lets you set each object's message, and a speak method that returns that message:

```
class Friend extends Person
{
  var $message;

  function set_message($msg)
  {
    $this->message = $msg;
  }
```

```
    function speak()
    {
      echo $this->message;
    }
  }
```

Now Friend objects will support the set_name, get_name, set_message, and speak methods. Here's an example, phpinheritcance.php, which shows this in action:

```
<html>
  <head>
    <title>
      Inheriting with constructors
    </title>
  </head>

  <body>
    <h1>Inheriting with constructors</h1>
    <?php
    class Person
    {
      var $name;

      function set_name($data)
      {
          $this->name = $data;
      }

      function get_name()
      {
          return $this->name;
      }
    }

    class Friend extends Person
    {
      var $message;

      function set_message($msg)
      {
        $this->message = $msg;
      }

      function speak()
      {
        echo $this->message;
      }
    }

    $tony = new Friend;
    $tony->set_name("Tony");
    $tony->set_message("Hiya from Tony.");
```

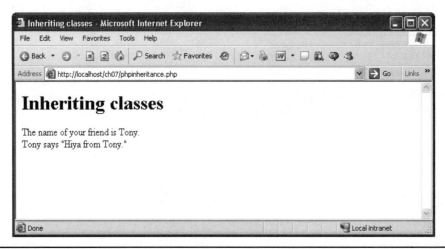

FIGURE 7-6   Inheriting classes

```
    echo "The name of your friend is ", $tony->get_name(), ".<br>";
    echo $tony->get_name(), " says \"", $tony->speak(), "\"<br>";
  ?>
 </body>
</html>
```

You can see the results in Figure 7-6, where the code has used all methods: set_name, get_name, set_message, and speak.

That's how inheritance works—you base one class on another, and the derived class inherits functionality from the base class. Inheriting properties and methods from the base class depends on the access modifiers you've used in the base class. Public members are visible in the derived class (and everywhere else), but members declared private in the base class won't be accessible in the derived class.

What if you want a member accessible in the base class—and in the derived class—but not to code outside the base class and derived classes? For that, you use protected access.

Protected Access

Using the protected keyword makes class members accessible only in the class they're declared in, and any class derived from that class. For example, you can make the set_name method protected in the Person class:

```
<?php
  class Person
  {
    var $name;

    protected function set_name($data)
    {
        $this->name = $data;
    }
```

```
    function get_name()
    {
        return $this->name;
    }
}
```

That means that only code inside Person and classes derived from it can call the set_name method. For example, this code won't work:

```
$tony = new Friend;
$tony->set_name("Tony");
```

To make set_name accessible to code outside the object, you might create a new method, set_name_public, which calls set_name internally, like this in the Friend class in phpprotected.php:

```
<html>
  <head>
    <title>
      Inheriting with constructors
    </title>
  </head>

  <body>
    <h1>Inheriting with constructors</h1>
    <?php
      class Person
      {
        var $name;

        protected function set_name($data)
        {
            $this->name = $data;
        }

        function get_name()
        {
            return $this->name;
        }
      }

      class Friend extends Person
      {
        var $message;

        function set_message($msg)
        {
          $this->message = $msg;
        }

        function speak()
        {
          echo $this->message;
        }
```

```
        function set_name_public($name)
        {
            $this->set_name($name);
        }
    }

    $tony = new Friend;
    $tony->set_name_public("Tony");
    $tony->set_message("Hiya from Tony.");

    echo "The name of your friend is ", $tony->get_name(), ".<br>";
    echo $tony->get_name(), " says \"", $tony->speak(), "\"<br>";
    ?>
  </body>
</html>
```

Now this works, because set_name_public has public access—any code can call it. That's the idea behind the protected access modifier—public access gives all code access to a member, private restricts access to the current class, and protected restricts access to the current class and any classes derived from that class.

Constructors and Inheritance

How about using constructors and inheritance? Specifically, how do you pass data back to the base class's constructor? For example, you saw a constructor for the Person class that took the person's name:

```
class Person
{
  var $name;

  function __construct($data)
  {
    $this->name = $data;
  }
```

How could you call this constructor from the Friend class, which is based on the Person class? You can do that like this in the Friend class's constructor—parent::__construct calls the parent class's (the Friend class's) constructor:

```
function __construct($data)
{
  parent::__construct($data);
}
```

And you can pass other data to this constructor as well—data targeted for the Friend class. You can see how this works in phpinherticonstructor.php:

```
<html>
  <head>
    <title>
      Inheriting with constructors
    </title>
  </head>
```

```
<body>
  <h1>Inheriting with constructors</h1>
  <?php
    class Person
    {
      var $name;

      function __construct($data)
      {
        $this->name = $data;
      }

      function set_name($data)
      {
          $this->name = $data;
      }

      function get_name()
      {
          return $this->name;
      }
    }

    class Friend extends Person
    {
      var $message;
      function __construct($data, $msg)
      {
        parent::__construct($data);
        $this->message = $msg;
      }

      function speak()
      {
        echo $this->message;
      }
    }

    $nancy = new Friend("Nancy", "Hi, Nancy here.");

    echo "The name of your friend is ", $nancy->get_name(), ".<br>";
    echo $nancy->get_name(), " says \"", $nancy->speak(), "\"<br>";
  ?>
  </body>
</html>
```

You can see the results in Figure 7-7, where the Friend constructor passed data back to the Person constructor.

Calling Base Class Methods

When you've inherited from another class, how do you call the methods in that base class? Normally, that's not a problem, because those methods are available to you to, simply

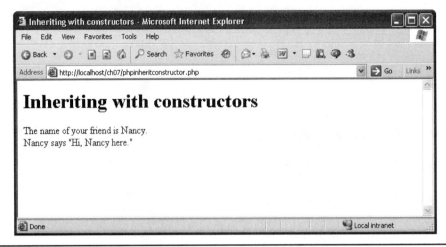

FIGURE 7-7   Using inheritance and constructors

because you've inherited them from the base class. But what if the base class has methods that are protected—and you want to make them public by letting any code call them?

Just as you saw with constructors, you can call base class methods by appending "parent::" in front of the base class method's name. Here's an example, phpbasemethods.php. Here, the methods get_name and set_name have been made protected in the Person class:

```php
<?php
  class Person
  {
    var $name;

    protected function set_name($data)
    {
        $this->name = $data;
    }

    protected function get_name()
    {
        return $this->name;
    }
  }
```

And the friend class has two methods, get_name_public and set_name_public, which call the protected methods using the parent:: syntax:

```html
<html>
  <head>
    <title>
      Calling base class methods
    </title>
  </head>
```

```php
<body>
  <h1>Calling base class methods</h1>
  <?php
    class Person
    {
      var $name;

      protected function set_name($data)
      {
          $this->name = $data;
      }

      protected function get_name()
      {
          return $this->name;
      }
    }

    class Friend extends Person
    {
      var $message;

      function set_message($msg)
      {
        $this->message = $msg;
      }

      function speak()
      {
        echo $this->message;
      }

      function set_name_public($data)
      {
          parent::set_name($data);
      }
      function get_name_public()
      {
          return parent::get_name();
      }
    }

    $britta = new Friend;
    $britta->set_name_public("Britta");
    $britta->set_message("Hello from Britta.");
    echo "The name of your friend is ", $britta->get_name_public(), ".<br>";
    echo $britta->get_name_public(), " says \"", $britta->speak(), "\"<br>";
  ?>
</body>
</html>
```

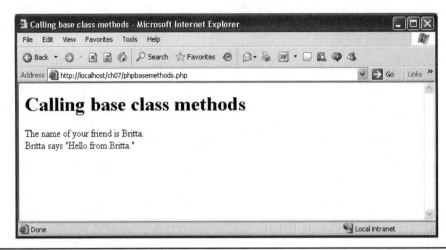

Figure 7-8   Calling base class methods

That's it—the code then creates a friend named Britta and uses get_name_public and set_name_public to call the protected versions of these methods, which the code does with the parent:: syntax. You can see the results in Figure 7-8.

Note   *You can also use the parent:: syntax to access base class properties.*

What do you do if you've inherited from a class that itself has inherited from another class? Can you use grandparent:: syntax? No, but you can simply prepend the member you want to access with the name of the class it's in. That would look like this in this example, where the member you're looking for is in the Person class:

```php
<?php
  class Person
  {
    var $name;

    protected function set_name($data)
    {
        $this->name = $data;
    }

    protected function get_name()
    {
        return $this->name;
    }
  }
```

```php
class Friend extends Person
{
  var $message;

  function set_message($msg)
  {
    $this->message = $msg;
  }

  function speak()
  {
    echo $this->message;
  }

  function set_name_public($data)
  {
      Person::set_name($data);
  }

  function get_name_public()
  {
      return Person::get_name();
  }
}
    .
    .
    .
```

Overriding Methods

In PHP, as with OOP in many languages, you can *override* methods. That means that you can redefine a base class method in a derived class.

Here's an example, phpoverride.php. This example overrides the set_name method in the Person base class:

```php
<?php
  class Person
  {
    var $name;

    function set_name($data)
    {
      $this->name = $data;
    }

    function get_name()
    {
      return $this->name;
    }
  }
```

This method is overridden in the Friend class, simply by redefining it. The overriding version of this method capitalizes the name before storing it:

```html
<html>
  <head>
    <title>
      Overriding methods
    </title>
  </head>

  <body>
    <h1>
        Overriding methods
    </h1>
    <?php
      class Person
      {
        var $name;

        function set_name($data)
        {
          $this->name = $data;
        }

        function get_name()
        {
          return $this->name;
        }
      }

      class Friend extends Person
      {
        var $name;

        function speak()
        {
          echo $this->name, " is speaking<br>";
        }

        function set_name($data)
        {
          $this->name = strtoupper($data);
        }
      }

      echo "Creating your new friend...<BR>";
      $friend = new Friend;
      $friend->set_name("Susan");
      $friend->speak();
      ?>
  </body>
</html>
```

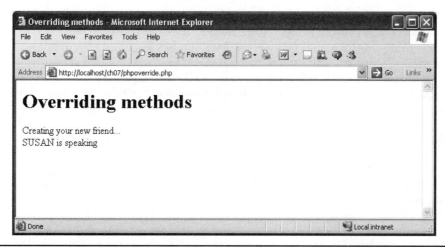

FIGURE 7-9   Overriding methods

That's it—now when you create a $susan object and give the object a name, that name is capitalized by the overridden version of the set_name method. You can see the results in Figure 7-9.

Overloading Methods

Besides overriding methods, you can also *overload* methods in PHP. Overriding a method means redefining it, but overloading it means creating an alternate version with a different argument list. In standard OOP languages, you overload a method by defining a new version of the method with a different argument list. Here's an example, where you define two versions of the set_name method, one that takes the person's name, and another that takes both the person's name and their message:

```
function set_name($data)
{
  $this->name = $data;
}

function set_name($data, $msg)
{
  $this->name = $data;
  $this->message = $msg;
}
```

Now you could call the set_name method with one or two arguments, and the OOP language would call the correct version of set_name, depending on how many arguments were passed:

```
$friend->set_name("Susan");
$friend->set_name("Ted", "Ted here");
```

That's how things work in standard OOP languages—but PHP is different.

In PHP, you implement method overloading with the __call method. In a class, this is the method that gets called when you call a method that doesn't exist.

How's that again? Say that you have a class that has a __call method, but no set_name method. When you call the set_name method on objects of that class, what actually gets called is the __call method. The __call method is passed the name of the missing method, as well as an array holding the argument list that was passed to that missing method:

```
function __call($method, $arguments)
{
        .
        .
        .

}
```

Because the arguments passed to the missing method are passed in an array, you can implement method overloading using the __call method. For example, if you wanted to overload the set_name method to be callable as both set_name($name) or set_name($name, $message), you could leave that method unwritten, and handle it with a __call method:

```
function __call($method, $arguments)
{
        .
        .
        .

}
```

In the __call method, you could first check if the method called (and not found) was indeed set_name:

```
function __call($method, $arguments)
{
   if($method == "set_name") {
        .
        .
        .

   }
}
```

The set_name method can be called with one or two arguments ($name or $name and $message), so you can check first if a single argument was passed:

```
function __call($method, $arguments)
{
   if($method == "set_name") {
```

```
      if(count($arguments) == 1){
            .
            .
            .
      }
    }
  }
```

If a single argument was passed, that's the person's name, and you can store it like this:

```
function __call($method, $arguments)
{
  if($method == "set_name"){

    if(count($arguments) == 1){
      $this->name = $arguments[0];
    }
  }
}
```

On the other hand, if two arguments were passed to the function, those arguments are $name and $message:

```
function __call($method, $arguments)
{
  if($method == "set_name"){

    if(count($arguments) == 1){
      $this->name = $arguments[0];
    }

    if(count($arguments) == 2){
      $this->name = $arguments[0];
      $this->message = $arguments[1];
    }

  }
}
```

That's how you handle overloading—calling the same method name with different numbers of arguments in PHP OOP. Now you can call set_name with one or two arguments, as you see in phpoverload.php:

```
<html>
  <head>
    <title>
      Overloading methods
    </title>
  </head>
```

```
<body>
  <h1>
      Overloading methods
  </h1>
  <?php
    class Friend
    {
      var $name;
      var $message;

      function speak()
      {
        echo $this->name, " says \"", $this->message, "\"<br>";
      }

      function set_message($msg)
      {
        $this->message = $msg;
      }

      function __call($method, $arguments)
      {
        if($method == "set_name"){

          if(count($arguments) == 1){
            $this->name = $arguments[0];
          }

          if(count($arguments) == 2){
            $this->name = $arguments[0];
            $this->message = $arguments[1];
          }

        }
      }
    }

    echo "Creating your new friend...<br>";
    $friend = new Friend;
    $friend->set_name("Susan");
    $friend->set_message("Hello from Susan");
    $friend->speak();

    $friend->set_name("Ted", "Ted here");
    $friend->speak();
  ?>
  </body>
</html>
```

You can see the results in Figure 7-10, where the code was able to call two different versions of the overloaded set_name method.

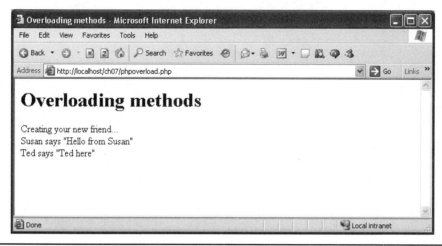

FIGURE 7-10   Overloading methods

Autoloading Classes

If you're going to create lots of classes, or if your class definitions are long ones, you might want to store them in separate files. You could explicitly include each such file, but there's an easier way: you can use the __autoload function.

This function is passed the names of any classes that PHP is looking for and can't find in the current file. That means you can load the missing class using require or include like this, where the class class_name is in a file class_name.php:

```
function __autoload($class_name)
{
    require $class_name . '.php';
}
```

Let's see this in action. You've seen examples with the Person class and the Friend class, so let's put those classes into external files. Here's Person.php (note that the <?php...?> markup is required):

```
<?php
  class Person
  {
    var $name;

    function set_name($data)
    {
        $this->name = $data;
    }
```

```php
        function get_name()
        {
            return $this->name;
        }
    }
?>
```

And here's Friend.php:

```php
<?php
  class Friend extends Person
  {
    var $message;

    function set_message($msg)
    {
        $this->message = $msg;
    }

    function speak()
    {
      echo $this->message;
    }
  }
?>
```

Now, in phpautoload.php, you can use the __autoload function to automatically load in Friend.php and Person.php as needed, like this:

```php
<html>
  <head>
    <title>
      Autoloading classes
    </title>
  </head>

  <body>
    <h1>
      Autoloading classes
    </h1>

    <?php
      function __autoload($class_name)
      {
        require $class_name . '.php';
      }

      $tony = new Friend;
      $tony->set_name("Tony");
      $tony->set_message("Hiya from Tony.");
```

```
      echo "The name of your friend is ", $tony->get_name(), ".<br>";
      echo $tony->get_name(), " says \"", $tony->speak(), "\"<br>";
    ?>
  </body>
</html>
```

You can see the results in Figure 7-11, where the Person and Friend classes were successfully loaded in as PHP needed them. That's a good technique to know, because as your classes become longer, you'll probably want to put them in separate files.

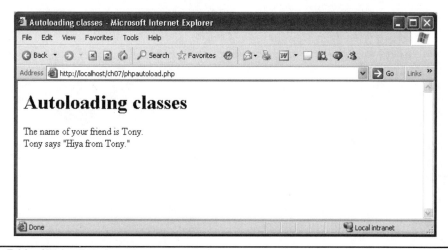

FIGURE 7-11   Autoloading classes

Advanced Object-Oriented Programming

The preceding chapter got the ball rolling with OOP. In this chapter, your guided tour continues, giving you all you need to become a PHP OOP-meister. Here, you're going to how to handle static class members, abstraction, interfaces, and reflection—all parts of any modern OOP-supporting language.

Let's get things started by working with static class members.

Creating Static Methods

Say that you wanted to create a Math utility class that you could store useful math routines in:

```php
<?php
  class Math
  {
    .
    .
    .
  }
?>
```

For example, you might place a method in the Math class named squarer, which displays the square of numbers you pass to it:

```php
<?php
  class Math
  {
    function squarer($op)
    {
      echo $op, "<sup>2</sup> = ", $op * $op, "<br>";
    }
  }
?>
```

Now you can create an object of the Math class and use its squarer method to display the squares of numbers like this in phpmath.php:

```
<html>
  <head>
    <title>
      Using the Math class
    </title>
  </head>

  <body>
    <h1>
      Using the Math class
    </h1>
    <?php
      class Math
      {
        function squarer($op)
        {
          echo $op, "<sup>2</sup> = ", $op * $op, "<br>";
        }
      }

      echo "Using a Math object...<br>";
      $math = new Math();
      echo $math->squarer(2);
    ?>
  </body>
</html>
```

And you can see the results in Figure 8-1.

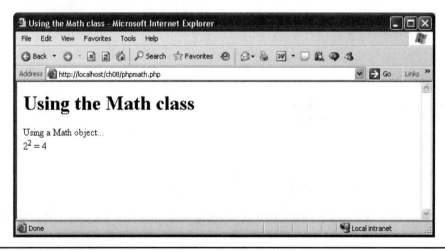

FIGURE 8-1   Using a Math object

That's fine as far as it goes, but why did you need to create a Math object like this?

```
echo "Using a Math object...<br>";
$math = new Math();
echo $math->squarer(2);
```

The Math class is just a utility class—shouldn't it be possible to just use the methods in it, like the squarer method, directly? Shouldn't you be able to simply call such methods on the *class*, not an *object* of that class?

Creating a Static Method

When you create static methods, you can do that—call the method without having to first create an object of that class. Static methods are class methods; they're meant to called on the class, not on an object. Let's see how this works by altering the Math class to support static methods, creating the Math class over again:

```
<?php
  class Math
  {
      .
      .
      .
  }
?>
```

For example, you might start with a static method named say_hi that displays a message:

```
<?php
  class Math
  {
    public function say_hi()
    {
      echo "The Math class says 'Hello there'. <br>";
    }
  }
?>
```

To make this method static, you have to use the static keyword in front of the function keyword:

```
<?php
  class Math
  {
    public static function say_hi()
    {
      echo "The Math class says 'Hello there'. <br>";
    }
  }
?>
```

Now you can access the say_hi method in the Math class—without needing to first create an object of that class—as Math::say_hi():

```php
<?php
  class Math
  {
    public static function say_hi()
    {
      echo "The Math class says 'Hello there'. <br>";
    }
  }

  echo "Using the Math class...<br>";
  Math::say_hi();
?>
```

You can see the results in Figure 8-2, where the call to the static method—also called a class method—worked.

Note the syntax here: Math::say_hi(). You can't use the -> operator here, as you would when working with an object, because no object is involved. Instead, you use the double-colon operator (::) also called the scope resolution operator (also called, very oddly, the Paamayim Nekudotayim in PHP—which stands for "double colon" in Hebrew).

Here's another tip: You don't actually have to use the static keyword to make a method static in PHP. If you use a method in a static way—that is, calling it using the class name instead of calling it as part of an object—PHP will treat the method as static. So this works— no static keyword:

```php
<?php
  class Math
  {
    public function say_hi()
```

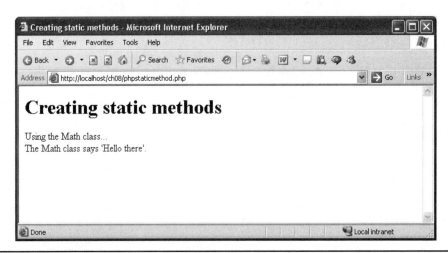

FIGURE 8-2   Calling a class method

```
    {
      echo "The Math class says 'Hello there'. <br>";
    }
  }

  echo "Using the Math class...<br>";            •
  Math::say_hi();
?>
```

However, it's a good idea to use the static keyword to keep things straight in your own code.

TIP *Can you also pass data to a static method? Certainly.*

Passing Data to a Static Method

Say that you wanted to write the squarer method and add it to the Math class. You pass that method the number you want to square:

```
<?php
  class Math
  {
    static $data;

    public static function say_hi()
    {
      echo "The Math class says 'Hello there'. <br>";
    }

    function squarer($op)
    {
      .
      .
      .
    }
  }
?>
```

And you can use the data passed to this method in code inside the method:

```
<?php
  class Math
  {
    static $data;

    public static function say_hi()
    {
      echo "The Math class says 'Hello there'. <br>";
    }

    function squarer($op)
    {
      echo $op, "<sup>2</sup> = ", $op * $op, "<br>";
    }
?>
```

Here's how to call and pass data to the squarer method in phpstaticmethods.php:

```html
<html>
  <head>
    <title>
      Creating static methods
    </title>
  </head>

  <body>
    <h1>
      Creating static methods
    </h1>
    <?php
      class Math
      {
        static $data;

        public static function say_hi()
        {
          echo "The Math class says 'Hello there'. <br>";
        }

        function squarer($op)
        {
          echo $op, "<sup>2</sup> = ", $op * $op, "<br>";
        }
      }

      echo "Using the Math class...<br>";
      Math::say_hi();
      Math::squarer(2);
    ?>
  </body>
</html>
```

You can see the results in Figure 8-3—the squarer method got your data and is displaying its square.

You can see that you can use static methods with classes—what about static properties?

Using Properties in Static Methods

Sometimes, you want to use properties when you do your work, and that's no problem when you're using objects. But can you use properties when you're just working with the class in code, not object? Yes, as long as they're static properties.

For example, say that you had a static method named set_data that's passed an argument:

```php
<?php
  class Math
  {
    public static function set_data($op)
    {
```

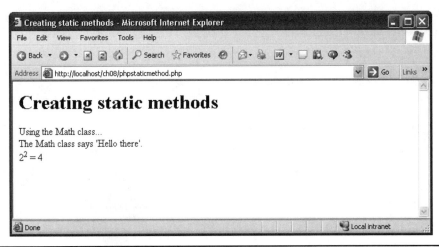

FIGURE 8-3   Creating an object

```
        .
        .
        .
      }
    }
  ?>
```

Now say that you want to save the data passed to this static method in a class property. Turns out that you can do that in PHP, even though no object is involved. You have to declare the property static this way:

```php
<?php
  class Math
  {
    static $data;

    public static function set_data($op)
    {
      .
      .
      .
    }
  }
?>
```

Now you're free to store data in that property. But how do you refer to that property in code? You can't use the $this->data syntax, because $this refers to the current object, and there is no object here. Instead, you have to use the keyword self when working with static properties in static methods. So here's how you can store the data passed to set_data in the $data property:

```php
<?php
  class Math
  {
    static $data;

    public static function set_data($op)
    {
      self::$data = $op;
        .
        .
        .
    }
  }
?>
```

And you can echo the value in that property to prove it's being handled correctly:

```php
<?php
  class Math
  {
    static $data;

    public static function set_data($op)
    {
      self::$data = $op;
      echo "self::\$data = ", self::$data, "<br>";
        .
        .
        .

    }
  }
?>
```

And you can do things like increment the value in $data like this:

```php
<?php
  class Math
  {
    static $data;

    public static function set_data($op)
    {
      self::$data = $op;
      echo "self::\$data = ", self::$data, "<br>";
      echo "Adding 1 to self::\$data <br>";
      self::$data++;
      echo "Now self::\$data = ", self::$data, "<br>";
    }
  }
?>
```

Here's how you can put the set_data method to work in phpstaticproperty.php, passing it a value of 5:

```
<html>
  <head>
    <title>
      Creating static properties
    </title>
  </head>

  <body>
    <h1>
        Creating static properties
    </h1>
    <?php
      class Math
      {
        static $data;

        public static function set_data($op)
        {
          self::$data = $op;
          echo "self::\$data = ", self::$data, "<br>";
          echo "Adding one to self::\$data <br>";
          self::$data++;
          echo "Now self::\$data = ", self::$data, "<br>";
        }
      }

      echo "Using the Math class...<br>";
      Math::set_data(5);
    ?>
  </body>
</html>
```

And you can see the results in Figure 8-4, where the static property did its thing.

Can you also use plain variables in static methods? Yes, you can. For example, you can create a new variable named $item, and assign the value in the $data property to it:

```
    <?php
      class Math
      {
        static $data;

        public static function set_data($op)
        {
          self::$data = $op;
          echo "self::\$data = ", self::$data, "<br>";
          echo "Adding one to self::\$data <br>";
          self::$data++;
          echo "Now self::\$data = ", self::$data, "<br>";
          echo "Assigning self::\$data to \$item. <br>";
          $item = self::$data;
```

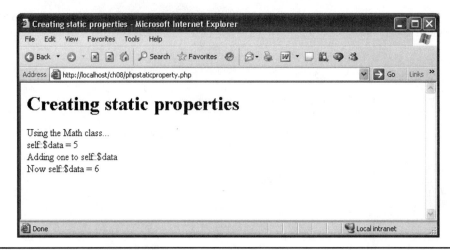

FIGURE 8-4 Creating a static property

```
              .
              .
              .
            }
          }
      ?>
```

And you might increment $item and display the results:

```
<html>
  <head>
    <title>
      Creating static properties
    </title>
  </head>

  <body>
    <h1>
      Creating static properties
    </h1>
    <?php
      class Math
      {
        static $data;

        public static function set_data($op)
        {
          self::$data = $op;
          echo "self::\$data = ", self::$data, "<br>";
          echo "Adding one to self::\$data <br>";
          self::$data++;
          echo "Now self::\$data = ", self::$data, "<br>";
          echo "Assigning self::\$data to \$item. <br>";
          $item = self::$data;
```

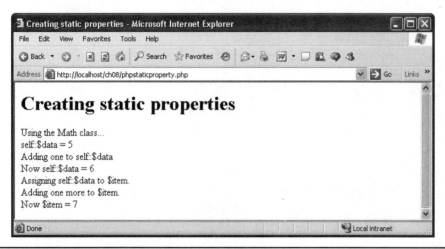

FIGURE 8-5   Using variables in static methods

```
        echo "Adding one more to \$item. <br>";
        $item++;
        echo "Now \$item = ", $item, "<br>";
      }
    }

    echo "Using the Math class...<br>";
    Math::set_data(5);
  ?>
  </body>
</html>
```

You can see the results in Figure 8-5, where you were successful in using variables in static methods.

Static Members and Inheritance

What happens with static members when inheritance is involved? Can you refer to static members of a base class from an inherited class? Yes, you can.

Here's an example, phpstaticinheritance.php. Let's add a static property, $message, containing a reassuring message, to our Math class:

```
<?php
  class Math
  {
    static $data;
    static $message = "No worries.";

    public static function say_hi()
    {
      echo "The Math class says 'Hello there'. <br>";
    }
```

```php
  public static function squarer($op)
  {
    echo $op, "<sup>2</sup> = ", $op * $op, "<br>";
  }
}
?>
```

Now you can extend the Math class in a new class, New_Math:

```php
<?php
  class Math
  {
    static $data;
    static $message = "No worries.";
      .
      .
      .
  }

  class New_Math extends Math
  {
      .
      .
      .
  }
?>
```

And you can access the Math class's static $message property from a method in New_Math—the show_message method:

```php
<?php
  class Math
  {
    static $data;
    static $message = "No worries.";
      .
      .
      .
  }

  class New_Math extends Math
  {
    public static function show_message()
    {
      echo "In New_Math, the message from the Math class is: '",
        Math::$message, "'<br>";
    }
  }
?>
```

Now you can call New_Math::show_message like this in phpstaticinheritance.php:

```html
<html>
  <head>
    <title>
```

```
      Creating static methods
    </title>
  </head>

  <body>
    <h1>
        Creating static methods
    </h1>
    <?php
      class Math
      {
        static $message = "No worries.";
          .
          .
          .
      }

      class New_Math extends Math
      {
        public static function show_message()
        {
          echo "In New_Math, the message from the Math class is: '",
            Math::$message, "'<br>";
        }
      }

      echo "Using the New_Math class...<br>";
      New_Math::show_message();
    ?>
  </body>
</html>
```

You can see the results in Figure 8-6, where the static $message property in the base class Math was indeed accessible from the static show_message method in the derived New_Math class. Cool.

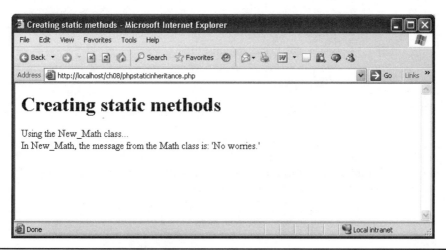

FIGURE 8-6   Using static members with inheritance

Creating Abstract Classes

PHP allows you to create abstract classes as well. You can't use abstract classes to created objects with directly. Instead, you have to inherit a class from the abstract class first. What use is that? You can mark particular methods in the abstract class as abstract, which means that the inheriting class has to define them before you can create objects of the inheriting class.

The idea is to force anyone who wants to use an abstract class to implement their own methods. For example, say that you're a publisher, and you have a Novel class that you send out to authors. That Novel class may have a standard method, get_publisher_info, that returns information about you as the publisher. It might also have an abstract method, get_text, that returns the text of the novel the author is going to write. Because get_text is abstract, the author has to implement the get_text method themselves, which is what you want—the author to write their own novel.

Let's take a look at this in phpabstract.php. You can start by creating the abstract class Novel (to contain abstract methods, a class must be abstract) that you, as the publisher, send out to authors:

```php
<?php
    abstract class Novel
    {
        .
        .
        .
    }
?>
```

This class may have a standard method, say get_publisher_info, that returns information about you, the publisher:

```php
<?php
    abstract class Novel
    {
        function get_publisher_info()
        {
            return "SteveCo Publishing <br>";
        }
        .
        .
        .
    }
?>
```

In addition, you can support a get_text method, that returns the text of the novel. That's the method you want the author to implement, so you make this method abstract. To do that, you don't give it a body, just end its declaration with a semicolon:

```php
<?php
  abstract class Novel
  {
    function get_publisher_info()
    {
      return "SteveCo Publishing <br>";
    }

    abstract function get_text();
  }
?>
```

The author can't create an object of the Novel class directly—they have to add code to the get_text method themselves. They might start by creating a new class, My_Novel, extending your abstract class Novel:

```php
<?php
  abstract class Novel
  {
    function get_publisher_info()
    {
      return "SteveCo Publishing <br>";
    }

    abstract function get_text();
  }

  class My_Novel extends Novel
  {
    .
    .
    .
  }
?>
```

To avoid complaints from PHP, this code has to implement the get_text function, which might look like this:

```php
<?php
  abstract class Novel
  {
    function get_publisher_info()
    {
      return "SteveCo Publishing <br>";
    }

    abstract function get_text();
  }
```

```
class My_Novel extends Novel
{
  public function get_text()
  {
    return "It was a dark and stormy night...";
  }
}
?>
```

Here's phpabstract.php, which creates and uses an object of the My_Novel class:

```
<html>
  <head>
    <title>
      Creating abstract classes
    </title>
  </head>

  <body>
    <h1>
      Creating abstract classes
    </h1>
    <?php
      abstract class Novel
      {
        function get_publisher_info()
        {
          return "SteveCo Publishing <br>";
        }

        abstract function get_text();
      }

      class My_Novel extends Novel
      {
        public function get_text()
        {
          return "It was a dark and stormy night...";
        }
      }

      $mynovel = new My_Novel();
      echo "This novel comes from ", $mynovel->get_publisher_info();
      echo "The novel says '", $mynovel->get_text(), "'<br>";
    ?>
  </body>
</html>
```

As you can see in Figure 8-7, the abstract class did its thing—the author needed to implement the abstract method get_text before creating any objects.

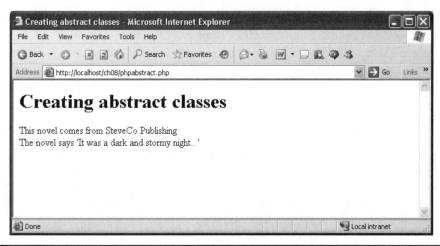

FIGURE 8-7   Using abstract classes

Creating Interfaces

In OOP, interfaces are a little like abstract classes—they specify what methods a class has to implement. However, interfaces are only specifications for methods; they can't include any code.

For example, you could have an interface named iDatabase that specifies methods a database class must implement—get_record and set_record, for example. Any database class that implemented the iDatabase interface would have to also implement the get_record and set_record methods.

Like most OOP-supporting languages, PHP doesn't support multiple inheritance—that is, you can't inherit from multiple classes at the same level, because you can't list multiple classes with the extends keyword. That is, you can do this:

```
class My_Novel extends Novel
{
    .
    .
    .
}
```

But you can't do this:

```
class My_Novel extends Novel, Novella, Story
{
    .
    .
    .
}
```

Using interfaces is sometimes touted as letting you use multiple inheritance, because you can implement multiple interfaces at the same time, like this:

```
class My_Novel implements Novel, Novella, Story
{
    .
    .
    .
}
```

However, don't be fooled—this is not multiple inheritance. Interfaces are simply specifications for methods, and interfaces don't include any code for those methods. Interfaces are useful when, for example, you want to create dozens of classes and to standardize the methods in each class. The names and the argument lists for the methods will be the same across all classes that implement the interface—although the actual code implementations of the methods may vary by class.

Here's an example, modifying the abstract Novel class you just saw into an interface, iNovel. To create an interface, you use the interface keyword:

```
<?php
    interface iNovel
    {
        .
        .
        .
    }
?>
```

Then you list the methods you want any class that implements this interface to contain. Note that as with abstract methods, you don't include any method body. In this case, you might add two methods to iNovel: get_dedication, which returns the novel's dedication, and get_text, which returns the movel's text:

```
<?php
    interface iNovel
    {
        function get_dedication();
        function get_text();
    }
?>
```

To implement this interface in the My_Novel class, you use the implements keyword:

```
<?php
    interface iNovel
    {
        function get_dedication();
        function get_text();
    }
```

```
class My_Novel implements iNovel
{
  .
  .
  .
}
?>
```

Since you've implemented the iNovel interface, you have to implement every method in that interface. Here, that's get_dedication and get_text, and that looks like this in My_Novel:

```
<?php
interface iNovel
{
  function get_dedication();
  function get_text();
}

class My_Novel implements iNovel
{
  public function get_dedication()
  {
    return "To my sweetie.";
  }

  public function get_text()
  {
    return "It was a dark and stormy night...";
  }
}
?>
```

Here's how you can create an object using My_Novel and put it to work:

```
<html>
  <head>
    <title>
      Using interfaces
    </title>
  </head>

  <body>
    <h1>
      Using interfaces
    </h1>
    <?php
    interface iNovel
    {
      function get_dedication();
      function get_text();
    }
```

```php
class My_Novel implements iNovel
{
  public function get_dedication()
  {
    return "To my sweetie.";
  }

  public function get_text()
  {
    return "It was a dark and stormy night...";
  }
}

$mynovel = new My_Novel();
echo "The novel is dedicated '", $mynovel->get_dedication(), "'<br>";
echo "The novel says '", $mynovel->get_text(), "'<br>";
?>
</body>
</html>
```

You can see the results in Figure 8-8, where the iNovel interface was implemented in the My_Novel class. Not bad.

Bear in mind that interfaces don't actually do all that much for you—they just let you specify the methods that implementing classes must implement. And that's fine if you want to maintain a consistent set of methods across multiple classes.

Want another interface example? Coming up next.

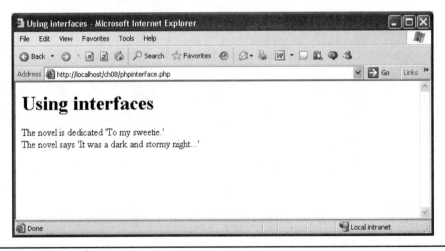

FIGURE 8-8   Using interfaces

Supporting Object Iteration

Want to allow your objects to contain collection of items so that you can loop over them using foreach? You can do that if you implement the PHP Iterator interface, which contains these methods:

- **public function current()**   Returns the current element in your collection
- **public function key()**   Returns the current key
- **public function next()**   Returns the next element
- **public function valid()**   Returns true if the current element is valid
- **public function rewind()**   Starts operations over from the beginning

Let's put this to work in a simple example, phpiterator, that creates objects you can use in foreach loops. The class here is going to be called DataHandler, and to make this a simple example, it's going to use an array internally, because arrays already support the methods of the Iterator interface, making our job easier.

First, you create the DataHandler class, implementing the PHP Iterator interface:

```php
<?php
  class DataHandler implements Iterator
  {
      .
      .
      .
  }
?>
```

This class is going to store an array internally that you pass to its constructor, and let you iterate over that array. Here's how the constructor stores the array as the private property $array:

```php
<?php
  class DataHandler implements Iterator
  {
      private $array = array();

      public function __construct($arr)
      {
          if (is_array($arr)) {
              $this->array = $arr;
          }
      }
      .
      .
      .
  }
?>
```

Now you can use the PHP array functions to write the Iterator methods—that is, to let you use arrays in foreach statements, arrays already implement those methods, so we'll make use of that fact here. For example, the DataHandler method current will just use the array method current on the private array $array, the key method uses the array method key on the private array $array and so on. Here's how to implement the Iterator methods in DataHandler:

```php
<?php
  class DataHandler implements Iterator
  {
      private $array = array();

      public function __construct($arr)
      {
          if (is_array($arr)) {
              $this->array = $arr;
          }
      }

      public function current()
      {
          return current($this->array);
      }

      public function key()
      {
          return key($this->array);
      }

      public function next()
      {
          return next($this->array);
      }

      public function valid()
      {
          return $this->current() !== false;
      }

      public function rewind()
      {
          reset($this->array);
      }
  }
?>
```

All that remains is to create an object of the DataHandler class, initializing it with an array, and then use a foreach loop to iterate over that object, which looks like this in phpiterator.php:

```html
<html>
  <head>
    <title>
      Object iteration
    </title>
  </head>
```

```
<body>
  <h1>
     Object iteration
  </h1>
  <?php
    class DataHandler implements Iterator
    {
        private $array = array();

        public function __construct($arr)
        {
            if (is_array($arr)) {
                $this->array = $arr;
            }
        }
        .
          .
            .
    }

    $new_array = array("a", "b", "c", "d", "e");
    $object = new DataHandler($new_array);

    echo "Iterating over the object: <br>";

    foreach ($object as $key => $value) {
        echo $key, ' => ', $value, "<br>";
    }
  ?>
  </body>
</html>
```

You can see the results in Figure 8-9, where the foreach loop had no trouble with the DataHandler object. Cool.

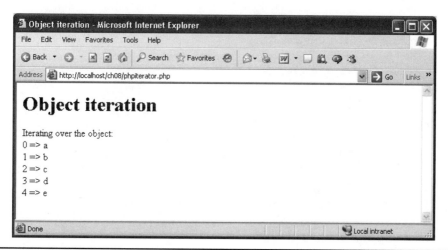

FIGURE 8-9   Object iteration

Comparing Objects

Comparing two objects in PHP takes a little thought. When using the comparison operator (==), object variables are compared simply—two objects are equal if they have the same attributes and values, and are objects of the same class. If you use the identity operator (===), objects are identical if and only if they refer to the same object.

Here's an example, phpcompare.php, that shows how this works. In this example, $object_1 is an instance of Class_1, $object_1a is another instance of Class_1, $object_1copy is a copy of $object_1, and $object_2 is an instance of Class_2:

```
<html>
  <head>
    <title>
      Comparing objects
    </title>
  </head>

  <body>
    <h1>
      Comparing objects
    </h1>
    <?php
      class Class_1
      {
        public $data;

        function __construct($item)
        {
          $this->data = $item;
        }
      }

      class Class_2
      {
        public $data;

        function __construct($item)
        {
          $this->data = $item;
        }
      }

      $object_1 = new Class_1("a");
      $object_1copy = $object_1;
      $object_1a = new Class_1("a");
      $object_2 = new Class_2("a");

      if($object_1 == $object_1a){
        echo '$object_1 == $object_1a is TRUE <br>';
      }
```

```
    else {
      echo '$object_1 == $object_1a is FALSE <br>';
    }

    if($object_1 == $object_2){
      echo '$object_1 == $object_2 is TRUE <br>';
    }
    else {
      echo '$object_1 == $object_2 is FALSE <br>';
    }

    if($object_1 === $object_1a){
      echo '$object_1 === $object_1a is TRUE <br>';
    }
    else {
      echo '$object_1 === $object_1a is FALSE <br>';
    }

    if($object_1 === $object_1copy){
      echo '$object_1 === $object_1copy is TRUE <br>';
    }
    else {
      echo '$object_1 === $object_1copy is FALSE <br>';
    }

  ?>
  </body>
</html>
```

You can see the results in Figure 8-10, where the various comparisons are working as they should.

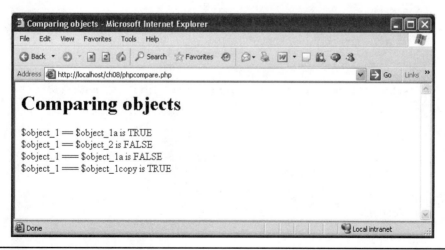

Figure 8-10   Comparing objects

Creating Class Constants

You can also create class constants in PHP classes. These are constants designed to be used by classes, not objects. Here's an example: phpconstant.php, which declares a Math class this way:

```php
<?php
  class Math
  {
       .
       .
       .
  }
?>
```

And you can define a constant in the Math class, pi:

```php
<?php
  class Math
  {
    const pi = 3.14159;
       .
       .
       .
  }
?>
```

Now you can refer to the constant pi in code inside the Math class as self::pi. You use the constant with self:: rather than $this-> because for class constants, there's no object involved. Here's how you might display self::pi using a public method, display_pi:

```php
<?php
  class Math
  {
    const pi = 3.14159;

    function display_pi()
    {
      echo  'Pi from inside the class (self::pi): ', self::pi , "<br>";
    }
  }
?>
```

Can you access pi outside the class? Yes, you can—as Math::pi. Note that it uses the class name, Math, not an object name:

```php
<?php
  class Math
  {
    const pi = 3.14159;
```

```
   function display_pi()
   {
      echo 'Pi from inside the class (self::pi): ', self::pi , "<br>";
   }
}

echo 'Pi from outside the class (Math::pi): ', Math::pi , "<br>";
   .
   .
   .
?>
```

You can also display pi using objects, if you call the public method display_pi:

```
<?php
   class Math
   {
      const pi = 3.14159;

      function display_pi()
      {
         echo 'Pi from inside the class (self::pi): ', self::pi , "<br>";
      }
   }

   echo 'Pi from outside the class (Math::pi): ', Math::pi , "<br>";
   $object = new Math();
   $object->display_pi();
      .
      .
      .
?>
```

However, you can't access the class constant pi using object expressions like $object::pi or $object->pi like this in phpconstant.php:

```
<html>
   <head>
      <title>
         Using class constants
      </title>
   </head>

   <body>
      <h1>
         Using class constants
      </h1>
      <?php
         class Math
         {
            const pi = 3.14159;
```

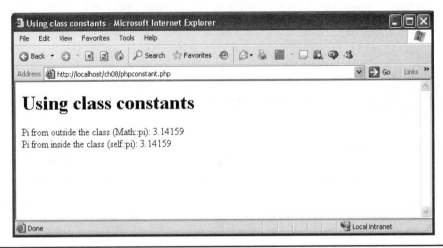

FIGURE 8-11   Using class constants

```
    function display_pi()
    {
       echo 'Pi from inside the class (self::pi): ', self::pi , "<br>";
    }
  }

  echo 'Pi from outside the class (Math::pi): ', Math::pi , "<br>";

  $object = new Math();
  $object->display_pi();

  //Neither of these will work:
  //echo $object::pi;
  //echo $object->pi;
  ?>
 </body>
</html>
```

You can see the results in Figure 8-11, where the value of the constant was indeed displayed.

So class constants are available for use inside the code in a class, and when prefixed with the class name and the scope resolution operator—but that's it.

Using the final Keyword

You may recall that you can override classes like this. In this example from the preceding chapter, the set_name method is being overridden in a new version that capitalizes the name:

```html
<html>
  <head>
    <title>
      Final methods
    </title>
  </head>

  <body>
    <h1>
        Final methods
    </h1>
    <?php
      class Person
      {
        var $name;

        function set_name($data)
        {
          $this->name = $data;
        }

        function get_name()
        {
          return $this->name;
        }
      }

      class Friend extends Person
      {
        var $name;

        function speak()
        {
          echo $this->name, " is speaking<br>";
        }

        function set_name($data)
        {
          $this->name = strtoupper($data);
        }
      }

      echo "Creating your new friend...<BR>";
      $friend = new Friend;
      $friend->set_name("Susan");
      $friend->speak();
      ?>
  </body>
</html>
```

What if you don't want to allow a method to be overridden? You can do that in PHP, as with other OOP-supporting languages, with the final keyword. All you have to do is to use this keyword when declaring a method you want to restrict, like this in the Person base class in phpfinal.php:

```
class Person
{
  var $name;

  final function set_name($data)
  {
    $this->name = $data;
  }

  function get_name()
  {
    return $this->name;
  }
}
```

Marking set_name as final should give us an error; you can see the results in Figure 8-12, where PHP is informing us that you can't override set_name, because it's final. Cool.

TIP *Using the final keyword is a good idea in classes you're going to give to others that they may inherit from, if you don't want any methods to be overridden.*

In fact, you can declare entire classes to be final, which means you can't extend them. Here's the way that looks:

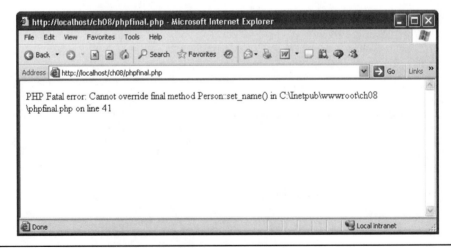

FIGURE 8-12   Disallowing a method override

```html
<html>
  <head>
    <title>
      Final classes
    </title>
  </head>

  <body>
    <h1>
      Final classes
    </h1>
    <?php
      final class Person
      {
        var $name;

        function set_name($data)
        {
          $this->name = $data;
        }

        function get_name()
        {
          return $this->name;
        }
      }

      class Friend extends Person
      {
        var $name;

        function speak()
        {
          echo $this->name, " is speaking<br>";
        }

        function set_name($data)
        {
          $this->name = strtoupper($data);
        }
      }

      echo "Creating your new friend...<BR>";
      $friend = new Friend;
      $friend->set_name("Susan");
      $friend->speak();
    ?>
  </body>
</html>
```

Now that the Person class has been declared final, this code will give you an error, because it attempts to override that class.

Cloning Objects

When you copy over objects, you have to give the process a little thought. You can use the clone keyword to make a copy of an object in PHP:

```
$object_copy = close $object_1;
```

This statement makes a copy of $object_1, $object_copy (if you just used the assignment operator, =, you'd end up with two variable names that pointed at the same object). However, there's an issue here: if $object_1 has some internal properties that themselves contain subobjects, the properties of the cloned object will also point to the same subobjects. And that might not be what you want—you might want the copy of the object to contain new subobjects. You can make that happen by using the __clone method.

Here's an example to make this clear, phpclone.php. You might have a class, BigClass, that contains two LittleClass objects:

```php
<?php
  class BigClass
  {
    public $little_1;
    public $little_2;

    public function __construct()
    {
      $this->little_1 = new LittleClass();
      $this->little_2 = new LittleClass();
    }
        .
        .
        .
    }
  }
?>
```

You can add a __clone method to the BigClass class that will expressly clone $little_1:

```php
<?php
  class BigClass
  {
    public $little_1;
    public $little_2;

    public function __construct()
    {
      $this->little_1 = new LittleClass();
      $this->little_2 = new LittleClass();
    }
```

```php
      function __clone()
      {
        $this->little_1 = clone $this->little_1;
      }
    }
  ?>
```

In LittleClass, you can give each instance a unique number, stored in the $number property, which is incremented each time you create a new LittleClass object:

```php
  <?php
    class LittleClass
    {
      static $counter = 0;
      public $number;

      public function __construct()
      {
          $this->number = ++self::$counter;
      }

      public function __clone() {
        $this->number = ++self::$counter;
      }
    }
  ?>
```

And you can add a __clone method in LittleClass that will increment $number when a LittleClass object is cloned:

```php
  <?php
    class LittleClass
    {
      static $counter = 0;
      public $number;

      public function __construct()
      {
          $this->number = ++self::$counter;
      }

      public function __clone() {
        $this->number = ++self::$counter;
      }
    }
  ?>
```

Now you can create an object of BigClass and then clone it—then take a look at the first object's properties and the clone's property like this:

```html
<html>
  <head>
    <title>
```

```
        Cloning objects
      </title>
   </head>

<body>
   <h1>
       Cloning objects
   </h1>
   <?php
     class BigClass
     {
       public $little_1;
       public $little_2;

       public function __construct()
       {
          $this->little_1 = new LittleClass();
          $this->little_2 = new LittleClass();
        }

        function __clone()
        {
          $this->little_1 = clone $this->little_1;
        }
      }

     class LittleClass
     {
       static $counter = 0;
       public $number;

       public function __construct()
       {
           $this->number = ++self::$counter;
       }

       public function __clone() {
         $this->number = ++self::$counter;
       }
     }

     $object_1 = new BigClass();
     $object_2 = clone $object_1;

     echo "\$object_1: <br>";
     print_r($object_1);

     echo "<br><br>";
     echo "\$object_2: <br>";
     print_r($object_2);

   ?>
   </body>
</html>
```

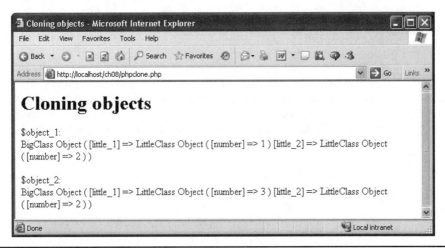

FIGURE 8-13 Cloning objects

You can see the results in Figure 8-13. Note that for $object_1, $little_1's $number = 1, and $little_2's $number = 2. For $object_2, $little_1's $number = 3, while $little_2's $number = 2. That is, $object_1's $little_2 and $object_2's $little_2 point to the same object. On the other hand, because there was a __clone method that handled $little_1 differently, $object_1's $little_1 and $object_2's $little_1 point to the different objects. Very nice.

Reflection

Using reflection in OOP means that you can examine your own code at run time. Here's an example, phpreflection.php, which shows how to get information about a method. The method in this case is named tracker:

```php
<?php
  function tracker()
  {
    static $counter = 10;
    $counter++;
    return $counter;
  }
?>
```

To get information about this method, you can use the ReflectionFunction class:

```php
<?php
  function tracker()
  {
    static $counter = 10;
    $counter++;
    return $counter;
  }
```

```
$method = new ReflectionFunction('tracker');
          .
          .
          .
    ?>
```

Now you can use this new object, $method, to find the name of the method it represents, the lines the method spans in code, what happens when you pass data to the method, what static properties the method has, and more. Here's what it looks like in phpreflection.php:

```html
<html>
  <head>
    <title>
      Reflection
    </title>
  </head>

  <body>
    <h1>
       Reflection
    </h1>
    <?php
      function tracker()
      {
        static $counter = 10;
        $counter++;
        return $counter;
      }

      $method = new ReflectionFunction('tracker');

      echo  "The method named  ", $method->getName();
      echo " is ", $method->isInternal() ? "PHP-defined <br>." :
        "user-defined. <br>";
      echo "It's in ", $method->getFileName(), "<br>";
      echo "It starts at line ", $method->getStartLine();
      echo " and ends at line ",  $method->getEndline(), "<br>";

      if ($method->getStaticVariables()){
        $statics = $method->getStaticVariables();
        echo "It has this static variable: ", var_export($statics, 1), "<br>";
      }

      echo "Invoking the method results in ", var_dump($method->invoke()), "<br>";
    ?>
  </body>
</html>
```

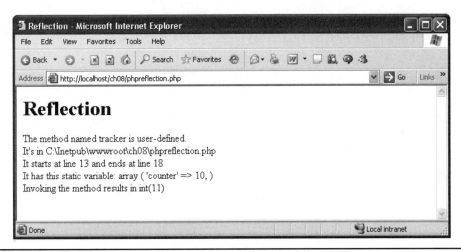

Figure 8-14   Using reflection

You can see the results in Figure 8-14, where, as you see, there's a lot of information about the tracker method.

NOTE *You can also perform reflection on classes, objects, properties, and more.*

File Handling

This chapter discusses file handling using PHP. Storing data on the server is especially powerful in Web applications, because it allows you to make data "persist"—that is, stick around between page accesses. Blogs, guest books, feedback pages—all are possible when you work with files on the server.

There's a lot of PHP technology coming up in this chapter, starting with opening files.

Opening Files Using fopen

To start working with a file in PHP, you must first open that file, as in most languages.

```
$filehandle = fopen (filename, mode [, use_include_path [, zcontext]])
```

In this function call, *filename* is the name of the file you're opening, *mode* indicates how you want to open the file (for example, to read from it or to write to it), *use_include_path* may be set to 1 or TRUE to specify that you want to search for the file in the PHP include path, and *zcontext* holds an optional file context (contexts modify or enhance the behavior of the data streams from and to files). Here are the possible modes:

- **'r'** Open for reading only.
- **'r+'** Open for reading and writing.
- **'w'** Open for writing only and truncate the file to zero length. If the file does not exist, attempt to create it.
- **'w+'** Open for reading and writing and truncate the file to zero length. If the file does not exist, attempt to create it.
- **'a'** Open for appending only. If the file does not exist, attempt to create it.
- **'a+'** Open for reading and writing, starting at the end of the file. If the file does not exist, attempt to create it.
- **'x'** Create and open for writing only. If the file already exists, the fopen call will fail by returning FALSE.
- **'x+'** Create and open for reading and writing. If the file already exists, the fopen call will fail by returning FALSE.

Note that different operating systems have different line-ending conventions. When you write a text file and want to insert a line break, you need to use the correct line-ending character(s) for your operating system. Unix-based systems use \n as the line ending character, Windows-based systems use \r\n as the line ending characters, and Macintosh-based systems use \r as the line ending character.

In Windows, you can use a text-mode translation flag ('t'), which will translate \n to \r\n when working with the file. In contrast, you can also use 'b' to force binary mode, which will not translate your data. To use these flags, specify either 'b' or 't' as the last character of the mode parameter, such as 'wt'.

Currently, the default mode is set to binary for all platforms that distinguish between binary and text mode. If you are having problems with your scripts, try using the 't' flag.

Here's an example, which opens the file /home/file.txt for reading (you can use forward slashes like this in path names even in Windows—you can also use backslashes if you escape them like this: \\):

```
$handle = fopen("/home/file.txt", "r");
```

When you open a file, you get a file handle, which represents an open file. From then on, you use this handle to work with the file. Now that the file has been opened, you can read from it using the various data-reading functions we'll cover in a few pages, such as fread.

This example opens a file for writing to:

```
$handle = fopen("/home/file.txt", "w");
```

This example opens a file for binary writing:

```
$handle = fopen("/home/file.txt", "wb");
```

In Windows, you should be careful to escape any backslashes used in the path to the file (or use forward slashes):

```
$handle = fopen("c:\\data\\file.txt", "r");
```

You're not limited to files in the local file system, either. Here's how you might open a file on a different Web site, as specified by URL:

```
$handle = fopen("http://www.superduperbigco.com/file.txt", "r");
```

You can also open files using the FTP protocol:

```
$handle = fopen("ftp://user:password@superduperbigco.com/file.txt", "w");
```

When you open a file, you get a file handle to work with, and you can pass that file handle to other file functions to work with the file.

Here's an example. Say that you have a file, file.txt, with these contents:

```
Here
is
your
data.
```

You might open this file for reading in phpfopen.php:

```php
<?php
  $handle = fopen("file.txt", "r");
     .
     .
     .
?>
```

If the open operation fails, fopen returns FALSE, so you can check if the file was opened like this in phpfopen.php:

```html
<html>
  <head>
    <title>
      Opening a file
    </title>
  </head>

  <body>
    <h1>
      Opening a file
    </h1>
    <?php
      $handle = fopen("file.txt", "r");
      if($handle){
        echo "File opened OK.";
      }
    ?>
  </body>
</html>
```

You can see the results in Figure 9-1, where the file file.txt was opened successfully.

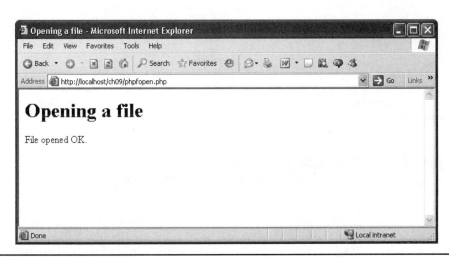

FIGURE 9-1 Opening a file

You can open URLs on the Internet with fopen as well, preparing you to read from Web pages, like this:

```
$handle = fopen("http://www.php.net", "r");
```

Okay, now the file was opened successfully—how do you read the text in it?

Looping over a File's Contents with feof

There are multiple lines in the file you're reading, file.txt, and you're going to see how to read those lines in, a line at a time. How do you loop over all the lines in the file, now that the file has been opened?

You can use a while loop, and the feof function. You pass this function a file handle, and it returns true if you're at the end of the file. So here's how you can loop over the file's contents, line by line in phpread.php:

```
<html>
  <head>
    <title>
      Reading from a file
    </title>
  </head>

  <body>
    <h1>
      Reading from a file
    </h1>
    <?php
      $handle = fopen("file.txt", "r");
      while (!feof($handle)){
            .
            .
            .
      }
    ?>
  </body>
</html>
```

To make this loop active, you have to actually read from the file (otherwise, you'll never reach the end of the file and this loop will never terminate). And you can do that with the fgets function.

Reading Text from a File Using fgets

You can use the fgets function to get a string of text from a file; here's how you use it in general:

```
fgets (handle [, length])
```

You pass this function the file handle corresponding to an open file, and an optional length. The function returns a string of up to length – 1 bytes read from the file corresponding to the file handle. Reading ends when length − 1 bytes have been read, on a newline (which is included in the return value), or on encountering the end of file, whichever comes first. If no length is specified, the length defaults to 1024 bytes.

Here's how you might read a line of text from the file, file.txt, if phpread.php:

```php
<?php
  $handle = fopen("file.txt", "r");
  while (!feof($handle)){
    $text = fgets($handle);
      .


      .


  }
?>
```

And you might echo the text that was read, line by line:

```html
<html>
  <head>
    <title>
      Reading from a file
    </title>
  </head>

  <body>
    <h1>
      Reading from a file
    </h1>
    <?php
      $handle = fopen("file.txt", "r");
      while (!feof($handle)){
        $text = fgets($handle);
        echo $text, "<br>";
      }
    ?>
  </body>
</html>
```

That opens the file and reads from it. There's one more step to take to complete the file-reading operation—closing the file.

Closing a File

When you're done with a file, you should close it in PHP. Closing the file frees up the resources connected with that file, and avoids conflicts later in your code in case you recycle file handle variables.

To close a file, you use fclose like this:

```php
fclose($filehandle);
```

This function returns TRUE if the file was closed successfully, and FALSE otherwise.

Here's how to put fclose to work in phpread.php:

```
<html>
  <head>
    <title>
      Reading from a file
    </title>
  </head>

  <body>
    <h1>
       Reading from a file
    </h1>
    <?php
      $handle = fopen("file.txt", "r");
      while (!feof($handle)){
        $text = fgets($handle);
        echo $text, "<BR>";
      }
      fclose($handle);
    ?>
  </body>
</html>
```

You can see the results in Figure 9-2, where the file file.txt was opened successfully, read from, and then closed.

That's one way of reading text—line by line. So how about character by character? Coming up next.

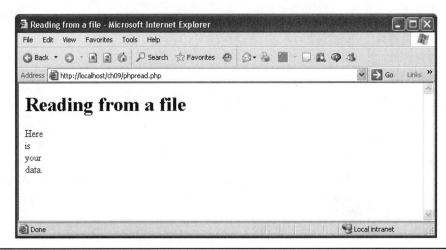

FIGURE 9-2   Reading from a file

Reading from a File Character by Character with fgetc

You can read individual characters from a text file using the fgetc function:

```
fgetc($filehandle);
```

This function returns the character read. It's a useful function for precision control over reading operations.

Here's an example, phpfgetc.php. You start by opening the file to read from, file.txt:

```php
<?php
    $handle = fopen("file.txt", "r");
    .
    .
    .
?>
```

You can read an individual character from file.txt like this:

```php
<?php
    $handle = fopen("file.txt", "r");

    $char = fgetc($handle)
    .
    .
    .
    }
?>
```

To loop over all the characters in the file, you can put the preceding statement in the condition of a while loop—when fgetc returns FALSE, there are no more characters to read:

```php
<?php
    $handle = fopen("file.txt", "r");

    while ($char = fgetc($handle)) {
    .
    .
    .
    }
?>
```

And you can echo each character as you read it:

```php
<?php
    $handle = fopen("file.txt", "r");

    while ($char = fgetc($handle)) {

        echo "$char";

    }
?>
```

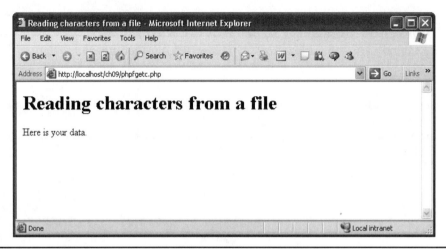

Figure 9-3   Reading characters from a file

You can see the results in Figure 9-3, where the file file.txt was opened and then read from, character by character.

That's fine as far as it goes, but what about newline characters? The file, file.txt, has these contents:

```
Here
is
your
data.
```

But as you can see in Figure 9-4, the newline characters from the file were simply sent to the browser, which doesn't display newline characters—you have to convert them to <br> elements instead. That looks like this in code:

```php
<?php
  $handle = fopen("file.txt", "r");

  while ($char = fgetc($handle)) {
    if($char == "\n"){
      $char = "<br>";
    }

    echo "$char";
  }
?>
```

All that's left is to close the file with fclose in phpfgetc.php:

```
<html>
  <head>
    <title>
      Reading characters from a file
    </title>
  </head>

  <body>
    <h1>
      Reading characters from a file
    </h1>
      <?php
        $handle = fopen("file.txt", "r");

        while ($char = fgetc($handle)) {
          if($char == "\n"){
            $char = "<br>";
          }
          echo "$char";
        }

        fclose($handle);
      ?>
  </body>
</html>
```

You can see the results in Figure 9-4, where the file file.txt was opened, read from character by character—including proper newline handling—and then closed.

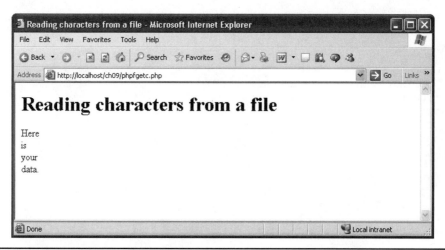

FIGURE 9-4   Reading characters from a file and handling newlines

Reading a Whole File at Once with file_get_contents

You can read the entire contents of a file with the file_get_contents function:

```
file_get_contents (filename [, use_include_path [, context [, offset [, maxlen]]]]
)
```

Here, *filename* is the name of the file, *use_include_path* is set to TRUE if you want to search PHP's include path, *context* is a context for the operation, *offset* is the offset into the file at which to start reading, and *maxlen* is the maximum length of data to read.

Here's an example, phpfilegetcontents.php. This example starts by reading the entire contents of the file file.txt into the variable $text:

```
<?php
  $text = file_get_contents("file.txt");
  .
  .
  .
?>
```

Then the code converts all newlines into <br> elements using the PHP function str_replace:

```
<?php
  $text = file_get_contents("file.txt");

  $fixed_text = str_replace("\n", "<br>", $text);
  .
  .
  .
?>
```

Finally, the converted text is echoed to the browser this way in phpfilegetcontents.php:

```
<html>
  <head>
    <title>
      Reading a whole file at once
    </title>
  </head>

  <body>
    <h1>
      Reading a whole file at once
    </h1>
    <?php
      $text = file_get_contents("file.txt");

      $fixed_text = str_replace("\n", "<br>", $text);
```

```
       echo $fixed_text;
     ?>
  </body>
</html>
```

You can see the results in Figure 9-5, where the file file.txt was opened, read from entirely, and then displayed.

Want to read a Web page all at once? Just open it up and read it, as here, where we're reading the PHP home page:

```
<html>
  <head>
    <title>
      Reading a whole file at once
    </title>
  </head>

  <body>
    <h1>
      Reading a whole file at once
    </h1>
      <?php
        $text = file_get_contents("http://www.php.net");

        $fixed_text = str_replace("\n", "<br>", $text);

        echo $fixed_text;
      ?>
  </body>
</html>
```

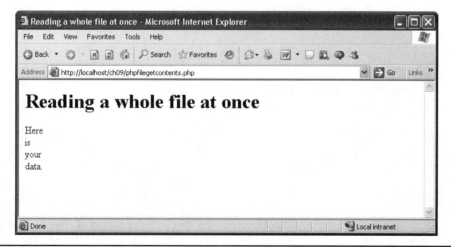

FIGURE 9-5   Reading a file all at once

Reading a File into an Array with file

You can use the file function to read a file into an array all at once; each line becomes an element in the array. Here's how to use the file function:

```
file (filename [, use_include_path [, context]] )
```

In this case, *filename* is the name of the file you want to read, *use_include_path* should be set to TRUE if you want to search the PHP include path for the file, and *context* is a context for the operation. This function returns an array or FALSE if the operation failed.

This function is extremely useful if you want to write your own database files. For example, suppose you wanted to keep students' scores in a database file—and you could read all those scores into an array with a single statement.

Here's an example, phpfarray.php, which reads file.txt into an array, $data. First, you can load the contents of that file into the array:

```
<?php
  $data = file('file.txt');
  .
  .
  .
?>
```

That's it—now you've been able to read an entire file into the $data array. Now each line in file.txt is an element in the $data array.

You can display the data now in the array with a foreach loop:

```
<?php
  $data = file('file.txt');

  foreach ($data as $line) {
    .
    .
    .
  }
?>
```

And all you've got to do is to display each line:

```
<?php
  $data = file('file.txt');

  foreach ($data as $line) {
    echo $line , "<br>";
  }
?>
```

In fact, you can do more than that—you can also display line numbers. Here's how that works in phpfarray.php:

```
<html>
  <head>
    <title>
      Reading a file into an array
    </title>
  </head>

  <body>
    <h1>
      Reading a file into an array
    </h1>
      <?php
        $data = file('file.txt');

        foreach ($data as $number => $line) {
            echo "Line $number: " , $line , "<br>";
        }
      ?>
  </body>
</html>
```

And you can see the result in Figure 9-6, where the entire file, file.txt, was read into an array and displayed.

You can also open Web pages and read them into arrays using the file function. Here's an example, phpurlarray.php, which reads http://www.php.net in and displays it:

```
<html>
  <head>
    <title>
      Reading a Web page into an array
    </title>
  </head>
```

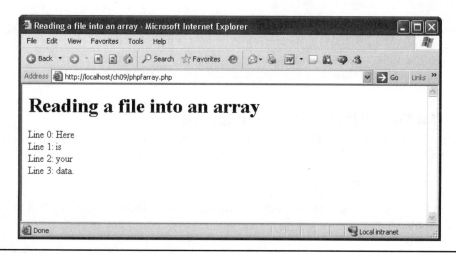

FIGURE 9-6   Reading a file into an array

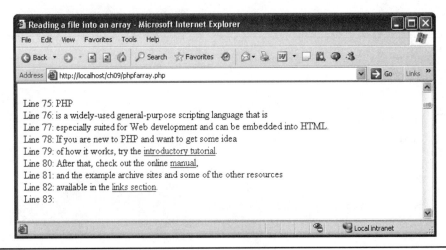

FIGURE 9-7   Reading an URL into an array

```
<body>
  <h1>
     Reading a Web page into an array
  </h1>
    <?php
      $data = file('http://www.php.net');

      foreach ($data as $number => $line) {
        echo "Line $number: " , $line , "<br>";
      }
    ?>
  </body>
</html>
```

You can see part of the result in Figure 9-7, where the URL was read in and its HTML displayed, line by line.

Here's one thing to note: each element in the array still has a newline character at the end of it. If you want to get rid of that newline character, you can use the rtrim PHP function.

Checking if a File Exists with file_exists

If you try working with a file that doesn't exist, you'll get an error. To prevent that, you can check if a file exists with the file_exists function:

```
file_exists (filename )
```

You pass this function a filename (which can include a path), and it returns TRUE if the file exists, FALSE otherwise.

Here's an example, phpfileexists.php. This example checks on a nonexistent file, does_
not_exist.txt:

```
<?php
  $filename = "does_not_exist.txt";
      .
      .
      .
  ?>
```

The code then checks if the file exists:

```
<?php
  $filename = "does_not_exist.txt";

  if (file_exists($filename)) {
      .
      .
      .
  }
      .
      .
      .
  ?>
```

If the file exists, you can read it in and display its contents:

```
<?php
  $filename = "does_not_exist.txt";

  if (file_exists($filename)) {
    $data = file($filename);

    foreach ($data as $number => $line) {
      echo "Line $number: " , $line , "<br>";
    }
  }
      .
      .
      .
  ?>
```

If the file doesn't exist, you can display a message to that effect—which beats an error
message from PHP:

```
<html>
  <head>
    <title>
      Checking if a file exists
    </title>
  </head>
```

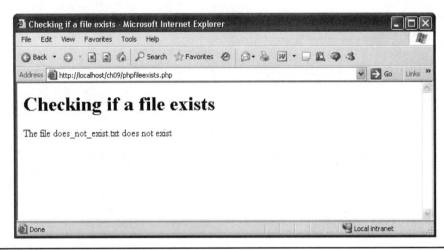

FIGURE 9-8 Checking if a file exists

```
<body>
  <h1>
     Checking if a file exists
  </h1>
    <?php
      $filename = "does_not_exist.txt";

      if (file_exists($filename)) {
        $data = file($filename);

        foreach ($data as $number => $line) {
          echo "Line $number: " , $line , "<br>";
        }
      }
      else {
        echo "The file $filename does not exist";
      }
    ?>
  </body>
</html>
```

You can see the result in Figure 9-8, where this example determined that the file didn't exist before trying to open it, and so didn't generate an error.

Getting File Size with filesize

You can get a file's size returned by the filesize function, returned as an integer:

```
filesize (filename )
```

You just pass the filename (including path if you want to add that) to filesize and you'll get an integer back or FALSE if the file doesn't exist.

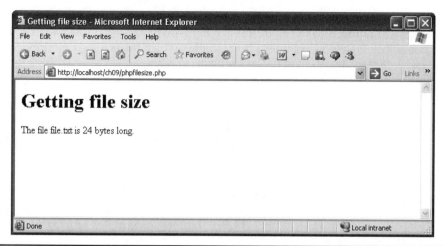

FIGURE 9-9   Reading a URL into an array

Here's an example, phpfilesize.php, which displays the size of file.txt:

```
<html>
  <head>
    <title>
      Getting file size
    </title>
  </head>

  <body>
    <h1>
      Getting file size
    </h1>
      <?php
        echo "The file file.txt is ", filesize("file.txt"), " bytes long.";
      ?>
  </body>
</html>
```

You can see the result in Figure 9-9, where this example determined the file was 24 bytes long.

You've seen a lot about how to handle text files—how about binary files?

Reading Binary Reads with fread

So far, the files you've seen here have been handled as text files, but it's simple to handle files in a binary way as well using functions like fread:

```
fread (handle, length)
```

This function reads up to *length* bytes from the file referenced by *handle*. Reading stops when *length* bytes have been read, of the EOF (end of file) is reached.

On systems like Windows, you should open files for binary reading, mode 'rb', to work with fread. Since adding 'b' to the mode does no harm on other systems, we'll include it here for portability. Here's an example, phpfread.php, which treats file.txt as a binary file. This example starts by opening file.txt for binary reading:

```php
<?php
  $handle = fopen("file.txt", "rb");
  .
  .
  .
?>
```

You can use filesize to determine the file's size, and read it all into a variable, $text, using fread:

```php
<?php
  $handle = fopen("file.txt", "rb");

  $text = fread($handle, filesize("file.txt"));
  .
  .
  .
?>
```

Now you can replace newlines with <br> elements:

```php
<?php
  $handle = fopen("file.txt", "rb");

  $text = fread($handle, filesize("file.txt"));

  $fixed_text = str_replace("\n", "<br>", $text);
  .
  .
  .
?>
```

And you can echo $text, forcing PHP to treat it as text:

```php
<?php
  $handle = fopen("file.txt", "rb");

  $text = fread($handle, filesize("file.txt"));

  $fixed_text = str_replace("\n", "<br>", $text);

  echo $fixed_text;
  .
  .
  .
?>
```

All that remains is to close the file, as you see in phpfread.php:

```
<html>
  <head>
    <title>
      Reading binary data
    </title>
  </head>

  <body>
    <h1>
      Reading binary data
    </h1>
      <?php
        $handle = fopen("file.txt", "rb");

        $text = fread($handle, filesize("file.txt"));

        $fixed_text = str_replace("\n", "<br>", $text);

        echo $fixed_text;

        fclose($handle);
      ?>
  </body>
</html>
```

You can see the result in Figure 9-10, where this example read file.txt in using a binary read operation.

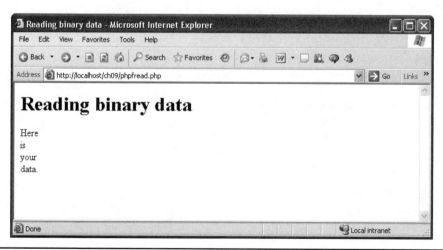

FIGURE 9-10   Reading binary data

Parsing Files with fscanf

You can also parse files with the fscanf function:

```
fscanf (handle, format)
```

This function takes a file handle, and a format string of the same type you'd use with sprintf.

Here's an example, phpfscaf.php, which reads this file, actors.txt, where the actors' first and last names are separated by tabs:

```
Cary    Grant
Myrna   Loy
Jimmy   Stewart
June    Allyson
```

You start this example by opening actors.txt:

```php
<?php
  $handle = fopen("actors.txt", "r");
   .
   .
   .
?>
```

The format in this case is "%s\t%s\n" (string, tab, string, newline character), so here's how you read and parse a line of data from a file into an array named $name in a while loop:

```php
<?php
  $handle = fopen("actors.txt", "r");

  while ($name = fscanf($handle, "%s\t%s\n")) {
    .
    .
    .
  }
?>
```

Next, you assign the values in the $name array to the variables $firstname and $lastname, and then display those names:

```html
<html>
  <head>
    <title>
      Parsing files
    </title>
  </head>

  <body>
    <h1>
      Parsing files
    </h1>
      <?php
        $handle = fopen("actors.txt", "r");
```

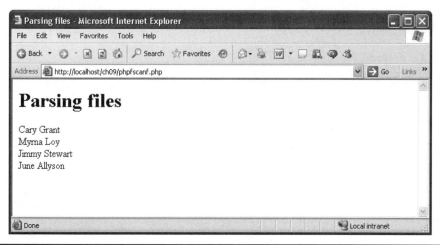

FIGURE 9-11   Parsing file data

```
    while ($name = fscanf($handle, "%s\t%s\n")) {
      list ($firstname, $lastname) = $name;
      echo $firstname, " ", $lastname, "<br>";
    }

    fclose($handle);
  ?>
 </body>
</html>
```

You can see the result in Figure 9-11, where the file actors.txt was parsed and the data in it displayed.

Parsing ini Files with parse_ini_file

Much like fscanf, parse_ini_file lets you parse files—in this case, .ini initialization files. Here's how you use parse_ini_file:

```
parse_ini_file (filename [, process_sections] )
```

This function loads in the ini file *filename* and returns the settings in it in an associative array. By setting the last process_sections parameter to TRUE, you get a multidimensional array, with the section names and settings included. The default for process_sections is FALSE.

Note that this function is not for use with the initialization file that PHP itself uses—php.ini. That file is parsed and read before PHP even starts.

CAUTION   *There are reserved words that must not be used as keys for ini files. These include: null, yes, no, true, and false. Values null, no, and false results in "", yes and true results in "1". Characters {}|&~![()" must not be used anywhere in the key.*

For example, here's a sample .ini file, sample.ini (note that you can start comments with semicolons in .ini files):

```
; This is a sample .ini file

[first_section]
first_color = red
second_color = white
third_color = blue

[second_section]
file = "/usr/local/code.data"
URL = "http://www.php.net"
```

Here's an example showing how to read sample.ini, phpparseinifile.php. You can read the contents of sample.ini into an array, $array:

```php
<?php
    $array = parse_ini_file("sample.ini");
        .
        .
        .
?>
```

Now you can recover the values in the .ini file using the $array array. For example, you can recover the value under the key first_color (which is "red") like this: $array["first_color"]. In this example, you can loop over the array, displaying the keys and their values:

```html
<html>
  <head>
    <title>
      Parsing .ini files
    </title>
  </head>

  <body>
    <h1>
      Parsing .ini files
    </h1>
      <?php
        $array = parse_ini_file("sample.ini");

        foreach ($array as $key => $value) {
          echo "$key => $value <br>";
        }
      ?>
  </body>
</html>
```

You can see the result in Figure 9-12, where the data in sample.ini was read in and displayed.

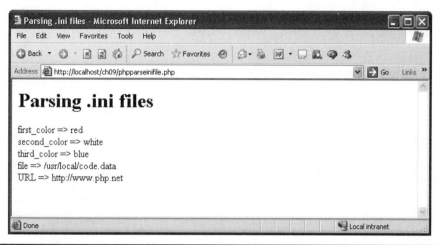

FIGURE 9-12   Parsing an .ini file

Getting File Info with stat

The stat function gives you information about a file:

```
stat (filename )
```

The function returns an array containing information that mostly makes sense on Unix machines. Here is the data stored in the returned array with these numerical indexes (you can also use the text keys given here in parentheses):

- **0 (dev)**   Device number
- **1 (ino)**   Inode number
- **2 (mode)**   Inode protection mode
- **3 (nlink)**   Number of links
- **4 (uid)**   Userid of owner
- **5 (gid)**   Groupid of owner
- **6 (rdev)**   Device type, if inode device
- **7 (size)**   Size in bytes
- **8 (atime)**   Time of last access (Unix timestamp)
- **9 (mtime)**   Time of last modification (Unix timestamp)
- **10 (ctime)**   Time of last inode change (Unix timestamp)
- **11 (blksize)**   Blocksize of filesystem I/O
- **12 (blocks)**   Number of blocks allocated

Most of these items only have meaning in Unix; if there are no counterparts in Windows, you'll get a value of -1.

Here's an example putting this to work, phpstat.php, which reports the size of the file file.txt. This example begins by using stat on file.txt:

```php
<?php
  $array = stat("file.txt");
  .
  .
  .
?>
```

And you can find the file file.txt size and display it this way:

```html
<html>
  <head>
    <title>
      Using stat
    </title>
  </head>

  <body>
    <h1>
       Using stat
    </h1>
      <?php
        $array = stat("file.txt");

        echo "The file is ", $array["size"]. " bytes long.";
      ?>
  </body>
</html>
```

You can see the result in Figure 9-13, where the file's size appears.

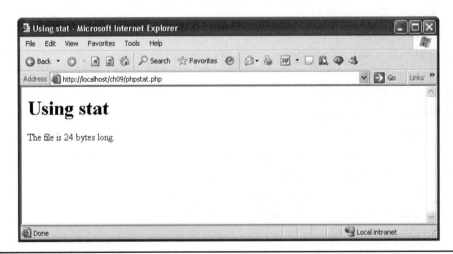

FIGURE 9-13   Finding a file's size

Setting the File Pointer's Location with fseek

PHP uses file pointers to keep track of where it is in a file, and where the next read or write operation occurs from. For example, when you open a file, the file pointer is set to the beginning of the file; when you open a file for appending, the file pointer is set the end of the file. You can use fseek to set the file pointer yourself:

```
fseek(handle, offset, [start_point]);
```

Here, *handle* is the handle of the file to set the file pointer in, *offset* is the number of bytes you want to set the pointer to, and *start_point* indicates a starting point for the pointer, which is one of these constants:

- **SEEK_SET**   The beginning of the file
- **SEEK_CUR**   The current pointer location
- **SEEK_END**   The end of the file

You can set the offset to negative values.

Copying Files with copy

You can copy files with the copy function:

```
copy (source, destination)
```

Here, *source* is the name of the source file, and *destination* is the name of the copy (including pathnames, if applicable). This function returns TRUE if it was successful, FALSE otherwise.

Here's an example, phpcopy.php. This example is going to make a copy of file.txt, copy.txt:

```
<?php
  $file = 'file.txt';
  $copy = 'copy.txt';
  .
  .
  .
?>
```

Here's where we try to make the copy, and report success if it worked:

```
<?php
  $file = 'file.txt';
  $copy = 'copy.txt';

  if (copy($file, $copy)) {
    echo "Copied $file.";
  }
  .
  .
  .
?>
```

If the copy operation failed, we can report that failure this way in phpcopy.php:

```
<html>
  <head>
    <title>
      Copying files
    </title>
  </head>

  <body>
    <h1>
        Copying files
    </h1>
      <?php
        $file = 'file.txt';
        $copy = 'copy.txt';

        if (copy($file, $copy)) {
          echo "Copied $file.";
        }
        else {
          echo "Could not copy $file.";
        }
      ?>
  </body>
</html>
```

You can see the result in Figure 9-14, where the file was copied, as planned.

NOTE *If you just want to move a file, use the rename function instead.*

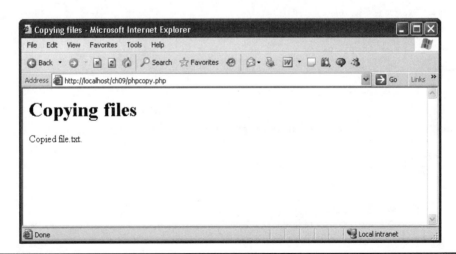

FIGURE 9-14 Copying files

Deleting Files with unlink

Want to delete a file? You can do that with the unlink function:

```
unlink (filename [, context] )
```

Here, *filename* is the name of the file, and *context* is an optional context. This function returns
TRUE if the file was deleted, FALSE otherwise.

You can find an example in phpunlink.php. If the code is successful in deleting copy.txt,
it says so:

```php
<?php
  if(unlink("copy.txt")){
    echo "Deleted the file.";
  }
  .
  .
  .
?>
```

And if the file couldn't be deleted, this example, phpunlink.php, also indicates that:

```
<html>
  <head>
    <title>
      Deleting files
    </title>
  </head>

  <body>
    <h1>
      Deleting files
    </h1>
      <?php
        if(unlink("copy.txt")){
          echo "Deleted the file.";
        }
        else {
          echo "Could not delete the file.";
        }
      ?>
  </body>
</html>
```

You can see the result in Figure 9-15, where the file was deleted.

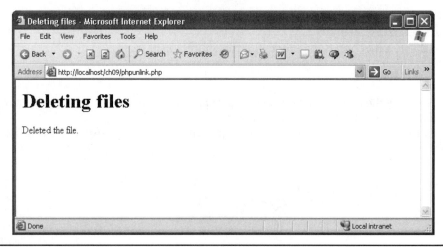

FIGURE 9-15 Deleting a file

Writing to a File with fwrite

What if you wanted to write a string to a file? You could use fwrite:

```
fwrite (handle, string [, length])
```

You pass fwrite a file handle, the string to write, and, optionally, the maximum length of data to write. This function returns the number of bytes written, or FALSE if there was an error.

Note that to set up your system to write files may take a little work, because of the file system protections involved. For example, in Windows, you have to right-click the folder where you want to write files, select Properties, click the Web Sharing tab, select the Share The Folder radio button, and enable writing. In Unix, make sure you have writing privileges in the folder you're writing to.

Here's an example, phpfwrite.php, which will write text to a file, data.txt. You start by opening the file for writing:

```
<?php
  $handle = fopen("data.txt", "w");
  .
  .
  .
?>
```

Then you can create the text string to write to the file, $text. Note that if you want multiline text, you're responsible for adding the newline characters yourself:

```
<?php
  $handle = fopen("data.txt", "w");
```

```
    $text = "Here\nis\nthe\ntext.";
    .
    .
    .
  ?>
```

Time to write the file with fwrite:

```php
<?php
  $handle = fopen("data.txt", "w");

  $text = "Here\nis\nthe\ntext.";

  fwrite($handle, $text);
?>
```

To make this better, you can check whether the write operation failed, like this in phpfwrite.php:

```php
<?php
  $handle = fopen("data.txt", "w");

  $text = "Here\nis\nthe\ntext.";

  if (fwrite($handle, $text) == FALSE) {
    echo "Can not write data.txt.";
  }
?>
```

If the operation was successful, you can indicate that to the user like this:

```html
<html>
  <head>
    <title>
      Writing files
    </title>
  </head>
  <body>
    <h1>
      Writing files
    </h1>

    <?php
      $handle = fopen("data.txt", "w");

      $text = "Here\nis\nthe\ntext.";

      if (fwrite($handle, $text) == FALSE) {
        echo "Can not write data.txt.";
      }
      else {
        echo "Created data.txt.";
      }
```

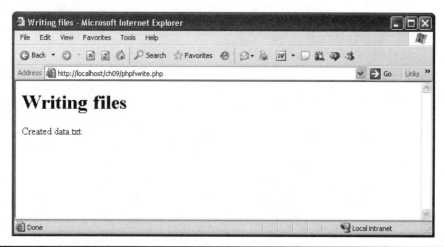

FIGURE 9-16   Writing a file

```
    fclose($handle);
  ?>
 </body>
</html>
```

You can see the result in Figure 9-16, where the file was written. Nice.
Here's the contents of data.txt:

```
Here
is
the
text.
```

TIP *Want to check if a file is writable before trying to write to it? Call is_writable, passing it the filename; this function will return TRUE if you can write to the file, FALSE otherwise.*

Reading and Writing Binary Files

You can write binary data with fwrite, and read it with fread, but it takes a little work. You can pack binary data into strings using the pack function, and unpack binary data using the unpack function.

Here's an example, phpwritebinary.php, that writes the number 512 to a file in binary (not string) format. If starts by opening the file for binary writing like this:

```
<?php
  $number = 512;
  $handle = fopen ("data.dat", "wb");
      .
      .
      .
  ?>
```

Next, it packs the data into long integer format like this:

```
pack ("L", $number);
```

Here are the formats for the pack function, such as "L" for long integer:

- **a**   NUL-padded string
- **A**   SPACE-padded string
- **h**   Hex string, low nibble first
- **H**   Hex string, high nibble first
- **c**   Signed char
- **C**   Unsigned char
- **s**   Signed short (always 16 bit, machine byte order)
- **S**   Unsigned short (always 16 bit, machine byte order)
- **n**   Unsigned short (always 16 bit, big endian byte order)
- **v**   Unsigned short (always 16 bit, little endian byte order)
- **i**   Signed integer (machine-dependent size and byte order)
- **I**   Unsigned integer (machine-dependent size and byte order)
- **l**   Signed long (always 32 bit, machine byte order)
- **L**   Unsigned long (always 32 bit, machine byte order)
- **N**   Unsigned long (always 32 bit, big endian byte order)
- **V**   Unsigned long (always 32 bit, little endian byte order)
- **f**   Float (machine-dependent size and representation)
- **d**   Double (machine-dependent size and representation)
- **x**   NUL byte
- **X**   Back up one byte
- **@**   NUL-fill to absolute position

Here's how this example writes this data to file:

```php
<?php
  $number = 512;
  $handle = fopen ("data.dat", "wb");
  if (fwrite ($handle, pack ("L", $number)) == FALSE) {

    .
    .
    .

  }
?>
```

And finally, this code indicates success or failure to the user like this in phpwritebinary.php:

```
<html>
  <head>
    <title>
      Writing binary files
    </title>
  </head>
  <body>
    <h1>
      Writing binary files
    </h1>

    <?php
      $number = 512;
      $handle = fopen ("data.dat", "wb");
      if (fwrite ($handle, pack ("L", $number)) == FALSE) {
        echo "Can not write data.dat.";
      }
      else {
        echo "Created data.dat. and stored $number.";
      }

      fclose ($handle);
    ?>
  </body>
</html>
```

You can see the result in Figure 9-17, where the binary file was written to.

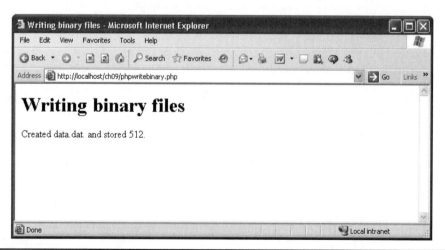

FIGURE 9-17   Writing a binary file

To read the binary data from the file, you can use the unpack function in phpbinaryread .php. First, you open the file for binary reading:

```php
<?php
  $handle = fopen ("data.dat", "rb");
     .
     .
     .
?>
```

Then use fread to read the binary data, indicating that you want four bytes (the length of a long integer):

```php
<?php
  $handle = fopen ("data.dat", "rb");
  $data = fread ($handle, 4);
     .
     .
     .
?>
```

Then you can use unpack to unpack the data into an array with an element under the index "data" containing a long value:

```php
<?php
  $handle = fopen ("data.dat", "rb");
  $data = fread ($handle, 4);
  $array = unpack ("Ldata", $data);
     .
     .
     .
?>
```

Now you can recover the binary data from the array using the key "data":

```php
<?php
  $handle = fopen ("data.dat", "rb");
  $data = fread ($handle, 4);
  $array = unpack ("Ldata", $data);
  $data = $array["data"];
     .
     .
     .
?>
```

All that remains is to display that data, in phpbinaryread.php:

```html
<html>
  <head>
    <title>
      Reading binary files
    </title>
  </head>
```

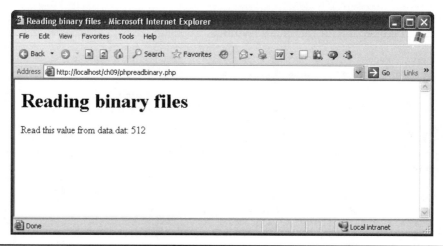

FIGURE 9-18 Reading from a binary file

```
<body>
  <h1>
    Reading binary files
  </h1>

  <?php
    $handle = fopen ("data.dat", "rb");
    $data = fread ($handle, 4);
    $array = unpack ("Ldata", $data);
    $data = $array["data"];
    echo "Read this value from data.dat: ", $data;
  ?>
  </body>
</html>
```

You can see the result in Figure 9-18, where the binary data was read from the file data. dat successfully.

Appending to Files with fwrite

You can also append data to files using fwrite if you open the file for appending explicitly. Here's an example, phpappend.php, which will append some text to the file data.txt. It starts by opening data.txt for appending:

```
<?php
  $handle = fopen("data.txt", "a");
     .
     .
     .
?>
```

And you put together the text to append to the file, which is

```
Here
is
more
text.
```

You can put this text into a variable, $text:

```php
<?php
    $handle = fopen("data.txt", "a");

    $text = "\nHere\nis\nmore\ntext.";
        .
        .
        .
?>
```

Now you use fwrite to append to data.txt—and let the user know if the operation failed:

```php
<?php
    $handle = fopen("data.txt", "a");

    $text = "\nHere\nis\nmore\ntext.";

    if (fwrite($handle, $text) == FALSE) {
        echo "Can not append to data.txt.";
    }
        .
        .
        .
?>
```

On the other hand, if the append operation was successful, you can let the user know that like this in phpappend.php:

```php
<html>
    <head>
        <title>
            Appending to files
        </title>
    </head>
    <body>
        <h1>
            Appending to files
        </h1>

    <?php
        $handle = fopen("data.txt", "a");

        $text = "\nHere\nis\nmore\ntext.";
```

```
      if (fwrite($handle, $text) == FALSE) {
        echo "Can not append to data.txt.";
      }
      else {
        echo "Appended to data.txt.";
      }

      fclose($handle);
    ?>
  </body>
</html>
```

You can see the result in Figure 9-19, where the file was appended to.
Here are the new contents of data.txt:

```
Here
is
the
text.
Here
is
more
text.
```

Cool.

TIP *Want to do the opposite, and truncate a file? Use ftruncate, specifying the new size of the file:*

```
ftruncate (handle, size)
```

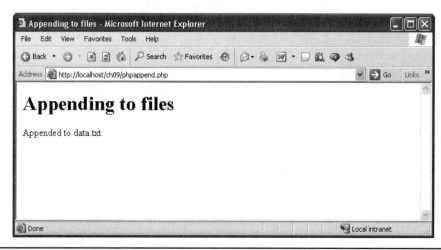

FIGURE 9-19   Appending to a file

Writing a File All at Once with file_put_contents

There's a shortcut if you want to write text to a file—use the file_put_contents function. This function writes a string to a file, and here's how you use it in general:

```
file_put_contents (filename, data [, flags [, context]])
```

In this case, *filename* is the name of the file you want to write, *data* is the string text to write, *flags* can be either FILE_USE_INCLUDE_PATH and/or FILE_APPEND, and *context* is a file context. The function returns the number of bytes that were written to the file, or FALSE if it couldn't write to the file.

Using this function is much the same as calling fopen, fwrite, and fclose automatically—you don't have to open or close the file yourself, and you don't need a file handle. Here's an example, phpfileputcontents.php. You start with the text to write to the file:

```php
<?php
  $text = "Here\nis\nthe\ntext.";
    .
    .
    .
?>
```

Next, you can use file_put_contents to write to the file data.txt:

```php
<?php
  $text = "Here\nis\nthe\ntext.";

  file_put_contents("data.txt", $text);
    .
    .
    .
?>
```

You can improve on this as you've seen before by checking the return value from the function. If there was a problem, you can let the user know:

```php
<?php
  $text = "Here\nis\nthe\ntext.";

  if (file_put_contents("data.txt", $text) == FALSE) {
    echo "Can not write data.txt.";
  }
    .
    .
    .
?>
```

Otherwise, you can let the user know that the operation was a success like this in phpfileputcontents.php:

```
<html>
  <head>
    <title>
      Writing files with file_put_contents
    </title>
  </head>
  <body>
    <h1>
      Writing files with file_put_contents
    </h1>

    <?php
      $text = "Here\nis\nthe\ntext.";

      if (file_put_contents("data.txt", $text) == FALSE) {
        echo "Can not write data.txt.";
      }
      else {
        echo "Wrote to data.txt.";
      }
    ?>
  </body>
</html>
```

Note that you don't need to close the file (or open it, for that matter). You can see the result in Figure 9-20, where the file was created.

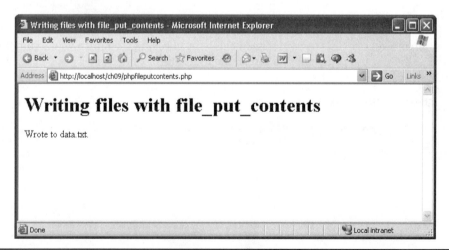

FIGURE 9-20   Writing a file with file_put_contents

Locking Files

In a multiuser environment, such as a Web server, multiple users may be accessing your scripts at the same time—which means multiple copies of the same script can operate at the same time. If your script(s) accesses files, there may be a conflict as two scripts, or two copies of the same script, tries to write to the same file at the same time. To fix that, use the file locking function, flock:

```
flock (handle, operation [, &wouldblock] )
```

Here, *handle* is the handle of the file you want to lock, and *operation* is one of these:

- To acquire a shared lock (reader), set operation to LOCK_SH.
- To acquire an exclusive lock (writer), set operation to LOCK_EX.
- To release a lock (shared or exclusive), set operation to LOCK_UN.

And the optional third argument is set to TRUE if the lock would block.

This function returns TRUE if it got a lock, FALSE otherwise.

You get a lock on files in an advisory way—all your file-accessing code must see if it can get a lock on a file before accessing that file. If your code can't get a lock on a file, some other code is using the file, and your present code should wait. Locks are advisory (except under Windows, where they are mandatory), which means that other code can work with locked files—and possibly mess things up—so you must be sure to try to get a lock before writing to a file. When you're done, unlock the file, giving other code access to it.

The flock function normally blocks (that is, doesn't return) until a lock can be secured. If you don't want to wait—and possibly hang your code—OR the constant LOCK_NB to the operation, such as: LOCK_EX | LOCK_NB. That will make the flock function return immediately, and if you didn't get a lock, you can wait a second (with the PHP sleep function like this: sleep(1), which makes the code pause for a second) and try again, timing out after, say, fifteen attempts.

Here's an example, phpflock.php, which locks the file data.txt before writing to it. You can open the file and attempt to get a lock like this:

```php
<?php
    $handle = fopen("data.txt", "w");

    $text = "Here\nis\nthe\ntext.";

    if (flock($handle, LOCK_EX | LOCK_NB)) {
        .
        .
        .
    }
?>
```

If you got the lock, you can write to the file and then unlock it:

```php
<?php
    $handle = fopen("data.txt", "w");
```

```
    $text = "Here\nis\nthe\ntext.";

    if (flock($handle, LOCK_EX | LOCK_NB)) {
      echo "Locked the file. <br>";
      if (fwrite($handle, $text) == FALSE) {
        echo "Can not write data.txt. <br>";
      }
      else {
        echo "Created data.txt. <br>";
      }
      flock($handle, LOCK_UN);
      echo "Unlocked the file. <br>";
    }
  ?>
```

This code only tries to lock the file once, and immediately shows an error if it can't, but you could loop over fifteen or twenty seconds, trying continuously to lock the file until you gave up.

If you couldn't get the lock, other code is using the file, and you should let the user know like this in phpflock.php:

```
<html>
  <head>
    <title>
      Locking and unlocking files
    </title>
  </head>
  <body>
    <h1>
      Locking and unlocking files
    </h1>

    <?php
      $handle = fopen("data.txt", "w");

      $text = "Here\nis\nthe\ntext.";

      if (flock($handle, LOCK_EX | LOCK_NB)) {
        echo "Locked the file. <br>";
        if (fwrite($handle, $text) == FALSE) {
          echo "Can not write data.txt. <br>";
        }
        else {
          echo "Created data.txt. <br>";
        }
        flock($handle, LOCK_UN);
        echo "Unlocked the file. <br>";
      }
      else {
        echo "Could not lock the file. <br>";
      }
```

```
    fclose($handle);
  ?>
  </body>
</html>
```

That's it; you can see the result in Figure 9-21, where the file was locked, written to, and unlocked. Very cool.

Just bear in mind that if you can't get a lock on a file, most likely some other code is using that file, and you should try again later.

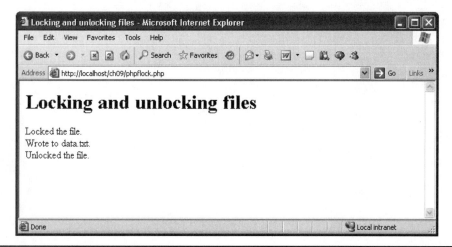

FIGURE 9-21   Locking and writing to a file

10

CHAPTER

Working with Databases

Connecting PHP to databases on the server is a natural, and this chapter discusses that connection. You're going to see how to connect PHP to database tables and the like in this chapter, updating data as you want in that database.

PHP comes with a lot of support for databases built in, and that's good, because one of the most popular ways to work with PHP is to handle databases on the server. You can see the databases that PHP supports in Table 10-1.

If you want to use the built-in PHP support for the various database servers in Table 10-1, you can find the manuals for them at www.php.net/*dbname*, where *dbname* is the database name, like mysql, sybase, mssql, and so on. For ODBC, use the name uodbc; for Oracle, oci8.

By far, the most frequently used database system with PHP is MySQL, so this chapter focuses on MySQL, which you can get for free from www.mysql.com, although other database servers are discussed as well. All these databases support PHP, and the only difference between them, for the most part, is how you connect to them—once you know how to work with MySQL, the process is easily generalized to other databases.

Adabas	Ingres	Oracle
dBase	InterBase	Ovrimos
Empress	FrontBase	PostgreSQL
FilePro	mSQL	Solid
Hyperwave Direct	MS-SQL	Sybase
IBM DB2	MySQL	Velocis
Informix	ODBC	Unix dbm

TABLE 10-1 PHP-Supported Databases

What Is a Database?

So, just what is a database? We'll take a look at what makes a database here briefly (and if you are already familiar with databases, tables, and so on, you can naturally skip this intro).

Databases organize data for easy access and use by programs. The most popular database construct is the table, and we'll take a look at tables here. Say, for example, that you're teaching PHP to a class of students and want to keep track of their scores. You might create a table with two columns, Name and Grade:

```
Name    Grade
```

You can store the name of the first student in the Name column, like this:

```
Name    Grade
Ann
```

This creates a table entry for Ann—that is, a new row. Each row in a database table is a *record,* and this record is for the student named Ann. Each column in a record is called a *field,* and you've given the Name field the value "Ann". Similarly, you can give Ann a grade in the Grade field:

```
Name    Grade
Ann     C
```

And you can add records for other students as well:

```
Name    Grade
Ann     C
Mark    B
Ed      A
Frank   A
Ted     A
Mabel   B
Ralph   B
Tom     B
```

What, then, is a database? In its most conventional form, a database is just a collection of one or more tables. And to access the data in those tables, you use SQL in PHP, which is coming up in the next topic.

Some Essential SQL

To interact with databases in PHP, you use Structured Query Language, SQL. We're going to take a look at some SQL here (note that the full SQL language is beyond the score of this book, which focuses on connecting to databases and so on in PHP—the SQL you use to work with your database is up to you).

For example, say that you had a database table named fruit, and you wanted to recover the records from that table. Here's what might be in that table at present:

```
Name        Number
apples      1020
oranges     3329
bananas     8582
pears       235
```

To work with this table in your code, you can execute an SQL statement, called an SQL *query,* on the table. This query will return all the records in the table:

```
SELECT * FROM FRUIT
```

Executing this query gives you a record set containing all matching records from the fruit table. Because you specified that you wanted to match the wildcard * here, all records in the fruit table are returned by this query. In PHP, that record set is returned as an array, and you can loop over that array in ways you're going to see in this chapter.

How's this look in PHP? How do you actually execute an SQL query in PHP? To interact with MySQL, you'd use the mysql_query function to execute that SQL query, something like this, which returns the entire fruit table and stores it in $result:

```
$query = "SELECT * FROM fruit";
$result = mysql_query($query) or die("Query failed: " . mysql_error());
```

Now $result holds an array with the records for the fruit table, and you can access the fields in each record by name.

How about some more SQL? You can also select specific fields from a table like this, where we're selecting the name and number fields from the fruit table:

```
SELECT name, number FROM fruit
```

Using the WHERE clause, you can set up selection criteria that the records in the record set generated by the query must meet. For example, to select all the records in the fruit table where the name field equals apples, you can execute this statement: SELECT * FROM fruit WHERE name= "apples".

You don't have to use an equal sign here; you can test fields using these operators:

- < (less than)
- <= (less than or equal to)
- > (greater than)
- >= (greater than or equal to)

You can use an IN clause to specify a set of values that fields can match. For example, here's how you can retrieve records that have values in the name field that match apples or oranges:

```
SELECT * FROM fruit WHERE name IN ("apples", "oranges")
```

You can also use logical operations on the clauses in your SQL statements. Here's an example where we're specifying two criteria: the name field must hold either "apples" or "oranges", and there must be some value in the number field. You use the NULL keyword to test if there's anything in a field:

```
SELECT * FROM fruit WHERE name NOT IN ("apples", "oranges") AND number IS NOT NULL
```

You can use these logical operators to connect clauses: AND, OR, and NOT. Using AND means that both clauses must be true, using OR means either one can be true, and using NOT flips the value of a clause from TRUE to FALSE or FALSE to TRUE.

As you might expect, you can also order the records in the record set produced by an SQL statement. Here's an example where we're ordering the records in the fruit table using the name field:

```
SELECT * FROM fruit ORDER BY name
```

You can also sort records in descending order with the DESC keyword:

```
SELECT * FROM fruit ORDER BY name DESC
```

You can use the DELETE statement to delete records like this, where we're removing all records from the fruit table that have name values that are not apples or oranges:

```
DELETE * FROM fruit WHERE name NOT IN ("apples", "oranges")
```

You use the UPDATE statement to update a database when you want to make changes. For example, here's how to change the value of the number field in the record that contains the number of apples:

```
UPDATE fruit SET number = "2006" WHERE name = "apples"
```

You can also insert new data into a table. Here's an example that inserts a new row into the fruit table:

```
INSERT INTO fruit (name, number) VALUES('apricots', '203')
```

Okay, we've gotten as much SQL under our belts as we'll need here. The next step is all about creating a database to work with in PHP.

Creating a MySQL Database

We're using MySQL databases in this chapter, and to have something to work with in code, we're going to create a database in MySQL now. You can get MySQL for free from www.mysql.com—and in fact, your system might already have it installed. To check if it's already installed, try this from a command prompt (remember, % stands for the generic command-line prompt in this book):

```
%mysql
```

If you see a response from MySQL, congratulations, you've already got it installed. Otherwise, you'll need to download and install it. In fact, MySQL used to come with PHP, but it no longer does because of licensing issues.

Depending on your system and MySQL version, you might have to start the MySQL server before working with MySQL. You can start the MySQL server with this command line:

```
%mysqld --console
```

On some systems, such as Windows with recent versions of MySQL, you don't need to start the MySQL server at all—it's already running. In that case, you'll get an error if you try to start the MySQL server a second time; the error will concern shared resources.

Next, you should start a MySQL session that's going to connect to the server, and which you can use to create your own database. You need a username and password to work with MySQL; say your username is "user" and your password is "password". You can start MySQL like this at the command prompt:

```
%mysql -u user -p
```

This will ask you to enter your password:

```
%mysql -u user -p
Enter password: ********
```

Once you've started a session, you'll see a response something like this:

```
%mysql -u user -p
Enter password: ********
Welcome to the MySQL monitor.  Commands end with ; or \g.
mysql>
```

The last line, mysql>, is a prompt for you to enter your commands.

If you don't have a username and password, enter **mysql -u root**, or just **mysql**, to start:

```
%mysql -u root
Welcome to the MySQL monitor.  Commands end with ; or \g.
mysql>
```

To get started, enter **SELECT VERSION(), CURRENT_DATE;** to confirm that MySQL is working:

```
mysql> SELECT VERSION(), CURRENT_DATE;
+-----------+--------------+
| VERSION() | CURRENT_DATE |
+-----------+--------------+
| 5.0.19-nt | 2007-05-10   |
+-----------+--------------+
1 row in set (0.01 sec)
```

This command gives you the MySQL version and the current date. Note that MySQL commands like this end with a semicolon.

MySQL comes with some databases built in—which you can check with the SHOW DATABASES; command:

```
mysql> SHOW DATABASES;
+-----------------------+
| Database              |
+-----------------------+
| mysql                 |
| test                  |
+-----------------------+
2 rows in set (0.08 sec)
```

These databases already exists in MySQL—mysql is a database that MySQL uses for internal administration, and test is a database for test purposes.

Database tables are stored inside databases, so the first step is to create a database. You might use this database to contain information about various fruits and vegetables, for example, and so you can create a database named, say, produce. You can create the produce database with the CREATE DATABASE command in the MySQL monitor:

```
mysql> CREATE DATABASE produce;
Query OK, 1 row affected (0.01 sec)
```

That creates a new, empty database, which you can see with the SHOW DATABASES; command:

```
mysql> CREATE DATABASE produce;
Query OK, 1 row affected (0.01 sec)

mysql> SHOW DATABASES;
+-----------------------+
| Database              |
+-----------------------+
| mysql                 |
| test                  |
| produce               |
+-----------------------+
3 rows in set (0.08 sec)
```

Now make the produce database the default database with the USE command like this in MySQL:

```
mysql> CREATE DATABASE produce;
Query OK, 1 row affected (0.01 sec)

mysql> SHOW DATABASES;
+-----------------------+
| Database              |
+-----------------------+
| mysql                 |
| test                  |
| produce               |
+-----------------------+
3 rows in set (0.08 sec)
```

```
mysql> USE produce
Database changed
```

Are there any tables in this new database? You can use the SHOW TABLES command to check that out:

```
mysql> USE produce
Database changed

mysql> SHOW TABLES;
Empty set (0.01 sec)
```

This response—"Empty set"—tells you that this database doesn't contain any tables yet.

Creating a New Table

You can change that by creating a new table, say fruits, to contain various fruits. To create a database table, you have to create the various fields in that table, which means setting their data format. Here are a few of the most popular data formats:

- **VARCHAR(*length*)**   Creates a variable-length string
- **INT**   Creates an integer
- **DECIMAL(totaldigits, decimalplaces)**   Creates a decimal value
- **DATETIME**   Creates a date and time object, such as 2008-11-15 20:00:00

Records in the fruit table will contain two 20-character strings—the name of a fruit, and the number of that fruit on hand. Here's how you create the fruit table in the MySQL monitor:

```
mysql> CREATE TABLE fruit (name VARCHAR(20), number VARCHAR(20));
Query OK, 0 rows affected (0.13 sec)
```

That creates the fruit table, which you can check with the SHOW TABLES; command like this:

```
mysql> CREATE TABLE fruit (name VARCHAR(20), number VARCHAR(20));
Query OK, 0 rows affected (0.13 sec)

mysql> SHOW TABLES;
+-------------------+
| Tables_in_produce |
+-------------------+
| fruit             |
+-------------------+
1 row in set (0.00 sec)
```

In fact, you can check on this table, getting the format of its fields with the DESCRIBE SQL command like this:

```
mysql> CREATE TABLE fruit (name VARCHAR(20), number VARCHAR(20));
Query OK, 0 rows affected (0.13 sec)

mysql> SHOW TABLES;
+-------------------+
| Tables_in_produce |
+-------------------+
| fruit             |
+-------------------+
1 row in set (0.00 sec)

mysql> DESCRIBE fruit;
+---------+-------------+------+-----+---------+-------+
| Field   | Type        | Null | Key | Default | Extra |
+---------+-------------+------+-----+---------+-------+
| name    | varchar(20) | YES  |     | NULL    |       |
| number  | varchar(20) | YES  |     | NULL    |       |
+---------+-------------+------+-----+---------+-------+
2 rows in set (0.01 sec)
```

Cool—now you've got a new database table, fruits. Time to stock it with some data.

Putting Data into the New Database

Say that you're keeping track of the fruit inventory at your local grocery store. You count this many fruits:

- apples   1020
- oranges   3329
- bananas   8582
- pears   235

Alright, how about storing that in the new fruit database table? You've got two fields in each record in the fruit table, as you can see in the MySQL description of the table:

```
mysql> DESCRIBE fruit;
+---------+-------------+------+-----+---------+-------+
| Field   | Type        | Null | Key | Default | Extra |
+---------+-------------+------+-----+---------+-------+
| name    | varchar(20) | YES  |     | NULL    |       |
| number  | varchar(20) | YES  |     | NULL    |       |
+---------+-------------+------+-----+---------+-------+
2 rows in set (0.01 sec)
```

So now you can insert two strings into the record for each kind of fruit—the name of the fruit, and the number of that fruit on hand. You can create records in the fruit table with the SQL INSERT command. For example, to insert a record for the number of apples on hand, you'd execute this command:

```
mysql> INSERT INTO fruit VALUES ('apples', '1020');
Query OK, 1 row affected (0.00 sec)
```

Great, that creates a new record for apples. You can check that new record with the SELECT * FROM fruit; command:

```
mysql> INSERT INTO fruit VALUES ('apples', '1020');
Query OK, 1 row affected (0.00 sec)

mysql> SELECT * FROM fruit;
+---------+--------+
| name    | number |
+---------+--------+
| apples  | 1020   |
+---------+--------+
1 row in set (0.00 sec)
```

As you can see, there is a new record for apples here.

Here's how you add the other fruits with INSERT statements:

```
mysql> INSERT INTO fruit VALUES ('apples', '1020');
Query OK, 1 row affected (0.00 sec)

mysql> INSERT INTO fruit VALUES ('oranges', '3329');
Query OK, 1 row affected (0.00 sec)

mysql> INSERT INTO fruit VALUES ('bananas', '8582');
Query OK, 1 row affected (0.00 sec)

mysql> INSERT INTO fruit VALUES ('pears', '235');
Query OK, 1 row affected (0.00 sec)
```

And you can check the new fruit table and its contents with SELECT * FROM fruit; like this:

```
mysql> SELECT * FROM fruit;
+---------+--------+
| name    | number |
+---------+--------+
| apples  | 1020   |
| oranges | 3329   |
| bananas | 8582   |
| pears   | 235    |
+---------+--------+
4 rows in set (0.00 sec)
```

That creates a database, produce, and a table in that database, fruit. You can quit the MySQL monitor like this:

```
mysql> SELECT * FROM fruit;
+---------+--------+
| name    | number |
+---------+--------+
| apples  | 1020   |
| oranges | 3329   |
| bananas | 8582   |
| pears   | 235    |
+---------+--------+
4 rows in set (0.00 sec)

mysql>quit
```

That creates your database—it's time to access it in PHP.

Accessing the Database in PHP

When you install PHP, you can select from a number of extensions. To install support for MySQL, click the Extensions node in the installer to open that node and select the MySQL node to install that extension. Your PHP installation may have already been installed with MySQL support—most installations on Web servers are.

The MySQL support in PHP consists of a number of functions you can call to interact with MySQL, and here they are:

- **mysql_affected_rows** Get the number of rows affected by the previous MySQL operation.
- **mysql_change_user** Change the logged-in user.
- **mysql_client_encoding** Return the name of the current character set.
- **mysql_close** Close a MySQL connection.
- **mysql_connect** Open a connection to a MySQL Server.
- **mysql_create_db** Create a MySQL database.
- **mysql_data_seek** Seek data in the database.
- **mysql_db_name** Get the name of the database.
- **mysql_db_query** Send a MySQL query.
- **mysql_drop_db** Drop (that is, delete) a MySQL database.
- **mysql_error** Return the text of the error message from the previous MySQL operation.
- **mysql_fetch_array** Fetch a result row as an associative array, a numeric array, or both.
- **mysql_fetch_assoc** Fetch a result row as an associative array.

- **mysql_fetch_row**   Get a result row as an enumerated array.
- **mysql_field_len**   Return the length of a given field.
- **mysql_field_name**   Get the name of the given field in a result.
- **mysql_field_seek**   Seek to a given field offset.
- **mysql_field_table**   Get the name of the table the given field is in.
- **mysql_field_type**   Get the type of the given field in a result.
- **mysql_get_server_info**   Get MySQL server info.
- **mysql_info**   Get information about the most recent query.
- **mysql_list_dbs**   List databases available on a MySQL server.
- **mysql_list_fields**   List MySQL table fields.
- **mysql_list_tables**   List the tables in a MySQL database.
- **mysql_num_fields**   Get the number of fields in result.
- **mysql_num_rows**   Get the number of rows in result.
- **mysql_pconnect**   Open a persistent connection to a MySQL server.
- **mysql_query**   Send a MySQL query.
- **mysql_result**   Get result data.
- **mysql_select_db**   Select a MySQL database.
- **mysql_tablename**   Get the table name of a field.

We're going to put these functions to work in this chapter. For example, you might put together an example, phpdatatable.php, which reads in and displays the fruit table from the produce database.

Connecting to the Database Server

PHP connects to databases using *connection* objects. To create a connection object for MySQL, use mysql_connect:

```
mysql_connect ( [server [, username [, password [, new_link [, client_flags]]]]] )
```

Here, *server* is the MySQL server, which can be URLs, port numbers, and so on. The *username* and *password* arguments are the MySQL username and password.

The new_link argument, if set to TRUE, forces PHP to establish a new link to the database, even if it already has such a link. Otherwise, if you try to open a second link to the database by calling mysql_connect a second time, PHP may use its already-established link instead.

The client_flags parameter can be a combination (created by Oring values together with the OR operator, |) of the following constants: MYSQL_CLIENT_SSL, MYSQL_CLIENT_COMPRESS, MYSQL_CLIENT_IGNORE_SPACE, or MYSQL_CLIENT_INTERACTIVE.

The mysql_connect function returns a connection object if successful, FALSE otherwise.

Okay, let's connect to MySQL from PHP using mysql_connect. In this case, MySQL and PHP are on the same machine, so the server is just "localhost". Here's how to create the connection object (fill in your own username and password, of course):

```
<?php
  $connection = mysql_connect("localhost","root","*********")
    .
    .
    .
```

Let's augment this a little, making it display a message if there was an error, and quit, using the die function:

```
<?php
  $connection = mysql_connect("localhost","root","*********")
    or die ("Couldn't connect to server");
    .
    .
    .
```

Connecting to the Database

Okay, we're connected to MySQL; the next step is to select the database you want to use. You select the database with the mysql_select_db, which works like this:

```
mysql_select_db (database_name [, link_identifier] )
```

Here, *database_name* is the name of the database, which is "produce" here, and *link_identifier* is the connection object. Here's how to put mysql_select_db to work in phpdatatable.php:

```
<?php
  $connection = mysql_connect("localhost","root","*********")
    or die ("Couldn't connect to server");

  $db = mysql_select_db("produce", $connection)
    or die ("Couldn't select database");
    .
    .
    .
?>
```

Great—you've connected to the database server, and you've selected the database you want to work with. Selecting the database is crucial—if you don't select a database before proceeding, you'll get errors.

Reading the Table

The goal of the phpdatatable.php example is to read and display the database table named fruit. To get that table returned from the MySQL server, you can send that server an SQL query using the mysql_query function:

```
mysql_query (query [, link_identifier] )
```

Here, *query* is the SQL query you want to send to the database server, and *link_identifier* is the connection object, representing the connection to that server; if you only have one connection open, PHP will use that connection.

For SELECT, SHOW, DESCRIBE, EXPLAIN, and other statements returning table data, mysql_query returns a resource on success, or FALSE on error. For other type of SQL statements, UPDATE, DELETE, DROP, and so on, mysql_query returns TRUE on success or FALSE on error. The returned result resource should be passed to mysql_fetch_array, and other functions for dealing with result tables, to access the returned data. And you can use mysql_num_rows to find out how many rows were returned for a SELECT statement.

The SQL for getting all records from the fruit table is "SELECT * FROM fruit", so that'll be our query:

```php
<?php
  $connection = mysql_connect("localhost","root","*********")
    or die ("Couldn't connect to server");

  $db = mysql_select_db("produce",$connection)
    or die ("Couldn't select database");

  $query = "SELECT * FROM fruit";
    .
    .
    .
?>
```

Now you can get a returned data table full of rows from the database like this with mysql_query:

```php
<?php
  $connection = mysql_connect("localhost","root","*********")
    or die ("Couldn't connect to server");

  $db = mysql_select_db("produce",$connection)
    or die ("Couldn't select database");

  $query = "SELECT * FROM fruit";

  $result = mysql_query($query)
    .
    .
    .
?>
```

Note that if the SQL query failed, you can end the application and display an error using the mysql_error function:

```php
<?php
  $connection = mysql_connect("localhost","root","*********")
    or die ("Couldn't connect to server");
```

```
$db = mysql_select_db("produce",$connection)
    or die ("Couldn't select database");

$query = "SELECT * FROM fruit";

$result = mysql_query($query)
    or die("Query failed: " . mysql_error());
    .
    .
    .

?>
```

Alright, you've made progress. Now it's time to decipher the data you've recovered from the database.

Displaying the Table Data

You can display the data from the fruit table in an HTML table in the Web page returned by this example. The two fields in the fruit table are name and number, so you can start by creating the HTML table with table headers Name and Number:

```
<?php
$connection = mysql_connect("localhost","root","*********")
    or die ("Couldn't connect to server");

$db = mysql_select_db("produce",$connection)
    or die ("Couldn't select database");

$query = "SELECT * FROM fruit";
$result = mysql_query($query)
    or die("Query failed: " . mysql_error());

echo "<table border='1'>";
echo "<tr>";
echo "<th>Name</th><th>Number</th>";
echo "</tr>";
    .
    .
    .

?>
```

Now it's time to start dealing with the result you got back from your SQL query. That's a PHP resource; it's the fruit table in code form. To extract the records from that table, you can use the mysql_fetch_array function—this function returns an array corresponding to the current record (that is, the current row) in the data table, and you can loop over the records using loops. Here's how to use mysql_fetch_array:

```
mysql_fetch_array (result [, result_type] )
```

Here, *result* is the resource returned by the mysql_query function—that's the data table you've recovered from the database. And *result_type* is the type of array that you want.

This value is a constant and can take the following values: MYSQL_ASSOC, MYSQL_NUM, and the default value of MYSQL_BOTH.

You can use mysql_fetch_array to fetch rows from the fruit table, and you might loop over those rows with a while loop. Here's how that looks, where you store each row from the table in a variable named $row:

```php
<?php
    $connection = mysql_connect("localhost","root","*********")
        or die ("Couldn't connect to server");

    $db = mysql_select_db("produce",$connection)
        or die ("Couldn't select database");

    $query = "SELECT * FROM fruit";
    $result = mysql_query($query)
        or die("Query failed: " . mysql_error());

    echo "<table border='1'>";
    echo "<tr>";
    echo "<th>Name</th><th>Number</th>";
    echo "</tr>";

    while ($row = mysql_fetch_array($result))
    {
        .
        .
        .
    }
?>
```

This assigns the current row from the fruit table to $row. You can access the name field in that row like this: $row['name'], and the number field in the row as $row['number'].

That means you can display the data in the current row's two fields, name and number, like this in phpdatatable.php:

```php
<?php
    $connection = mysql_connect("localhost","root","*********")
        or die ("Couldn't connect to server");

    $db = mysql_select_db("produce",$connection)
        or die ("Couldn't select database");

    $query = "SELECT * FROM fruit";
    $result = mysql_query($query)
        or die("Query failed: " . mysql_error());

    echo "<table border='1'>";
    echo "<tr>";
    echo "<th>Name</th><th>Number</th>";
    echo "</tr>";
```

```
    while ($row = mysql_fetch_array($result))
    {
      echo "<tr>";
      echo "<td>", $row['name'], "</td><td>", $row['number'], "</td>";
      echo "</tr>";
    }
          .
          .
          .

  ?>
```

All that's left is to close the connection to the database.

Closing the Connection

You can close the connection to the database with mysql_close:

```
mysql_close ( [link_identifier] )
```

Here, *link_identifier* is the connection object that represents the connection to the database. Here's how you close the connection in phpdatatable.php:

```
<html>
  <head>
    <title>
        Displaying tables with MySQL
    </title>
  </head>

  <body>
    <h1>Displaying tables with MySQL</h1>

    <?php
      $connection = mysql_connect("localhost","root","********")
        or die ("Couldn't connect to server");

      $db = mysql_select_db("produce",$connection)
        or die ("Couldn't select database");

      $query = "SELECT * FROM fruit";
      $result = mysql_query($query)
        or die("Query failed: " . mysql_error());

      echo "<table border='1'>";
      echo "<tr>";
      echo "<th>Name</th><th>Number</th>";
      echo "</tr>";

      while ($row = mysql_fetch_array($result))
      {
        echo "<tr>";
        echo "<td>", $row['name'], "</td><td>", $row['number'], "</td>";
        echo "</tr>";
      }
```

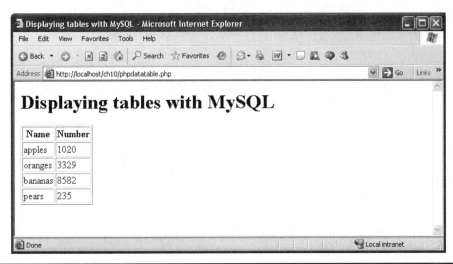

FIGURE 10-1   The fruit table

```
    echo "</table>";

    mysql_close($connection);
  ?>
 </body>
</html>
```

You can see the results appear in Figure 10-1, where you can see the whole fruit table. Very cool.

Okay, you've been successful in recovering data from a database table. Excellent. Now how about modifying that data?

Updating Databases

If someone buys your products online, you'll need to update your database. Say, for example, that someone purchases a pear from you online, which means that you go from 235 pears in stock to 234:

- apples   1020
- oranges   3329
- bananas   8582
- pears   234

How would you make this change from PHP to the fruit table? You would connect to the produce database and use an SQL UPDATE query to make the change.

You can see how this works in phpdataupdate.php. First, you get a connection to the database server (put in your own username and password, of course):

```php
<?php
    $connection = mysql_connect("localhost","root","*********")
        or die ("Couldn't connect to server");
        .
        .
        .
```

Then you select the produce database:

```php
<?php
    $connection = mysql_connect("localhost","root","*********")
        or die ("Couldn't connect to server");

    $db = mysql_select_db("produce",$connection)
        or die ("Couldn't select database");
        .
        .
        .
```

So how do you update the number of pears? You can use the UPDATE SQL statement "UPDATE fruit SET number = 234 WHERE name = 'pears'" like this:

```php
<?php
    $connection = mysql_connect("localhost","root","*********")
        or die ("Couldn't connect to server");

    $db = mysql_select_db("produce",$connection)
        or die ("Couldn't select database");

    $query = "UPDATE fruit SET number = 234 WHERE name = 'pears'";
        .
        .
        .
```

Now you can execute this SQL with mysql_query:

```php
<?php
    $connection = mysql_connect("localhost","root","********")
        or die ("Couldn't connect to server");

    $db = mysql_select_db("produce",$connection)
        or die ("Couldn't select database");

    $query = "UPDATE fruit SET number = 234 WHERE name = 'pears'";

    $result = mysql_query($query)
        or die("Query failed: ".mysql_error());
        .
        .
        .
```

Okay, now let's confirm that the change was made to the fruit table, updating the number of pears. You can display the new contents of the fruit table this way in phpdataupdate.php:

```
<html>
  <head>
    <title>
      Updating databases
    </title>
  </head>

  <body>
    <h1>Updating databases</h1>

    <?php
      $connection = mysql_connect("localhost","root","********")
        or die ("Couldn't connect to server");

      $db = mysql_select_db("produce",$connection)
        or die ("Couldn't select database");

      $query = "UPDATE fruit SET number = 234 WHERE name = 'pears'";

      $result = mysql_query($query)
        or die("Query failed: ".mysql_error());

      $query = "SELECT * FROM fruit";

      $result = mysql_query($query)
        or die("Query failed: " . mysql_error());

      echo "<table border='1'>";
      echo "<tr>";
      echo "<th>Name</th><th>Number</th>";
      echo "</tr>";

      while ($row = mysql_fetch_array($result))
      {
        echo "<tr>";
        echo "<td>", $row['name'], "</td><td>", $row['number'], "</td>";
        echo "</tr>";
      }

      echo "</table>";

      mysql_close($connection);
    ?>
  </body>
</html>
```

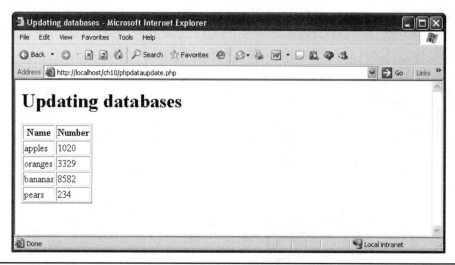

FIGURE 10-2 Updating the fruit table

You can see the results in Figure 10-2, where the number of pears has been updated to 234. Very nice.

Okay, so far so good. Now you've been able to read data from a database, and update that data. What about inserting some new data?

Inserting New Data Items into a Database

Business is good, and you decide to start adding more fruit to your Web site, starting with apricots. Your first shipment is 203 apricots, so you might add that to your stock of fruit:

- apples   1020
- oranges   3329
- bananas   8582
- pears   234
- **apricots**   **203**

But there's no record for apricots, so it's time to add one, which you can do with the INSERT SQL statement in a new example, phpdatainsert.php.

First, you connect to the database server:

```php
<?php
  $connection = mysql_connect("localhost","root","stoic8888")
    or die ("Couldn't connect to server");
     .
     .
     .
```

Then select the fruit database:

```php
<?php
  $connection = mysql_connect("localhost","root","stoic8888")
    or die ("Couldn't connect to server");

  $db = mysql_select_db("produce", $connection)
    or die ("Couldn't select database");
    .
    .
    .
```

You can insert a new record into a table with the SQL INSERT statement. To insert a new record for apricots into the fruit table, you can execute this SQL statement: "INSERT INTO fruit (name, number) VALUES('apricots', '203')":

```php
<?php
  $connection = mysql_connect("localhost","root","stoic8888")
    or die ("Couldn't connect to server");

  $db = mysql_select_db("produce", $connection)
    or die ("Couldn't select database");

  $query = "INSERT INTO fruit (name, number) VALUES('apricots', '203')";

  $result = mysql_query($query)
    or die("Query failed: " . mysql_error());
    .
    .
    .
```

If successful, that inserts a new record into the database table fruit. You can confirm that by displaying the fruit table in phpdatainsert.php:

```html
<html>
  <head>
    <title>
      Inserting new data
    </title>
  </head>

  <body>
    <h1>Inserting new data</h1>

    <?php
      $connection = mysql_connect("localhost","root","stoic8888")
        or die ("Couldn't connect to server");

      $db = mysql_select_db("produce",$connection)
        or die ("Couldn't select database");

      $query = "INSERT INTO fruit (name, number) VALUES('apricots', '203')";
```

```
$result = mysql_query($query)
  or die("Query failed: " . mysql_error());

$query = "SELECT * FROM fruit";

$result = mysql_query($query)
  or die("Query failed: " . mysql_error());

echo "<table border='1'>";
echo "<tr>";
echo "<th>Name</TH><TH>Number</th>";
echo "</tr>";

while ($row = mysql_fetch_array($result))
{
  echo "<TR>";
  echo "<td>", $row['name'], "</td><td>", $row['number'], "</td>";
  echo "</tr>";
}

echo "</TABLE>";

mysql_close($connection);
?>
</body>
</html>
```

And you can see the results in Figure 10-3, where a new record has been added for apricots. Cool. 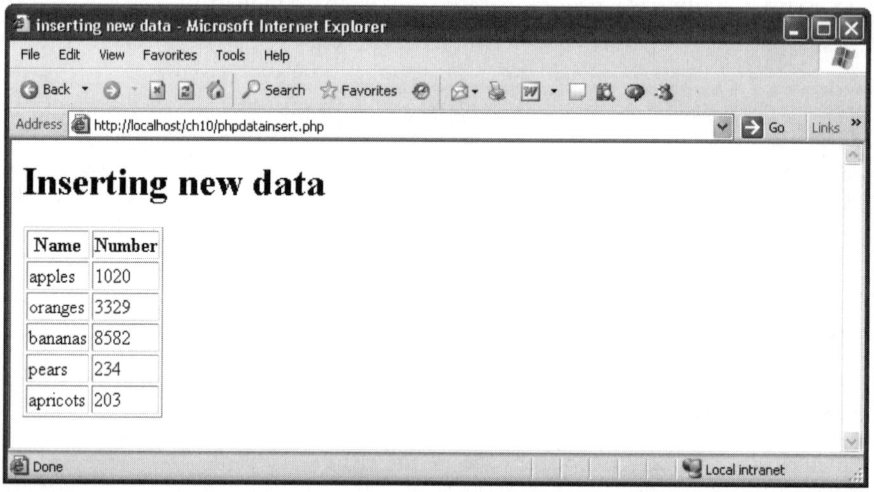

FIGURE 10-3   Insert a new record into the fruit table

Deleting Records

Now say that your supply of apricots has dried up, so you need to remove them from being offered on your Web site. How do you delete a record? You can use the SQL DELETE statement.

Here's an example, phpdatadelete.php, which removes the apricots record from the fruit table. You start as usual, by connecting to the database server and selecting the produce database this way:

```php
<?php
    $connection = mysql_connect("localhost","root","")
        or die ("Couldn't connect to server");

    $db = mysql_select_db("produce",$connection)
        or die ("Couldn't select database");
        .
        .
        .
```

Now you can delete the apricots record from the fruit table using the SQL DELETE FROM fruit WHERE name = 'apricots'":

```php
<?php
    $connection = mysql_connect("localhost","root","")
        or die ("Couldn't connect to server");

    $db = mysql_select_db("produce",$connection)
        or die ("Couldn't select database");

    $query = "DELETE FROM fruit WHERE name = 'apricots'";
        .
        .
        .
?>
```

And you can execute the query on the database:

```php
<?php
    $connection = mysql_connect("localhost","root","")
        or die ("Couldn't connect to server");

    $db = mysql_select_db("produce",$connection)
        or die ("Couldn't select database");

    $query = "DELETE FROM fruit WHERE name = 'apricots'";

    $result = mysql_query($query)
        or die("Query failed: " . mysql_error());
        .
        .
        .
?>
```

And you can display the newly modified table in phpdatadelete.php:

```
<html>
  <head>
    <title>
      Deleting records
    </title>
  </head>

  <body>
    <h1>Deleting records</h1>

    <?php
      $connection = mysql_connect("localhost","root","*******")
        or die ("Couldn't connect to server");

      $db = mysql_select_db("produce",$connection)
        or die ("Couldn't select database");

      $query = "DELETE FROM fruit WHERE name = 'apricots'";

      $result = mysql_query($query)
        or die("Query failed: " . mysql_error());

      $query = "SELECT * FROM fruit";

      $result = mysql_query($query)
        or die("Query failed: " . mysql_error());

      echo "<table border='1'>";
      echo "<tr>";
      echo "<th>Name</th><th>Number</th>";
      echo "</tr>";

      while ($row = mysql_fetch_array($result))
      {
        echo "<tr>";
        echo "<td>", $row['name'], "</td><td>", $row['number'], "</td>";
        echo "</tr>";
      }

      echo "</table>";

      mysql_close($connection);
    ?>
  </body>
</html>
```

You can see the results in Figure 10-4, where apricots have been deleted. Cool.

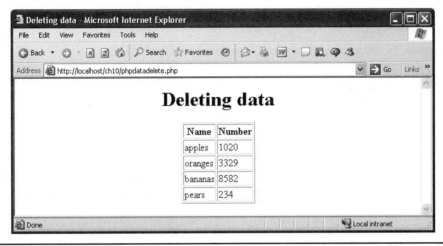

FIGURE **10-4** Deleting records

Creating New Tables

You can also create your own database tables using PHP and SQL. Here's an example, phpcreatetable.php, which creates a new table named vegetables with these records:

- Name   Number
- corn   2083
- spinach   1993
- beets   437

You start by connecting to the server, as usual, and by selecting the produce database:

```php
<?php
  $connection = mysql_connect("localhost","root","********")
    or die ("Couldn't connect to server");

  $db = mysql_select_db("produce",$connection)
    or die ("Couldn't select database");
    .
    .
    .
?>
```

You can create tables using the SQL CREATE statement. For example, to create a new vegetables table with name and number fields, you could execute the SQL "CREATE TABLE vegetables (name VARCHAR(20), number VARCHAR(20))":

```php
<?php
  $connection = mysql_connect("localhost","root","********")
    or die ("Couldn't connect to server");
```

```php
$db = mysql_select_db("produce",$connection)
  or die ("Couldn't select database");

$query = "CREATE TABLE vegetables (name VARCHAR(20),
  number VARCHAR(20))";

$result = mysql_query($query)
  or die("Query failed: " . mysql_error());
     .
     .
     .
?>
```

It's time to stock the new table with some vegetables, which you can do with the SQL INSERT statement. Here's how you might insert a new record for corn, for example:

```php
<?php
$connection = mysql_connect("localhost","root","********")
  or die ("Couldn't connect to server");

$db = mysql_select_db("produce",$connection)
  or die ("Couldn't select database");

$query = "CREATE TABLE vegetables (name VARCHAR(20),
  number VARCHAR(20))";

$result = mysql_query($query)
  or die("Query failed: " . mysql_error());

$query = "INSERT INTO vegetables (name, number) VALUES(
  'corn', '2083')";

$result = mysql_query($query)
  or die("Query failed: " . mysql_error());
     .
     .
     .
?>
```

And here's how to create the other two records in the vegetables table:

```php
<?php
$connection = mysql_connect("localhost","root","********")
  or die ("Couldn't connect to server");

$db = mysql_select_db("produce",$connection)
  or die ("Couldn't select database");

$query = "CREATE TABLE vegetables (name VARCHAR(20),
  number VARCHAR(20))";

$result = mysql_query($query)
  or die("Query failed: " . mysql_error());

$query = "INSERT INTO vegetables (name, number) VALUES(
  'corn', '2083')";
```

```
   $result = mysql_query($query)
     or die("Query failed: " . mysql_error());

   $query = "INSERT INTO vegetables (name, number)
     VALUES('spinach', '1993')";

   $result = mysql_query($query)
     or die("Query failed: " . mysql_error());

   $query = "INSERT INTO vegetables (name, number)
     VALUES('beets', '437')";

   $result = mysql_query($query)
     or die("Query failed: " . mysql_error());
      .
      .
      .

  ?>
```

Finally, you can display the new table like this in phpcreatetable.php:

```
<html>
  <head>
    <title>
      Creating a new table
    </title>
  </head>

  <body>
    <h1>
      Creating a new table
    </h1>
    <?php
      $connection = mysql_connect("localhost","root","*******")
        or die ("Couldn't connect to server");

      $db = mysql_select_db("produce",$connection)
        or die ("Couldn't select database");

      $query = "CREATE TABLE vegetables (name VARCHAR(20),
        number VARCHAR(20))";

      $result = mysql_query($query)
        or die("Query failed: " . mysql_error());

      $query = "INSERT INTO vegetables (name, number) VALUES(
        'corn', '2083')";

      $result = mysql_query($query)
        or die("Query failed: " . mysql_error());

      $query = "INSERT INTO vegetables (name, number)
        VALUES('spinach', '1993')";

      $result = mysql_query($query)
        or die("Query failed: " . mysql_error());
```

```
$query = "INSERT INTO vegetables (name, number)
  VALUES('beets', '437')";

$result = mysql_query($query)
  or die("Query failed: " . mysql_error());

$query = "SELECT * FROM vegetables";

$result = mysql_query($query)
  or die("Query failed: " . mysql_error());

echo "<table border='1'>";
echo "<tr>";
echo "<th>Name</th><th>Number</th>";
echo "</tr>";

while ($row = mysql_fetch_array($result))
{
  echo "<tr>";
  echo "<td>", $row['name'], "</td><td>",
    $row['number'], "</td>";
  echo "</tr>";
}

echo "</table>";

mysql_close($connection);
?>
</body>
</html>
```

You can see the results in Figure 10-5, where the new table appears. Very nice.

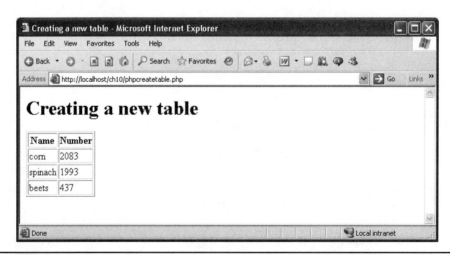

FIGURE 10-5   Creating a new table

Creating a New Database

You can even create entirely new databases, with their own tables, using PHP and SQL. For example, you might create a new database, foods, with a snacks table that has these records:

- Name   Number
- tacos   218
- pizza   193
- cheeseburgers   112

Here's how to do that in phpcreatedatabase.php. First, connect to the database server:

```php
<?php
    $connection = mysql_connect("localhost","root","*******")
        or die ("Couldn't connect to server");
        .
        .
        .
?>
```

Now you can create a whole new database, foods, with the SQL "CREATE DATABASE IF NOT EXISTS foods":

```php
<?php
    $connection = mysql_connect("localhost","root","*******")
        or die ("Couldn't connect to server");

    $query = "CREATE DATABASE IF NOT EXISTS foods";

    $result = mysql_query($query)
        or die("Query failed: " . mysql_error());
        .
        .
        .
?>
```

Next, you select the foods database:

```php
<?php
    $connection = mysql_connect("localhost","root","*******")
        or die ("Couldn't connect to server");

    $query = "CREATE DATABASE IF NOT EXISTS foods";

    $result = mysql_query($query)
        or die("Query failed: " . mysql_error());

    $db = mysql_select_db("foods", $connection)
        or die ("Couldn't select database");
        .
        .
        .
?>
```

Then it's time to create the snacks table:

```php
<?php
  $connection = mysql_connect("localhost","root","*******")
    or die ("Couldn't connect to server");

  $query = "CREATE DATABASE IF NOT EXISTS foods";

  $result = mysql_query($query)
    or die("Query failed: " . mysql_error());

  $db = mysql_select_db("foods", $connection)
    or die ("Couldn't select database");

  $query = "CREATE TABLE snacks (name VARCHAR(20), number
    VARCHAR(20))";

  $result = mysql_query($query)
    or die("Query failed: " . mysql_error());
    .
    .
    .
?>
```

And then you stock the snacks table with some snacks:

```php
<?php
  $connection = mysql_connect("localhost","root","*******")
    or die ("Couldn't connect to server");

  $query = "CREATE DATABASE IF NOT EXISTS foods";

  $result = mysql_query($query)
    or die("Query failed: " . mysql_error());

  $db = mysql_select_db("foods", $connection)
    or die ("Couldn't select database");

  $query = "CREATE TABLE snacks (name VARCHAR(20), number
    VARCHAR(20))";

  $result = mysql_query($query)
    or die("Query failed: " . mysql_error());

  $query = "INSERT INTO snacks (name, number)
    VALUES('tacos', '218')";

  $result = mysql_query($query)
    or die("Query failed: " . mysql_error());

  $query = "INSERT INTO snacks (name, number)
    VALUES('pizza', '193')";
```

```
    $result = mysql_query($query)
      or die("Query failed: " . mysql_error());

    $query = "INSERT INTO snacks (name, number)
      VALUES('cheeseburgers', '112')";

    $result = mysql_query($query)
      or die("Query failed: " . mysql_error());
        .
        .
        .

  ?>
```

Now you can display the new snacks table:

```
<html>
  <head>
    <title>
    Creating a new database
    </title>
  </head>

  <body>
    <h1>
    Creating a new database
    </h1>

    <?php
      $connection = mysql_connect("localhost","root","*******")
        or die ("Couldn't connect to server");

      $query = "CREATE DATABASE IF NOT EXISTS foods";

      $result = mysql_query($query)
        or die("Query failed: " . mysql_error());

      $db = mysql_select_db("foods", $connection)
        or die ("Couldn't select database");

      $query = "CREATE TABLE snacks (name VARCHAR(20), number
        VARCHAR(20))";

      $result = mysql_query($query)
        or die("Query failed: " . mysql_error());

      $query = "INSERT INTO snacks (name, number)
        VALUES('tacos', '218')";

      $result = mysql_query($query)
        or die("Query failed: " . mysql_error());

      $query = "INSERT INTO snacks (name, number)
        VALUES('pizza', '193')";
```

```
    $result = mysql_query($query)
      or die("Query failed: " . mysql_error());

    $query = "INSERT INTO snacks (name, number)
      VALUES('cheeseburgers', '112')";

    $result = mysql_query($query)
      or die("Query failed: " . mysql_error());
    $query = "SELECT * FROM snacks";

    $result = mysql_query($query)
      or die("Query failed: " . mysql_error());

    echo "<table border='1'>";
    echo "<tr>";
    echo "<th>Name</th><th>Number</th>";
    echo "</tr>";

    while ($row = mysql_fetch_array($result))
    {
      echo "<tr>";
      echo "<td>", $row['name'], "</td><td>",
        $row['number'], "</td>";
      echo "</tr>";
    }
    echo "</table>";

    mysql_close($connection);
  ?>
  </body>
</html>
```

You can see the results in Figure 10-6, where the new table in the new database appears.

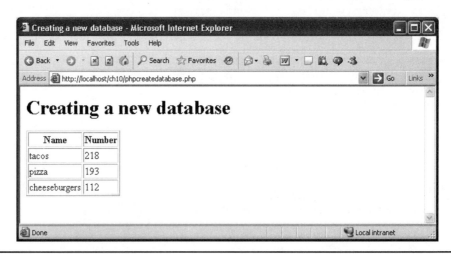

FIGURE 10-6   Creating a new database

Sorting Your Data

You can keep going with your database work using SQL in PHP—anything possible with databases is possible with SQL. Here's another example, phpsortdata.php, that uses SQL to sort the data in the fruit table before displaying it:

```
<html>
  <head>
    <title>
      Sorting your data
    </title>
  </head>

  <body>
    <h1>
      Sorting your data
    </h1>

    <?php
      $connection = mysql_connect("localhost","root","*******")
        or die ("Couldn't connect to server");

      $db = mysql_select_db("produce",$connection)
        or die ("Couldn't select database");

      $query = "SELECT * FROM fruit ORDER BY name";

      $result = mysql_query($query)
        or die("Query failed: " . mysql_error());

      echo "<table border='1'>";
      echo "<tr>";
      echo "<th>Name</th><th>Number</th>";
      echo "</TR>";

      while ($row = mysql_fetch_array($result))
      {
        echo "<tr>";
        echo "<td>", $row['name'], "</td><td>",
          $row['number'], "</td>";
        echo "</tr>";
      }

      echo "</table>";

      mysql_close($connection);
    ?>
  </body>
</html>
```

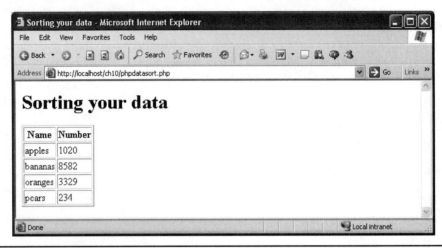

FIGURE 10-7 Sorting your data

You can see the results in Figure 10-7, where your data was sorted.

Now that you can use SQL with PHP, your database capabilities are unlimited.

## 11

CHAPTER

Sessions, Cookies, and FTP

There's a lot of PHP power coming up in this chapter—sessions, cookies, FTP, e-mail, and more. These topics are of central interest of PHP programmers, so this chapter is going to be an interesting one.

By its very nature, the Internet is a stateless place—that is, Web pages don't store data. The next time you load most Web pages into a browser is the same as the first—the Web page is reinitialized and is displayed anew. However, the Web has become a more serious place in terms of programming, and that means writing Web applications that work in a multipage way: and that means storing data about the user that persists from page to page. You're going to see two ways of doing that in this chapter: sessions and cookies. And we're going to start with cookies.

Setting a Cookie

Cookies are those text segments that you can store on the user's computer, and PHP has good support for setting and reading cookies. Those segments of text can persist even when the user's computer is turned off, so you can store information about the user easily. That's great when you want to customize a Web application—the user might choose a color scheme, for example. Cookies are used for all kinds of purposes, from the benign to the more sinister—such as tracking what ads a user has already seen and responded to. Setting and reading cookies in PHP is not hard.

You set cookies on the user's machine with the PHP setcookie function:

```
setcookie(name [, value [, expire [, path [, domain [, secure]]]]])
```

Here is what the parameters mean:

- *name* The name of the cookie.
- *value* The value of the cookie. (This value is stored on the clients computer, so do not store sensitive information.)
- *expire* The time the cookie expires. This is the number of seconds since January 1, 1970. You'll most likely set this with the PHP time function plus the number of seconds before you want it to expire.
- *path* The path on the server in which the cookie will be available on.

- *domain*   The domain for which the cookie is available.
- *secure*   Indicates that the cookie should only be transmitted over a secure HTTPS connection. When set to 1, the cookie will only be set if a secure connection exists. The default is 0.

Want a real simple cookie example? Here it is, phpsetcookie.php. This example sets a cookie named message to the text "No worries.":

```php
<?php
  setcookie("message", "No worries.");
?>
```

Here's what this PHP looks like in phpsetcookie.php:

```html
<html>
  <head>
    <title>
      Setting a cookie
    </title>
    <?php
      setcookie("message", "No worries.");
    ?>
  </head>

  <body>
    <h1>
      Setting a cookie
    </h1>
    The cookie was set.

    Go to <a href="phpgetcookie.php">phpgetcookie.php</a> to read it.
  <body>
</html>
```

And you can see the results in Figure 11-1, where the cookie was set.

This PHP page includes a hyperlink to another page, phpgetcookie.php, where the cookie will be read:

```html
<html>
        .

        .

        .
  <body>
    <h1>
      Setting a cookie
    </h1>
    The cookie was set.

    Go to <a href="phpgetcookie.php">phpgetcookie.php</a> to read it.
  <body>
</html>
```

And that page—phpgetcookie.php—is coming up next.

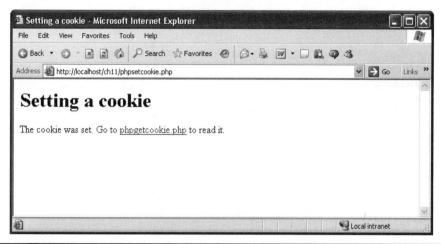

FIGURE 11-1   Setting a cookie

Reading a Cookie

When you set a cookie, it won't be visible to your scripts until the next time you load a page. That's because the cookie is sent to the server from the user's machine, so immediately after you set a cookie, you won't be able to read it; you need to get a page back from the browser first. Note also that cookies are sent in the HTTP headers in pages sent to you by the browser, and if your cookie-handling page is in domain A (such as www.ultragiantbigco.com), only the cookies that came from domain A are sent to you.

Once the cookies have been set, they can be accessed on the next page load with the $_COOKIE array. We set a cookie named message in the previous topic—and we'll read it here. The values of cookies are automatically loaded into the global array named $_COOKIES, much as the values of Web page data are stored in $_REQUEST, which makes this process easy.

In phpgetcookie.php, you can start by checking if the cookie was set (avoiding an error when you try to display $_COOKIE['message'] and the cookie wasn't set):

```php
<?php
  if (isset($_COOKIE['message'])) {
    .

    .

    .
  }
?>
```

If the cookie was indeed set, you can display its text like this:

```php
<?php
  if (isset($_COOKIE['message'])) {
    echo $_COOKIE['message'];
  }
?>
```

Here's what this looks like in phpgetcookie.php:

```
<html>
  <head>
    <title>
      Reading a cookie
    </title>
  </head>

  <body>
    <h1>
      Reading a cookie
    </h1>
      The cookie says:
      <?php
        if (isset($_COOKIE['message'])) {
          echo $_COOKIE['message'];
        }
      ?>
  <body>
</html>
```

You can see the results in Figure 11-2, where the cookie was read.

Okay, that lets you set cookies and read them. However, this cookie will be deleted as soon as the user closes their browser. How can you set a cookie's expiration time? That's coming up next.

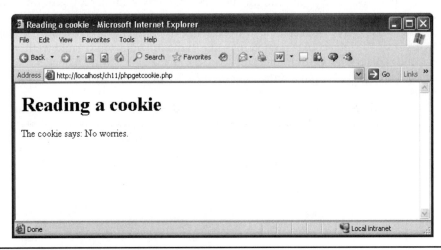

FIGURE 11-2 Reading a cookie

Setting Cookies' Expiration

You can set cookie's expiration time when you create the cookie with the setcookie function:

```
setcookie(name [, value [, expire [, path [, domain [, secure]]]]])
```

Here, the time stored in this parameter is a Unix timestamp, holding the number of seconds since January 1, 1970, and specifying the time when the cookie should be deleted. To get the current number of seconds since January 1, 1970, you can use the PHP time function. For example, to specify that a cookie should be deleted in an hour, you can do something like this, where you specify an expiration time of time() + 3600 seconds:

```php
<?php
    setcookie("mycookie", $value, time() + 3600);
?>
```

Here's an example, phpsetexpiration.php, which sets a cookie with an expiration date of thirty days from now, by setting the expiration to time()+60*60*24*30:

```php
<?php
  setcookie("message", "No worries for 30 days.", time()+60*60*24*30);
?>
```

Here's how that looks in phpsetexpiration.php:

```html
<html>
  <head>
    <title>
      Setting a cookie's expiration time
    </title>
    <?php
      setcookie("message", "No worries for 30 days.", time()+60*60*24*30);
    ?>
  </head>

  <body>
    <h1>
      Setting a cookie's expiration time
    </h1>
      The cookie has been set to expire in 30 days. Go to
      <a href="phpgetcookie.php">phpgetcookie.php</a> next.
  <body>
</html>
```

You can see the results in Figure 11-3, where the cookie was set for 30 days.

When you click the hyperlink in this example, you're taken to the cookie-reading page, phpreadcookie.php, and you can see the cookie's text in Figure 11-4.

You might even want more cookie control—for example, you can delete cookies, and that's coming up next.

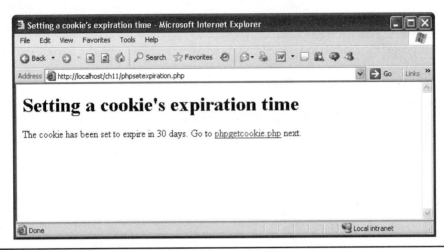

FIGURE 11-3   Setting a cookie for thirty days

Deleting Cookies

Want to delete a cookie? Whether or not you can depends on the browser you're dealing with. You can set the expiration time of a cookie to some time in the past, and that should theoretically make the browser delete the cookie, but the browser may not delete the cookie until the user closes the browser—and possibly not even then. So a wise precaution is to first set the text for the cookie to an empty string, "":

```php
<?php
  setcookie("message", "");
?>
```

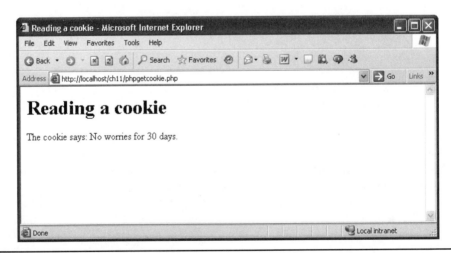

FIGURE 11-4   Reading a cookie

Then set the expiration time to some time in the past as well:

```php
<?php
  setcookie("message", "", time() - 3600);
?>
```

That's it—that's how you delete a cookie; there is no special deletecookie function. Here's what this looks like in phpdeletecookie.php:

```html
<html>
  <head>
    <title>
      Deleting cookies
    </title>
    <?php
      setcookie("message", "", time() - 3600);
    ?>
  </head>

  <body>
    <h1>
      Deleting cookies
    </h1>

    Cookie was deleted. Check that at
    <a href="phpgetcookie.php">phpgetcookie.php</a>.
  <body>
</html>
```

You can see the results in Figure 11-5, where the cookie was deleted.

You can see what the phpgetcookie.php page says about the deleted cookie in Figure 11-6—it couldn't find the cookie.

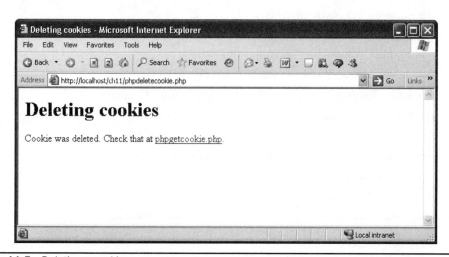

FIGURE 11-5   Deleting a cookie

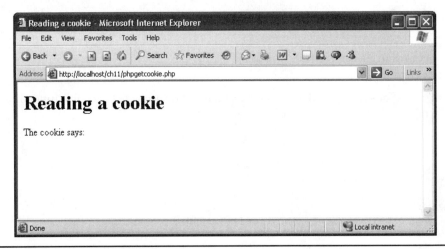

FIGURE 11-6   Trying to read a deleted cookie

Working with FTP

Using FTP is great on the Internet for moving files around to various servers. This can be a great means of deploying code, getting configuration data from other sources, reading Web pages, and more. Here is the FTP support built into PHP (the functions with nb in their names are non-blocking—they don't wait to complete their task before returning):

- **ftp_alloc**   Allocates space for a file to be uploaded
- **ftp_cdup**   Changes to the parent directory
- **ftp_chdir**   Changes directories on an FTP server
- **ftp_chmod**   Set permissions on a file via FTP
- **ftp_close**   Closes an FTP connection
- **ftp_connect**   Opens an FTP connection
- **ftp_delete**   Deletes a file on the FTP server
- **ftp_exec**   Requests execution of a program on the FTP server
- **ftp_fget**   Downloads a file from the FTP server and saves to an open file
- **ftp_fput**   Uploads from an open file to the FTP server
- **ftp_get_option**   Retrieves run-time behaviors of the current FTP stream
- **ftp_get**   Downloads a file from the FTP server
- **ftp_login**   Logs in to an FTP connection
- **ftp_mdtm**   Returns the last modified time of the given file
- **ftp_mkdir**   Creates a directory
- **ftp_nb_continue**   Continues retrieving/sending a file

- **ftp_nb_fget**   Retrieves a file from the FTP server and writes it to an open file
- **ftp_nb_fput**   Stores a file from an open file to the FTP server
- **ftp_nb_get**   Retrieves a file from the FTP server and writes it to a local file
- **ftp_nb_put**   Stores a file on the FTP server
- **ftp_nlist**   Returns a list of files in the given directory
- **ftp_put**   Uploads a file to the FTP server
- **ftp_pwd**   Returns the current directory name
- **ftp_quit**   An alias of ftp_close
- **ftp_raw**   Sends an arbitrary command to an FTP server
- **ftp_rawlist**   Returns a detailed list of files in the given directory
- **ftp_rename**   Renames a file on the FTP server
- **ftp_rmdir**   Removes a directory
- **ftp_set_option**   Set miscellaneous run-time FTP options
- **ftp_site**   Sends a SITE command to the server
- **ftp_size**   Returns the size of the given file
- **ftp_ssl_connect**   Opens a Secure SSL-FTP connection
- **ftp_systype**   Returns the system type identifier of the remote FTP server

Here's an example, phpftp.php. This example will log in to a remote directory and get a directory listing. It starts by connecting to the remote server using ftp_connect:

```
ftp_connect(host [, port [, timeout]])
```

This function opens an FTP connection to the given *host* (note that host shouldn't have any trailing slashes and shouldn't be prefixed with ftp://). The *port* parameter specifies an alternate port to connect to; if it is omitted or set to zero, then the default FTP port, 21, will be used. The *timeout* parameter specifies the timeout for all subsequent network operations. If omitted, the default value is 90 seconds. This function returns an FTP stream on success, or FALSE on error.

Here's how the code in phpftp.php connects (put in your own server here):

```
<?php
  $connect = ftp_connect("ftp.ispname.com");
    .
    .
    .
?>
```

Next, you have to log in to the FTP server, and you can use ftp_login for that.

```
ftp_login(ftp_stream, username, password)
```

This function passes your *username* and *password* to the FTP server, and it returns TRUE on success or FALSE on failure. If you get a result of TRUE, you're logged in to the FTP server.

Here's how phpftp.php uses ftp_login to log in (fill in your own name and password):

```php
<?php
  $connect = ftp_connect("ftp.ispname.com");

  $result = ftp_login($connect, "username", "password");
     .

     .

     .

?>
```

Okay, so far, so good. The goal of phpftp.php is to get a directory listing of a remote directory on the server, and in this example, that directory will be named code22. You can use the ftp_nlist function to get the listing of the remote directory:

```
array ftp_nlist(ftp_stream, directory)
```

Here, *ftp_stream* is the connection object you got from ftp_connect, and *directory* is the remote directory you want the listing of. This function returns an array of filenames from the specified directory on success or FALSE on error.

Here's how to get a directory listing of the code22 directory:

```php
<?php
  $connect = ftp_connect("ftp.ispname.com");

  $result = ftp_login($connect, "username", "password");

  $array = ftp_nlist($connect, "code22");
     .

     .

     .

?>
```

Now you can loop over the array of filenames, $array, listing the filenames:

```php
<?php
  $connect = ftp_connect("ftp.ispname.com");

  $result = ftp_login($connect, "username", "password");

  $array = ftp_nlist($connect, "code22");

  foreach($array as $value){
    echo $value, "<br>";
  }
?>
```

Cool. Here's what this PHP looks like in phpftp.php:

```html
<html>
  <head>
    <title>
```

```
      Reading a remote directory with FTP
    </title>
  </head>

  <body>
    <h1>
      Reading a remote directory with FTP
    </h1>

    This is what is in the remote directory:
    <br>
    <br>
    <?php
      $connect = ftp_connect("ftp.ispname.com");

      $result = ftp_login($connect, "username", "password");

      $array = ftp_nlist($connect, "code22");

      foreach($array as $value){
        echo $value, "<br>";
      }
    ?>
  <body>
</html>
```

You can see what the phpftp.php page gives you in Figure 11-7—it connected to the remote directory and displayed the directory's files. Not bad.

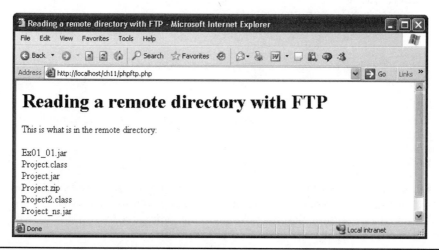

FIGURE 11-7   Getting a remote directory listing with FTP

Downloading Files with FTP

How about downloading a file using FTP? This next example, ftpget.php, does exactly that. This example starts by connecting to a server (use your own server here):

```php
<?php
  $connect = ftp_connect("ftp.ispname.com");
    .
    .
    .
?>
```

Then it attempts to log in (use your own username and password here):

```php
<?php
  $connect = ftp_connect("ftp.ispname.com");

  $result = ftp_login($connect, "username", "password");
    .
    .
    .
?>
```

If logging in didn't work, you can inform the user and exit the application:

```php
<?php
  $connect = ftp_connect("ftp.ispname.com");

  $result = ftp_login($connect, "username", "password");

  if(!$result){
    echo "Could not connect.";
    exit;
  }
    .
    .
    .
?>
```

On the other hand, if the user was able to log in, it's time to download the file. For that, use ftp_get:

```
ftp_get(ftp_stream, local_file, remote_file, mode [, pos])
```

This function retrieves *remote_file* from the FTP server and saves it to *local_file* locally (which can include a pathname). The transfer *mode* specified must be either FTP_ASCII or FTP_BINARY. The *pos* argument is the position in the remote file to start downloading from. This function returns TRUE on success or FALSE on failure.

Here's how to download the file a.php and save it as script.php locally:

```php
<?php
  $connect = ftp_connect("ftp.ispname.com");
```

```
$result = ftp_login($connect, "username", "password");

if(!$result){
  echo "Could not connect.";
  exit;
}

$result = ftp_get($connect, "script.php", "a.php", FTP_ASCII);
  .
  .
  .
```

Did you actually get the file? You can check by seeing if $result is true or false. If $result is TRUE, you got the file; if FALSE, you didn't:

```
<?php
$connect = ftp_connect("ftp.ispname.com");

$result = ftp_login($connect, "username", "password");

if(!$result){
  echo "Could not connect.";
  exit;
}

$result = ftp_get($connect, "script.php", "a.php", FTP_ASCII);

if($result){
  echo "Got the file.";
}
else {
  echo "Did not get the file.";
}
  .
  .
  .
?>
```

Finally, it's a good idea to close the FTP connection, which you can do with ftp_close like this in phpftpget.php:

```
<html>
  <head>
    <title>
      Downloading a file with FTP
    </title>
  </head>

  <body>
    <h1>Downloading a file with FTP</h1>
    Downloading the file....
    <br>
    <?php
```

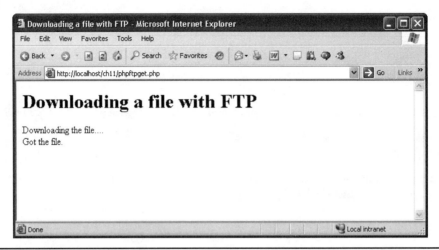

FIGURE 11-8 Downloading a file with FTP

```
      $connect = ftp_connect("ftp.ispname.com");

      $result = ftp_login($connect, "username", "password");

      if(!$result){
        echo "Could not connect.";
        exit;
      }

      $result = ftp_get($connect, "script.php", "a.php", FTP_ASCII);

      if($result){
        echo "Got the file.";
      }
      else {
        echo "Did not get the file.";
      }

      ftp_close($connect);
    ?>
  <body>
</html>
```

You can see the results in Figure 11-8—the application connected to the remote server and downloaded the file. Excellent.

Uploading Files with FTP

You just saw how to download files with FTP and PHP; you can upload files as well. All it takes is ftp_put:

```
ftp_put(ftp_stream, remote_file, local_file, mode [, pos])
```

This function stores *local_file* (which can be specified with a pathname) on the FTP server, as *remote_file*. The transfer mode specified must be either FTP_ASCII or FTP_BINARY. The *pos* argument specifies the place to start reading data from in the local file. The function returns TRUE on success or FALSE on failure.

Here's an example, phpftpput.php, which uploads itself. It starts by connecting to the FTP server:

```php
<?php
  $connect = ftp_connect("ftp.ispname.com");
      .
      .
      .
?>
```

Then you can log in:

```php
<?php
  $connect = ftp_connect("ftp.ispname.com");

  $result = ftp_login($connect, "username", "password");
      .
      .
      .
?>
```

And you can display the results of the connection attempt if it failed, exiting the program this way:

```php
<?php
  $connect = ftp_connect("ftp.ispname.com");

  $result = ftp_login($connect, "username", "password");

  if(!$result){
    echo "Could not connect.";
    exit;
  }
      .
      .
      .
?>
```

Now you can upload the file using ftp_put:

```php
<?php
  $connect = ftp_connect("ftp.ispname.com");

  $result = ftp_login($connect, "username", "password");
      .
      .
      .
?>
```

And you can check the results of this operation, reporting on success to the user:

```php
<?php
    $connect = ftp_connect("ftp.ispname.com");

    $result = ftp_login($connect, "username", "password");

    if(!$result){
        echo "Could not connect.";
        exit;
    }

    $result = ftp_put($connect, "phpftpput.php", "phpftpput.php", FTP_
ASCII);

    if($result){
        echo "Uploaded the file.";
    }
        .
        .
        .
?>
```

Or, if the operation failed, you can report that as well. Finally, you can close the connection as well:

```html
<html>
  <head>
    <title>
      Uploading a file with FTP
    </title>
  </head>

  <body>
    <h1>
      Uploading a file with FTP
    </h1>
    Uploading the file....
    <br>
    <?php
        $connect = ftp_connect("ftp.ispname.com");

        $result = ftp_login($connect, "username", "password");

        if(!$result){
            echo "Could not connect.";
            exit;
        }

        $result = ftp_put($connect, "phpftpput.php", "phpftpput.php", FTP_ASCII);
```

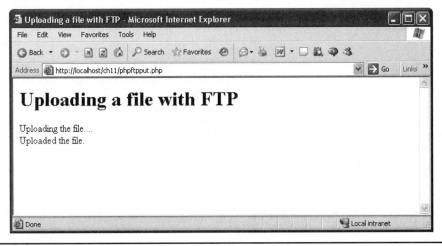

FIGURE 11-9   Uploading a file with FTP

```
    if($result){
      echo "Uploaded the file.";
    }
    else {
      echo "Did not upload the file.";
    }

    ftp_close($connect);
  ?>
 <body>
</html>
```

Okay, you can see the results in Figure 11-9—the application connected to the remote server and uploaded the file.

Deleting a File with FTP

Want to get rid of a file on the FTP server? Use ftp_delete:

```
ftp_delete (ftp_stream, path)
```

Here, *ftp_stream* is the connection object, and *path* is the name of the file—including its path—on the server to delete. This function returns TRUE on success and FALSE on failure.

In this example, phpftpdelete.php, you have to connect and log in first:

```
  <?php
    $connect = ftp_connect("ftp.ispname.com");

    $result = ftp_login($connect, "username", "password");

    if(!$result){
```

```
      echo "Could not connect.";
      exit;
   }
      .
      .
      .
```

Then you can delete the file you uploaded before, phpftpput.php:

```php
<?php
   $connect = ftp_connect("ftp.ispname.com");

   $result = ftp_login($connect, "username", "password");

   if(!$result){
     echo "Could not connect.";
     exit;
   }

   $result = ftp_delete($connect, "phpftpput.php");
      .
      .
      .

?>
```

If the file was deleted, you can report that:

```php
<?php
   $connect = ftp_connect("ftp.ispname.com");

   $result = ftp_login($connect, "username", "password");

   if(!$result){
     echo "Could not connect.";
     exit;
   }

   $result = ftp_delete($connect, "phpftpput.php");

   if($result){
     echo "Deleted the file.";
   }
      .
      .
      .

?>
```

Otherwise, you can report failure. Either way, you should close the FTP connection like this in phpftpdelete.php:

```html
<html>
  <head>
    <title>
      Deleting a file with FTP
```

```
    </title>
  </head>

  <body>
    <h1>
      Deleting a file with FTP
    </h1>
    Deleting the file....
    <br>
    <?php
      $connect = ftp_connect("ftp.ispname.com");

      $result = ftp_login($connect, "username", "password");

      if(!$result){
        echo "Could not connect.";
        exit;
      }

      $result = ftp_delete($connect, "phpftpput.php");

      if($result){
        echo "Deleted the file.";
      }
      else {
        echo "Did not delete the file.";
      }

      ftp_close($connect);
    ?>
  <body>
</html>
```

You can see the results in Figure 11-10—the file was indeed deleted.

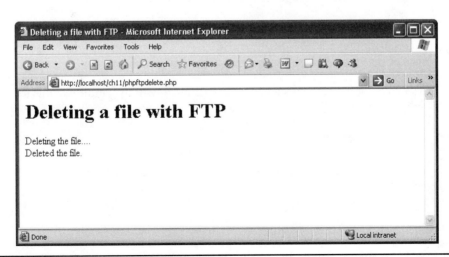

FIGURE 11-10   Deleting a file with FTP

Creating and Removing Directories with FTP

You can also create and delete directories on remote FTP servers using PHP. You create directories using ftp_mkdir (for "make directory"):

```
ftp_mkdir (ftp_stream, directory )
```

And you can delete directories using ftp_rmdir (for "remove directory"):

```
ftp_rmdir (ftp_stream, directory )
```

For both functions, *ftp_stream* is the FTP connection object, and *directory* is the affected directory.

Here's an example, phpftpdir.php. After connecting and logging in, the code attempts to create a new directory named backup with ftp_mkdir, and lets the user know if it was successful:

```php
<?php
  $connect = ftp_connect("ftp.ispname.com");

  $result = ftp_login($connect, "username", "password");

  if(!$result){
    echo "Could not connect.";
    exit;
  }

  $result = ftp_mkdir($connect, "backup");

  if($result){
    echo "Created the directory. <br>";
  }
  else {
    echo "Could not create the directory. <br>";
  }
     .
     .
     .
?>
```

And after creating the new directory, you can delete it with ftp_rmdir like this in phpftpdir.php:

```html
<html>
  <head>
    <title>
      Creating and removing directories with FTP
    </title>
  </head>

  <body>
    <h1>
      Creating and removing directories with FTP
    </h1>
```

```php
<?php
  $connect = ftp_connect("ftp.ispname.com");

  $result = ftp_login($connect, "username", "password");

  if(!$result){
    echo "Could not connect.";
    exit;
  }

  $result = ftp_mkdir($connect, "backup");

  if($result){
    echo "Created the directory. <br>";
  }
  else {
    echo "Could not create the directory. <br>";
  }

  $result = ftp_rmdir($connect, "backup");

  if($result){
    echo "Removed the directory. <br>";
  }
  else {
    echo "Could not remove the directory. <br>";
  }

  ftp_close($connect);
?>
<body>
</html>
```

You can see the results in Figure 11-11—the directory was created and then deleted.

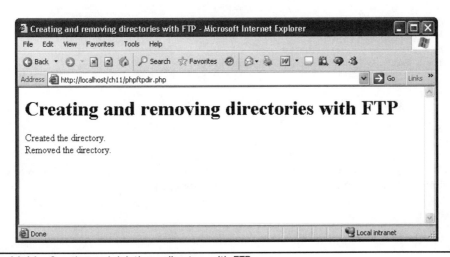

FIGURE 11-11   Creating and deleting a directory with FTP

Sending E-mail

Your PHP scripts can send e-mail as well. To enable e-mail, edit this section in the PHP initialization file, php.ini:

```
[mail function]
; For Win32 only.
SMTP = localhost
; For Win32 only.
sendmail_from = me@localhost.com
; For Unix only.  You may supply arguments as well (default: "sendmail -t -i").
;sendmail_path =
```

Windows users should list the SMTP host they want to use (such as mail.ispname.com or smtp.ispname.com) and set their return address. Linux and Unix users may not have to make any changes if the sendmail utility is already in their path, but if things don't work as they are, uncomment the sendmail_path and set it to the appropriate value (such as /usr/bin/sendmail).

To send mail, you use the mail function:

```
mail(to, subject, message [, additional_headers [, additional_parameters]])
```

This sends mail to the e-mail address in *to*, with subject *subject*, and message *message*. You can also set additional mail headers and parameters to sendmail.

You can see an example here—phpemail.html and phpemail.php. The phpemail.html page lets the user enter the e-mail they want to send, and posts it to phpemail.php:

```
<html>
  <head>
    <title>
      Send email
    </title>
  </head>

  <body>
    <h1>Send email</h1>
    <br>
    <form method="post" action="phpemail.php">
        .
        .
        .
    </form>
  <body>
</html>
```

In this page, the user can enter their comments in a text area named message, and click the Submit button to send those comments to phpemail.php:

```
<html>
  <head>
    <title>
```

```
        Send email
      </title>
  </head>

  <body>
    <h1>Send email</h1>
    <br>
    <form method="post" action="phpemail.php">
      Please type your comments and click Submit:
      <br>
      <textarea name="message" cols="50" rows="5"></textarea>
      <br>
      <br>
      <input type="submit" value="Submit">
    </form>
  <body>
</html>
```

You can see this page in Figure 11-12, where the user has entered an e-mail message.

The phpemail.php script reads the message sent by the user—that is, $_REQUEST["message"]—and mails it this way:

```
<html>
  <head>
    <title>
      Your email was sent
    </title>
  </head>
```

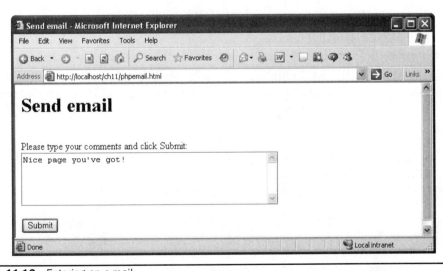

FIGURE 11-12   Entering an e-mail

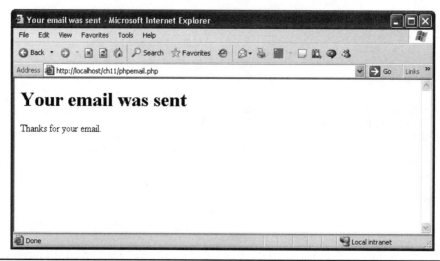

Your email was sent

FIGURE 11-13   Sending e-mail

```
<body>
  <h1>Your email was sent</h1>
  Thanks for your email.
  <br>
  <?php
    mail("steve@ispname.com", "Web mail", $_REQUEST["message"]);
  ?>
<body>
</html>
```

You can see the results in Figure 11-13, where the e-mail was sent.

Sending Advanced E-mail

You can also send e-mail with additional headers, such as a cc header and a bcc header. Here's how that works in phpadvemail.html and phpadvemail.php. Here's phpadvemail.html, which allows the user to enter their e-mail:

```
<html>
  <head>
    <title>
      Send email with headers
    </title>
  </head>

  <body>
    <h1>Send email with headers</H1>

    <form method="post" action="phpadvemail.php">
      Please type your comments and click Submit:
      <br>
      <br>
```

```
      <textarea name="message" cols="50" rows="5"></textarea>
      <br>
      <input type="submit" value="Submit">
    </form>
  <body>
</html>
```

And you can include text fields for cc and bcc headers as well:

```
<html>
  <head>
    <title>
      Send email with headers
    </title>
  </head>

  <body>
    <h1>Send email with headers</H1>

    <form method="post" action="phpadvemail.php">
      Please type your comments and click Submit:
      <br>
      cc: <input type="text" name="cc">
      bcc: <input type="text" name="bcc">
      <br>
      <textarea name="message" cols="50" rows="5"></textarea>
      <br>
      <input type="submit" value="Submit">
    </form>
  <body>
</html>
```

You can see this page in Figure 11-14, where the user has entered an e-mail, along with cc and bcc e-mail addresses.

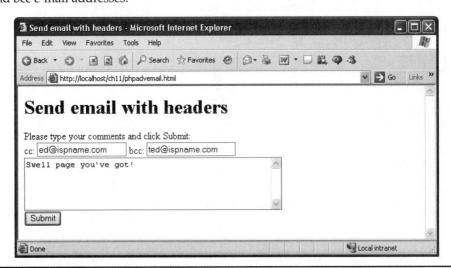

FIGURE 11-14   Entering e-mail with headers

The user's e-mail message and cc and bcc headers is sent to phpadvemail.php. To use the e-mail headers, you assemble them into a text string, separated by "\r\n". For example, if the user entered a cc header, you can add that to a string named $headers this way:

```php
<?php
  $headers = "";

  if(isset($_REQUEST["cc"])){
    $headers .= "cc:" . $_REQUEST["cc"] . "\r\n";
  }
    .
    .
    .
```

And you can get the bcc header as well, if there was one:

```php
<?php
  $headers = "";

  if(isset($_REQUEST["cc"])){
    $headers .= "cc:" . $_REQUEST["cc"] . "\r\n";
  }

  if(isset($_REQUEST["bcc"])){
    $headers .= "bcc:" . $_REQUEST["bcc"] . "\r\n";
  }
    .
    .
    .
?>
```

Finally, you can send the e-mail, along with the headers in phpadvemail.php:

```html
<html>
  <head>
    <title>
      Your email was sent
    </title>
  </head>

  <body>
    <h1>Your email was sent</h1>
    Thanks for your email with headers.
    <br>
    <?php
      $headers = "";

      if(isset($_REQUEST["cc"])){
        $headers .= "cc:" . $_REQUEST["cc"] . "\r\n";
      }
```

FIGURE 11-15   Sending e-mail with headers

```
    if(isset($_REQUEST["bcc"])){
      $headers .= "bcc:" . $_REQUEST["bcc"] . "\r\n";
    }

    $result = mail("steve@ispname.com", "Web mail", $_REQUEST["message"],
      $headers);
  ?>
  <body>
</html>
```

You can see the results in Figure 11-15, where the e-mail—complete with cc and bcc headers—was sent.

Adding Attachments to E-mail

You can also send attachments with your e-mail from PHP, although that takes some additional work. Here's an example, phpemailattachments.php, that sends an image file, image.jpg.

We'll start by storing the needed data for this e-mail in various variables—note that $attachment contains the name of the image file to attach, and $attachment_MIME_type contains the MIME (the Multipurpose Internet Mail Extension type) of the attachment:

```
  <?php
    $to = "steve@ispname.com";
    $subject = "Web mail";
    $message = "This email has an attachment.";
    $attachment = "image.jpg";
    $attachment_MIME_type = "image/jpeg";
      .
      .
      .
```

Now you can work on the attachment, encoding it for inclusion in the message. This is where it takes a little work, because you have to create a multipart form. You can start by reading in the attachment's data into a variable named $data:

```php
<?php
    $to = "steve@ispname.com";
    $subject = "Web mail";
    $message = "This email has an attachment.";
    $attachment = "image.jpg";
    $attachment_MIME_type = "image/jpeg";

    $handle = fopen ($attachment, "rb");
    $data = fread ($handle, filesize($attachment));
    fclose ($handle);
        .
        .
        .
```

Now we're going to work on creating our multipart form, starting with the boundary that separates the e-mail message from the attachment data:

```php
<?php
    $to = "steve@ispname.com";
    $subject = "Web mail";
    $message = "This email has an attachment.";
    $attachment = "image.jpg";
    $attachment_MIME_type = "image/jpeg";

    $handle = fopen ($attachment, "rb");
    $data = fread ($handle, filesize($attachment));
    fclose ($handle);

    $boundary = "---Multipart_Boundary---";

    $headers = "\nMIME-Version: 1.0\n" .
    "Content-Type: multipart/mixed;\n" .
    " boundary=\"" . $boundary . "\"";
        .
        .
        .
```

Now you have to encode the binary attachment data into text that e-mail uses, and you can do that using the PHP chunk_split and base64_encode functions:

```php
<?php
    $to = "steve@ispname.com";
    $subject = "Web mail";
    $message = "This email has an attachment.";
    $attachment = "image.jpg";
    $attachment_MIME_type = "image/jpeg";
```

```
$handle = fopen ($attachment, "rb");
$data = fread ($handle, filesize($attachment));
fclose ($handle);

$boundary = "---Multipart_Boundary---";

$headers = "\nMIME-Version: 1.0\n" .
"Content-Type: multipart/mixed;\n" .
" boundary=\"" . $boundary . "\"";

$data = chunk_split(base64_encode($data));
     .
     .
     .
```

Then you can assemble the text of the message, including the text-encoded attachment, and mail the whole like so:

```
<?php
$to = "steve@ispname.com";
     .
     .
     .

$boundary = "---Multipart_Boundary---";

$headers = "\nMIME-Version: 1.0\n" .
"Content-Type: multipart/mixed;\n" .
" boundary=\"" . $boundary . "\"";

$data = chunk_split(base64_encode($data));

$text = "--" . $boundary . "\n" .
"Content-Type:text/plain\nContent-Transfer-Encoding: 7bit\n\n" .
$message . "\n\n--" . $boundary . "\n" .
"Content-Type: " . $attachment_MIME_type . ";\n name=\"" .
$attachment . "\"\nContent-Transfer-Encoding: base64\n\n" .
$data . "\n\n--" . $boundary . "--\n";

$result = mail($to, $subject, $text, $headers);
     .
     .
     .
?>
```

Finally, you can report to the user what happened, like this in phpemailattachments .php:

```
<html>
  <head>
    <title>
```

```
        Sending email with attachments
      </title>
   </head>

   <body>
     <h1>
        Sending email with attachments
     </h1>
     <?php
       $to = "steve@ispname.com";
       $subject = "Web mail";
       $message = "This email has an attachment.";
       $attachment = "image.jpg";
       $attachment_MIME_type = "image/jpeg";

       $handle = fopen ($attachment, "rb");
       $data = fread ($handle, filesize($attachment));
       fclose ($handle);

       $boundary = "---Multipart_Boundary---";

       $headers = "\nMIME-Version: 1.0\n" .
       "Content-Type: multipart/mixed;\n" .
       " boundary=\"" . $boundary . "\"";

       $data = chunk_split(base64_encode($data));

       $text = "--" . $boundary . "\n" .
       "Content-Type:text/plain\nContent-Transfer-Encoding: 7bit\n\n" .
       $message . "\n\n--" . $boundary . "\n" .
       "Content-Type: " . $attachment_MIME_type . ";\n name=\"" .
       $attachment . "\"\nContent-Transfer-Encoding: base64\n\n" .
       $data . "\n\n--" . $boundary . "--\n";

       $result = @mail($to, $subject, $text, $headers);
       if($result) {
         echo "The email was sent.";
       } else {
         echo "The email was not sent.";
       }
     ?>
   <body>
</html>
```

Cool. You can see the results in Figure 11-16, where the e-mail, including the attachment, was sent.

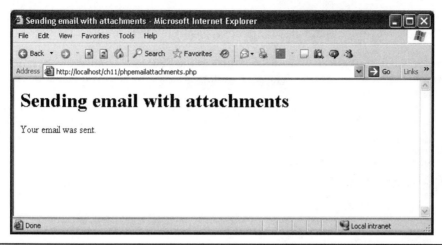

FIGURE 11-16   Sending e-mail with attachments

Storing Data in Sessions

By their very nature, Web pages hold only temporary data, unless you specifically store your data on the server. One way of storing data on the server is to use *sessions*. Using sessions, you can store and retrieve data by name. To work with a session, you start by calling session_start:

```
session_start();
     .
     .
     .
```

To store data in the session, use the $_SESSION array. For example, here we're storing "Rear Window" under the key "movie":

```
session_start();
$_SESSION['movie'] = "Rear Window";
     .
     .
     .
```

Now in another page access (either of the same or a different page), you can access the data under the key "movie" using $_SESSION again:

```
session_start();
$movie = $_SESSION['movie'];
     .
     .
     .
```

So as you can see, you're able to preserve data between page accesses. That data isn't preserved forever—it times out at some point, typically 30–180 minutes, depending on your PHP installation.

Session behavior is affected by these settings in the PHP initialization file, php.ini—note for example that you can set how long session data is stored by setting a value for session .cache_expire in minutes:

- session.save_path "/tmp"
- session.name "PHPSESSID"
- session.save_handler "files"
- session.auto_start "0"
- session.gc_probability "1"
- session.gc_divisor "100"
- session.gc_maxlifetime "1440"
- session.serialize_handler "php"
- session.cookie_lifetime "0"
- session.cookie_path "/"
- session.cookie_domain ""
- session.cookie_secure ""
- session.use_cookies "1"
- session.use_only_cookies "0"
- session.referer_check ""
- session.entropy_file ""
- session.entropy_length "0"
- session.cache_limiter "nocache"
- session.cache_expire "180"
- session.use_trans_sid "0" PHP_INI_SYSTEM | PHP_INI_PERDIR

In particular, you might note that all data for a particular session will be stored in a file in the directory specified by the session.save_path item. A file for each session (whether or not any data is associated with that session) will be created.

Okay, time for an example, phpsession.php, which stores the purchase total the user has made in the session data. First, you start with session_start:

```
<?php
  session_start();
    .
    .
    .
?>
```

Then you can store the user's purchase total with the session key "purchase":

```php
<?php
  session_start();
  $_SESSION['purchase'] = "39.25";
?>
```

Here's what it looks like in phpsession.php:

```html
<html>
  <head>
    <title>
      Storing data in sessions
    </title>
  </head>

  <body>
    <h1>
      Storing data in sessions
    </h1>

    <?php
      session_start();
      $_SESSION['purchase'] = "39.25";
    ?>

    Stored your purchase, $39.35.
    <br>
    To read your purchase in a new page, <a href="phpsession2.php"> click
      here</a>.
  </body>
</html>
```

You can see the results in Figure 11-17, where the user's purchase total was stored in the session.

This script, phpsession.php, has a hyperlink to another page, phpsession2.php, which reads the session data and displays it. In phpsession2.php, you start with session_start:

```php
<?php
  session_start();
      .
      .
      .
?>
```

The information you want is stored with the key "purchase"—but before trying to display it, you should check if an entry exists in the $_SESSION array with that key to avoid errors:

```php
<?php
  session_start();
```

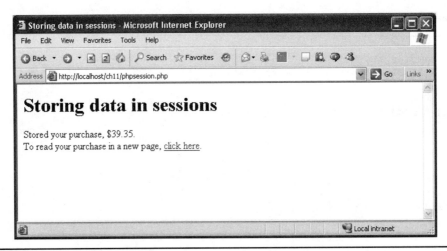

FIGURE 11-17   Saving data in a session

```
if(isset($_SESSION["purchase"])){
    .
    .
    .
}
?>
```

If the data you're looking for exists, you can display it like this:

```
<?php
session_start();

if(isset($_SESSION["purchase"])){
    echo "Welcome. You have purchased \$" . $_SESSION['purchase'] . " worth.";
}
?>
```

Here's how this looks in phpsession2.php:

```
<html>
  <head>
    <title>
      Retrieving data from sessions
    </title>
  </head>

  <body>
    <h1>
      Retrieving data from sessions
    </h1>
```

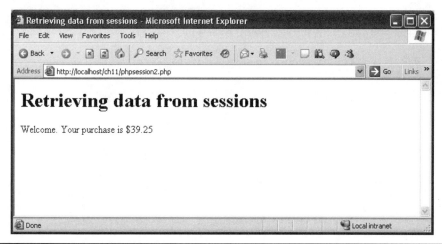

FIGURE **11-18**   Retrieving data from sessions

```php
<?php
  session_start();

  if(isset($_SESSION["purchase"])){
    echo "Welcome. You have purchased \$" . $_SESSION['purchase'] . " worth.";
  }
  ?>
</body>
</html>
```

And you can see the results in Figure 11-18, where the data stored in the session was successfully retrieved.

Writing a Hit Counter Using Sessions

Here's another example showing how sessions preserve data between page accesses: a Web hit counter, indicating how many times the user has been to a Web page (don't use this as a true Web counter, because it's only supposed to demonstrate how sessions work—after the user is inactive for the session time-out period, the data in the session will be dumped).

Here's how this example, phpcounter.php, starts:

```php
<?php
  session_start();
    .
    .
    .
  ?>
```

If the user has been here before, the page will have stored data in the session under the key "count", so you can check if there is any such data:

```php
<?php
  session_start();

  if (!isset($_SESSION['count'])) {
    .
    .
    .
  }
?>
```

If there is not any data in the session under the key "count", you can store data in the session, setting it to 0:

```php
<?php
  session_start();

  if (!isset($_SESSION['count'])) {
    $_SESSION['count'] = 0;
    .
    .
    .
  }
?>
```

Otherwise, you can increment the value stored in the session. Then that value is displayed by the page:

```php
<html>
  <head>
    <title>
      A session hit counter
    </title>
  </head>

  <body>
    <h1>
      A session hit counter
    </h1>
      Hello there. You have been here
      <?php
        session_start();

        if (!isset($_SESSION['count'])) {
          $_SESSION['count'] = 0;
        } else {
          $_SESSION['count']++;
        }
        echo $_SESSION['count'];
```

FIGURE 11-19   Starting the hit counter

```
    ?>
    times before.
  <body>
</html>
```

And you can see the results in Figure 11-19, where the user has just browsed to the page, and the hit counter is set to 0.

After the user reloads the page a few times, you can see the results in Figure 11-20, where the hit counter data was saved in the session.

FIGURE 11-20   Using the hit counter

Ajax

A jax is a hot topic, and the foundation of what's been called Web 2.0. Using Ajax techniques, you can create Web-based applications that have the look and feel of desktop applications. The primary difference is that Ajax applications don't refresh the entire browser display every time the user does something, which is a very Web-centric way of doing things. Using Ajax, you can communicate with the server behind the scenes, download data, and display it in some specific part of the Web page, without having to reload the whole page.

Ajax (the name stands for Asynchronous JavaScript and XML) relies on using JavaScript in the browser. The most common language on the server to use with Ajax is PHP, so this technology merits our attention.

Getting Started with Ajax

Here's an Ajax example to get things rolling—there's considerable client-side (that is, browser-side) technology to learn here. This example, will be called index.html, and it appears in Figure 12-1.

This simple example just fetches the contents of a text file, data.txt, from the server when you click the button. The difference between this application and a normal Web page is that when you click the button, the page doesn't blink and redisplay—all that happens is that the text "The fetched message will appear here." is overwritten with the contents of data.txt fetched from the server—"Hello from Ajax.", as you can see in Figure 12-2.

This application looks and works like a desktop application—when you do something in a word processor, type a character for example, the whole page doesn't flash and flicker when that new character is displayed. That's what Ajax brings to Web programming—no

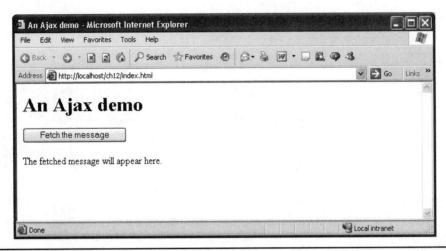

FIGURE 12-1   An Ajax demo

longer does the whole page have to be reloaded when the user does something and you need to interact with the server. The entire interaction with the server can take place behind the scenes, downloading and uploading data, and just specific sections of the Web page will be updated instead of the whole page being reloaded.

We'll take a look at how to work with Ajax, using it to fetch the contents of a text file, before moving on to using Ajax with PHP, seeing how to send data to PHP scripts using Ajax techniques, and reading what those scripts send back to you.

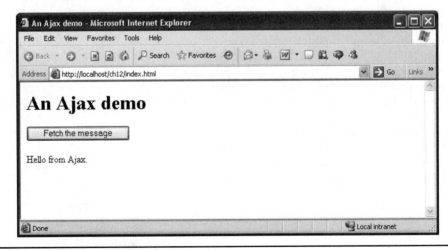

FIGURE 12-2   Fetching a message using Ajax

Writing Ajax

Here's what our first example, index.html, looks like—we'll spend a little time understanding how Ajax works with this example:

```html
<html>
  <head>
    <title>An Ajax demo</title>

    <script language = "javascript">
      var XMLHttpRequestObject = false;

      if (window.XMLHttpRequest) {
        XMLHttpRequestObject = new XMLHttpRequest();
      } else if (window.ActiveXObject) {
        XMLHttpRequestObject = new
          ActiveXObject("Microsoft.XMLHTTP");
      }

      function getData(dataSource, divID)
      {
        if(XMLHttpRequestObject) {
          var obj = document.getElementById(divID);
          XMLHttpRequestObject.open("GET", dataSource);

          XMLHttpRequestObject.onreadystatechange = function()
          {
            if (XMLHttpRequestObject.readyState == 4 &&
              XMLHttpRequestObject.status == 200) {
                obj.innerHTML = XMLHttpRequestObject.responseText;
            }
          }

          XMLHttpRequestObject.send(null);
        }
      }
    </script>
  </head>

  <body>
    <h1>An Ajax demo</h1>


    <form>
      <input type = "button" value = "Fetch the message"
        onclick = "getData('data.txt', 'targetDiv')">
    </form>

    <div id="targetDiv">
      <p>The fetched message will appear here.</p>
    </div>

  </body>
</html>
```

Okay, it's time to take this example apart—you're going to learn how to write full Ajax/ PHP applications here. The action here takes place when the user clicks the button with the caption "Fetch the message", and here's what that button looks like in the HTML form in index.html:

```
<body>

  <h1>An Ajax demo</h1>

  <form>
    <input type = "button" value = "Fetch the message"
      onclick = "getData('data.txt', 'targetDiv')">
  </form>

</body>
```

This button is connected to a JavaScript function, getData, and passes two arguments to that function—"data.txt", the name of the file on the server to fetch, and "targetDiv", which is the name of the <div> element to display the downloaded text in. Here's what that <div> element, which currently displays "The fetched message will appear here.", looks like in index.html:

```
<body>

  <h1>An Ajax demo</h1>

  <form>
    <input type = "button" value = "Fetch the message"
      onclick = "getData('data.txt', 'targetDiv')">
  </form>

  <div id="targetDiv">
    <p>The fetched message will appear here.</p>
  </div>

</body>
```

When the text in data.txt is downloaded, it'll be displayed in this <div> element, targetDiv, as you can see in Figure 12-2.

The real action in this application takes place in the JavaScript, including the getData function.

Creating the XMLHttpRequest Object

Ajax revolves around the XMLHttpRequest object available in most modern browsers. This is the object that lets you connect to the server behind the scenes, passing data to PHP scripts on the server, and reading the responses from those scripts.

The JavaScript in this example starts by creating an XMLHttpRequest object and storing it in a variable named XMLHttpRequestObject. The JavaScript code, contained in an HTML <script> element, starts by declaring that variable and setting it to false (so that if we are unsuccessful in creating an XMLHttpRequest object, this variable will be left holding FALSE, which subsequent code can test):

```
<script language = "javascript">
  var XMLHttpRequestObject = false;
       .
       .
       .
</script>
```

Now you've got to create the XMLHttpRequest object—a process that differs, depending on what browser you're dealing with. You can start out by attempting to create this object in the Netscape Navigator (version 7.0 and later), Apple Safari (version 1.2 and later), and Firefox using window.XMLHttpRequest, if that object exists, which you can test this way:

```
<script language = "javascript">
  var XMLHttpRequestObject = false;

  if (window.XMLHttpRequest) {
     .
     .
     .
  }
</script>
```

If window.XMLHttpRequest exists, you can create a new XMLHttpRequest object this way, using the expression new XMLHttpRequest():

```
<script language = "javascript">
  var XMLHttpRequestObject = false;

  if (window.XMLHttpRequest) {
    XMLHttpRequestObject = new XMLHttpRequest();
  }
</script>
```

That takes care of Firefox, Navigator, and Safari. You now have an XMLHttpRequest object, ready to use in those browsers.

What about the Internet Explorer? In Internet Explorer, you create XMLHttpRequest objects as an ActiveX object, so you first test to see if you can create ActiveX objects:

```
<script language = "javascript">
  var XMLHttpRequestObject = false;

  if (window.XMLHttpRequest) {
    XMLHttpRequestObject = new XMLHttpRequest();
  } else if (window.ActiveXObject) {
     .
     .
     .
  }
</script>
```

If you can create ActiveX objects, you can create a new XMLHttpRequest object using the expression ActiveXObject("Microsoft.XMLHTTP") in Internet Explorer:

```
<script language = "javascript">
  var XMLHttpRequestObject = false;

  if (window.XMLHttpRequest) {
    XMLHttpRequestObject = new XMLHttpRequest();
  } else if (window.ActiveXObject) {
    XMLHttpRequestObject = new
      ActiveXObject("Microsoft.XMLHTTP");
  }
</script>
```

At this point, then, you've been able to create an XMLHttpRequest object for all major browsers. The major properties and methods of this object are the same across the browsers—you can see all properties and methods of this object by browser in Tables 12-1 to 12-6.

Property	Description
onreadystatechange	Contains the name of the event handler that should be called when the value of the readyState property changes. Read/write.
readyState	Contains state of the request. Read-only.
responseBody	Contains a response body, which is one way HTTP responses can be returned. Read-only.
responseStream	Contains a response stream, a binary stream to the server. Read-only.
responseText	Contains the response body as a string. Read-only.
responseXML	Contains the response body as XML. Read-only.
status	Contains the HTTP status code returned by a request. Read-only.
statusText	Contains the HTTP response status text. Read-only.

TABLE 12-1 XMLHttpRequest Object Properties for Internet Explorer

Method	Description
abort	Aborts the HTTP request.
getAllResponseHeaders	Returns all the HTTP headers.
getResponseHeader	Returns the value of an HTTP header.
open	Opens a request to the server.
send	Sends an HTTP request to the server.
setRequestHeader	Sets the name and value of an HTTP header.

TABLE 12-2 XMLHttpRequest Object Methods for Internet Explorer

Property	Description
channel	Contains the channel used to perform the request. Read-only.
readyState	Contains state of the request. Read-only.
responseText	Contains the response body as a string. Read-only.
responseXML	Contains the response body as XML. Read-only.
status	Contains the HTTP status code returned by a request. Read-only.
statusText	Contains the HTTP response status text. Read-only.

TABLE 12-3   XMLHttpRequest Object Properties for Mozilla, Firefox, and Netscape Navigator

Method	Description
abort	Aborts the HTTP request.
getAllResponseHeaders	Returns all the HTTP headers.
getResponseHeader	Returns the value of an HTTP header.
openRequest	Native (nonscript) method to open a request.
overrideMimeType	Overrides the MIME type the server returns.

TABLE 12-4   XMLHttpRequest Object Methods for Mozilla, Firefox, and Netscape Navigator

Property	Description
onreadystatechange	Contains the name of the event handler that should be called when the value of the readyState property changes. Read/write.
readyState	Contains state of the request. Read-only.
responseText	Contains the response body as a string. Read-only.
responseXML	Contains the response body as XML. Read-only.
status	Contains the HTTP status code returned by a request. Read-only.
statusText	Contains the HTTP response status text. Read-only.

TABLE 12-5   XMLHttpRequest Object Properties for Apple Safari

Method	Description
abort	Aborts the HTTP request.
getAllResponseHeaders	Returns all the HTTP headers.
getResponseHeader	Returns the value of an HTTP header.
open	Opens a request to the server.
send	Sends an HTTP request to the server.
setRequestHeader	Sets the name and value of an HTTP header.

TABLE 12-6   XMLHttpRequest object methods for Apple Safari

Okay, now you have an XMLHttpRequest object—the next step is to open it, preparing you to interact with the server.

Opening the XMLHttpRequest Object

To work with an XMLHttpRequest object and connect to the server, you first have to open that object. That happens in this example's code in the getData function, which is passed the name of the file to fetch from the server (as the dataSource argument) and the name of the <div> element to display the fetched text in (as the divID argument):

```
<script language = "javascript">
  var XMLHttpRequestObject = false;

  if (window.XMLHttpRequest) {
    XMLHttpRequestObject = new XMLHttpRequest();
  } else if (window.ActiveXObject) {
    XMLHttpRequestObject = new
      ActiveXObject("Microsoft.XMLHTTP");
  }

  function getData(dataSource, divID)
  {
    .
    .
    .
  }
</script>
```

Now you can check if the XMLHttpRequest object-creation code has been successful in creating an XMLHttpRequest object. That creation code, being outside any JavaScript function, runs as soon as the page loads, so you can test if you've been able to create an XMLHttpRequest object this way in the getData function:

```
<script language = "javascript">
  var XMLHttpRequestObject = false;

  if (window.XMLHttpRequest) {
    XMLHttpRequestObject = new XMLHttpRequest();
  } else if (window.ActiveXObject) {
    XMLHttpRequestObject = new
      ActiveXObject("Microsoft.XMLHTTP");
  }

  function getData(dataSource, divID)
  {
    if(XMLHttpRequestObject) {
      .
      .
      .
    }
  }
</script>
```

It's time to open the XMLHttpRequest object, which configures it for use with the server (it does not connect the object to the server); here's how you use that method:

```
open("method", "URL"[, asyncFlag[, "userName"[, "password"]]])
```

Here are what these various parameters mean:

- **method**   This is the HTTP method used to open the connection, such as GET, POST, PUT, HEAD, or PROPFIND.
- **URL**   This is the requested URL.
- **asyncFlag**   A Boolean value indicating whether the call is asynchronous. The default is true.
- **userName**   The user name.
- **password**   The password.

Here's how to open the XMLHttpRequest object in this example, index.html, configuring that object to use the GET method to connect to the server, and to download data.txt (which is passed to the getData function in the dataSource argument):

```
<script language = "javascript">
  var XMLHttpRequestObject = false;

  if (window.XMLHttpRequest) {
    XMLHttpRequestObject = new XMLHttpRequest();
  } else if (window.ActiveXObject) {
    XMLHttpRequestObject = new
      ActiveXObject("Microsoft.XMLHTTP");
  }

  function getData(dataSource, divID)
  {
    if(XMLHttpRequestObject) {

      XMLHttpRequestObject.open("GET", dataSource);
      .
      .
      .
    }
  }
</script>
```

You've configured the XMLHttpRequest object, which sets it up to work with the server. Next, you have to make provisions to handle the data downloaded from the server.

Handling Downloaded Data

Ajax does its work *asynchronously*, which means it doesn't wait for the data to return from the server before letting the browser attend to other tasks. Specifically, it means that you must create a *callback* function. That callback function is called when the data is downloaded, so you put the code that handles the download in that callback function.

You connect the callback function to the XMLHttpRequest object by using that object's onreadystatechange property. A function *assigned* to that property will be called when data download events occur.

Here's how you assign a function to the XMLHttpRequest object's onreadystatechange property:

```
<script language = "javascript">
  var XMLHttpRequestObject = false;

  if (window.XMLHttpRequest) {
    XMLHttpRequestObject = new XMLHttpRequest();
  } else if (window.ActiveXObject) {
    XMLHttpRequestObject = new
      ActiveXObject("Microsoft.XMLHTTP");
  }

  function getData(dataSource, divID)
  {
    if(XMLHttpRequestObject) {
      XMLHttpRequestObject.open("GET", dataSource);

      XMLHttpRequestObject.onreadystatechange = function()
      {
        .
        .
        .
      }

    }
  }
</script>
```

When this function is called, the download status of your data has changed, and you check that using two additional XMLHttpRequest object properties—readyState and status. The readyState property tells you how the data downloading is coming. Here are the possible values for this property—a value of 4 is what you want to see, because that means that the data has been fully downloaded:

- 0 uninitialized
- 1 loading
- 2 loaded
- 3 interactive
- 4 complete

The status property is the property that contains the actual status of the download. This is actually the normal HTTP status code that you get when you try to download Web pages—for example, if the data you're looking for wasn't found, you'll get a value of 404 in the status property. Here are some of the possible values—note that you'll want to see a value of 200 here, which means that the download completed normally:

- **200**   OK
- **201**   Created
- **204**   No Content
- **205**   Reset Content
- **206**   Partial Content
- **400**   Bad Request
- **401**   Unauthorized
- **403**   Forbidden
- **404**   Not Found
- **405**   Method Not Allowed
- **406**   Not Acceptable
- **407**   Proxy Authentication Required
- **408**   Request Timeout
- **411**   Length Required
- **413**   Requested Entity Too Large
- **414**   Requested URL Too Long
- **415**   Unsupported Media Type
- **500**   Internal Server Error
- **501**   Not Implemented
- **502**   Bad Gateway
- **503**   Service Unavailable
- **504**   Gateway Timeout
- **505**   HTTP Version Not Supported

In the function connected to the onreadystatechange property, then, you can check if your data has been downloaded by checking if the readyState property equals 4:

```
<script language = "javascript">
  function getData(dataSource, divID)
  {
    if(XMLHttpRequestObject) {

      XMLHttpRequestObject.open("GET", dataSource);

      XMLHttpRequestObject.onreadystatechange = function()
      {
        if (XMLHttpRequestObject.readyState == 4 &&
          .
          .
          .
      }
    }
  }
</script>
```

And you can check if everything went okay by seeing if the status property holds 200:

```
<script language = "javascript">
  function getData(dataSource, divID)
  {
    if(XMLHttpRequestObject) {
      var obj = document.getElementById(divID);
      XMLHttpRequestObject.open("GET", dataSource);

      XMLHttpRequestObject.onreadystatechange = function()
      {
        if (XMLHttpRequestObject.readyState == 4 &&
          XMLHttpRequestObject.status == 200) {
          .
          .
          .
        }
      }
    }
  }
</script>
```

If you got the data from the server, you can display it in the targetDiv element in the Web page with just a little Dynamic HTML, no page refresh needed. Here's how targetDiv is defined in the Web page:

```
<body>

  <h1>An Ajax demo</h1>

  <form>
    <input type = "button" value = "Fetch the message"
      onclick = "getData('data.txt', 'targetDiv')">
  </form>

  <div id="targetDiv">
    <p>The fetched message will appear here.</p>
  </div>

</body>
```

You can get a JavaScript object corresponding to that <div> element like this:

```
<script language = "javascript">
  function getData(dataSource, divID)
  {
    if(XMLHttpRequestObject) {
      var obj = document.getElementById(divID);
      XMLHttpRequestObject.open("GET", dataSource);

      XMLHttpRequestObject.onreadystatechange = function()
      {
        if (XMLHttpRequestObject.readyState == 4 &&
          XMLHttpRequestObject.status == 200) {
```

```
                 .
                 .
                 .
           }
        }

        XMLHttpRequestObject.send(null);
      }
    }
  </script>
```

And when your data is downloaded successfully, you can display that data in the
<div> element—when you use XMLHttpRequest objects, your text is downloaded to the
responseText property, so this is how you handle that download in this example:

```
  <script language = "javascript">
    function getData(dataSource, divID)
    {
      if(XMLHttpRequestObject) {
        var obj = document.getElementById(divID);
        XMLHttpRequestObject.open("GET", dataSource);

        XMLHttpRequestObject.onreadystatechange = function()
        {
          if (XMLHttpRequestObject.readyState == 4 &&
            XMLHttpRequestObject.status == 200) {
              obj.innerHTML = XMLHttpRequestObject.responseText;
          }
        }

        XMLHttpRequestObject.send(null);
      }
    }
  </script>
```

Starting the Download

Okay, you've set everything up for the download—you've opened the XMLHttpRequest
object to configure it, and have set up the callback function. Now you need to start the
connection to the server and the whole download process.

You do that with the XMLHttpRequest send method. When you're using the GET
method, you pass a value of null to the send method like this:

```
  <script language = "javascript">
    var XMLHttpRequestObject = false;

    if (window.XMLHttpRequest) {
      XMLHttpRequestObject = new XMLHttpRequest();
    } else if (window.ActiveXObject) {
      XMLHttpRequestObject = new
        ActiveXObject("Microsoft.XMLHTTP");
    }
```

```
    function getData(dataSource, divID)
    {
      if(XMLHttpRequestObject) {
        var obj = document.getElementById(divID);
        XMLHttpRequestObject.open("GET", dataSource);

        XMLHttpRequestObject.onreadystatechange = function()
        {
          if (XMLHttpRequestObject.readyState == 4 &&
            XMLHttpRequestObject.status == 200) {
              obj.innerHTML = XMLHttpRequestObject.responseText;
          }
        }

        XMLHttpRequestObject.send(null);
      }
    }
  </script>
```

That connects to the server and starts the download. As you're going to see, when you use the POST method, you pass the data you want to send to the server, if any, to the send method.

That completes this example—you've initializes the XMLHttpRequest object, set up a callback function to handle the data download, and started the data access.

Creating XMLHttpRequest Objects

So far, you've created XMLHttpRequest objects this way:

```
  <script language = "javascript">
    var XMLHttpRequestObject = false;

    if (window.XMLHttpRequest) {
      XMLHttpRequestObject = new XMLHttpRequest();
    } else if (window.ActiveXObject) {
      XMLHttpRequestObject = new
        ActiveXObject("Microsoft.XMLHTTP");
    }
  </script>
```

However, some browsers support different versions of XMLHttpRequest objects, and you might find that you want to use a more advanced version (note that the preceding code will work fine for us in this book). Internet Explorer, for example, supports these more recent versions: MSXML2.XMLHTTP, MSXML2.XMLHTTP.3.0, MSXML2.XMLHTTP.4.0, or MSXML2.XMLHTTP.5.0.

Here's how to create an XMLHttpRequest object using MSXML2.XMLHTTP, for example. JavaScript supports a try/catch construct that you can use to handle errors, so you can try creating an MSXML2.XMLHTTP object using a try block like this:

```
  <script language = "javascript">
    var XMLHttpRequestObject = false;
```

```
try {
    XMLHttpRequestObject = new ActiveXObject("MSXML2.XMLHTTP");
}
    .
    .
    .
```

</script>

If there was an error—if the browser couldn't create a MSXML2.XMLHTTP object—you can catch that error in a catch block and try again by creating a standard Microsoft.XMLHTTP object:

```
<script language = "javascript">
    var XMLHttpRequestObject = false;

    try {
        XMLHttpRequestObject = new ActiveXObject("MSXML2.XMLHTTP");
    } catch (exception1) {
        try {
            XMLHttpRequestObject = new
            ActiveXObject("Microsoft.XMLHTTP");
        }
            .
            .
            .
    }
```

</script>

And if that didn't work, you can make sure that XMLHttpRequestObject is set to false:

```
<script language = "javascript">
    var XMLHttpRequestObject = false;

    try {
        XMLHttpRequestObject = new ActiveXObject("MSXML2.XMLHTTP");
    } catch (exception1) {
        try {
            XMLHttpRequestObject = new
            ActiveXObject("Microsoft.XMLHTTP");
        } catch (exception2) {
            XMLHttpRequestObject = false;
        }
    }
```

</script>

If XMLHttpRequestObject is left holding FALSE after all that code, you're not dealing with the Internet Explorer, and you can create an XMLHttpRequest object for other browsers like this:

```
<script language = "javascript">
    var XMLHttpRequestObject = false;
```

```
    try {
      XMLHttpRequestObject = new ActiveXObject("MSXML2.XMLHTTP");
    } catch (exception1) {
      try {
        XMLHttpRequestObject = new
         ActiveXObject("Microsoft.XMLHTTP");
      } catch (exception2) {
        XMLHttpRequestObject = false;
      }
    }

    if (!XMLHttpRequestObject && window.XMLHttpRequest) {
      XMLHttpRequestObject = new XMLHttpRequest();
    }
</script>
```

This code will create an MSXML2.XMLHTTP XMLHttpRequest object if it can in the Internet Explorer, or a Microsoft.XMLHTTP if it can't.

So far, you've just downloaded a text file, but Ajax is most often used with PHP on the server, so let's get to some of that.

Ajax with Some PHP

Say you had a PHP script named data.php, which echoed some text like this:

```
<?php
    echo 'This text was fetched from the server with Ajax and PHP.';
?>
```

You can download the echoed text using Ajax like this in a new version of index.html, index2.html:

```
<html>
  <head>
    <title>An Ajax and PHP demo</title>

    <script language = "javascript">
      var XMLHttpRequestObject = false;

      if (window.XMLHttpRequest) {
        XMLHttpRequestObject = new XMLHttpRequest();
      } else if (window.ActiveXObject) {
        XMLHttpRequestObject = new
          ActiveXObject("Microsoft.XMLHTTP");
      }

      function getData(dataSource, divID)
      {
        if(XMLHttpRequestObject) {
          var obj = document.getElementById(divID);
          XMLHttpRequestObject.open("GET", dataSource);
```

```
        XMLHttpRequestObject.onreadystatechange = function()
        {
          if (XMLHttpRequestObject.readyState == 4 &&
            XMLHttpRequestObject.status == 200) {
              obj.innerHTML = XMLHttpRequestObject.responseText;
          }
        }

        XMLHttpRequestObject.send(null);
      }
    }
  </script>
</head>

<body>

  <H1>An Ajax and PHP demo</H1>

  <form>
    <input type = "button" value = "Fetch the message"
      onclick = "getData('data.php', 'targetDiv')">
  </form>

  <div id="targetDiv">
    <p>The fetched message will appear here.</p>
  </div>

</body>
</html>
```

Passing Data to the Server with GET

How about sending some data to the server? You've got to encode the data you send to the server yourself in Ajax applications—you can't rely on that being done automatically by an HTML form, as when you send data using HTML controls.

In this example, we're going to send data to the server under the parameter name "data". If the data parameter holds "1" (note that this is the string "1", not the number 1, because all data you send to PHP scripts from Web pages is text), the script, choosem.php, sends back this message:

```
<?
  if ($_REQUEST["data"] == "1") {
    echo 'You sent the server a value of 1';
  }
    .
    .
    .
?>
```

On the other hand, if the data you send is "2", the script choosem.php echoes this message:

```
<?
  if ($_REQUEST["data"] == "1") {
    echo 'You sent the server a value of 1';
  }
  if ($_REQUEST["data"] == "2") {
    echo 'You sent the server a value of 2';
  }
?>
```

When you use the GET method of fetching data from the server, data is sent from Web pages back to the server using URL encoding, which means that data is appended to the URL that is read from the server. For example, if you were using the GET method and you had a standard Web page with a text field named "a" that contained the number 5, a text field named "b" that contained the number 6, and a text field named "c" that contained the text "Now is the time", all that data would be encoded and added to the URL you're accessing. The names of the text fields, a, b, and c, are the parameters you're sending to the server, and the text in each text field is the data assigned to each parameter.

When data is URL encoded, a question mark (?) is added to the end of the URL, and the data, in name=data format, is added after that question mark. Spaces in text are converted to a plus sign (+), and you separate pairs of name=data items with ampersands (&). So to encode the data from the "a", "b", and "c" text fields and send it to http://www.servername .com/user/scriptname, you'd use this URL:

```
http://www.servername.com/user/scriptname?a=5&b=6&c=Now+is+the+time
```

That means that to send the data parameter holding "1" to choosem.php, you can use an URL like this:

```
choosem.php?data=1
```

You can modify the Ajax page you've seen so far in this chapter to interact with choosem.php if you put in two buttons—the first sends the data parameter with "1" using URL encoding:

```
<form>
  <input type = "button" value = "Fetch message 1"
    onclick = "getData('choosem.php?data=1', 'targetDiv')">
       .
       .
       .
</form>
```

And the second button sends the value "2" to choosem.php:

```
<form>
  <input type = "button" value = "Fetch message 1"
    onclick = "getData('choosem.php?data=1', 'targetDiv')">
```

```
      <input type = "button" value = "Fetch message 2"
        onclick = "getData('choosem.php?data=2', 'targetDiv')">
    </form>
```

Here's what all this looks like in index3.html:

```
<html>
  <head>
    <title>Sending Ajax data with GET</title>

    <script language = "javascript">
      var XMLHttpRequestObject = false;

      if (window.XMLHttpRequest) {
        XMLHttpRequestObject = new XMLHttpRequest();
      } else if (window.ActiveXObject) {
        XMLHttpRequestObject = new
          ActiveXObject("Microsoft.XMLHTTP");
      }

      function getData(dataSource, divID)
      {
        if(XMLHttpRequestObject) {
          var obj = document.getElementById(divID);
          XMLHttpRequestObject.open("GET", dataSource);

          XMLHttpRequestObject.onreadystatechange = function()
          {
            if (XMLHttpRequestObject.readyState == 4 &&
              XMLHttpRequestObject.status == 200) {
                obj.innerHTML = XMLHttpRequestObject.responseText;
            }
          }

          XMLHttpRequestObject.send(null);
        }
      }
    </script>
  </head>

<body>

  <h1>Sending Ajax data with GET</h1>

  <form>
    <input type = "button" value = "Fetch message 1"
      onclick = "getData('choosem.php?data=1', 'targetDiv')">
    <input type = "button" value = "Fetch message 2"
      onclick = "getData('choosem.php?data=2', 'targetDiv')">
  </form>
```

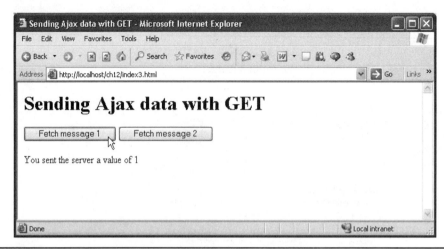

FIGURE 12-3 Sending "1" to the server with GET

```
<div id="targetDiv">
  <p>The fetched message will appear here.</p>
</div>

</body>
</html>
```

You can see the result in Figure 12-3, where the user clicked the "Fetch message 1" button. In Figure 12-4, the user clicked the "Fetch message 2" button.

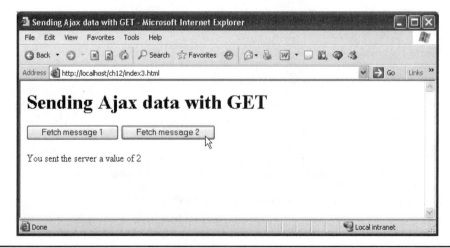

FIGURE 12-4 Sending "2" to the server with GET

Passing Data to the Server with POST

We've written choose.php this way, using $_REQUEST instead of $_GET or $_POST to read data sent to this script:

```
<?
  if ($_REQUEST["data"] == "1") {
    echo 'You sent the server a value of 1';
  }
  if ($_REQUEST["data"] == "2") {
    echo 'You sent the server a value of 2';
  }
?>
```

That means that chhosem.php is set to be used with the POST method, not just GET. But how do you send data to PHP scripts using POST?

First, because you're not sending data URL-encoded anymore, you have to change the two buttons in the form from this:

```
<form>
  <input type = "button" value = "Fetch message 1"
    onclick = "getData('choosem.php?data=1', 'targetDiv')">
  <input type = "button" value = "Fetch message 2"
    onclick = "getData('choosem.php?data=2', 'targetDiv')">
</form>
```

to this, where the data—"1" or "2"—is sent to the getData function as the function's third argument:

```
<form>
  <input type = "button" value = "Fetch message 1"
    onclick = "getData('choosem.php', 'targetDiv', 1)">
  <input type = "button" value = "Fetch message 2"
    onclick = "getData('choosem.php', 'targetDiv', 2)">
</form>
```

Now you've got to modify the getData function to take three arguments:

```
function getData(dataSource, divID, data)
{
    .
    .
      .
}
```

And you've also got to change this line, which specifies the GET method:

```
function getData(dataSource, divID, data)
{
  if(XMLHttpRequestObject) {
    var obj = document.getElementById(divID);
    XMLHttpRequestObject.open("GET", dataSource);
```

```
         .
         .
         .
     }
```

to use the POST method instead:

```
     function getData(dataSource, divID, data)
     {
       if(XMLHttpRequestObject) {
         var obj = document.getElementById(divID);
         XMLHttpRequestObject.open("POST", dataSource);
         .
         .
         .
     }
```

There's more to switching to the POST method than just that, however—you also have to indicate to the server-side code that you're going to be encoding data the way POST encodes that data, which means you have to include this line of code:

```
     function getData(dataSource, divID, data)
     {
       if(XMLHttpRequestObject) {
         var obj = document.getElementById(divID);
         XMLHttpRequestObject.open("POST", dataSource);
         XMLHttpRequestObject.setRequestHeader('Content-Type',
           'application/x-www-form-urlencoded');
         .
         .
         .
       }
     }
```

Finally, you use the send method to send the data to the server. You send the server a data string that is the same as the one you'd append to the end of the URL with the GET method, but when using POST, you pass that string to the send method:

```
     function getData(dataSource, divID, data)
     {
       if(XMLHttpRequestObject) {
         var obj = document.getElementById(divID);
         XMLHttpRequestObject.open("POST", dataSource);
         XMLHttpRequestObject.setRequestHeader('Content-Type',
           'application/x-www-form-urlencoded');

         XMLHttpRequestObject.onreadystatechange = function()
         {
           if (XMLHttpRequestObject.readyState == 4 &&
             XMLHttpRequestObject.status == 200) {
               obj.innerHTML = XMLHttpRequestObject.responseText;
         }
       }
```

```
        XMLHttpRequestObject.send("data=" + data);
      }
    }
```

Here's what it all looks like in index4.html:

```
<html>
  <head>
    <title>Sending Ajax data with POST</title>

    <script language = "javascript">
      var XMLHttpRequestObject = false;

      if (window.XMLHttpRequest) {
        XMLHttpRequestObject = new XMLHttpRequest();
      } else if (window.ActiveXObject) {
        XMLHttpRequestObject = new
          ActiveXObject("Microsoft.XMLHTTP");
      }

      function getData(dataSource, divID, data)
      {
        if(XMLHttpRequestObject) {
          var obj = document.getElementById(divID);
          XMLHttpRequestObject.open("POST", dataSource);
          XMLHttpRequestObject.setRequestHeader('Content-Type',
            'application/x-www-form-urlencoded');

          XMLHttpRequestObject.onreadystatechange = function()
          {
            if (XMLHttpRequestObject.readyState == 4 &&
              XMLHttpRequestObject.status == 200) {
                obj.innerHTML = XMLHttpRequestObject.responseText;
            }
          }

          XMLHttpRequestObject.send("data=" + data);
        }
      }
    </script>
  </head>

  <body>

    <h1>Sending Ajax data with POST</h1>

    <form>
      <input type = "button" value = "Fetch message 1"
        onclick = "getData('choosem.php', 'targetDiv', 1)">
      <input type = "button" value = "Fetch message 2"
        onclick = "getData('choosem.php', 'targetDiv', 2)">
    </form>
```

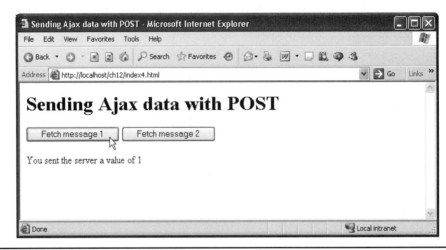

FIGURE 12-5 Sending "1" to the server with POST

```
<div id="targetDiv">
  <p>The fetched message will appear here.</p>
</div>

</body>
</html>
```

You can see the result in Figure 12-5, where the user clicked the "Fetch message 1" button, sending "1" to the server via POST.

So far, you've simply downloaded straight text, using the responseText property of the XMLHttpRequest object. But doesn't Ajax stand for Asynchronous JavaScript and XML? How about handling some XML? That's coming up next.

Handling XML

Say that you wanted to set up an online store that sold various items—a book on PHP, a television, a radio, and so on. You could store the items for sale in various XML files—products1.xml, products2.xml, and so on, and then download their contents using Ajax.

For example, here's what products1.xml might look like. You start with an XML declaration, as all XML files must have:

```
<?xml version = "1.0" ?>
        .
        .
        .
```

This XML declaration says that the document is an XML document, and that it's written in XML version 1.0. Next, all XML documents need a document element—that is, an XML element that contains all the other elements in the document. You make up your own elements in XML, so you might use a document element named <items> to store the items you have for sale like this:

```
<?xml version = "1.0" ?>
<items>
        .
        .
        .

</items>
```

And you can store the actual items for sale inside <item> elements like this:

```
<?xml version = "1.0" ?>
<items>
  <item>PHP book</item>
  <item>Television</item>
  <item>Radio</item>
</items>
```

That completes products1.xml. You can also have other lists of items for sale, as here in products2.xml, which lists Soda, Cheese, and Salami:

```
<?xml version = "1.0" ?>
<items>
  <item>Soda</item>
  <item>Cheese</item>
  <item>Salami</item>
</items>
```

Okay, now you have the two XML files that store the items for sale. How about downloading those XML files using Ajax? We'll put this to work in a page called store.html.

You can display two buttons in the store.html page—one for the first list of products, and one for the second list of products. For example, the first button would download products.1xml by calling a JavaScript function named getproducts1:

```
<form>
  <input type = "button" value = "Select products 1"
    onclick = "getproducts1()">
    .
    .
    .
</form>
```

And the second button will download the second list of items, products2.xml, by calling a JavaScript function named getproducts2:

```
<form>
  <input type = "button" value = "Select products 1"
    onclick = "getproducts1()">
  <input type = "button" value = "Select products 2"
    onclick = "getproducts2()">
</form>
```

In addition, we might display the downloaded items for sale in a <select> drop-down list control named productsList:

```
<form>
  <select size="1" id="productsList">
    <option>Select an item</option>
  </select>
  <br>
  <br>
  <input type = "button" value = "Select products 1"
    onclick = "getproducts1()">
  <input type = "button" value = "Select products 2"
    onclick = "getproducts2()">
</form>
```

And when the user selects a displayed item, you can indicate which one they selected in the page, which we'll do in a JavaScript function named setproducts, called when the user makes a selection in the <select> control:

```
<form>
  <select size="1" id="productsList"
    onchange="setproducts()">
    <option>Select an item</option>
  </select>
  <br>
  <br>
  <input type = "button" value = "Select products 1"
    onclick = "getproducts1()">
  <input type = "button" value = "Select products 2"
    onclick = "getproducts2()">
</form>
```

Okay, that sets up the controls in the page. Time to get to some Ajax, starting by creating the XMLHttpRequest object we're going to use to communicate with the server in JavaScript:

```
<html>
  <head>

    <title>Using Ajax with XML</title>

    <script language = "javascript">

      var XMLHttpRequestObject = false;

      if (window.XMLHttpRequest) {
        XMLHttpRequestObject = new XMLHttpRequest();
      } else if (window.ActiveXObject) {
        XMLHttpRequestObject = new ActiveXObject("Microsoft.XMLHTTP");
      }

          .
          .
          .
```

We're going to use a function named getproducts1 to fetch products1.xml and display the items in that XML document in the <select> control. The getproducts1 function starts by checking if the XMLHttpRequest object exists:

```
function getproducts1()
{
  if(XMLHttpRequestObject) {
    .
    .
    .
  }
}
```

If the XMLHttpRequest object exists, you can open it, indicating that you want to fetch products1.xml:

```
function getproducts1()
{
  if(XMLHttpRequestObject) {
    XMLHttpRequestObject.open("GET", "products1.xml");
    .
    .
    .
  }
}
```

Now you can download the XML here just as you downloaded text earlier—except this time, the downloaded data is XML, which means you use the responseXML property of the XMLHttpRequest object, not the responseText property:

```
function getproducts1()
{
  if(XMLHttpRequestObject) {
    XMLHttpRequestObject.open("GET", "products1.xml");

    XMLHttpRequestObject.onreadystatechange = function()
    {
      if (XMLHttpRequestObject.readyState == 4 &&
        XMLHttpRequestObject.status == 200) {
        var xmlDocument = XMLHttpRequestObject.responseXML;
        .
        .
        .
      }
    }
  }
}
```

The responseXML property holds your XML data in the form of a JavaScript XML document object. You can extract the <item> elements from that document object by using the getElementsByTagName method, which returns an array of <item> elements, which we'll store in a variable named products:

```
<html>
  <head>

    <title>Using Ajax with XML</title>

    <script language = "javascript">

      var products;
            .
            .
            .

      function getproducts1()
      {
        if(XMLHttpRequestObject) {
          XMLHttpRequestObject.open("GET", "products1.xml");

          XMLHttpRequestObject.onreadystatechange = function()
          {
            if (XMLHttpRequestObject.readyState == 4 &&
              XMLHttpRequestObject.status == 200) {
            var xmlDocument = XMLHttpRequestObject.responseXML;
            products = xmlDocument.getElementsByTagName("item");
              .
              .
              .
            }
          }
        }
      }
```

Alright, now the products variable stores an array of <item> elements. You can call a new function, listproducts, we'll write that will display the text in those elements in the <select> control in the page:

```
      function getproducts1()
      {
        if(XMLHttpRequestObject) {
          XMLHttpRequestObject.open("GET", "products1.xml");

          XMLHttpRequestObject.onreadystatechange = function()
          {
            if (XMLHttpRequestObject.readyState == 4 &&
              XMLHttpRequestObject.status == 200) {
            var xmlDocument = XMLHttpRequestObject.responseXML;
            products = xmlDocument.getElementsByTagName("item");
            listproducts();
            }
          }
        }
```

And the last step is to send a value of null to the XMLHttpRequest object to start
the download:

```
function getproducts1()
{
  if(XMLHttpRequestObject) {
    XMLHttpRequestObject.open("GET", "products1.xml");

    XMLHttpRequestObject.onreadystatechange = function()
    {
      if (XMLHttpRequestObject.readyState == 4 &&
        XMLHttpRequestObject.status == 200) {
      var xmlDocument = XMLHttpRequestObject.responseXML;
      products = xmlDocument.getElementsByTagName("item");
      listproducts();
      }
    }

    XMLHttpRequestObject.send(null);
  }
}
```

That completes the function getproducts1; the getproducts2 function downloads the
products2.xml document:

```
function getproducts2()
{
  if(XMLHttpRequestObject) {
    XMLHttpRequestObject.open("GET", "products2.xml");

    XMLHttpRequestObject.onreadystatechange = function()
    {
      if (XMLHttpRequestObject.readyState == 4 &&
        XMLHttpRequestObject.status == 200) {
      var xmlDocument = XMLHttpRequestObject.responseXML;
      products = xmlDocument.getElementsByTagName("item");
      listproducts();
      }
    }

    XMLHttpRequestObject.send(null);
  }
}
```

Excellent. Now you can write the listproducts function that lists the products for sale, as
stored in the products array. The products array holds these elements:

```
<item>PHP book</item>
<item>Television</item>
<item>Radio</item>
```

You can access them as products[0], products[1], products[2]. But that's not the end
of the story—how do you access the text inside each element? That's one of the tricks of

working with XML in JavaScript—to access the text inside each XML element, say products[0], you have to use the expression products[0].firstChild. That expression returns the first text node inside the element, and that text node holds the text we want. To access the text inside the text node, you would use the expression products[0].firstChild.data. Here, then, is how you can stock the <select> control with <option> elements whose captions are the products for sale:

```
function listproducts ()
{
  var loopIndex;
  var selectControl = document.getElementById('productsList');

  for (loopIndex = 0; loopIndex < products.length; loopIndex++ )
  {
    selectControl.options[loopIndex] = new
      Option(products[loopIndex].firstChild.data);
  }
}
```

We're almost done—all that's left is to write the setproducts function, which is called when the user makes a selection in the <select> control displaying the items for sale. You can display the item the user selected in a <div> element named targetDiv like this in setproducts:

```
function setproducts()
{
  document.getElementById('targetDiv').innerHTML =
    "You selected " + products[document.getElementById
      ('productsList').selectedIndex].firstChild.data;
}
```

As you can see, it takes a little extra effort to handle XML in Ajax. You can see store.html in Figure 12-6.

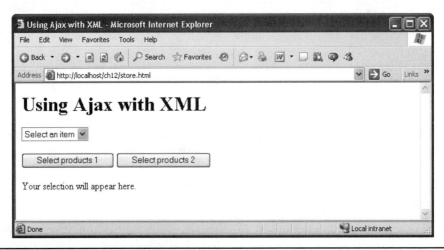

Using Ajax with XML - Microsoft Internet Explorer
File   Edit   View   Favorites   Tools   Help
Back •   •   Search   Favorites
Address   http://localhost/ch12/store.html   Go   Links »

Using Ajax with XML

Select an item

Select products 1   Select products 2

Your selection will appear here.

Done   Local intranet

FIGURE 12-6   store.html

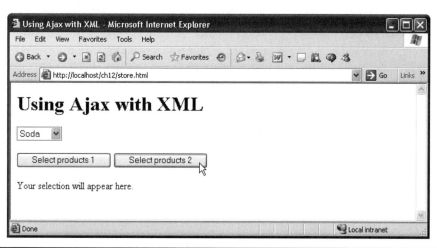

FIGURE 12-7   Downloading products using XML

When the user clicks the "Select products 2" button, those products are downloaded using XML and Ajax and displayed in the <select> control, as you can see in Figure 12-7.

And when the user selects an item, that item is displayed in the page, as you see in Figure 12-8.

That gives you an indication of how to handle XML with Ajax. Now it's time to add PHP to this picture.

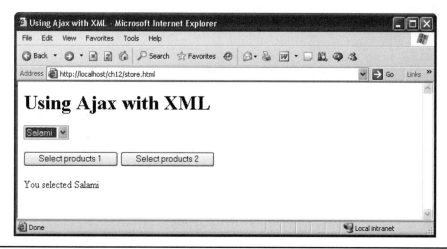

FIGURE 12-8   Selecting a product

Handling XML with PHP

Let's convert store.html into a new example, store2.html, that reads its XML from a PHP script, products.php. The products.php script is responsible for returning both the first XML document:

```
<?xml version = "1.0" ?>
<items>
   <item>PHP book</item>
   <item>Television</item>
   <item>Radio</item>
</items>
```

as well as the second one:

```
<?xml version = "1.0" ?>
<items>
   <item>Soda</item>
   <item>Cheese</item>
   <item>Salami</item>
</items>
```

To indicate which XML document you want, you can send a parameter, items, to products.php. When items equals "1", the script will return the first XML document, when items equals "2", the script will return the second XML document.

We'll write products.php first—which brings up the question: how exactly do you return an XML document from a PHP script? The way to do that is to set the Content-type header of the data sent to the browser to "text/xml", using the PHP header function:

```
<?php
header("Content-type: text/xml");
         .
         .
         .
?>
```

This necessary step lets the browser know that XML is coming. Now you can read the items parameter and load an array named $items accordingly:

```
<?php
header("Content-type: text/xml");

if ($_REQUEST["items"] == "1")
  $items = array('PHP book', 'Television', 'Radio');
if ($_REQUEST["items"] == "2")
  $items = array('Soda', 'Cheese', 'Salami');
         .
         .
         .
?>
```

Now you've got to assemble a proper XML document to send to the browser, starting with the XML declaration:

```php
<?php
header("Content-type: text/xml");

if ($_REQUEST["items"] == "1")
  $items = array('PHP book', 'Television', 'Radio');
if ($_REQUEST["items"] == "2")
  $items = array('Soda', 'Cheese', 'Salami');

echo '<?xml version="1.0" ?>';
        .
        .
        .
?>
```

And you can send the document element, which is <items>:

```php
<?php
header("Content-type: text/xml");

if ($_REQUEST["items"] == "1")
  $items = array('PHP book', 'Television', 'Radio');
if ($_REQUEST["items"] == "2")
  $items = array('Soda', 'Cheese', 'Salami');

echo '<?xml version="1.0" ?>';

echo '<items>';
        .
        .
        .
echo '</items>';
?>
```

Now you can loop over the items for sale, creating an <item> element for each this way:

```php
<?php
header("Content-type: text/xml");

if ($_REQUEST["items"] == "1")
  $items = array('PHP book', 'Television', 'Radio');
if ($_REQUEST["items"] == "2")
  $items = array('Soda', 'Cheese', 'Salami');

echo '<?xml version="1.0" ?>';

echo '<items>';
foreach ($items as $value)
{
  echo '<item>';
  echo $value;
  echo '</item>';
}
echo '</items>';
?>
```

The modifications in store2.html are relatively minor; all you have to do is to make sure you send the correct value for the items parameter to the products.php script—"1" or "2". You make that change in the getproducts1 and getproducts2 functions—for example, here's how you send a value of "1" to products.php in the getproducts1 function:

```
function getproducts1()
{
  if(XMLHttpRequestObject) {
    XMLHttpRequestObject.open("GET", "products.php?items=1");

    XMLHttpRequestObject.onreadystatechange = function()
    {
      if (XMLHttpRequestObject.readyState == 4 &&
        XMLHttpRequestObject.status == 200) {
      var xmlDocument = XMLHttpRequestObject.responseXML;
      products = xmlDocument.getElementsByTagName("item");
      listproducts();
      }
    }

    XMLHttpRequestObject.send(null);
  }
}
```

And that's all you need—the rest of store2.html is the same as store.html. You can see store2.html at work in Figure 12-9.

Very cool.

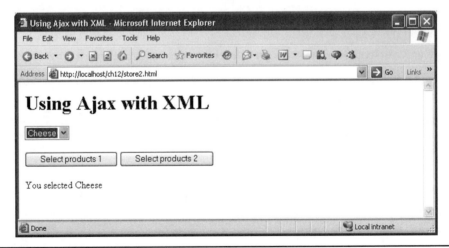

FIGURE 12-9   Selecting a product in store2.html

Advanced Ajax

The preceding chapter got the ball rolling with Ajax and PHP, and this chapter turns to some more required skills to use Ajax. For example, the preceding chapter used a single XMLHttpRequest object to communicate with the server. But what if the user clicks a button a second time before the first Ajax operation is complete? The code will innocently use the same XMLHttpRequest object for another request to the server—before the first request comes back.

That's not a big problem with the examples you've seen, since they download static data, but what if you were connection to a changing database? Or what if you had twenty Ajax-enabled buttons in your Web page, but used only one XMLHttpRequest object to fetch your data? Clearly, you should create and use one XMLHttpRequest object for each server request.

There's more coming up here as well. For example, Ajax is restricted to fetching data from the same server that the Ajax-enabled Web page itself comes from. That is, if your Ajax page is http://www.myajax.com/mypage.com, then you're going to have trouble accessing data from any other domain than http://www.myajax.com using Ajax. We'll discuss this behavior—and how to get around it—in this chapter.

There are other topics here as well. For example, besides downloading text or XML using Ajax, a common thing to do with Ajax is to download JavaScript that you execute in the browser. That's how you connect to a Google Ajax API (application programming interface)—Google Suggest, which you're going to see here.

Besides all that, you're going to see how to use Ajax with HTTP head requests, allowing you to check if files exist on the server, what their length and creation date is, and more. And you'll also see how to defeat caching in browsers like the Internet Explorer, and many other topics as you start getting into serious Ajax.

Handling Concurrent Ajax Requests with Multiple XMLHttpRequest Objects

As you recall from the preceding chapter, we created only a single XMLHttpRequest object, even though some of our examples, like store.html—shown next—give the user the option of clicking two buttons. That means the user could theoretically click a second button before their first Ajax request had been completed, and that is a problem. Here's what that looks

like in store.html—note that there's only one XMLHttpRequest object, and that same object
is used no matter what button the user clicks:

```html
<html>
  <head>

    <title>Using Ajax with XML</title>

    <script language = "javascript">

      var products;

      var XMLHttpRequestObject = false;

      if (window.XMLHttpRequest) {
        XMLHttpRequestObject = new XMLHttpRequest();
      } else if (window.ActiveXObject) {
        XMLHttpRequestObject = new ActiveXObject("Microsoft.XMLHTTP");
      }

      function getproducts1()
      {
        if(XMLHttpRequestObject) {
          XMLHttpRequestObject.open("GET", "products1.xml");

          XMLHttpRequestObject.onreadystatechange = function()
          {
            if (XMLHttpRequestObject.readyState == 4 &&
              XMLHttpRequestObject.status == 200) {
            var xmlDocument = XMLHttpRequestObject.responseXML;
            products = xmlDocument.getElementsByTagName("item");
            listproducts();
            }
          }

          XMLHttpRequestObject.send(null);
        }
      }

      function getproducts2()
      {
        if(XMLHttpRequestObject) {
          XMLHttpRequestObject.open("GET", "products2.xml");

          XMLHttpRequestObject.onreadystatechange = function()
          {
            if (XMLHttpRequestObject.readyState == 4 &&
              XMLHttpRequestObject.status == 200) {
            var xmlDocument = XMLHttpRequestObject.responseXML;
            products = xmlDocument.getElementsByTagName("item");
            listproducts();
            }
          }
```

```
            XMLHttpRequestObject.send(null);
         }
      }

      function listproducts ()
      {
        var loopIndex;
        var selectControl = document.getElementById('productsList');

        for (loopIndex = 0; loopIndex < products.length; loopIndex++ )
        {
            selectControl.options[loopIndex] = new
               Option(products[loopIndex].firstChild.data);
        }
      }

      function setproducts()
      {
        document.getElementById('targetDiv').innerHTML =
          "You selected " + products[document.getElementById
            ('productsList').selectedIndex].firstChild.data;
      }

    </script>
  </head>

  <body>

    <h1>Using Ajax with XML</h1>

    <form>
      <select size="1" id="productsList"
        onchange="setproducts()">
        <option>Select an item</option>
      </select>
      <br>
      <br>
      <input type = "button" value = "Select products 1"
        onclick = "getproducts1()">
      <input type = "button" value = "Select products 2"
        onclick = "getproducts2()">
    </form>

    <div id="targetDiv" width =100 height=100>
      Your selection will appear here.
    </div>
  </body>
</html>
```

This is a problem we should address, and it's a common problem with Ajax applications. Knowing how to deal with it is crucial to Ajax programming. There are several solutions, which you'll see here. The first such solution is to use multiple XMLHttpRequest objects.

Here's how to modify store.html to use two XMLHttpRequest objects. The process is not hard: all you have to do is to create two XMLHttpRequest objects—XMLHttpRequestObject and XMLHttpRequestObject2—and then use one object in the functions that connect to the server—getproducts1 and getproducts2:

```
<html>
  <head>

    <title>Using two XMLHttpRequest objects</title>

    <script language = "javascript">

      var products;

      var XMLHttpRequestObject = false;
      var XMLHttpRequestObject2 = false;

      if (window.XMLHttpRequest) {
        XMLHttpRequestObject = new XMLHttpRequest();
      } else if (window.ActiveXObject) {
        XMLHttpRequestObject = new ActiveXObject("Microsoft.XMLHTTP");
      }

      if (window.XMLHttpRequest) {
        XMLHttpRequestObject2 = new XMLHttpRequest();
      } else if (window.ActiveXObject) {
        XMLHttpRequestObject2 = new ActiveXObject("Microsoft.XMLHTTP");
      }

      function getproducts1()
      {
        if(XMLHttpRequestObject) {
          XMLHttpRequestObject.open("GET", "products1.xml");

          XMLHttpRequestObject.onreadystatechange = function()
          {
            if (XMLHttpRequestObject.readyState == 4 &&
              XMLHttpRequestObject.status == 200) {
            var xmlDocument = XMLHttpRequestObject.responseXML;
            products = xmlDocument.getElementsByTagName("item");
            listproducts();
            }
          }

          XMLHttpRequestObject.send(null);
        }
      }

      function getproducts2()
      {
        if(XMLHttpRequestObject2) {
          XMLHttpRequestObject2.open("GET", "products2.xml");

          XMLHttpRequestObject2.onreadystatechange = function()
          {
            if (XMLHttpRequestObject2.readyState == 4 &&
```

```
            XMLHttpRequestObject2.status == 200) {
          var xmlDocument = XMLHttpRequestObject2.responseXML;
          products = xmlDocument.getElementsByTagName("item");
          listproducts();
          }
        }

        XMLHttpRequestObject2.send(null);
      }
    }

    function listproducts ()
    {
      var loopIndex;
      var selectControl = document.getElementById('productsList');

      for (loopIndex = 0; loopIndex < products.length; loopIndex++ )
      {
          selectControl.options[loopIndex] = new
            Option(products[loopIndex].firstChild.data);
      }
    }

    function setproducts()
    {
      document.getElementById('targetDiv').innerHTML =
        "You selected " + products[document.getElementById
          ('productsList').selectedIndex].firstChild.data;
    }

    </script>
  </head>
  <body>

    <h1>Using two XMLHttpRequest objects</h1>

    <form>
      <select size="1" id="productsList"
        onchange="setproducts()">
        <option>Select an item</option>
      </select>
      <br>
      <br>
      <input type = "button" value = "Select products 1"
        onclick = "getproducts1()">
      <input type = "button" value = "Select products 2"
        onclick = "getproducts2()">
    </form>

    <div id="targetDiv" width =100 height=100>
      Your selection will appear here.
    </div>
  </body>
</html>
```

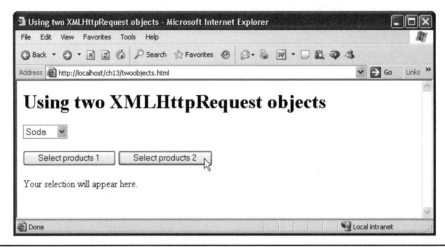

FIGURE 13-1   Using two XMLHttpRequest objects

You can see the results in Figure 13-1, where each of the two buttons uses a different XMLHttpRequest object.

This approach is an improvement, but it also has issues—what if you needed a thousand such objects, would you want to add code to explicitly create each one? Hardly. You might try creating an array of XMLHttpRequest objects instead, coming up next.

Handling Concurrent Ajax Requests with an XMLHttpRequest Array

To handle the case where you might need dozens of XMLHttpRequest objects to handle dozens of requests, you could store those objects in an array, XMLHttpRequestObjects:

```
var XMLHttpRequestObjects = new Array();
```

And then when you needed a new XMLHttpRequest object, you could create one, adding it to the array with the JavaScript push method:

```
var XMLHttpRequestObjects = new Array();

function getproducts1()
{
  if (window.XMLHttpRequest) {
    XMLHttpRequestObjects.push(new XMLHttpRequest());
  } else if (window.ActiveXObject) {
    XMLHttpRequestObjects.push(new ActiveXObject("Microsoft.XMLHTTP"));
  }
  .
  .
  .
```

Here's a new Ajax-enabled page, array.html, that puts this to work, creating the store example using an array of XMLHttpRequest objects in case you have multiple concurrent Ajax calls:

```html
<html>
  <head>

    <title>Using XMLHttpRequest arrays</title>

    <script language = "javascript">

      var products;
      var index = 0;
      var XMLHttpRequestObjects = new Array();

      function getproducts1()
      {
        if (window.XMLHttpRequest) {
          XMLHttpRequestObjects.push(new XMLHttpRequest());
        } else if (window.ActiveXObject) {
        XMLHttpRequestObjects.push(new ActiveXObject("Microsoft.XMLHTTP"));
        }

        index = XMLHttpRequestObjects.length - 1;

        if(XMLHttpRequestObjects[index]) {
          XMLHttpRequestObjects[index].open("GET", "products1.xml");

          XMLHttpRequestObjects[index].onreadystatechange = function()
          {
            if (XMLHttpRequestObjects[index].readyState == 4 &&
              XMLHttpRequestObjects[index].status == 200) {
            var xmlDocument = XMLHttpRequestObjects[index].responseXML;
            products = xmlDocument.getElementsByTagName("item");
            listproducts();
            }
          }

          XMLHttpRequestObjects[index].send(null);
        }
      }

      function getproducts2()
      {
        if (window.XMLHttpRequest) {
          XMLHttpRequestObjects.push(new XMLHttpRequest());
        } else if (window.ActiveXObject) {
        XMLHttpRequestObjects.push(new
          ActiveXObject("Microsoft.XMLHTTP"));
        }

        index = XMLHttpRequestObjects.length - 1;
```

```
        if(XMLHttpRequestObjects[index]) {
          XMLHttpRequestObjects[index].open("GET", "products2.xml");

          XMLHttpRequestObjects[index].onreadystatechange = function()
          {
            if (XMLHttpRequestObjects[index].readyState == 4 &&
              XMLHttpRequestObjects[index].status == 200) {
            var xmlDocument = XMLHttpRequestObjects[index].responseXML;
            products = xmlDocument.getElementsByTagName("item");
            listproducts();
            }
          }

          XMLHttpRequestObjects[index].send(null);
        }
      }

    function listproducts ()
    {
      var loopIndex;
      var selectControl = document.getElementById('productsList');

      for (loopIndex = 0; loopIndex < products.length; loopIndex++ )
      {
          selectControl.options[loopIndex] = new
              Option(products[loopIndex].firstChild.data);
      }
    }

  function setproducts()
  {
    document.getElementById('targetDiv').innerHTML =
      "You selected " + products[document.getElementById
        ('productsList').selectedIndex].firstChild.data;
  }

  </script>
</head>

<body>

  <h1>Using XMLHttpRequest arrays</h1>

  <form>
    <select size="1" id="productsList"
      onchange="setproducts()">
      <option>Select an item</option>
    </select>
    <br>
    <br>
    <input type = "button" value = "Select products 1"
      onclick = "getproducts1()">
    <input type = "button" value = "Select products 2"
      onclick = "getproducts2()">
```

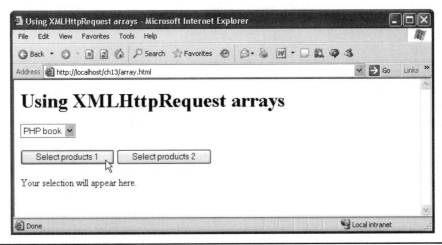

FIGURE **13-2**   Using an XMLHttpRequest array

```
    </form>

    <div id="targetDiv" width =100 height=100>
      Your selection will appear here.
    </div>
  </body>
</html>
```

You can see the results in Figure 13-2, where each of the two buttons uses a different XMLHttpRequest object from the array.

This technique works, but you may end up with large arrays of XMLHttpRequest objects, and it's up to you to delete unused objects. Both the techniques you've seen—multiple XMLHttpRequest objects and XMLHttpRequest object arrays—work, and you'll see them used, but perhaps the best solution to handling concurrent Ajax requests is to use JavaScript inner functions, coming up next.

Handling Concurrent Ajax Requests with JavaScript Inner Functions

What's an inner function? It's a function that's contained inside another function, like this:

```
function outer(data)
{
  var variable1 = data;

  function inner(variable2)
  {
    alert(variable1 + variable2)
  }
}
```

Now say you call the outer function with a value of 4 like this: outer(4). That sets the variable variable1 in this function to 4. It turns out that the inner function has access to the outer function's data—even after the call to the outer function has finished. So if you were now to call the inner function, passing a value of 5, that would set variable2 in the inner function to 5—and variable1 is still set to 4. So the result of calling the inner function would be 4 + 5 = 9, which is the value that would be displayed by the JavaScript alert function in this case.

Here's the good part: Every time you call the outer function, a *new* copy of that function is created, which means a new value will be stored as variable1. And the inner function will have access to that value. So if you make the shift from thinking in terms of variable1 and start thinking in terms of the variable XMLHttpRequestObject, you can see that each time a function like this is called, JavaScript will create a new copy of the function with a new XMLHttpRequest object, and that object will be available to any inner functions.

That's what you want in this case, because the code you've been writing already uses an anonymous inner function, connected to the onreadystatechange property in the getData function. To make this work like the preceding example, where a new XMLHttpRequest object is created each time you call the functionsgetproducts1 or getproducts2, all you have to do is to put the code that creates and fills the variable XMLHttpRequestObject *inside the getproducts1 and getproducts2 functions.* Once you've done that, a new XMLHttpRequest object will be created each time you call the function, and the anonymous inner function will use that new object automatically. That means the whole solution to the problem of multiple concurrent requests looks like this in inner.html:

```
<html>
  <head>

    <title>Using Ajax with inner functions</title>

    <script language = "javascript">

      var products;

      function getproducts1()
      {
        var XMLHttpRequestObject = false;

        if (window.XMLHttpRequest) {
          XMLHttpRequestObject = new XMLHttpRequest();
        } else if (window.ActiveXObject) {
          XMLHttpRequestObject = new ActiveXObject("Microsoft.XMLHTTP");
        }

        if(XMLHttpRequestObject) {
          XMLHttpRequestObject.open("GET", "products1.xml");

          XMLHttpRequestObject.onreadystatechange = function()
          {
            if (XMLHttpRequestObject.readyState == 4 &&
              XMLHttpRequestObject.status == 200) {
            var xmlDocument = XMLHttpRequestObject.responseXML;
            products = xmlDocument.getElementsByTagName("item");
            listproducts();
```

```
        }
      }

      XMLHttpRequestObject.send(null);
    }
  }

  function getproducts2()
  {
    var XMLHttpRequestObject = false;

    if (window.XMLHttpRequest) {
      XMLHttpRequestObject = new XMLHttpRequest();
    } else if (window.ActiveXObject) {
      XMLHttpRequestObject = new ActiveXObject("Microsoft.XMLHTTP");
    }

    if(XMLHttpRequestObject) {
      XMLHttpRequestObject.open("GET", "products2.xml");

      XMLHttpRequestObject.onreadystatechange = function()
      {
        if (XMLHttpRequestObject.readyState == 4 &&
          XMLHttpRequestObject.status == 200) {
        var xmlDocument = XMLHttpRequestObject.responseXML;
        products = xmlDocument.getElementsByTagName("item");
        listproducts();
        }
      }

      XMLHttpRequestObject.send(null);
    }
  }

  function listproducts ()
  {
    var loopIndex;
    var selectControl = document.getElementById('productsList');

    for (loopIndex = 0; loopIndex < products.length; loopIndex++ )
    {
        selectControl.options[loopIndex] = new
          Option(products[loopIndex].firstChild.data);
    }
}

function setproducts()
{
  document.getElementById('targetDiv').innerHTML =
    "You selected " + products[document.getElementById
      ('productsList').selectedIndex].firstChild.data;
}

</script>
```

```
    </head>

    <body>

      <h1>Using Ajax with inner functions</h1>

      <form>
        <select size="1" id="productsList"
          onchange="setproducts()">
          <option>Select an item</option>
        </select>
        <br>
        <br>
        <input type = "button" value = "Select products 1"
          onclick = "getproducts1()">
        <input type = "button" value = "Select products 2"
          onclick = "getproducts2()">
      </form>

      <div id="targetDiv" width =100 height=100>
        Your selection will appear here.
      </div>
    </body>
</html>
```

You can see the results in Figure 13-3, where the example uses inner functions to automatically create a new XMLHttpRequest object for each Ajax request.

Besides downloading text and XML in Ajax, you can download other types of data as well. You're going to see how to download JavaScript—a commonly used technique—in this chapter, as well as images.

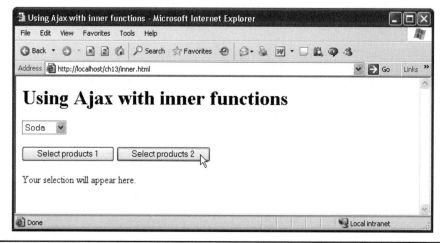

FIGURE 13-3   Using inner functions

NOTE *Images? Isn't Ajax limited to downloading text data such as XML? It turns out that when you download images, you actually download the* name *of the image, and rely on Dynamic HTML in the browser to actually download the image.*

Downloading Images Using Ajax

Here's an example showing how to download images using Ajax, image.html. This example relies on a PHP script, imageName.php, which you can send a parameter named "image" to. That parameter can take the values "1" or "2" and will return the name of a different image, Image1.jpg, or Image2.jpg, accordingly:

```php
<?php
  if ($_REQUEST["image"] == "1"){
    echo "Image1.jpg";
  }
  if ($_REQUEST["image"] == "2"){
    echo "Image2.jpg";
  }
?>
```

And you can add two buttons to the page, "Show image 1" and "Show image 2". Each button is connected to the JavaScript function getData, which we've been using to download data using Ajax. The first button calls imageName.php with the image parameter set to "1", and the second button calls imageName.php with the image parameter set to "2":

```
<form>
  <input type = "button" value = "Show image 1"
    onclick = "getData('imageName.php?image=1', callback)">
  <input type = "button" value = "Show image 2"
    onclick = "getData('imageName.php?image=2', callback)">
</form>
```

So how do you use the downloaded image name to force the browser to download an image? You do that by writing an <img> element in the Web page. For that reason, image. html includes a target <div> element, targetDiv:

```
<div id="targetDiv">
  <p>The fetched image will appear here.</p>
</div>
```

In JavaScript, there's a function named callback that is passed the name of the image file to download. It writes the new <img> element in the targetDiv <div> element like this:

```
function callback(text)
{
  document.getElementById("targetDiv").innerHTML =
    "<img src= " + text + ">";
}
```

When the new <img> element appears in the page, the browser downloads the required image. Here's how it all looks in image.html:

```
<html>
  <head>
    <title>Downloading images using Ajax</title>

    <script language = "javascript">

      function getData(dataSource, callback)
      {
        var XMLHttpRequestObject = false;

        if (window.XMLHttpRequest) {
          XMLHttpRequestObject = new XMLHttpRequest();
        } else if (window.ActiveXObject) {
          XMLHttpRequestObject = new
            ActiveXObject("Microsoft.XMLHTTP");
        }

        if(XMLHttpRequestObject) {
          XMLHttpRequestObject.open("GET", dataSource);

          XMLHttpRequestObject.onreadystatechange = function()
          {
            if (XMLHttpRequestObject.readyState == 4 &&
              XMLHttpRequestObject.status == 200) {
                callback(XMLHttpRequestObject.responseText);
                delete XMLHttpRequestObject;
                XMLHttpRequestObject = null;
            }
          }

          XMLHttpRequestObject.send(null);
        }
      }

      function callback(text)
      {
        document.getElementById("targetDiv").innerHTML =
          "<img src= " + text + ">";
      }

    </script>
  </head>

  <body>

    <H1>Downloading images using Ajax</H1>

    <form>
      <input type = "button" value = "Show image 1"
        onclick =
```

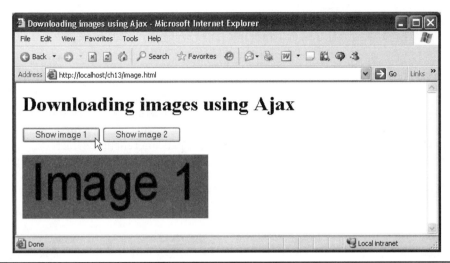

FIGURE 13-4   Downloading images with Ajax

```
        "getData('imageName.php?image=1', callback)">
    <input type = "button" value = "Show image 2"
      onclick =
        "getData('imageName.php?image=2', callback)">
  </form>

  <div id="targetDiv">
    <p>The fetched image will appear here.</p>
  </div>

  </body>
</html>
```

You can see the results in Figure 13-4, where the user has clicked the Show image 1 button, and the application has loaded Image1.jpg. Clicking Show image 2 would display Image2.jpg.

Now you're downloading images using Ajax and PHP. Not bad. Now let's take a look at handling JavaScript downloads.

Downloading JavaScript with Ajax

Sometimes when you use Ajax, the site you're connecting to will return JavaScript, and it's worthwhile knowing how to handle that. A notable example of this is connecting to Google Suggest, which searches for matches to keywords the user types as they type them; Google Suggest is coming up in this chapter.

You can send any kind of JavaScript back from the server to the Ajax-enabled JavaScript. Here's a short example, javascript.html and javascript.php. In javascript.html, there's a

JavaScript function named display, and javascript.php simply echoes that function call as a JavaScript statement:

```php
<?php
    echo 'display()';
?>
```

When the code in javascript.html reads this JavaScript statement, "display()", it'll execute that statement, which will call the display function, displaying a message.

You start javascript.html with a button calling the getData function, which we've been using to download Ajax data, passing it the name of the PHP script to access, javascript.php:

```
<form>
  <input type = "button" value = "Download the JavaScript"
    onclick = "getData('javascript.php')">
</form>
```

Here's the key—when you download JavaScript from a PHP script, you can use the JavaScript eval function to execute that JavaScript. That JavaScript will be downloaded into the XMLHttpRequest object's responseText property, so you can execute it like this in getData:

```
function getData(dataSource)
{
  if(XMLHttpRequestObject) {

    XMLHttpRequestObject.open("GET", dataSource);

    XMLHttpRequestObject.onreadystatechange = function()
    {
      if (XMLHttpRequestObject.readyState == 4 &&
        XMLHttpRequestObject.status == 200) {

          eval(XMLHttpRequestObject.responseText);
      }
    }

    XMLHttpRequestObject.send(null);
  }
}
```

Finally, you need to write a display function in javascript.html that will be called when the JavaScript downloaded from javascript.php is executed. That looks like this in our complete Ajax application, javascript.html, where the display function displays the message "Success" in the page:

```
<html>
  <head>
    <title>Downloading JavaScript with Ajax</title>

    <script language = "javascript">
      var XMLHttpRequestObject = false;
```

```
      if (window.XMLHttpRequest) {
        XMLHttpRequestObject = new XMLHttpRequest();
      } else if (window.ActiveXObject) {
        XMLHttpRequestObject = new ActiveXObject("Microsoft.XMLHTTP");
      }

      function getData(dataSource)
      {
        if(XMLHttpRequestObject) {

          XMLHttpRequestObject.open("GET", dataSource);

          XMLHttpRequestObject.onreadystatechange = function()
          {
            if (XMLHttpRequestObject.readyState == 4 &&
              XMLHttpRequestObject.status == 200) {

                eval(XMLHttpRequestObject.responseText);
            }
          }

          XMLHttpRequestObject.send(null);
        }
      }

      function display()
      {
        var targetDiv = document.getElementById("targetDiv");

        targetDiv.innerHTML = "Success";
      }
    </script>
  </head>

  <body>

    <h1>Downloading JavaScript with Ajax</h1>

    <form>
      <input type = "button" value = "Download the JavaScript"
        onclick = "getData('javascript.php')">
    </form>

    <div id="targetDiv">
      <p>The data will go here.</p>
    </div>

  </body>
</html>
```

You can see the results in Figure 13-5, where javascript.html appears.

When the user clicks the button, the JavaScript is downloaded from javascript.php and executed, giving you a message of success, as you can see in Figure 13-6.

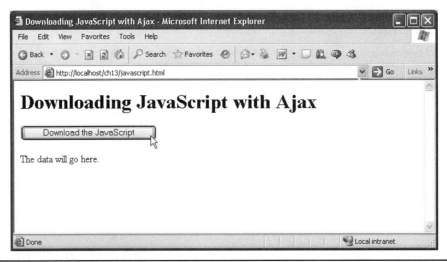

FIGURE 13-5 javascript.html

Connecting to Google Suggest

Take a look at Figure 13-7, which shows the Google Suggest page you can find at http://www.google.com/webhp?complete=1&hl=en.

Now type something in the text field, and Google will look up what you're searching for as you type, giving you the drop-down box that appears in Figure 13-8.

That's a prime example of Ajax—the items in the drop-down list box were fetched behind the scenes using Ajax, and then displayed in the page.

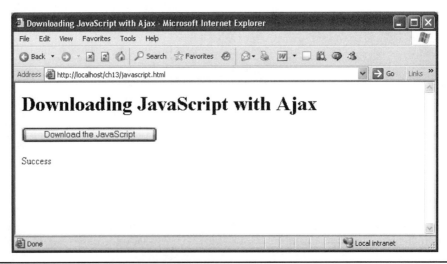

FIGURE 13-6 Downloading and executing JavaScript

FIGURE 13-7   Google Suggest

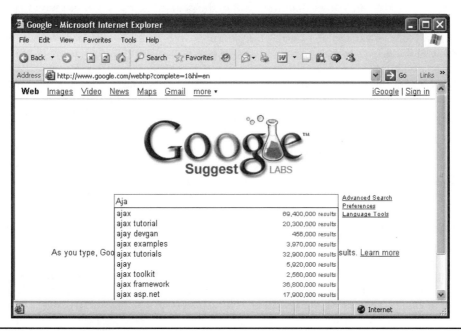

FIGURE 13-8   Using Google Suggest

So how can you connect to Google Suggest? Say that you've stored the partial search term in a variable named searchTerm—you could then connect to Google Suggest at this URL:

```
"http://www.google.com/complete/search?hl=en&js=true&qu=" + searchTerm;
```

How does Google Suggest communicate with you? It will send back JavaScript code that calls a function named sendRPCDone. Here are the parameters passed to that function:

```
sendRPCDone(unusedVariable, searchTerm, arrayTerm, arrayResults, unusedArray)
```

So what does the JavaScript call you get back from Google Suggest actually look like? Well, if you're searching for "ajax", this is the kind of JavaScript you'll get back from Google:

```
sendRPCDone(frameElement, "ajax", new Array("ajax", "ajax amsterdam",

"ajax fc", "ajax ontario", "ajax grips", "ajax football club", "ajax public
library", "ajax football", "ajax soccer", "ajax pickering transit"), new
Array("3,840,000 results", "502,000 results", "710,000 results", "275,000
results", "8,860 results", "573,000 results", "40,500 results", "454,000
results", "437,000 results", "10,700
results"), new Array(""));
```

You take it from there, writing your own sendRPCDone function that will display the results sent back to you from Google Suggest.

We're going to write an example, google.html, that will connect to Google Suggest using Ajax and PHP. Why is PHP needed here? That has to do with an Ajax issue—using Ajax, you can't access domains other than the domain the page came from without having the browser display warnings. More on this is coming up.

You can see our version of a Google Suggest page in Figure 13-9. It looks and acts just like the real thing, except that we're going to do it ourselves, putting Ajax to work with the help of some PHP.

The google.html example starts with a text field that calls a JavaScript function named connectGoogleSuggest each time a typed key is released by tying it to the text field's onkeyup event:

```
<body>
  <h1>Connecting to Google Suggest</h1>

  Search for <input id = "textField" type = "text"
    name = "textField" onkeyup = "connectGoogleSuggest(event)">
        .
        .
        .
</body>
```

In the connectGoogleSuggest function, you can check if there's any text to send to Google Suggest, and if so, send that text to google.php as the parameter qu (for query). You can get the text to send using the text field's value property:

```
function connectGoogleSuggest(keyEvent)
{
  var input = document.getElementById("textField");
```

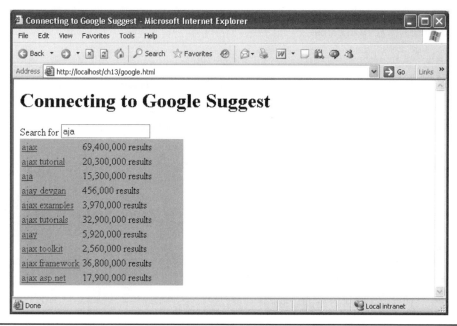

FIGURE 13-9   google.html

```
        if (input.value) {
          getData("google.php?qu=" + input.value);
        }
           .
           .
           .
      }
```

On the other hand, if there's nothing to send, the user has presumably deleted all text in the text field, in which case you want to clear the displayed drop-down list of matches from Google Suggest. Those matches are actually going to be displayed in a drop-down list, which is actually an HTML table, inserted into a <div> element, targetDiv, right under the text field:

```
<body>
  <h1>Connecting to Google Suggest</h1>

  Search for <input id = "textField" type = "text"
    name = "textField" onkeyup = "connectGoogleSuggest(event)">

  <div id = "targetDiv"><div></div></div>

</body>
```

In the connectGoogleSuggest function, you can clear the drop-down list if the user has deleted all search text, like this:

```
function connectGoogleSuggest(keyEvent)
{
  var input = document.getElementById("textField");

  if (input.value) {
    getData("google.php?qu=" + input.value);
  }
  else {
    var targetDiv = document.getElementById("targetDiv");

    targetDiv.innerHTML = "<div></div>";
  }
}
```

So when the user enters some search text, that text is passed to google.php by the getData function—and when Google Suggest returns JavaScript to execute, we'll execute that JavaScript using the JavaScript eval function:

```
function getData(dataSource)
{
  var XMLHttpRequestObject = false;

  if (window.XMLHttpRequest) {
    XMLHttpRequestObject = new XMLHttpRequest();
  } else if (window.ActiveXObject) {
    XMLHttpRequestObject = new ActiveXObject("Microsoft.XMLHTTP");
  }

  if(XMLHttpRequestObject) {
    XMLHttpRequestObject.open("GET", dataSource);

    XMLHttpRequestObject.onreadystatechange = function()
    {
      if (XMLHttpRequestObject.readyState == 4 &&
        XMLHttpRequestObject.status == 200) {
          eval(XMLHttpRequestObject.responseText);
      }
    }

    XMLHttpRequestObject.send(null);
  }
}
```

Alright, it's time for google.php to take over. This is the script that connects to Google Suggest and downloads JavaScript for the application to execute.

Here's the key to this application: why not just connect to Google Suggest directly from google.html? Why do you have to go through the intermediary of google.php? You need google.php because of the mentioned quirk in Ajax: using Ajax, you can't access any other domain other than the one your page comes from without seeing warning dialogs from the browser. Those warning dialogs are there for security—the browser thinks your page is doing something it shouldn't.

To avoid those warning dialogs, and still connect to other domains using Ajax, you need to relay your request through some server-side code. That way, the browser only sees you accessing a script in the same domain as your main page. But that script can connect to another site, and the browser won't know a thing about it.

The URL you want to access Google Suggest is http://www.google.com/complete/ search, and you send it the user's partially typed search term using the parameter qu. And you can open that URL from PHP using fopen. So here's how you send Google Suggest the partially typed search term the user has typed, getting a file handle that represents the response in google.php:

```php
<?php
  $filehandle =
    fopen("http://www.google.com/complete/search?hl=en&js=true&qu=" . $_GET["qu"],
      "r");
              .
              .
              .
?>
```

Now you've got a file handle that represents Google Suggest's JavaScript response to the partially typed search term you sent it. You can loop over that response using a while loop and feof:

```php
<?php
  $filehandle =
    fopen("http://www.google.com/complete/search?hl=en&js=true&qu=" . $_GET["qu"],
      "r");
  while (!feof($filehandle)){
              .
              .
              .
  }
?>
```

And you can download, and echo, Google Suggest's response to your query line by line like this:

```php
<?php
  $filehandle =
    fopen("http://www.google.com/complete/search?hl=en&js=true&qu=" . $_GET["qu"],
      "r");

  while (!feof($filehandle)){
    $download = fgets($filehandle);
    echo $download;
  }
?>
```

All that remains is to close the connection to Google Suggest:

```php
<?php
  $filehandle =
    fopen("http://www.google.com/complete/search?hl=en&js=true&qu=" . $_GET["qu"],
      "r");

  while (!feof($filehandle)){
    $download = fgets($filehandle);
    echo $download;
  }

  fclose($filehandle);
?>
```

Okay, that uses PHP to solve the problem of not being able to access other domains than your page's home domain with Ajax. This script connects to Google Suggest and gets Google's response to what the user has typed.

That response is in JavaScript form, as you've seen, something like this:

```
sendRPCDone(frameElement, "ajax", new Array("ajax", "ajax amsterdam",
"ajax fc", "ajax ontario", "ajax grips", "ajax football club", "ajax public
library", "ajax football", "ajax soccer", "ajax pickering transit"), new
Array("3,840,000 results", "502,000 results", "710,000 results", "275,000
results", "8,860 results", "573,000 results", "40,500 results", "454,000
results", "437,000 results", "10,700
results"), new Array(""));
```

And the google.html page executes that JavaScript with the eval function:

```
XMLHttpRequestObject.onreadystatechange = function()
{
  if (XMLHttpRequestObject.readyState == 4 &&
    XMLHttpRequestObject.status == 200) {
      eval(XMLHttpRequestObject.responseText);
  }
}
```

You're responsible for writing sendRPCDone yourself. Here's how Google defines the parameters of this function:

```
function sendRPCDone(unusedVariable, searchTerm, arrayTerm,
  arrayResults, unusedArray)
{
  .
  .
  .
}
```

Here's what the parameters are:

- **unusedVariable**   An unused variable
- **searchTerm**   The user's search term
- **arrayTerm**   An array of matching terms
- **arrayResults**   The number of matches to each array term
- **unusedArray**   An unused array

This information is going to be displayed in an HTML table inside the targetDiv element in the page's body:

```
<body>
  <h1>Connecting to Google Suggest</h1>

  Search for <input id = "textField" type = "text"
    name = "textField" onkeyup = "connectGoogleSuggest(event)">

  <div id = "targetDiv"><div></div></div>

</body>
```

The purpose of the sendRPCDone function is to create the HTML table in a variable named data showing the results and display it:

```
function sendRPCDone(unusedVariable, searchTerm, arrayTerm,
    arrayResults, unusedArray)
{
  var data = "<table>";
    .
    .
    .
  data += "</table>";

  var targetDiv = document.getElementById("targetDiv");

  targetDiv.innerHTML = data;
}
```

You can loop over the results from Google this way:

```
function sendRPCDone(unusedVariable, searchTerm, arrayTerm,
    arrayResults, unusedArray)
{
  var data = "<table>";
  var loopIndex;

  if (arrayResults.length != 0) {
    for (var loopIndex = 0; loopIndex < arrayResults.length;
      loopIndex++) {
        .
        .
```

```
      }
    }

    data += "</table>";

    var targetDiv = document.getElementById("targetDiv");

    targetDiv.innerHTML = data;
  }
```

In each line of the HTML table, you can display a hyperlink to the search term (in case the user decides that's the term they want to search for) and the number of matches Google found for that term:

```
function sendRPCDone(unusedVariable, searchTerm, arrayTerm,
  arrayResults, unusedArray)
{
  var data = "<table>";
  var loopIndex;

  if (arrayResults.length != 0) {
    for (var loopIndex = 0; loopIndex < arrayResults.length;
      loopIndex++) {
      data += "<tr><td>" +
      "<a href='http://www.google.com/search?q=" +
      arrayTerm[loopIndex] + "'>" + arrayTerm[loopIndex] +
      '</a></td><td>' + arrayResults[loopIndex] + "</td></tr>";
    }
  }

  data += "</table>";

  var targetDiv = document.getElementById("targetDiv");

  targetDiv.innerHTML = data;
}
```

You can also style the targetDiv element with a background color like this in a <style> element to make it stand out:

```
<head>
  <title>Connecting to Google Suggest</title>
  <style>
  #targetDiv {
    background-color: #FFAAAA;
    width: 40%;
  }
  </style>
       .
       .
       .
</head>
```

And that completes google.html—with this page and google.php, you've been able to connect to Google Suggest, download JavaScript, and run that JavaScript. Here's the full google.html:

```html
<html>
  <head>
    <title>Connecting to Google Suggest</title>
    <style>
    #targetDiv {
      background-color: #FFAAAA;
      width: 40%;
    }
    </style>

    <script language = "javascript">
      function getData(dataSource)
      {
        var XMLHttpRequestObject = false;

        if (window.XMLHttpRequest) {
          XMLHttpRequestObject = new XMLHttpRequest();
        } else if (window.ActiveXObject) {
          XMLHttpRequestObject = new ActiveXObject("Microsoft.XMLHTTP");
        }

        if(XMLHttpRequestObject) {
          XMLHttpRequestObject.open("GET", dataSource);

          XMLHttpRequestObject.onreadystatechange = function()
          {
            if (XMLHttpRequestObject.readyState == 4 &&
              XMLHttpRequestObject.status == 200) {
                eval(XMLHttpRequestObject.responseText);
            }
          }

          XMLHttpRequestObject.send(null);
        }
      }

      function connectGoogleSuggest(keyEvent)
      {
        var input = document.getElementById("textField");

        if (input.value) {
          getData("google.php?qu=" + input.value);
        }
        else {
          var targetDiv = document.getElementById("targetDiv");

          targetDiv.innerHTML = "<div></div>";
        }
      }
```

```
    function sendRPCDone(unusedVariable, searchTerm, arrayTerm,
      arrayResults, unusedArray)
    {
      var data = "<table>";
      var loopIndex;

      if (arrayResults.length != 0) {
        for (var loopIndex = 0; loopIndex < arrayResults.length;
          loopIndex++) {
          data += "<tr><td>" +
          "<a href='http://www.google.com/search?q=" +
          arrayTerm[loopIndex] + "'>" + arrayTerm[loopIndex] +
          '</a></td><td>' + arrayResults[loopIndex] + "</td></tr>";
        }
      }

      data += "</table>";

      var targetDiv = document.getElementById("targetDiv");

      targetDiv.innerHTML = data;
    }
  </script>
</head>

<body>
  <h1>Connecting to Google Suggest</h1>

  Search for <input id = "textField" type = "text"
    name = "textField" onkeyup = "connectGoogleSuggest(event)">

    <div id = "targetDiv"><div></div></div>

</body>
</html>
```

One of the key issues here was getting around the Ajax restriction of not being able to connect to other domains.

Connecting to Other Domains Using Ajax

Knowing how to connect to other domains using Ajax is a valuable skill, as you can see in the Google Suggest example. The key is to relay the request to another domain using a PHP script on the server.

You can adapt google.php to perform this action. You open the other domain using fopen, and then read that domain's response line by line using fgets and feof. When everything is done, you close the foreign URL:

```php
<?php
  $filehandle =
    fopen("http://www.google.com/complete/search?hl=en&js=true&qu=" . $_GET["qu"],
      "r");
```

```
while (!feof($filehandle)){
  $download = fgets($filehandle);
  echo $download;
}

fclose($filehandle);
?>
```

Logging in with Ajax and PHP

Here's another thing Ajax is often used for, and PHP is involved: checking logins. For example, you can check a user's login behind the scenes, or let them choose their own username or password. Here's an example, log.html, which lets the user choose a username—and if that username has already been taken, log.html informs the user of that fact. You can see how this works in Figure 13-10—the application checks the person's entered username as they type it, and if it's already taken, as here, it informs them of the fact.

This example reads keys as the user types them, calling a JavaScript function named checker that checks the new username:

```
<body>

  <H1>Choose a username</H1>

  Enter a username: <input id = "textField" type = "text"
   name = "textField" onkeyup = "checker()">

    <div id = "targetDiv"><div></div></div>

</body>
```

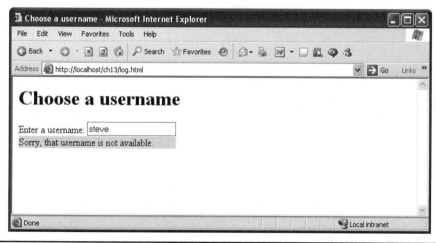

FIGURE 13-10   Checking a username

The checker function calls the getData function with the URL log.php, sending the username the user is entering to log.php using the parameter name "qu":

```
function checker()
{
  var targetDiv = document.getElementById("targetDiv");
  targetDiv.innerHTML = "<div></div>";

  if (document.getElementById("textField").value) {
    getData("log.php?qu=" +
      document.getElementById("textField").value);
  }
}
```

The getData function connects to the server and downloads the results:

```
function getData(dataSource)
{
  if(XMLHttpRequestObject) {
    XMLHttpRequestObject.open("GET", dataSource);

    XMLHttpRequestObject.onreadystatechange = function()
    {
      if (XMLHttpRequestObject.readyState == 4 &&
        XMLHttpRequestObject.status == 200) {
        .
        .
        .
      }
    }

    XMLHttpRequestObject.send(null);
  }
}
```

The PHP script in this case is going to return "OK" if the chosen username is okay, and "notOK" if the username has already been taken. If the username has already been taken, this example displays the message "Sorry, that username is not available." in a <div> element:

```
function getData(dataSource)
{
  if(XMLHttpRequestObject) {
    XMLHttpRequestObject.open("GET", dataSource);

    XMLHttpRequestObject.onreadystatechange = function()
    {
      if (XMLHttpRequestObject.readyState == 4 &&
        XMLHttpRequestObject.status == 200) {
          if(XMLHttpRequestObject.responseText == "notOK"){
        var targetDiv = document.getElementById("targetDiv");

        targetDiv.innerHTML =
          "<div>Sorry, that username is not available.</div>";
```

```
            }
        }
    }

    XMLHttpRequestObject.send(null);
    }
}
```

The PHP script, log.php, checks the username passed to it using the parameter qu and returns the text "notOK" if the username has already been taken:

```
<?php
    if ($_GET["qu"] == "steve"){
        echo "notOK";
    }

        .
        .
        .

?>
```

Otherwise, it returns "OK":

```
<?php
    if ($_GET["qu"] == "steve"){
        echo "notOK";
    }
    else {
        echo "OK";
    }
?>
```

And that's all you need.

Getting Data with Head Requests and Ajax

You can also use Ajax to check on files on the server before working with them. Here's an example, head.html, which reads the HTTP headers sent back from the server for the file head.html itself, and lists those headers, as you can see in Figure 13-11.

As you can see in the figure, when you make a head request for a file, you get back information like this, which gives the server, the last-modified date of the file, and its length:

```
Server: Microsoft-IIS/5.1 Date: Mon, 28 May 2007 17:57:54 GMT Content-Type: text/
html Accept-Ranges: bytes Last-Modified: Mon, 28 May 2007 17:57:49 GMT ETag:
"3c058b451a1c71:a2f" Content-Length: 1266
```

It's worth taking a look at working with head requests in Ajax, and this example, head. html, shows how they work. This example starts with the button you see in the figure, tied to the getData function:

```
<body>

    <h1>Getting header info</h1>
```

```
<form>
  <input type = "button" value = "Get header data"
    onclick = "getData('head.html', 'targetDiv')">
</form>

<div id="targetDiv">
  <div></div>
</div>

</body>
```

In the getData function, you specify that you want head information by specifying that you want to open the document using the HEAD method (not GET or POST):

```
function getData(dataSource, divID)
{
  if(XMLHttpRequestObject) {
    var targetDiv = document.getElementById(divID);
    XMLHttpRequestObject.open("HEAD", dataSource);
      .
      .
      .
}
```

And when your data is downloaded, you can recover the head data using the XMLHttpRequest object's getAllResponseHeaders method:

```
function getData(dataSource, divID)
{
  if(XMLHttpRequestObject) {
    var targetDiv = document.getElementById(divID);
    XMLHttpRequestObject.open("HEAD", dataSource);

    XMLHttpRequestObject.onreadystatechange = function()
    {
      if (XMLHttpRequestObject.readyState == 4 &&
        XMLHttpRequestObject.status == 200) {
          targetDiv.innerHTML =
            XMLHttpRequestObject.getAllResponseHeaders();
      }
    }

    XMLHttpRequestObject.send(null);
  }
}
```

This code gives you the results you see in Figure 13-11. Cool.

You can use the getAllResponseHeaders method to read all headers from the server, but you can also use getResponseHeader method to read the value of any particular header. Here's an example, lastModified.html, that checks its own last-modified date and displays it, as you can see in Figure 13-12.

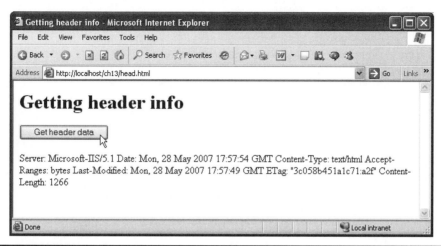

Figure 13-11   Getting header info

You make this work by calling the XMLHttpRequest object's getResponseHeader method like this: getResponseHeader("Last-Modified"). That's the way you use this method—you pass it the name of the header you're interested in. Here's how lastModified. html puts this to work:

```
<html>
  <head>
    <title>Getting a document's last-modified date</title>

    <script language = "javascript">
```

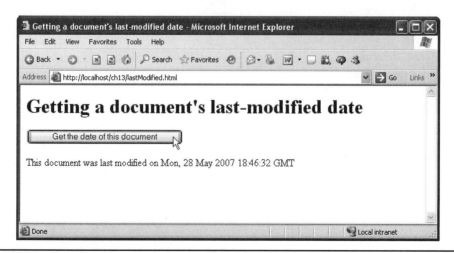

Figure 13-12   Checking a document's last-modified date

```
      var XMLHttpRequestObject = false;

      if (window.XMLHttpRequest) {
        XMLHttpRequestObject = new XMLHttpRequest();
      } else if (window.ActiveXObject) {
        XMLHttpRequestObject = new ActiveXObject("Microsoft.XMLHTTP");
      }

      function getData(dataSource, divID)
      {
        if(XMLHttpRequestObject) {
          var targetDiv = document.getElementById(divID);
          XMLHttpRequestObject.open("HEAD", dataSource);

          XMLHttpRequestObject.onreadystatechange = function()
          {
            if (XMLHttpRequestObject.readyState == 4 &&
              XMLHttpRequestObject.status == 200) {
                targetDiv.innerHTML =  "This document was last modified on " +
                  XMLHttpRequestObject.getResponseHeader(
                    "Last-Modified");
            }
          }
          XMLHttpRequestObject.send(null);
        }
      }
    </script>
  </head>

<body>

  <H1>Getting a document's last-modified date</H1>

  <form>
    <input type = "button" value = "Get the date of this document"
      onclick = "getData('lastModified.html', 'targetDiv')">
  </form>

  <div id="targetDiv">
    <div></div>
  </div>

  </body>
</html>
```

Drawing Images on the Server

This chapter is all about using PHP to create graphics on the server. Using PHP, you can draw just about anything and send it back to the browser in a variety of graphics formats—JPEG, PNG, etc.

To make this work, you have to install support for GD2 in PHP. That happens in a variety of ways—check the PHP install directions for your operating system. For example, you might have to check the CD2 check box when asked what options you want to install.

Just what graphics functions are available? Here's the list:

Function	Description
gd_info	Retrieve information about the GD library
getimagesize	Return size of an image
image_type_to_extension	Return file extension for image
image_type_to_mime_type	Return Mime-Type for image-type returned by getimagesize, exif_read_data, exif_thumbnail, exif_imagetype
image2wbmp	Send image to browser or file
imagealphablending	Set the blending for an image
imageantialias	Set if antialias functions will be used or not
imagearc	Draw an arc
imagechar	Draw a character horizontally
imagecharup	Draw a character vertically
imagecolorallocate	Allocate a color for an image
imagecolorallocatealpha	Allocate a color for an image
imagecolorat	Return the index of the color of a pixel
imagecolorclosest	Return the index of the closest color to the given color
imagecolorclosestalpha	Return the index of the closest color to the given color and alpha setting

Function	Description
imagecolorclosesthwb	Return the index of the color that has the hue, whiteness, and blackness nearest to the given color
imagecolordeallocate	De-allocate a color
imagecolorexact	Return the index of the given color
imagecolorexactalpha	Return the index of the given color and alpha setting
imagecolormatch	Make the colors of the palette version of an image more closely match the true color version
imagecolorresolve	Return the index of the given color or its closest possible alternative
imagecolorresolvealpha	Return the index of the given color and alpha setting or its closest possible alternative
imagecolorset	Set the color for the given palette index
imagecolorsforindex	Return the colors for an index
imagecolorstotal	Return the number of colors in an image's palette
imagecolortransparent	Set a color as transparent
imageconvolution	Apply a 3 x 3 convolution matrix
imagecopy	Copy just part of an image
imagecopymerge	Copy and merge part of an image
imagecopymergegray	Copy and merge part of an image with gray scale
imagecopyresampled	Copy and resize part of an image, using resampling
imagecopyresized	Copy and resize part of an image
imagecreate	Create a new image
imagecreatefromgd	Create a new image from GD file or URL
imagecreatefromgd2	Create a new image from GD2 file or URL
imagecreatefromgd2part	Create a new image from a given part of GD2 file or URL
imagecreatefromgif	Create a new image from GIF file
imagecreatefromjpeg	Create a new image from JPEG file
imagecreatefrompng	Create a new image from PNG file
imagecreatefromstring	Create a new image from the image stream
imagecreatefromwbmp	Create a new image from WBMP file
imagecreatefromxbm	Create a new image from XBM file
imagecreatefromxpm	Create a new image from XPM file
imagecreatetruecolor	Create a new true color image
imagedashedline	Draw a dashed line
imagedestroy	Destroy an image
imageellipse	Draw an ellipse

Function	Description
imagefill	Flood fill
imagefilledarc	Draw a partial ellipse and fill it
imagefilledellipse	Draw a filled ellipse
imagefilledpolygon	Draw a filled polygon
imagefilledrectangle	Draw a filled rectangle
imagefilltoborder	Flood fill to specific color
imagefilter	Apply a filter to an image
imagefontheight	Return font height
imagefontwidth	Return font width
imageftbbox	Give the bounding box of text
imagefttext	Write text to the image
imagegammacorrect	Apply a gamma correction
imagegd	Send GD image to browser or file
imagegd2	Send GD2 image to browser or file
imagegif	Send image to browser or file
imageinterlace	Enable or disable interlace operations
imageistruecolor	Determine whether an image is a true color image
imagejpeg	Send image to browser or file
imagelayereffect	Set the alpha blending flag to use layering effects
imageline	Draw a line
imageloadfont	Load a new font
imagepalettecopy	Copy the palette from an image
imagepng	Send a PNG image to either the browser or a file
imagepolygon	Draws a polygon
imagepsbbox	Specify the bounding box of text using PostScript Type1 fonts
imagepsencodefont	Change the character encoding of a font
imagepsextendfont	Extend or condense a font
imagepsfreefont	Free memory currently used by a PostScript Type 1 font
imagepsloadfont	Load a PostScript Type 1 font
imagepsslantfont	Slant a font
imagepstext	Draws text using PostScript Type1 fonts
imagerectangle	Draw a rectangle
imagerotate	Rotate an image to a given angle

Function	Description
imagesavealpha	Set the flag to save full alpha channel information when saving PNG images
imagesetbrush	Set the brush image for line drawing
imagesetpixel	Set a single pixel
imagesetstyle	Set the style for line drawing
imagesetthickness	Set the thickness for line drawing
imagesettile	Set the tile image for filling
imagestring	Draw a string horizontally
imagestringup	Draw a string vertically
imagesx	Return image width
imagesy	Return image height
imagetruecolortopalette	Convert a true color image to a palette image
imagettfbbox	Give the bounding box of a text using TrueType fonts
imagettftext	Write text to the image using TrueType fonts
imagetypes	Return the image types supported
imagewbmp	Send image to browser or file
imagexbm	Send XBM image to browser or file
iptcembed	Embed binary IPTC data into a JPEG image
iptcparse	Parse a binary IPTC block
jpeg2wbmp	Convert JPEG image file to a WBMP file
png2wbmp	Convert PNG image file to a WBMP file

Okay, let's get started by creating a simple image.

Creating an Image

To create an image in memory to work with, you start with the GD2 imagecreate function:

```
imagecreate(x_size, y_size)
```

The *x_size* and *y_size* parameters are in pixels.
Here's how we create a first image:

```
$image_height = 100;
$image_width = 300;

$image = imagecreate($image_width, $image_height);
    .
    .
    .
```

Next, to set colors to be used in the image, you use the imagecolorallocate function:

```
imagecolorallocate (image, red, green, blue )
```

You pass this function the image you're working with, as well as the red, green, and blue components as 0–255 values. For example, if you want solid red, you'd pass imagecolorallocate a red value of 255, and blue and green values of 0.

The first time you call imagecolorallocate, this function sets the background color; subsequent calls set various drawing colors. Here's how we set the background color to light gray (red = 200, green = 200, blue = 200):

```
$image = imagecreate($image_width, $image_height);

$back_color = imagecolorallocate($image, 200, 200, 200);
    .
    .
    .
```

To send a JPEG image back to the browser, you have to tell the browser that you're doing so with the header function to set the image's type, and then you send the image with the imagejpeg function like this:

```
$image_height = 100;
$image_width = 300;

$image = imagecreate($image_width, $image_height);

$back_color = imagecolorallocate($image, 200, 200, 200);

header('Content-Type: image/jpeg');
imagejpeg($image);
    .
    .
    .
```

Here are some of the image-creating functions for various image formats you can use:

- **imagegif**   Output a GIF image to browser or file.
- **imagejpeg**   Output a JPEG image to browser or file.
- **imagewbmp**   Output a WBMP image to browser or file.
- **imagepng**   Output a PNG image to either the browser or a file.

After sending the image, you can destroy the image object with the imagedestroy function; all this is shown in phpimage.php:

```
<?php
  $image_height = 100;
  $image_width = 300;

  $image = imagecreate($image_width, $image_height);

  $back_color = imagecolorallocate($image, 200, 200, 200);
```

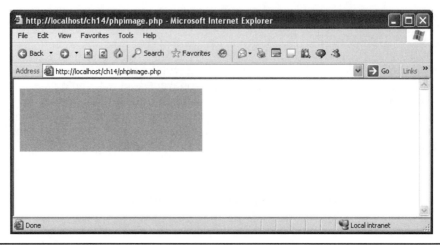

FIGURE 14-1   Creating a box image on the server

```
header('Content-Type: image/jpeg');

imagejpeg($image);
imagedestroy($image);

?>
```

You can see the results in Figure 14-1. As you see, all that appears is a background box in this example. However, we've made progress—that's a real image you see in the figure.

On the other hand, it's a rare Web page that displays simply an image. Usually, that image appears in an HTML page.

Displaying Images in HTML Pages

The image created by phpimage.php is a standard JPEG image, so there's no reason you can't embed it in a Web page. How would you do that? With a standard <img> element, of course. For example, if you had a JPEG on the server, image.jpg, you could display it this way in a Web page:

```
<img src="image.jpg">
```

In the same way, you can give the name of the script that generates a JPEG image, phpimage.php, as the src attribute like this:

```
<img src="phpimage.php">
```

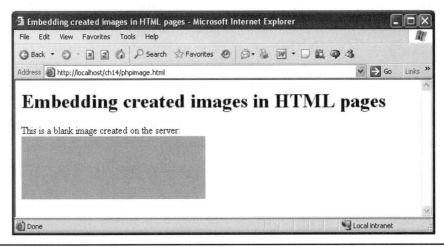

FIGURE 14-2   Displaying a box image in a Web page

Here's what a Web page, phpimage.html, that displays the blank box created by phpimage.php looks like:

```
<html>
  <head>
    <title>
      Embedding created images in HTML pages
    </title>
  </head>

  <body>
    <h1>
      Embedding created images in HTML pages
    </h1>
      This is a blank image created on the server:
      <br>
      <img src="phpimage.php">
  </body>
</html>
```

You can see the results in Figure 14-2, where the JPEG image created by phpimage.php appears, embedded in an HTML page. Not bad.

Okay, that creates a basic image and displays it. How about drawing some actual graphics?

Drawing Lines

You can draw lines with the imageline function:

```
imageline(image, x1, y1, x2, y2, color)
```

This function draws a line from (*x1, y1*) to (*x2, y2*) (the top left of the image is (0, 0), and all measurements are in pixels) in image *image* using drawing color *color*.

Time to draw some lines in a new script, phpline.php. This example starts by creating the same background in the image you've already seen:

```php
<?php
    $image_height = 100;
    $image_width = 300;

    $image = imagecreate($image_width, $image_height);

    $back_color = imagecolorallocate($image, 200, 200, 200);
        .
        .
        .
?>
```

Now we'll set the drawing color for the lines. In this case, we'll use black, which has a red, green, and blue color value of 0:

```php
<?php
    $image_height = 100;
    $image_width = 300;

    $image = imagecreate($image_width, $image_height);

    $back_color = imagecolorallocate($image, 200, 200, 200);

    $draw_color = imagecolorallocate($image, 0, 0, 0);
        .
        .
        .
?>
```

Then you can draw some lines with imageline:

```php
<?php
    $image_height = 100;
    $image_width = 300;

    $image = imagecreate($image_width, $image_height);

    $back_color = imagecolorallocate($image, 200, 200, 200);

    $draw_color = imagecolorallocate($image, 0, 0, 0);

    imageline($image, 40, 20, 90, 80, $draw_color);

    imageline($image, 30, 90, 250, 10, $draw_color);

    imageline($image, 110, 20, 140, 90, $draw_color);
        .
```

```
        .
        .
        .
?>
```

And you can send the image back to the browser and then destroy the image this way:

```php
<?php
    $image_height = 100;
    $image_width = 300;

    $image = imagecreate($image_width, $image_height);

    $back_color = imagecolorallocate($image, 200, 200, 200);

    $draw_color = imagecolorallocate($image, 0, 0, 0);

    imageline($image, 40, 20, 90, 80, $draw_color);

    imageline($image, 30, 90, 250, 10, $draw_color);

    imageline($image, 110, 20, 140, 90, $draw_color);

    header('Content-Type: image/jpeg');

    imagejpeg($image);

    imagedestroy($image);
?>
```

Here's what a Web page, phpline.html, that displays the lines created by phpline.php looks like:

```html
<html>
  <head>
    <title>
      Drawing lines
    </title>
  </head>

  <body>
    <h1>
      Drawing lines
    </h1>
      These lines were drawn on the server:
      <br>
      <img src="phpline.php">
  </body>
</html>
```

You can see the results in Figure 14-3, where the lines created by phpline.php appear in an HTML page. Cool.

You can adjust the parameters of lines like these; for example, you can draw thicker lines, and that's coming up next.

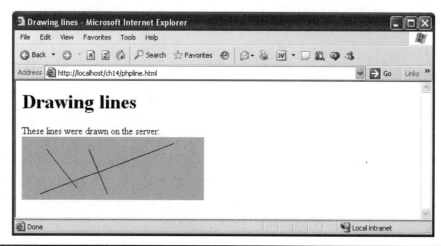

FIGURE 14-3   Displaying lines in a Web page

Setting Line Thickness

You can set the drawing thickness when you create an image, using the imagesetthickness function:

```
imagesetthickness(image, thickness)
```

When you call this function and pass an image to it, it sets the drawing width for that image, in pixels. For example, you might set the thickness of lines in phpline.php to 6 pixels (instead of the default 1 pixel) like this in phpthickline.php:

```php
<?php
    $image_height = 100;
    $image_width = 300;

    $image = imagecreate($image_width, $image_height);
    imagesetthickness($image, 6);

    $back_color = imagecolorallocate($image, 200, 200, 200);

    $draw_color = imagecolorallocate($image, 0, 0, 0);

    imageline($image, 40, 20, 90, 80, $draw_color);

       .
       .
       .

    imagedestroy($image);
?>
```

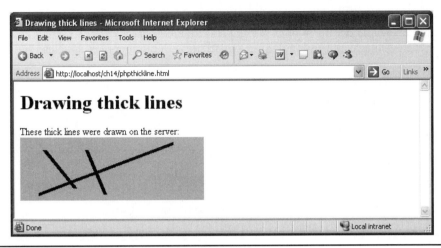

FIGURE 14-4   Displaying thick lines in a Web page

Here's what a Web page, phpthickline.html, that displays the thicker lines created by phpthickline.php might look like:

```
<html>
  <head>
    <title>
      Drawing thick lines
    </title>
  </head>

  <body>
    <h1>
      Drawing thick lines
    </h1>
      These thick lines were drawn on the server:
      <br>
      <img src="phpthickline.php">
  </body>
</html>
```

And You can see the results in Figure 14-4, where the thick lines appear in an HTML page.

Drawing Rectangles

You can draw plenty of figures using lines alone, but there are far more GD functions to consider. One of them, imagerectangle, draws rectangles:

```
imagerectangle(image, x1, y1, x2, y2, color)
```

This function creates a rectangle of color *color* in image *image* starting at upper-left coordinate *x1, y1* and ending at bottom-right coordinate *x2, y2*.

Here's an example, phprectangle.php, which draws a number of rectangles:

```php
<?php

    $image_height = 100;

    $image_width = 300;

    $image = imagecreate($image_width, $image_height);

    $back_color = imagecolorallocate($image, 200, 200, 200);

    $draw_color = imagecolorallocate($image, 0, 0, 0);

    imagerectangle($image, 30, 20, 50, 90, $draw_color);

    imagerectangle($image, 70, 20, 140, 90, $draw_color);

    imagerectangle($image, 170, 20, 270, 90, $draw_color);

    imagerectangle($image, 10, 40, 280, 80, $draw_color);

    header('Content-Type: image/jpeg');

    imagejpeg($image);

    imagedestroy($image);
?>
```

And here's how you might embed those rectangles in a Web page, phprectangle.html:

```html
<html>
  <head>
    <title>
      Drawing rectangles
    </title>
  </head>

  <body>
    <h1>
      Drawing rectangles
    </h1>
      These rectangles were drawn on the server:
      <br>
      <img src="phprectangle.php">
  </body>
</html>
```

You can see the results in Figure 14-5, where the rectangles appear.

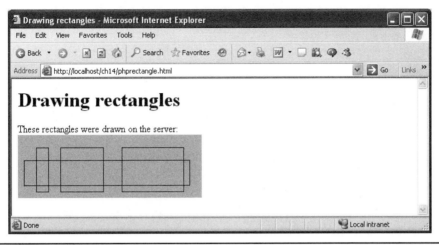

FIGURE 14-5   Displaying rectangles in a Web page

Drawing Ellipses

Want to draw circles or ellipses? Use the imageellipse function:

```
imageellipse(image, cx, cy, w, h, color)
```

Here's how it works. This function draws an ellipse centered at *cx, cy* in the image represented by *image*. The *w* and *h* values specify the ellipse's width and height, respectively. The color of the ellipse is specified by *color*. This function is pretty close to imagerectangle, but instead of specifying the upper-left and lower-right corners, you specify the center of the ellipse, and its width and height.

Here's an example, phpellipse.php, which draws ellipses:

```php
<?php

    $image_height = 100;
    $image_width = 300;

    $image = imagecreate($image_width, $image_height);

    $back_color = imagecolorallocate($image, 200, 200, 200);

    $draw_color = imagecolorallocate($image, 0, 0, 0);

    imageellipse($image, 100, 40, 150, 50, $draw_color);

    imageellipse($image, 150, 50, 150, 50, $draw_color);

    imageellipse($image, 200, 60, 150, 50, $draw_color);

    header('Content-Type: image/jpeg');
```

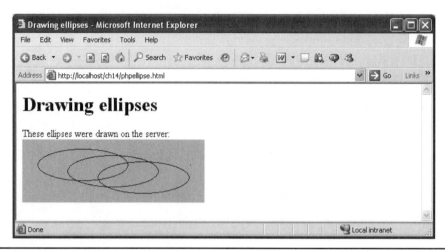

FIGURE 14-6   Displaying ellipses in a Web page

```
    imagejpeg($image);

    imagedestroy($image);
?>
```

And here's how you can embed those ellipses in a Web page, phpellipse.html:

```
<html>
  <head>
    <title>
      Drawing ellipses
    </title>
  </head>

  <body>
    <h1>
      Drawing ellipses
    </h1>
      These ellipses were drawn on the server:
      <br>
      <img src="phpellipse.php">
  </body>
</html>
```

You can see the results in Figure 14-6, where the ellipses appear.

Drawing Arcs

How about arcs? The imagearc function lets you draw arcs, which include partial circles and partial ellipses, as well as complete circles and ellipses:

```
imagearc(image, cx, cy, w, h, s, e, color)
```

This function is designed to draw arcs centered at *cx, cy* in the image represented by image. The *w* and *h* values specify the ellipse's width and height, respectively, while the start and end points are specified in degrees indicated by the *s* and *e* arguments (here, 0° is located at the three-o'clock position). The arc itself is drawn clockwise.

Here's how you can draw a smiley face using arcs:

```
imagearc($image, 150, 50, 50, 50, 30, 150, $drawing_color);

imagearc($image, 150, 50, 70, 70, 0, 360, $drawing_color);

imagearc($image, 135, 45, 20, 20, 190, -10, $drawing_color);

imagearc($image, 165, 45, 20, 20, 190, -10, $drawing_color);

imagearc($image, 135, 42, 10, 10, -10, 190, $drawing_color);

imagearc($image, 165, 42, 10, 10, -10, 190, $drawing_color);
```

And here's what that looks like in phparc.php:

```php
<?php
    $image_height = 100;
    $image_width = 300;

    $image = imagecreate($image_width, $image_height);

    $backcolor = imagecolorallocate($image, 200, 200, 200);

    $drawing_color = imagecolorallocate($image, 0, 0, 0);

    imagearc($image, 150, 50, 50, 50, 30, 150, $drawing_color);

    imagearc($image, 150, 50, 70, 70, 0, 360, $drawing_color);

    imagearc($image, 135, 45, 20, 20, 190, -10, $drawing_color);

    imagearc($image, 165, 45, 20, 20, 190, -10, $drawing_color);

    imagearc($image, 135, 42, 10, 10, -10, 190, $drawing_color);

    imagearc($image, 165, 42, 10, 10, -10, 190, $drawing_color);

    header("Content-type: image/jpeg");

    imagejpeg($image);

    imagedestroy($image);

?>
```

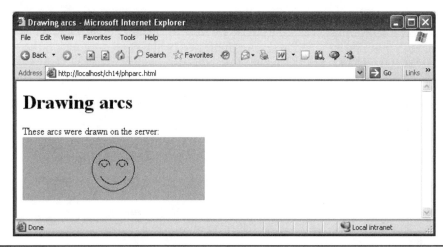

FIGURE 14-7   Displaying arcs in a Web page

Here's what the HTML page, phparc.html, that displays these arcs looks like:

```
<html>
  <head>
    <title>
      Drawing arcs
    </title>
  </head>

  <body>
    <h1>
      Drawing arcs
    </h1>
      These arcs were drawn on the server:
      <br>
      <img src="phparc.php">
  </body>
</html>
```

The smiley face appears in Figure 14-7. Cute.

Drawing Polygons

If you want to draw your own figures, you can trace them together using multiple lines if you want, but there's an easier way; you can use the imagepolygon function to draw a polygon simply by passing it an array of points. Here's how you use this function in general:

```
imagepolygon(image, points, num_points, color)
```

This function creates a polygon in an image. The *points* parameter is an array containing the polygon's vertices, (*points*[0] = x0, *points*[1] = y0, *points*[2] = x1, *points*[3] = y1, and so on). The *num_points* parameter holds the total number of points in the polygon, and *color* is the drawing color you want to use.

This is a good function for drawing complex figures—all you have to do is to supply the vertices of the polygon in an array, such as an array named $points:

```
$points = array(
    0  => 120, 1  => 60,
    2  => 130, 3  => 60,
    4  => 150, 5  => 80,
    6  => 170, 7  => 40,
    8  => 150, 9  => 40,
    10 => 110, 11 => 20,
    12 => 110, 13 => 90
);
```

Here's what that array looks like in phppolygon.php, which uses imagepolygon:

```
<?php
    $points = array(
        0  => 120, 1  => 60,
        2  => 130, 3  => 60,
        4  => 150, 5  => 80,
        6  => 170, 7  => 40,
        8  => 150, 9  => 40,
        10 => 110, 11 => 20,
        12 => 110, 13 => 90
    );

    $image_height = 100;
    $image_width = 300;

    $image = imagecreate($image_width, $image_height);
    $back_color = imagecolorallocate($image, 200, 200, 200);

    $draw_color = imagecolorallocate($image, 0, 0, 0);

    imagepolygon($image, $points, 7, $draw_color );

    header('Content-type: image/jpeg');

    imagejpeg($image);

    imagedestroy($image);
?>
```

Here's what the HTML page, phpolygon.html, that displays this polygon looks like:

```
<html>
  <head>
    <title>
```

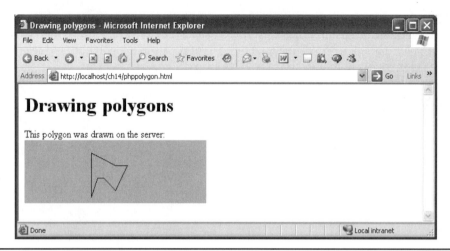

FIGURE 14-8   Displaying a polygon in a Web page

```
    Drawing polygons
  </title>
</head>

<body>
  <h1>
    Drawing polygons
  </h1>
    This polygon was drawn on the server:
    <br>
    <img src="phppolygon.php">
</body>
</html>
```

The polygon that this example draws appears in Figure 14-8.

Filling in Figures

In addition to just drawing figures in outline, you can also fill in figures with color using various functions that draw filled-in figures, such as these:

- **imagefilledarc**   Draw a partial ellipse and fill it
- **imagefilledellipse**   Draw a filled ellipse
- **imagefilledpolygon**   Draw a filled polygon
- **imagefilledrectangle**   Draw a filled rectangle

For example, take a look at imagefilledrectangle:

```
imagefilledrectangle(image, x1, y1, x2, y2, color)
```

This function creates a filled rectangle of color *color* in image *image* starting at upper-left coordinate *x1, y1* and ending at bottom-right coordinate *x2, y2*.

Here's an example putting imagefilledrectangle to work, modifying our earlier example phprectangle.php into phpfilledrectangle.php. The difference is that this version fills its rectangles in color—red in this case. Here's what the code looks like:

```php
<?php

    $image_height = 100;
    $image_width = 300;

    $image = imagecreate($image_width, $image_height);

    $back_color = imagecolorallocate($image, 200, 200, 200);

    $draw_color = imagecolorallocate($image, 255, 0, 0);

    imagefilledrectangle($image, 30, 20, 50, 90, $draw_color);

    imagefilledrectangle($image, 70, 20, 140, 90, $draw_color);

    imagefilledrectangle($image, 170, 20, 270, 90, $draw_color);

    header('Content-Type: image/jpeg');

    imagejpeg($image);

    imagedestroy($image);
?>
```

Here's the HTML page, phpfilledrectangle.html, that displays these filled rectangles:

```html
<html>
  <head>
    <title>
      Drawing filled rectangles
    </title>
  </head>

  <body>
    <h1>
      Drawing filled rectangles
    </h1>
      These filled rectangles was drawn on the server:
      <br>
      <img src="phpfilledrectangle.php">
  </body>
</html>
```

The filled rectangles that this example draws appear in Figure 14-9. They're in black and white here, but on the screen, they're red. Nice.

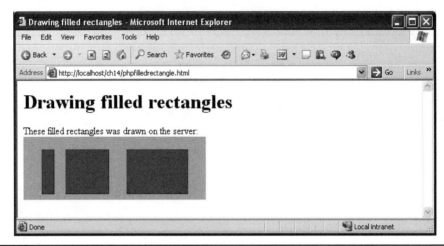

FIGURE **14-9**   Displaying filled rectangles in a Web page

Drawing Individual Pixels

Want more graphics power? You can set individual pixels using the imagesetpixel method:

```
imagesetpixel(image, x, y, color)
```

As you'd expect, this function draws a pixel at *x, y* in image *image* of color *color.*
Here's an example, phppixel.php, which draws a dotted line using imagesetpixel. To draw that line, this example simply uses a for loop:

```
for($loop_index = 50; $loop_index < 270; $loop_index += 3){

    imagesetpixel($image, $loop_index, $loop_index / 3, $drawing_color);

}
```

Here's what this for loop looks like in phppixel.php:

```
<?php
    $image_height = 100;
    $image_width = 300;

    $image = imagecreate($image_width, $image_height);

    $back_color = imagecolorallocate($image, 200, 200, 200);

    $drawing_color = imagecolorallocate($image, 0, 0, 0);

    for($loop_index = 50; $loop_index < 270; $loop_index += 3){

        imagesetpixel($image, $loop_index, $loop_index / 3, $drawing_color);

    }
```

```
header("Content-type: image/jpeg");

imagejpeg($image);

imagedestroy($image);
?>
```

And here is the HTML page, phppixel.html, that displays these pixels:

```
<html>
  <head>
    <title>
      Drawing pixels
    </title>
  </head>

  <body>
    <h1>
      Drawing pixels
    </h1>
      These pixels were drawn on the server:
      <br>
      <img src="phppixel.php">
  </body>
</html>
```

The pixels that this example draws appear in Figure 14-10.

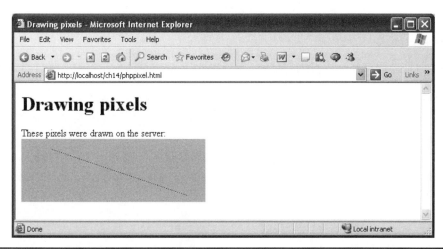

FIGURE 14-10   Displaying pixels in a Web page

Drawing Text

How about drawing text? There are a number of functions that draw text, such as imagestring:

```
imagestring(image, font, x, y, s, color)
```

This function draws the string *s* in the image specified by *image* with the upper-left corner at coordinates *x, y* in color *color.* The graphics package comes with built-in fonts—if *font* is 1, 2, 3, 4, or 5, a built-in font is used. You can also register your own fonts with the GD2 package using the imageloadfont function. Note that since we're working with graphics, this text is drawn as an image, not as editable text such as would appear in a text field.

Say you wanted to display some text centered in an image in an example, phptext.php. You might want to use font number 4, and display the text "No troubles.":

```php
<?php

    $font_number = 4;

    $text = "No troubles.";
        .
        .
        .
?>
```

How can you adjust the size of the image to center this text? You can make the image twice as wide as the text, using the imagefontwidth function to determine the width of each character in your font, and multiplying by 2 * strlen($text) to find the width the image should be:

```php
<?php

    $font_number = 4;

    $text = "No troubles.";

    $width = 2 * strlen($text) * imagefontwidth($font_number);
        .
        .
        .
?>
```

And you might make the image three times as high as the text is—which you can find out with the imagefontwidth function:

```php
<?php

    $font_number = 4;

    $text = "No troubles.";
```

```
    $width = 2 * strlen($text) * imagefontwidth($font_number);

    $height = 3 * imagefontheight($font_number);
        .
        .
        .

?>
```

Next, you can create the image and the background and drawing colors:

```
<?php

    $font_number = 4;

    $text = "No troubles.";

    $width = 2 * strlen($text) * imagefontwidth($font_number);

    $height = 3 * imagefontheight($font_number);

    $image = imagecreate($width, $height);

    $back_color = imagecolorallocate($image, 200, 200, 200);

    $drawing_color = imagecolorallocate($image, 0,   0,   0);
        .
        .
        .

?>
```

Next, you can find the *x* and *y* positions at which to start the text so that it will appear centered in the image:

```
<?php

$font_number = 4;

$text = "No troubles.";

$width = 2 * strlen($text) * imagefontwidth($font_number);

$height = 3 * imagefontheight($font_number);

$image = imagecreate($width, $height);

$back_color = imagecolorallocate($image, 200, 200, 200);

$drawing_color = imagecolorallocate($image, 0,   0,   0);

$x_position = ($width - (strlen($text) * imagefontwidth($font_number)))/ 2;

$y_position = ($height - imagefontheight($font_number)) / 2;
```

```
        .
        .
        .
?>
```

And then you can draw the text, like this in phppixel.php:

```php
<?php
    $font_number = 4;

    $text = "No troubles.";

    $width = 2 * strlen($text) * imagefontwidth($font_number);

    $height = 3 * imagefontheight($font_number);

    $image = imagecreate($width, $height);

    $back_color = imagecolorallocate($image, 200, 200, 200);

    $drawing_color = imagecolorallocate($image, 0,   0,   0);

    $x_position = ($width - (strlen($text) * imagefontwidth($font_number)))/ 2;

    $y_position = ($height - imagefontheight($font_number)) / 2;

    imagestring($image, $font_number, $x_position, $y_position, $text,
        $drawing_color);

    header('Content-Type: image/jpeg');

    imagejpeg($image);

    imagedestroy($image);
?>
```

And here is the HTML page, phptext.html, that displays the new text:

```html
<html>
  <head>
    <title>
      Drawing text
    </title>
  </head>

  <body>
    <h1>
      Drawing text
    </h1>
      This text was drawn on the server:
```

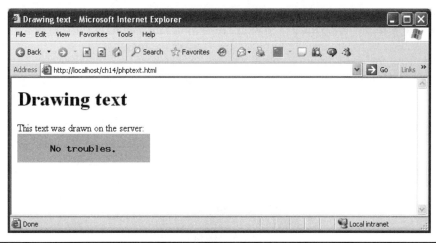

FIGURE 14-11   Displaying centered text in a Web page

```
      <br>
      <img src="phptext.php">
  </body>
</html>
```

The centered text that this example draws appears in Figure 14-11.

Drawing Vertical Text

You can draw text with imagestring—horizontally, anyway. What about drawing text vertically, as when you want to label the y axis of a graph? You can use the imagestringup function:

```
imagestringup(image, font, x, y, s, color)
```

This function draws the string *s* vertically in the image specified by *image* at coordinates *x*, *y* in color *color*. If font is 1, 2, 3, 4, or 5, a built-in font is used. You can also register your own fonts with the GD2 package using the imageloadfont function.

Here's an example, phpverticaltext.php, which draws some vertical text. It starts by selecting a font number and setting the text to display:

```
<?php

    $font_number = 4;
    $text = "No troubles.";
        .
        .
        .

?>
```

You have to then determine the dimensions of the image in which to display the text. For example, you can make the image width three times the height of the font you've selected, and make the image height twice the width of the text that's going to be displayed, as well as selecting a red drawing color:

```php
<?php
    $font_number = 4;
    $text = "No troubles.";

    $width = 3 * imagefontheight($font_number);

    $height = 2 * strlen($text) * imagefontwidth($font_number);

    $image = imagecreate($width, $height);

    $back_color = imagecolorallocate($image, 200, 200, 200);

    $drawing_color = imagecolorallocate($image, 255,    0,    0);
        .
        .
        .
?>
```

That creates the image and selects the drawing color. You can center the image with a little math, and draw the text using imagestringup this way:

```php
<?php
    $font_number = 4;
    $text = "No troubles.";

    $width = 3 * imagefontheight($font_number);

    $height = 2 * strlen($text) * imagefontwidth($font_number);

    $image = imagecreate($width, $height);

    $back_color = imagecolorallocate($image, 200, 200, 200);

    $drawing_color = imagecolorallocate($image, 255,    0,    0);

    $x_position = ($width - imagefontheight($font_number)) / 2;

    $y_position = ($height + (strlen($text) * imagefontwidth($font_number)))/2;

    imagestringup($image, $font_number, $x_position, $y_position, $text,
        $drawing_color);
        .
        .
        .
?>
```

And you can send the new image to the browser this way in phpverticaltext.php:

```php
<?php

    $font_number = 4;
    $text = "No troubles.";

    $width = 3 * imagefontheight($font_number);

    $height = 2 * strlen($text) * imagefontwidth($font_number);

    $image = imagecreate($width, $height);

    $back_color = imagecolorallocate($image, 200, 200, 200);

    $drawing_color = imagecolorallocate($image, 255,   0,   0);

    $x_position = ($width - imagefontheight($font_number)) / 2;

    $y_position = ($height + (strlen($text) * imagefontwidth($font_number)))/2;

    imagestringup($image, $font_number, $x_position, $y_position, $text,
        $drawing_color);

    header('Content-Type: image/jpeg');

    imagejpeg($image);

    imagedestroy($image);

?>
```

That completes phpverticaltext.php; here is the HTML page, phpverticaltext.html, that displays that text:

```html
<html>
  <head>
    <title>
      Drawing vertical text
    </title>
  </head>

  <body>
    <h1>
      Drawing vertical text
    </h1>
      This text was drawn on the server:
      <br>
      <img src="phpverticaltext.php">
  </body>
</html>
```

The vertical text that this example draws appears in Figure 14-12. Cool.

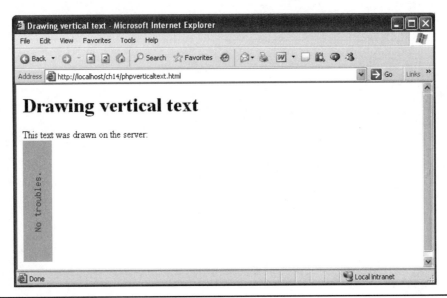

FIGURE **14-12**   Displaying vertical text in a Web page

Working with Image Files

You can create graphics image objects from existing image files using these functions:

- **imagecreatefromgif**   Create a new image from a GIF file or URL
- **imagecreatefromjpeg**   Create a new image from a JPEG file or URL
- **imagecreatefrompng**   Create a new image from a PNG file or URL
- **imagecreatefromwbmp**   Create a new image from a WBMP file or URL
- **imagecreatefromxbm**   Create a new image from an XBM file or URL
- **imagecreatefromxpm**   Create a new image from an XPM file or URL

This is great when you want to embed images in Web pages but also want to add something to them yourself, such as a copyright notice. You can add an image of yourself, or a logo, inside another image. As an example, we'll use imagecreatefromjpeg here, loading an existing JPEG image, image.jpg, and adding a smiley face and a border to it. Here's how you use this function:

```
imagecreatefromjpeg (string filename)
```

This function returns an image identifier representing the image obtained from the given filename, and it returns an empty string on failure.

We're going to modify the JPEG image you see in Figure 14-3, image.jpg, adding the smiley face you created earlier in the chapter, as well as a border around the whole image.

Hi there!

FIGURE 14-13   A JPEG image that will be modified

The PHP file, phpjpg.php, starts as you'd expect, by creating an image in memory from the file image.jpg:

```php
<?php

    $image = imagecreatefromjpeg ("image.jpg");
        .
        .
        .

?>
```

That loads the image, image.jpg, into the object $image (in practice, don't forget to add error-handling code in case PHP can't find your image file). You can draw a border inside this image—but it would help if you knew the image's dimensions.

You can find those dimensions with the imagesx and imagesy functions, which return the *x* and *y* size of an image. And you can use the imagerectangle function to create the border; here's how to draw that border ten pixels inside the image:

```php
<?php

$image = imagecreatefromjpeg ("image.jpg");

$back_color = imagecolorallocate($image, 200, 200, 200);

$draw_color = imagecolorallocate($image, 0, 0, 0);

imagerectangle($image, 10, 10, imagesx($image) - 10, imagesy($image) - 10,
    $draw_color);
    .
    .
    .

?>
```

And you can add the smiley face to the image as well like this in phpjpg.php:

```php
<?php
$image = imagecreatefromjpeg ("image.jpg");

$back_color = imagecolorallocate($image, 200, 200, 200);
```

```
$draw_color = imagecolorallocate($image, 0, 0, 0);

imagerectangle($image, 10, 10, imagesx($image) - 10, imagesy($image) - 10,
    $draw_color);

imagearc($image, 50, 50, 50, 50, 30, 150, $drawing_color);

imagearc($image, 50, 50, 70, 70, 0, 360, $drawing_color);

imagearc($image, 35, 45, 20, 20, 190, -10, $drawing_color);

imagearc($image, 65, 45, 20, 20, 190, -10, $drawing_color);

imagearc($image, 35, 42, 10, 10, -10, 190, $drawing_color);

imagearc($image, 65, 42, 10, 10, -10, 190, $drawing_color);

header('Content-Type: image/jpeg');

imagejpeg($image);

imagedestroy($image);
?>
```

Here is the HTML page, phpjpg.html, that displays the modified image:

```
<html>
  <head>
    <title>
      Using images
    </title>
  </head>

  <body>
    <h1>
      Using images
    </h1>
      This image was modified on the server:
      <br>
      <img src="phpjpg.php">
  </body>
</html>
```

And you can see the result in Figure 14-14, where the original JPEG image was modified as you wanted.

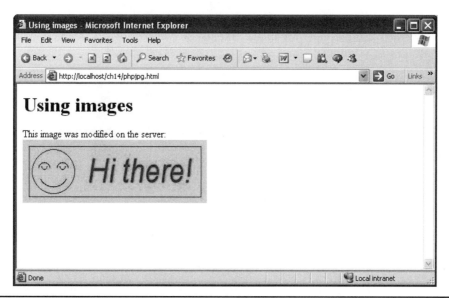

FIGURE 14-14   Displaying a modified image in a Web page

Tiling Images

You can also use one image to tile another image, by appearing repeatedly in the background, with the imagesettile function. Here's how you use this function:

```
imagesettile(image, tile)
```

This function sets the tile image to be used by all region-filling functions (such as imagefilledrectangle and imagefilledpolygon) when filling with the special color IMG_COLOR_TILED.

How about an example? This script, phptile.php, starts by creating an image that will be tiled. Here, we'll use imagecreatetruecolor to give the created image the full range of colors possible, rather than imagecreate, which might inadvertently restrict the number of colors available in the tiles (when there's any doubt about restricting colors, you should use imagecreatetruecolor instead of the more simple imagecreate):

```php
<?php
    $image_width = 300;
    $image_height = 200;

    $image = imagecreatetruecolor($image_width, $image_height);
        .
        .
        .
?>
```

Now we'll create the tile, $tile, that will appear inside the image stored in $image. In this case, we can tile the smiley-face image you just saw created by first reading in image.jpg with imagecreatefromjpeg :

```php
<?php
    $image_width = 300;
    $image_height = 200;

    $image = imagecreatetruecolor($image_width, $image_height);

    $tile = imagecreatefromjpeg ('image.jpg');
        .
        .
        .
?>
```

You can add the smiley face to this tile with imagearc:

```php
<?php
    $image_width = 300;
    $image_height = 200;

    $image = imagecreatetruecolor($image_width, $image_height);

    $tile = imagecreatefromjpeg ('image.jpg');

    imagearc($tile, 50, 50, 50, 50, 30, 150, $drawing_color);

    imagearc($tile, 50, 50, 70, 70, 0, 360, $drawing_color);

    imagearc($tile, 35, 45, 20, 20, 190, -10, $drawing_color);

    imagearc($tile, 65, 45, 20, 20, 190, -10, $drawing_color);

    imagearc($tile, 35, 42, 10, 10, -10, 190, $drawing_color);

    imagearc($tile, 65, 42, 10, 10, -10, 190, $drawing_color);
        .
        .
        .
?>
```

That completes the creation of the tile image, and you can set $tile as the tile for $image with imagesettile:

```php
<?php
    $image_width = 300;
    $image_height = 200;

    $image = imagecreatetruecolor($image_width, $image_height);

    $tile = imagecreatefromjpeg ('image.jpg');
```

```
      .
      .
      .
   imagearc($tile, 65, 42, 10, 10, -10, 190, $drawing_color);

   imagesettile($image, $tile);
      .
      .
      .
?>
```

And you can now draw a filled rectangle that will use this tile if you set the fill style to IMG_COLOR_TILED:

```
<?php
   $image_width = 300;
   $image_height = 200;

   $image = imagecreatetruecolor($image_width, $image_height);

   $tile = imagecreatefromjpeg ('image.jpg');
      .
      .
      .
   imagearc($tile, 65, 42, 10, 10, -10, 190, $drawing_color);

   imagesettile($image, $tile);

   imagefilledrectangle ($image, 0, 0, $image_width, $image_height,
      IMG_COLOR_TILED);
      .
      .
      .
?>
```

All that's left is to display the image and then destroy it in phptile.php:

```
<?php
   $image_width = 300;
   $image_height = 200;

   $image = imagecreatetruecolor($image_width, $image_height);

   $tile = imagecreatefromjpeg ('image.jpg');
      .
      .
      .
   imagearc($tile, 65, 42, 10, 10, -10, 190, $drawing_color);

   imagesettile($image, $tile);

   imagefilledrectangle ($image, 0, 0, $image_width, $image_height,
      IMG_COLOR_TILED);
```

```
        Header("Content-type: image/jpeg");

        imagejpeg($image);

        imagedestroy ($image);
        imagedestroy ($tile);
?>
```

And here is the HTML page, phptile.html, that displays the tiled image:

```
<html>
  <head>
    <title>
      Tiling images
    </title>
  </head>

  <body>
    <h1>
      Tiling images
    </h1>
      This image was tiled on the server:
      <br>
      <img src="phptile.php">
  </body>
</html>
```

And you can see the result in Figure 14-15, where the tiled image appears.

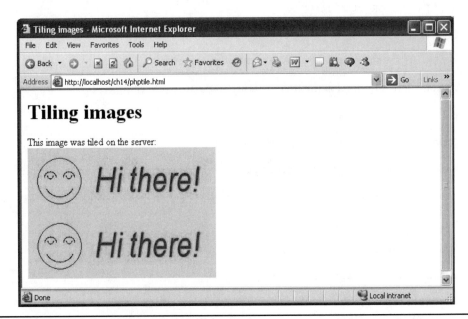

FIGURE **14-15**   Displaying a tiled image in a Web page

Copying Images

There's more graphics manipulation power available; for example, the imagecopy function lets you copy all of, or part of, an image:

```
imagecopy (dest_image, src_image, dest_x, dest_y, src_x, src_y, src_w, src_h)
```

This function copies a part of *src_image* onto *dest_image* starting at the *x, y* coordinates *src_x*, *src_y* with a width of *src_w* and a height of *src_h*. The portion defined will be copied onto the *x, y* coordinates, *dest_x* and *dest_y*.

Copying images lets you perform all kinds of tricks—for example, here's a script, phpflip.php, that flips an image horizontally. It starts by reading in image.jpg, adding a smiley face to it, and then creating a blank image, $image_new, of the same size:

```php
<?php
    $image_original = imagecreatefromjpeg("image.jpg");

    imagearc($image_original, 50, 50, 50, 50, 30, 150, $drawing_color);

    imagearc($image_original, 50, 50, 70, 70, 0, 360, $drawing_color);

    imagearc($image_original, 35, 45, 20, 20, 190, -10, $drawing_color);

    imagearc($image_original, 65, 45, 20, 20, 190, -10, $drawing_color);

    imagearc($image_original, 35, 42, 10, 10, -10, 190, $drawing_color);

    imagearc($image_original, 65, 42, 10, 10, -10, 190, $drawing_color);

    $image_width = imagesx($image_original);

    $image_height = imagesy($image_original);

    $image_new = imagecreate($image_width, $image_height);
        .
        .
        .
?>
```

Here's where you can flip the image, which the code does by copying the original image over and flipping it, pixel by pixel, into the flipped image:

```php
for ($col = 0 ; $col < $image_width ; $col++)
{
    for ($row = 0 ; $row < $image_height ; $row++)
    {
        imagecopy($image_new, $image_original, $image_width - $col - 1,
            $row, $col, $row, 1, 1);
    }
}
```

Here is the HTML page, phpflip.html, that displays the flipped image:

```
<html>
  <head>
    <title>
      Flipping images
    </title>
  </head>

  <body>
    <h1>
      Flipping images
    </h1>
      This image was flipped on the server:
      <br>
      <img src="phpflip.php">
  </body>
</html>
```

You can see the result in Figure 14-16, where the flipped image appears.

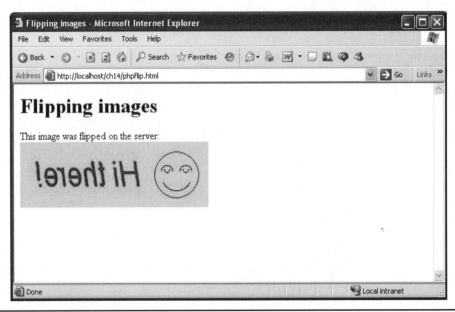

FIGURE 14-16 Displaying a flipped image in a Web page

XML and RSS

This chapter takes a look at XML and RSS. There's a lot of support built in for XML in PHP, and we're going to take a look at it in this chapter.

We're going to start by creating some XML on the server and sending it back to the browser.

Creating XML

How do you create XML on the server and send it back to the browser? As you recall, we tackled this problem in Chapter 12, where we created some XML and sent it to the browser. We'll take a look at this script, phpitems.php, here.

The key point when creating XML in PHP is to set the content-type header to an XML type, such as text/xml:

```
<?php
header("Content-type: text/xml");
        .
        .
        .
?>
```

This example let you construct two XML documents, depending on whether the items parameter you pass to it holds "1" or "2". Here's what you get with "1":

```
<?xml version = "1.0" ?>
<items>
  <item>PHP book</item>
  <item>Television</item>
  <item>Radio</item>
</items>
```

and here's what you get with "2":

```
<?xml version = "1.0" ?>
<items>
  <item>Soda</item>
```

```
  <item>Cheese</item>
  <item>Salami</item>
</items>
```

In phpitems.php, this is how you handle the items parameter—by using one of two different arrays of data:

```php
<?php
header("Content-type: text/xml");

if ($_REQUEST["items"] == "1")
  $items = array('PHP book', 'Television', 'Radio');
if ($_REQUEST["items"] == "2")
  $items = array('Soda', 'Cheese', 'Salami');
      .
      .
      .

?>
```

Now you have to echo the document's XML declaration, <?xml version="1.0" ?>, required for all XML documents (legal versions currently are only 1.0 or 1.1):

```php
<?php
header("Content-type: text/xml");

if ($_REQUEST["items"] == "1")
  $items = array('PHP book', 'Television', 'Radio');
if ($_REQUEST["items"] == "2")
  $items = array('Soda', 'Cheese', 'Salami');

echo '<?xml version="1.0" ?>';
      .
      .
      .

?>
```

The document element, <items>, contains all the other elements, as is always the case for document elements in XML documents:

```php
<?php
header("Content-type: text/xml");

if ($_REQUEST["items"] == "1")
  $items = array('PHP book', 'Television', 'Radio');
if ($_REQUEST["items"] == "2")
  $items = array('Soda', 'Cheese', 'Salami');

echo '<?xml version="1.0" ?>';

echo '<items>';
```

```
    .
    .
    .
?>
```

And you're free to echo the data in the $items array to the browser in <item> elements, and then end the XML document by closing the document element with an </items> tag:

```php
<?php
header("Content-type: text/xml");

if ($_REQUEST["items"] == "1")
  $items = array('PHP book', 'Television', 'Radio');
if ($_REQUEST["items"] == "2")
  $items = array('Soda', 'Cheese', 'Salami');

echo '<?xml version="1.0" ?>';

echo '<items>';

foreach ($items as $value)
{
  echo '<item>';
  echo $value;
  echo '</item>';
}

echo '</items>';
?>
```

You can take a look at this script by passing it a value for the items parameter, as in this URL: http://localhost/ch15/phpitems.php?items=1. The results appear in Figure 15-1, where you can see our XML.

Cool.

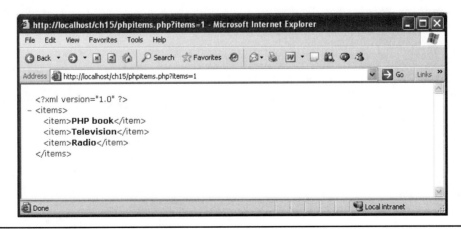

FIGURE 15-1   Creating XML on the server

Creating RSS

An XML dialect that is very common to use with PHP is RSS—Really Simple Syndication, which lets you distribute news feeds that people can take a look at in RSS readers. That's something you'll often see in PHP, because using PHP, you can automate the RSS-creation process. For example, you can write a PHP script to scan your blog and create an RSS feed from it.

Here's an example that creates an RSS feed, phprss.php. For simplicity, we'll embed the RSS data in this example script, but of course it could scan a blog or any other file to get the news items.

This script has to supply a title, an URL, and a description for each news item; here's the RSS document we're going to create in this example, which will be readable by RSS readers:

```
<?xml version="1.0" ?>
<rss version="2.0">
<channel>
  <title>Vital News</title>
  <link>http://url</link>
  <description>The most vital news stories anywhere</description>
  <language>en-us</language>
  <copyright>Copyright 2007</copyright>
  <webMaster>webmaster@url</webMaster>

  <item>
    <title>Snow in August</title>
    <link>http://url</link>
    <description>It's snowing in August. Is this still the northern
      hemisphere?</description>
  </item>

  <item>
    <title>Trees are green</title>
    <link>http://url</link>
    <description>Scientists determine that trees are green. Sky suspected to be
      blue.</description>
  </item>

  <item>
    <title>Stock market goes up and down</title>
    <link>http://url</link>
    <description>Yes, the stock market went up and down today. Like
      always.</description>
  </item>
  </channel>
</rss>
```

You can create a multidimensional array, $items, to hold the data in the news items in phprss.php:

```php
<?php
  $items[0] = array('Snow in August',
    'http://url',
    "It's snowing in August. Is this still the northern hemisphere?"
  );

  $items[1] = array('Trees are green',
    'http://url',
    'Scientists determine that trees are green. Sky suspected to be blue.'
  );

  $items[2] = array('Stock market goes up and down',
    'http://url',
    'Yes, the stock market went up and down today. Like always.'
  );
        .
        .
        .

?>
```

You can also set up the document by using the header function to make it XML, as well as including XML and RSS declarations; in this case, we're going to use RSS version 2.0, the current version:

```php
<?php
  $items[0] = array('Snow in August',
    'http://url',
    "It's snowing in August. Is this still the northern hemisphere?"
  );
        .
        .
        .

  header('Content-type: text/xml');

  echo '<?xml version="1.0" ?>';

  echo '<rss version="2.0">';
        .
        .
        .
?>
```

And you can echo the <channel>, <title>, and other elements that start the document off:

```php
<?php
  $items[0] = array('Snow in August',
    'http://url',
    "It's snowing in August. Is this still the northern hemisphere?"
```

```
    );

              .
              .
              .

    header('Content-type: text/xml');

    echo '<?xml version="1.0" ?>';

    echo '<rss version="2.0">';

    echo '<channel>';

    echo '<title>Vital News</title>';
    echo '<link>http://url</link>';
    echo '<description>The most vital news stories anywhere</description>';
    echo '<language>en-us</language>';
    echo '<copyright>Copyright 2007</copyright>';
    echo '<webMaster>webmaster@url</webMaster>';

              .
              .
              .

?>
```

Finally, you can echo the actual data in the feed, and end the document:

```
<?php
  $items[0] = array('Snow in August',
    'http://url',
    "It's snowing in August. Is this still the northern hemisphere?"
  );

  $items[1] = array('Trees are green',
    'http://url',
    'Scientists determine that trees are green. Sky suspected to be blue.'
  );

              .
              .
              .

  echo '<webMaster>webmaster@url</webMaster>';

  foreach ($items as $data) {
    echo '<item>';
    echo "<title>{$data[0]}</title>";
    echo "<link>{$data[1]}</link>";
    echo "<description>{$data[2]}</description>";
    echo '</item>';
  }
```

```
    echo '</channel>';

    echo '</rss>';
?>
```

You can see the RSS document this example, phprss.php, creates in Figure 15-2. And you can take a look at our new RSS feed in an RSS reader in Figure 15-3. Very cool. Now you're able to create RSS feeds using PHP that users can read in RSS readers.

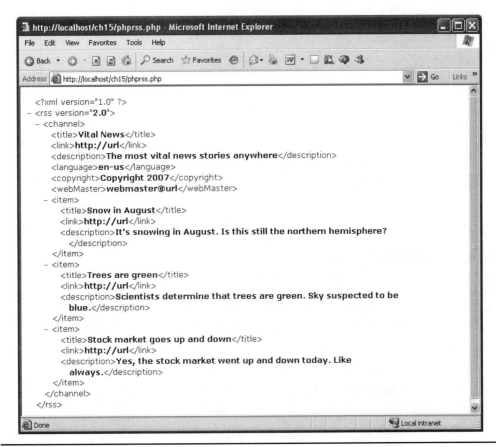

FIGURE 15-2   Creating RSS on the server

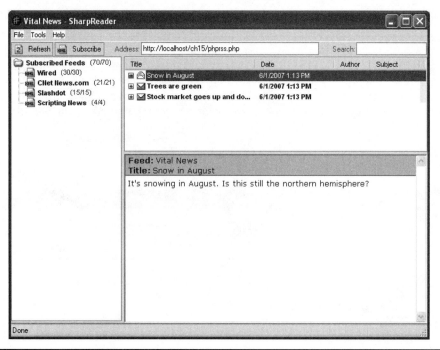

FIGURE 15-3 Reading RSS in an RSS reader

Using the SimpleXML Functions

PHP 5 comes with a great library of functions built in for handling XML—there are the SimpleXML functions, the XML parser functions, the DOM functions, XMLReader functions, and so on. We don't have space in this chapter to look at all the XML support in PHP, but we'll cover the most popular, starting with the SimpleXML functions. Here they are:

- **simplexml_import_dom**   Returns a SimpleXMLElement object from a DOM node.
- **simplexml_load_file**   Loads an XML file into an object
- **simplexml_load_string**   Loads a string of XML into an object
- **SimpleXMLElement->__construct()**   Creates a new SimpleXMLElement object
- **SimpleXMLElement->addAttribute()**   Adds an attribute to a SimpleXML element
- **SimpleXMLElement->addChild()**   Adds a child element to the XML node
- **SimpleXMLElement->asXML()**   Returns an XML string based on a SimpleXML element
- **SimpleXMLElement->attributes()**   Gets an element's attributes
- **SimpleXMLElement->children()**   Gets the children of given node

- **SimpleXMLElement->getDocNamespaces()**   Returns namespaces declared in document
- **SimpleXMLElement->getName()**   Gets the name of an XML element
- **SimpleXMLElement->getNamespaces()**   Returns the namespaces used in document
- **SimpleXMLElement->registerXPathNamespace()**   Creates a prefix/ns for the next XPath query
- **SimpleXMLElement->xpath()**   Executes an XPath query on XML data

You can use these functions to parse and edit XML documents on the fly. Here's the XML document you'll see for the following few examples, event.xml. This XML document lists an event, the National Awards event, and its attendees:

```
<?xml version="1.0"?>
<events>
    <event type="fundraising">
        <event_title>National Awards</event_title>
        <event_number>3</event_number>
        <subject>Pet Awards</subject>
        <date>5/5/2007</date>
        <people>
            <person attendance="present">
                <first_name>June</first_name>
                <last_name>Allyson</last_name>
            </person>
            <person attendance="absent">
                <first_name>Virginia</first_name>
                <last_name>Mayo</last_name>
            </person>
            <person attendance="present">
                <first_name>Jimmy</first_name>
                <last_name>Stewart</last_name>
            </person>
        </people>
    </event>
</events>
```

You can load this XML document into a SimpleXML object using the simplexml_load_file function like this:

```
<?php
  $xml = simplexml_load_file("event.xml");
      .
      .
      .
?>
```

Now the document is loaded into the $xml object. Here's where the simple in SimpleXML comes into play. Each element in event.xml—with the exception of the document element—becomes a property of that object.

For example, say you wanted to extract the date from event.xml:

```
<?xml version="1.0"?>
<events>
    <event type="fundraising">
        <event_title>National Awards</event_title>
        <event_number>3</event_number>
        <subject>Pet Awards</subject>
        <date>5/5/2007</date>
            .
            .
            .
```

You can access the text in that date as $xml->event->date:

```
<?php
    $xml = simplexml_load_file("event.xml");

    echo "<h1>Extracting simple data from an XML document</h1>";

    echo "The date of the event is " . $xml->event->date;
?>
```

And you can see the results of this example in Figure 15-4, where the date has been successfully extracted from event.xml.

The SimpleXML functions can also read XML data from a string if you pass that string to the SimpleXMLElement constructor. For example, you might have a script that loads the text in event.xml into a string named $xmlstr:

```
<?php
$xmlstr = <<<XML
<?xml version="1.0"?>
<events>
    <event type="fundraising">
        <event_title>National Awards</event_title>
        <event_number>3</event_number>
        <subject>Pet Awards</subject>
```

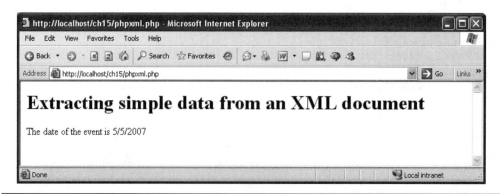

FIGURE 15-4   Extracting data from event.xml

```
        <date>5/5/2007</date>
        <people>
            <person attendance="present">
                <first_name>June</first_name>
                <last_name>Allyson</last_name>
            </person>
            <person attendance="absent">
                <first_name>Virginia</first_name>
                <last_name>Mayo</last_name>
            </person>
            <person attendance="present">
                <first_name>Jimmy</first_name>
                <last_name>Stewart</last_name>
            </person>
        </people>
    </event>
</events>
XML;
?>
```

Now you can include event.php in a new script, phpxml2.php:

```
<?php
    include 'event.php';

        .
        .
        .

?>
```

This introduces the $xmlstr into the code of phpxml2.php, and you can pass that string, including the XML text it contains, to the SimpleXMLElement constructor:

```
<?php
    include 'event.php';

    $xml = new SimpleXMLElement($xmlstr);

        .
        .
        .

?>
```

This creates the same object in $xml as if you had used the simplexml_load_file function, passing that function event.xml. Now you can extract the data in the <date> element as before:

```
<?php
    include 'event.php';

    $xml = new SimpleXMLElement($xmlstr);

    echo "<h1>Extracting simple data from an XML string</h1>";

    echo $xml->event->date;
?>
```

This script, phpxml2.php, gives you the same results as phpxml.php.

How do you handle the case where a document has more than one of the same element? For example, what if you wanted to extract the first and last names of each person from these three <person> elements?

```xml
<?xml version="1.0"?>
<events>
    <event type="fundraising">
        <event_title>National Awards</event_title>
        <event_number>3</event_number>
        <subject>Pet Awards</subject>
        <date>5/5/2007</date>
        <people>
            <person attendance="present">
                <first_name>June</first_name>
                <last_name>Allyson</last_name>
            </person>
            <person attendance="absent">
                <first_name>Virginia</first_name>
                <last_name>Mayo</last_name>
            </person>
            <person attendance="present">
                <first_name>Jimmy</first_name>
                <last_name>Stewart</last_name>
            </person>
        </people>
    </event>
</events>
```

You can't just use the terminology $people->person—how would SimpleXML know what <person> element you wanted? It turns out that SimpleXML handles this by letting you use array terminology, like this: $people->person[0], $people->person[1], $people->person[2], and so on, making things easy.

You can loop over multiple elements of the same name using foreach as well. In this example, we'll do exactly that to extract all the event attendees' names in phpparse.php. This script starts by loading the event.xml file:

```php
<?php
  $xml = simplexml_load_file("event.xml");
       .
       .
       .
?>
```

You can get an object corresponding to the <event> element:

```php
<?php
  $xml = simplexml_load_file("event.xml");

  echo "<h1>Parsing data from an XML document</h1>";

  echo "Here are the people who attended the event: <br>";
```

```
  $event = $xml->event;

         .
         .
         .

?>
```

And you can get an object corresponding to the <people> element this way:

```
<?php
  $xml = simplexml_load_file("event.xml");

  echo "<h1>Parsing data from an XML document</h1>";

  echo "Here are the people who attended the event: <br>";

  $event = $xml->event;

  $people = $event->people;

         .
         .
         .

?>
```

You can echo the people in an unordered list, so surround the code to display the people with <ul> and </ul>:

```
<?php
  $xml = simplexml_load_file("event.xml");

  echo "<h1>Parsing data from an XML document</h1>";

  echo "Here are the people who attended the event: <br>";

  $event = $xml->event;

  $people = $event->people;

  echo "<ul>";

         .
         .
         .

  echo "</ul>";
?>
```

And you loop over all <person> elements using a foreach loop, easily accessing the text in the person's <first_name> and <last_name> elements this way (is the HTML code for a non-breaking space):

```
<?php
  $xml = simplexml_load_file("event.xml");

  echo "<h1>Parsing data from an XML document</h1>";
```

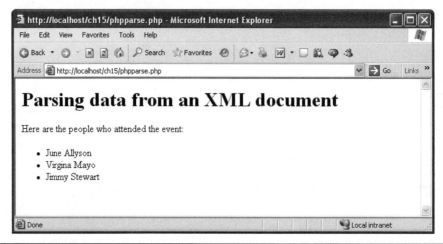

FIGURE 15-5   Extracting names from event.xml

```
   echo "Here are the people who attended the event: <br>";

   $event = $xml->event;

   $people = $event->people;

   echo "<ul>";

   foreach ($people->person as $person){
     echo "<li>", $person->first_name, ' ', $person->last_name , "</li>";
   }

   echo "</ul>";
?>
```

And you can see the results of this example in Figure 15-5, where people's names have been extracted from event.xml.

Extracting Attributes

How about extracting attributes from a document using SimpleXML? Turns out that's easy—you just use array notation.

For example, what if you wanted to extract the attendance attribute's value for each <person> element?

```
<?xml version="1.0"?>
<events>
    <event type="fundraising">
        <event_title>National Awards</event_title>
        <event_number>3</event_number>
        <subject>Pet Awards</subject>
        <date>5/5/2007</date>
```

```
    <people>
        <person attendance="present">
            <first_name>June</first_name>
            <last_name>Allyson</last_name>
        </person>
        <person attendance="absent">
            <first_name>Virgina</first_name>
            <last_name>Mayo</last_name>
        </person>
        <person attendance="present">
            <first_name>Jimmy</first_name>
            <last_name>Stewart</last_name>
        </person>
    </people>
  </event>
</events>
```

You can extract the attendance attribute's value for a <person> element like this: $person['attendance'], where $person holds the <person> element. Here's an example, phpattribute.php, that extracts the attendance attributes and displays them. As in the previous example, phpparse.php, you can display each person—in this case, each person's attendance—using an unordered HTML list:

```php
<?php
  $xml = simplexml_load_file("event.xml");

  echo "<h1>Parsing attributes from an XML document</h1>";

  echo "Here are the people who attended the event: <br>";

  $event = $xml->event;

  $people = $event->people;

  echo "<ul>";
        .
        .
        .
  echo "</ul>";
?>
```

And you can display everyone's attendance like this:

```php
<?php
  $xml = simplexml_load_file("event.xml");

  echo "<h1>Parsing attributes from an XML document</h1>";

  echo "Here are the people who attended the event: <br>";

  $event = $xml->event;

  $people = $event->people;

  echo "<ul>";
```

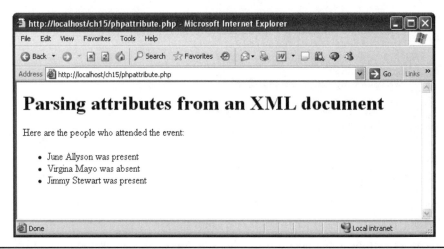

FIGURE 15-6 Extracting names from event.xml

```
foreach ($people->person as $person){
  echo "<li>", $person->first_name, ' ', $person->last_name, " was ",
    $person['attendance'], "</li>";
}

  echo "</ul>";
?>
```

You can see the results in Figure 15-6, where everyone's attendance attributes have been extracted from event.xml. Cool.

Using XPath

XPath is an XML specification for a special language that lets you search XML documents. A full discussion of XPath is beyond the scope of this book. Briefly, to use XPath, you consider an XML document as a tree of nodes; here are the legal node types:

- element
- attribute
- text
- CDATA section
- entity reference
- entity
- processing instruction

When you execute an XPath expression on a node, that node is called the context node. Here are a few XPath examples—say that you have this XML document:

```
<?xml version="1.0" encoding ="UTF-8"?>
<states>

    <state>
        <name>California</name>
        <population units="people">33871648</population><!--2000 census-->
        <capital>Sacramento</capital>
        <bird>Quail</bird>
        <flower>Golden Poppy</flower>
        <area units="square miles">155959</area>
    </state>

    <state>
        <name>Massachusetts</name>
        <population units="people">6349097</population><!--2000 census-->
        <capital>Boston</capital>
        <bird>Chickadee</bird>
        <flower>Mayflower</flower>
        <area units="square miles">7840</area>
    </state>

    <state>
        <name>New York</name>
        <population units="people">18976457</population><!--2000 census-->
        <capital>Albany</capital>
        <bird>Bluebird</bird>
        <flower>Rose</flower>
        <area units="square miles">47214</area>
    </state>

</states>
```

Then these XPath expression yield the following results:

- ***** Matches all element children of the context node.
- ***/*/state** Matches all <state> great-grandchildren of the context node.
- **.** Matches the context node.
- **..** Matches the parent of the context node.
- **../@units** Matches the units attribute of the parent of the context node.
- **.//state** Matches all <state> element descendants of the context node.
- **//state** Matches all the <state> descendants of the root node.
- **//state/name** Matches all the <name> elements that have an <state> parent.
- **/states/state[4]/name[3]** Matches the third <name> element of the fourth <state> element of the <states> element.

- **@*** Matches all the attributes of the context node.
- **@units** Matches the units attribute of the context node.
- **state** Matches the <state> element children of the context node.
- **state[@nickname and @units]** Matches all the <state> children of the context node that have both a nickname attribute and an units attribute.
- **state[@units = "people"]** Matches all <state> children of the context node that have a units attribute that has the value "people".
- **state[7]** Matches the seventh <state> child of the context node.
- **state[7][@units = "people"]** Matches the seventh <state> child of the context node if that child has a units attribute with value "people".
- **state[last()]** Matches the last <state> child of the context node.
- **state[name]** Matches the <state> children of the context node that themselves have <name> children.
- **state[name="Massachusetts"]** Matches the <state> child nodes of the context node that have <name> children whose text value is "Massachusetts".
- **states//state** Matches all <state> element descendants of the <states> element children of the context node.
- **text()** Matches all child text nodes of the context node.

Let's take a look at this in code. If you want to create an array of all <person> elements—no matter where they are in the event.xml document—you can use the XPath expression //person. Here, then, is how you can loop over all <person> elements in event. xml—without having to navigate to those <person> elements by working your way down through the <event> and <people> elements:

```php
<?php
$xml = simplexml_load_file("event.xml");

echo "<h1>Using XPath in an XML document</h1>";

echo "Here are the people who attended the event: <br>";

echo "<ul>";

foreach ($xml->xpath('//person') as $person){
    .
    .
    .
}

echo "</ul>";
?>
```

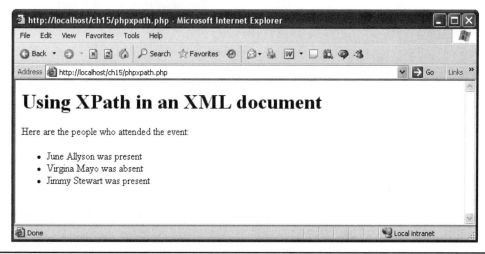

FIGURE 15-7   Using XPath in event.xml

And you can list each person and their attendance at the event like this:

```php
<?php
  $xml = simplexml_load_file("event.xml");

  echo "<h1>Using XPath in an XML document</h1>";

  echo "Here are the people who attended the event: <br>";

  echo "<ul>";

  foreach ($xml->xpath('//person') as $person){
    echo "<li>", $person->first_name, ' ', $person->last_name, " was ",
      $person['attendance'], "</li>";
  }

  echo "</ul>";
?>
```

You can see the results in Figure 15-7, where the XPath expression was successful in extracting all <person>elements.

Modifying XML Elements and Attributes

You can also modify elements and attributes using SimpleXML—all you have to do is to assign a new values to the element or attribute. Here's an example, phpmodify.php, which assigns the name "Myrna Loy" to each <person> element in event.xml:

```php
<?php
  $xml = simplexml_load_file("event.xml");

  echo "<h1>Modifying elements in an XML document</h1>";
```

```
  echo "Here are the people who attended the event: <br>";

  $event = $xml->event;

  $people = $event->people;

  foreach ($people->person as $person){
    $person->first_name = "Myrna";
    $person->last_name = "Loy";
  }
          .
          .
          .

?>
```

Then this example displays the text in each <person> element—which will be Myrna Loy three times:

```
<?php
  $xml = simplexml_load_file("event.xml");

  echo "<h1>Modifying elements in an XML document</h1>";

  echo "Here are the people who attended the event: <br>";

  $event = $xml->event;

  $people = $event->people;

  foreach ($people->person as $person){
    $person->first_name = "Myrna";
    $person->last_name = "Loy";
  }

  echo "<ul>";

  foreach ($people->person as $person){
    echo "<li>", $person->first_name, ' ', $person->last_name, " was ",
      $person['attendance'], "</li>";
  }

  echo "</ul>";
?>
```

You can see the results in Figure 15-8, where every <person> element was indeed changed to contain Myrna Loy.

As you can see, it's possible to make all elements contain Myrna Loy, but that's not the best way to indicate that she attended the event. How about adding a Myrna Loy element, instead of overwriting all the others?

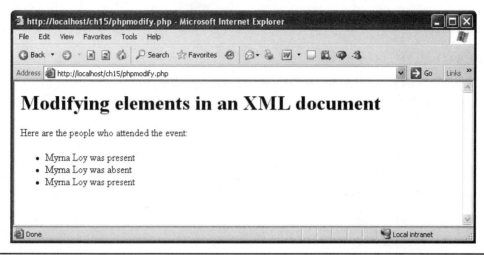

FIGURE 15-8 Modifying elements in event.xml

Adding New Elements and Attributes

You can create new elements using the SimpleXML package in PHP. For example, you can add an element to event.xml for Myrna Loy:

```
<?xml version="1.0"?>
<events>
    <event type="fundraising">
        <event_title>National Awards</event_title>
        <event_number>3</event_number>
        <subject>Pet Awards</subject>
        <date>5/5/2007</date>
        <people>
            <person attendance="present">
                <first_name>June</first_name>
                <last_name>Allyson</last_name>
            </person>
            <person attendance="absent">
                <first_name>Virginia</first_name>
                <last_name>Mayo</last_name>
            </person>
            <person attendance="present">
                <first_name>Jimmy</first_name>
                <last_name>Stewart</last_name>
            </person>
            <person attendance="present">
                <first_name>Myrna</first_name>
                <last_name>Loy</last_name>
```

```
            </person>
         </people>
      </event>
</events>
```

You start this new example, phpadd.php, by getting an object corresponding to the <people> element:

```
<?php
   $xml = simplexml_load_file("event.xml");

   echo "<h1>Adding elements in an XML document</h1>";

   echo "Here are the people who attended the event: <br>";

   $event = $xml->event;

   $people = $event->people;
      .
      .
      .

?>
```

You can add a <person> element as a child of the current <people> element using the addChild method:

```
<?php
   $xml = simplexml_load_file("event.xml");

   echo "<h1>Adding elements in an XML document</h1>";
   echo "Here are the people who attended the event: <br>";

   $event = $xml->event;

   $people = $event->people;

   $person = $people->addChild('person');
      .
      .
      .

?>
```

And you can add <first_name> and <last_name> child elements to the new <person> element like this, specifying the text data for each new child element:

```
<?php
   $xml = simplexml_load_file("event.xml");

   echo "<h1>Adding elements in an XML document</h1>";
```

```
    echo "Here are the people who attended the event: <br>";

    $event = $xml->event;

    $people = $event->people;

    $person = $people->addChild('person');

    $person->addChild('first_name', 'Myrna');
    $person->addChild('last_name', 'Loy');
              .
              .
              .
?>
```

Finally, you can add a new attendance attribute to the <person> element with the addAttribute method, and then display all the elements:

```php
<?php
    $xml = simplexml_load_file("event.xml");

    echo "<h1>Adding elements in an XML document</h1>";

    echo "Here are the people who attended the event: <br>";

    $event = $xml->event;

    $people = $event->people;

    $person = $people->addChild('person');

    $person->addChild('first_name', 'Myrna');
    $person->addChild('last_name', 'Loy');

    $person->AddAttribute('attendance', 'present');

    echo "<ul>";

    foreach ($people->person as $person){
      echo "<li>", $person->first_name, ' ', $person->last_name, " was ",
        $person['attendance'], "</li>";
    }

    echo "</ul>";
?>
```

You can see the results in Figure 15-9, where the new Myrna Loy <person> element was added.

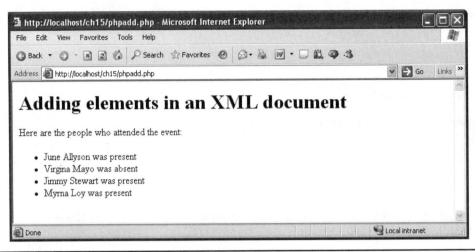

FIGURE 15-9 Adding elements to event.xml

Sending XML to the Browser

What if, after you make your modifications to an XML document, you want to send the modified XML document to a browser? It's going to take some work to decipher the XML document in its entirety from the SimpleXML object and send it, element by element, attribute by attribute, back to the browser.

Fortunately, there's an easier way—you can use the asXML method to echo the entire SimpleXML object as an XML document. Here's an example, phpasxml.php, that reads in event.xml, modifies it, and sends it back to the browser using asXML:

```php
<?php
  $xml = simplexml_load_file("event.xml");

  $event = $xml->event;

  $people = $event->people;

  $person = $people->addChild('person');

  $person->addChild('first_name', 'Myrna');
  $person->addChild('last_name', 'Loy');

  $person->AddAttribute('attendance', 'present');

  header("Content-type: text/xml");
  echo $xml->asXML();

?>
```

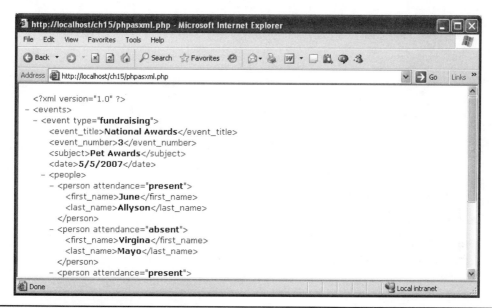

FIGURE 15-10   Sending XML to browsers

You can see the results in Figure 15-10, where this script did indeed send the complete XML document to the browser. Very useful.

Interacting with Other PHP XML Packages

SimpleXML is only one of the XML packages supported by PHP. You can connect SimpleXML to some of these other packages, such as the DOM (Document Object Model) package. Here's an example, phpsimpledom.php, that shows how to import a DOM object into SimpleXML using the simplexml_import_dom function.

This example starts by creating a new DOM XML document object, $dom:

```php
<?php
  $dom = new domDocument;
       .
       .
       .
?>
```

Then it loads an XML text string into the DOM object using the loadXML method:

```php
<?php
  $dom = new domDocument;
```

```
$dom->loadXML(
  '<people><person><first_name>Myrna</first_name></person></people>');
    .
    .
    .
?>
```

You can check if the DOM object was indeed created successfully:

```
<?php
  $dom = new domDocument;

  $dom->loadXML(
    '<people><person><first_name>Myrna</first_name></person></people>');

  if (!$dom) {
     echo 'Error';
     exit;
  }
    .
    .
    .
?>
```

That creates a DOM object, with its own methods and properties. You can convert that into a SimpleXML object using the simplexml_import_dom function, and then dump the object as XML back to the browser:

```
<?php
  $dom = new domDocument;

  $dom->loadXML(
    '<people><person><first_name>Myrna</first_name></person></people>');

  if (!$dom) {
     echo 'Error';
     exit;
  }

  $xml = simplexml_import_dom($dom);

  header("Content-type: text/xml");

  echo $xml->asXML();
?>
```

You can see the results in Figure 15-11, where this script converted a PHP XML DOM object into a SimpleXML one.

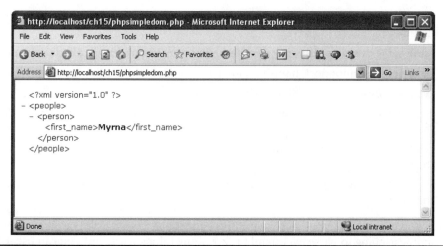

FIGURE 15-11   Converting a PHP DOM object into a SimpleXML one

Parsing with the XML Parser Functions

You can use the PHP XML Parser functions to parse XML; these functions act much like an XML SAX (Simple API for XML) parser, if you're familiar with SAX. Here are the XML Parser functions:

- **xml_error_string**   Return the XML parser error string
- **xml_get_current_byte_index**   Return the current byte index for the XML parser
- **xml_get_current_column_number**   Return the current column number for the XML parser
- **xml_get_current_line_number**   Return the current line number for the XML parser
- **xml_get_error_code**   Return the XML parser error code
- **xml_parse_into_struct**   Parse the XML data into an array
- **xml_parse**   Start parsing an XML document
- **xml_parser_create_ns**   Create an XML parser with namespace support
- **xml_parser_create**   Create an XML parser object
- **xml_parser_free**   Free an XML parser in memory
- **xml_parser_get_option**   Return options from the XML parser
- **xml_parser_set_option**   Set options in the XML parser
- **xml_set_character_data_handler**   Register character data handler
- **xml_set_default_handler**   Register default handler
- **xml_set_element_handler**   Register start and end element handlers

- **xml_set_end_namespace_decl_handler**   Register end namespace declaration handler

- **xml_set_external_entity_ref_handler**   Register external entity reference handler

- **xml_set_notation_decl_handler**   Register notation declaration handler

- **xml_set_object**   Use XML Parser within an object

- **xml_set_processing_instruction_handler**   Register processing instruction (PI) handler

- **xml_set_start_namespace_decl_handler**   Register start namespace declaration handler

- **xml_set_unparsed_entity_decl_handler**   Register unparsed entity declaration handler

Here's an example showing how to put these functions to work, phpxmlparser.php. This example is going to parse event.xml to show how things work, but you can use it to parse any XML document, and when you know how to parse XML documents, you can extract any data you want.

When you use the XML Parser functions, the XML data is parsed and passed to a series of callback functions. For example, when the XML parser sees the beginning of an XML element, it passes that element on to the callback function you've set up to handle the beginnings of elements. When the parser sees text, it passes that on to the text-handling function, and so on.

This example, phpxmlparser.php, starts by storing the name of the file to parse in $file, and you can modify this line to parse any XML document:

```
<?php
  $file = "event.xml";
        .
        .
        .

?>
```

One thing that the XML Parser functions don't handle is the XML declarations at the beginning of each XML document, so we'll print out a standard XML declaration (the PHP documentation for the XML Parser functions say that you can use a default handler—coming up soon—to read XML declarations, but in fact that does not work):

```
<?php
  $file = "event.xml";

  echo "<h1>Parsing XML with XML Parser functions</h1>";
  echo "Here is the parsed file: <br><br>";

  echo "&lt;?xml version='1.0'?&gt; <br>";
        .
        .
        .

?>
```

Next, you create an XML parser object, using the xml_parser_create function:

```php
<?php
  $file = "event.xml";

  echo "<h1>Parsing XML with XML Parser functions</h1>";
  echo "Here is the parsed file: <br><br>";

  echo "&lt;?xml version='1.0'?&gt; <br>";

  $xml_parser_object = xml_parser_create();
            .
            .
            .

?>
```

Next, you have to register your callback functions with the XML parser object. These are the functions that will handle the elements, attributes, text, and so on encountered by the parser as it reads through the XML document.

For example, to set the handler functions that will handle the beginning and end of elements, you use the xml_set_element_handler function. You pass the XML parser object to this function, as well as the callback function you want to handle the start of elements, startElement here, as well as the function to handle the end of elements, endElement here:

```php
<?php
  $file = "event.xml";

  echo "<h1>Parsing XML with XML Parser functions</h1>";
  echo "Here is the parsed file: <br><br>";

  echo "&lt;?xml version='1.0'?&gt; <br>";

  $xml_parser_object = xml_parser_create();

  xml_set_element_handler($xml_parser_object, "startElement", "endElement");
            .
            .
            .

?>
```

To handle the text data inside the elements, you register a callback function with the XML parser using the xml_set_character_data_handler function, and we'll use a function named text here. And to handle any other data that the XML parser encounters that you haven't set up a handler for, you can register a default handler with the xml_set_default_handler function. That default handler for us is going to be a function called defaultHandler:

```php
<?php
  $file = "event.xml";

  echo "<h1>Parsing XML with XML Parser functions</h1>";
  echo "Here is the parsed file: <br><br>";

  echo "&lt;?xml version='1.0'?&gt; <br>";
```

```php
$xml_parser_object = xml_parser_create();

xml_set_element_handler($xml_parser_object, "startElement", "endElement");

xml_set_character_data_handler($xml_parser_object, "text");

xml_set_default_handler($xml_parser_object, "defaultHandler");
        .
        .
        .
?>
```

You're responsible for opening the XML document and feeding it to the parser, so you start the process by opening the XML document and getting a file handle for it, $handle:

```php
<?php
  $file = "event.xml";
        .
        .
        .
  xml_set_default_handler($xml_parser_object, "defaultHandler");

  if (!($handle = fopen($file, "r"))) {
    die("Error.");
  }
        .
        .
        .
?>
```

Now you can read in some XML data, 1024 bytes at a time, with fread:

```php
<?php
  $file = "event.xml";
        .
        .
        .
  xml_set_default_handler($xml_parser_object, "defaultHandler");

  if (!($handle = fopen($file, "r"))) {
    die("Error.");
  }

  while ($xml_data = fread($handle, 1024)) {
        .
        .
        .
  }
  }
        .
        .
        .
?>
```

You pass the XML data to the XML parser's xml_parse function, passing it the XML parser object, the text data to parse, and a TRUE/FALSE argument that indicates whether or not you've passed all the XML data to xml_parse. You can determine if you've passed all the data to xml_parse with feof, so here's how you pass the XML data to the parser:

```php
<?php
  $file = "event.xml";
         .
         .
         .
  xml_set_default_handler($xml_parser_object, "defaultHandler");

  if (!($handle = fopen($file, "r"))) {
    die("Error.");
  }

  while ($xml_data = fread($handle, 1024)) {
    if (!xml_parse($xml_parser_object, $xml_data, feof($handle))) {
         .
         .
         .
    }
  }
         .
         .
         .
?>
```

If xml_parse returns a value of FALSE, there was an error. You can determine what the error was with the xml_error_string function, to which you pass the error code—and you can get the error code by passing the XML parser object to the xml_get_error_code function. You can also get the line number in the XML document at which the error occurred with the xml_get_current_line_number function, and display that as well:

```php
<?php
  $file = "event.xml";
         .
         .
         .
  xml_set_default_handler($xml_parser_object, "defaultHandler");

  if (!($handle = fopen($file, "r"))) {
    die("Error.");
  }

  while ($xml_data = fread($handle, 1024)) {
    if (!xml_parse($xml_parser_object, $xml_data, feof($handle))) {
      die(sprintf("Error %s on line %d",
        xml_error_string(xml_get_error_code($xml_parser_object)),
        xml_get_current_line_number($xml_parser_object)));
    }
  }
         .
         .
         .
?>
```

At this point, the parser will call your callback functions. All that's left—besides writing those callback functions—is to finish with the parser by calling xml_parser_free and closing the XML document with fclose:

```php
<?php
  $file = "event.xml";
        .
        .
        .
  while ($xml_data = fread($handle, 1024)) {
    if (!xml_parse($xml_parser_object, $xml_data, feof($handle))) {
      die(sprintf("Error %s on line %d",
        xml_error_string(xml_get_error_code($xml_parser_object)),
        xml_get_current_line_number($xml_parser_object)));
    }
  }

  xml_parser_free($xml_parser_object);

  fclose($handle);
        .
        .
        .
?>
```

We'll start with the defaultHandler function, which handles any XML data not handled by the other handlers you may have set up. We've registered a default handler function named defaultHandler with the XML parser; the defaultHandler function is passed the parser object and the unhandled XML text, so we'll just echo that text to the browser:

```php
<?php
  $file = "event.xml";
        .
        .
        .
  function defaultHandler($parser, $text)
  {
    echo $text, "<br>";
  }
        .
        .
        .
?>
```

That handles any XML data not handled by our other handlers. You can set up the startElement and endElement handlers next. The startElement handler is called when the parser encounters the opening tag of an XML element. The parser object, name of the element, and a hash containing its attributes is passed to startElement.

We're going to indent the parsed XML, and we'll keep track of the indentation level with a variable named $indent. The first order of business in startElement is to echo the indentation whitespace—two non-breaking spaces for each level of indentation:

```php
<?php
  $file = "event.xml";
  $indent = 0;
       .
       .
       .
  function startElement($parser, $name, $attrs)
  {
    global $indent;
    for ($i = 0; $i < $indent; $i++) {
      echo "    ";
    }
       .
       .
       .
  }
?>
```

The XML parser converts all element names to uppercase, but they're actually lowercase in event.xml, so we'll convert the name of each element back to lowercase with strtolower:

```php
<?php
  $file = "event.xml";
  $indent = 0;
       .
       .
       .
  function startElement($parser, $name, $attrs)
  {
    global $indent;
    for ($i = 0; $i < $indent; $i++) {
      echo "    ";
    }
    $lower = strtolower($name);
       .
       .
       .
  }
?>
```

The attributes of the current XML element, if any, are passed to startElement in a hash we've named $attrs, where the keys are the names of the attributes and the values are the attribute values. You can loop over that hash like this, assembling a text string that holds the attributes and their values like this: "attr1 = value1 attr2 = value2 ...":

```php
<?php
  $file = "event.xml";
  $indent = 0;

        .
        .
        .

  function startElement ($parser, $name, $attrs)
  {
    global $indent;
    for ($i = 0; $i < $indent; $i++) {
        echo "    ";
    }
    $lower = strtolower($name);
    $att_string = "";
    foreach ($attrs as $key => $value) {
      $att_string .= strtolower($key) . " = \"" . $value . "\"";
    }

        .
        .
        .

  }
?>
```

All that's left is to echo the opening tag of the current element—complete with attributes and their values—to the browser, and then increase the indentation level for any nested elements:

```php
<?php
  $file = "event.xml";
  $indent = 0;

        .
        .
        .

  function startElement ($parser, $name, $attrs)
  {
    global $indent;
    for ($i = 0; $i < $indent; $i++) {
        echo "    ";
    }
    $lower = strtolower($name);
    $att_string = "";
    foreach ($attrs as $key => $value) {
      $att_string .= strtolower($key) . " = \"" . $value . "\"";

    }
    echo "&lt;${lower} ${att_string}&gt; <br>";
    $indent++;
  }
?>
```

That handles the start tag of elements—how about the end tag? That's handled by a function we've called endElement, which is called when the parser encounters the end tag of an element. First, we display the indentation string in endElement:

```php
<?php
  function endElement($parser, $name)
  {
    global $indent;
    $indent--;
    for ($i = 0; $i < $indent; $i++) {
        echo "    ";
    }



        .
        .
        .


  }
?>
```

Then we display the element's closing tag, after first converting the element name back to lowercase:

```php
<?php
  function endElement($parser, $name)
  {
    global $indent;
    $indent--;
    for ($i = 0; $i < $indent; $i++) {
        echo "    ";
    }
    $lower = strtolower($name);
    echo "&lt;/${lower}&gt; <br>";
  }
?>
```

Okay, we've handled opening and closing tags for XML elements. The final task in this example is to handle the text inside every element, which is done in the function we've called text. This function is passed the parser object and the text the parser has encountered:

```php
<?php
  function text($parser, $text)
  {


        .
        .
        .


?>
```

The text method gets passed all the non-markup text in the XML document—and that includes the whitespace used for indentation in that document. For example, take a look at event.xml:

```
<?xml version="1.0"?>
<events>
    <event type="fundraising">
        <event_title>National Awards</event_title>
        <event_number>3</event_number>
        <subject>Pet Awards</subject>
        <date>5/5/2007</date>
        <people>
            <person attendance="present">
                <first_name>June</first_name>
                <last_name>Allyson</last_name>
            </person>
                .
                .
                .

</events>
```

Note the whitespace between the <events> tag and the <event> tag—that's reported as text to our text function. As is the text between the <event> and <event_title> tags, and so on. We don't want to display this whitespace in our parsed version of this file—we're handling the indentation ourselves. To avoid responding to text that's purely whitespace, you can use a regular expression. In particular, you can insist that at least one non-whitespace character (which you can check with the regular expression "/S") must appear in the text passed to us before we'll display it like this:

```
<?php
  function text($parser, $text)
  {
    if(preg_match("/\S/", $text)){
        .
        .
        .

    }
  }
?>
```

Now you can echo the indentation string and echo the non-whitespace text the parser found:

```
<?php
  function text($parser, $text)
  {
    global $indent;
    if(preg_match("/\S/", $text)){
```

```
        for ($i = 0; $i < $indent; $i++) {
          echo "    ";
        }
        echo "$text <br>";
      }
    }
?>
```

Okay, that completes the XML parser. You can see it at work in Figure 15-12, where the entire parsed version of event.xml appears. Excellent.

That completes this example, and that also completes our book on PHP. Happy programming!

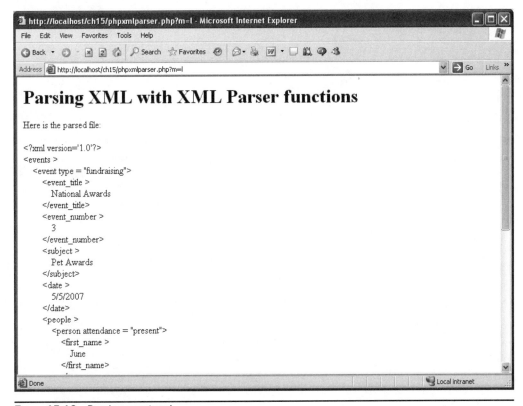

FIGURE 15-12   Parsing event.xml

Index

Symbols

$a & $b operator, 52
$a ^ $b operator, 52
$a | $b operator, 52
$a << $b operator, 52
$a >> $b operator, 52
$items array, 541
%= operator, 47
&= operator, 47
*= operator, 47
.= operator, 47
/= operator, 47
\n control character, 17
^= operator, 47
| = operator, 47
~ $a operator, 52
+= operator, 47
<<= operator, 47
-= operator, 47
>>= operator, 47

A

abort method, 438–439
abs function, 43
abstract classes, 294–297
access
    class member, 264–266
    MySQL database
        closing connection, 376–377
        connecting to database, 372
        connecting to server, 371–372
        displaying table data, 374–376
        overview, 370–371
        reading tables, 372–374
    to properties and methods, 253–257

access modifiers, 253
accessor methods, 252
acos function, 43
acosh function, 43
action attributes, 162
Adabas, 361
addAttribute method, 559
addChild method, 558
addcslashes function, 82
addslashes function, 82
advanced e-mails, 418–421
Ajax (Asynchronous JavaScript and XML),
    433–500
    concurrent requests
        JavaScript inner functions,
            475–479
        multiple XMLHttpRequest
            objects, 467–472
        XMLHttpRequest arrays,
            472–475
    connecting to other domains, 494–496
    downloading
        images, 479–481
        JavaScript, 481–484
    GET method, 450–453
    Google Suggest, 484–494
    handling downloaded data,
        441–445
    head requests, 497–500
    logging in, 495–497
    overview, 433–434
    PHP and, 448–449
    POST method, 453–456
    starting downloads, 445–447
    warning dialogs, 489

Ajax (Asynchronous JavaScript and XML) (*cont.*)
    writing, 435–436
    XML, 456–466
    XMLHttpRequest objects, 436–441, 446–448
alignment specifiers, 89
alternate syntax, 80
AND clause, 364
"and" logical operators, 62
API (application programming interface), Google Ajax, 467
append operations, 352–354
Apple Safari, 437, 439
application programming interface (API), Google Ajax, 467
arcs, 514–516
arguments, 132–135
array function, 105
array internal data type, 38
array notation, 550–552
array pointers, 116–117
array_change_key_case function, 104
array_chunk function, 104
array_combine function, 104
array_count_values function, 104
array_diff function, 104
array_diff_assoc function, 104
array_diff_uassoc function, 104
array_fil function, 104
array_filter function, 104
array_flip function, 104, 119
array_intersect function, 104
array_intersect_assoc function, 104
array_key_exists function, 105
array_keys function, 105
array_map function, 105
array_merge function, 105
array_merge_recursive function, 105
array_multisort function, 105
array_pad function, 105
array_pop function, 105
array_push function, 105
array_rand function, 105
array_reduce function, 105
array_reverse function, 105
array_search function, 105
array_shift function, 105

array_slice function, 105, 117
array_splice function, 105
array_sum function, 105, 119
array_udiff function, 105
array_udiff_assoc function, 105
array_udiff_uassoc function, 105
array_unique function, 105, 120
array_unshift function, 105
array_values function, 105
array_walk function, 105
arrays, 92–121
    associative, 112
    building, 92–95
    comparing, 112
    custom, 215–218
    deleting elements in, 97–99
    explode function, 107
    extracting data from, 107–108
    flipping, 120
    functions, 104–106, 119–121
    handling with loops, 99–104
    implode function, 106–107
    modifying data in, 95–97
    multidimensional, 112–115
    navigating, 116–117
    operators, 110–112
    overview, 81
    passing to functions, 127–130
    reading files into, 330–332
    returning to functions, 137–139
    sorting, 109–110
    splitting and merging, 117–119
    superglobal, 203
    XMLHttpRequest, 472–475
arsort function, 105
asin function, 43
asinh function, 43
asort function, 105, 110
assignment operators, 28, 46–48
associative arrays, 112
Asynchronous JavaScript and XML. *See* Ajax
atan function, 43
atan2 function, 43
atanh function, 43
attachments, e-mail, 421–425
attributes, and SimpleXML functions
    adding, 557–560
    extracting, 550–552
    modifying, 555–557

'AUTH_TYPE' server variable, 204
__autoload function, 277
autoloading classes, 277–279

━━━ **B** ━━━

base class methods, 267–271
base_convert function, 43
bcc headers, 418–421
bin2hex function, 82
binary files, 335–337, 348–352
bindec function, 43
bitwise operators, 51–52
boolean data type, 37
boxes
    box images, 506
    check, 170–172
    JavaScript alert, 239
    list, 175–179
break statements, 68, 77–78
browsers, 203–243
    data validation, 221–223, 237–240
    determining user, 206–209
    form data, 212–220
        dumping, 212–215
        handling on one page, 218–220
        handling with custom arrays,
            215–218
    HTML tags in user input, 241–243
    HTTP headers, 205–206, 209–212
    overview, 203
    persisting user data, 234–237
    required data, 223–234
        entered by user, 223–226
        numbers, 227–230
        text, 230–234
    server variables, 203–205
buttons, 191–201
    overview, 191–192
    persistence of data, 192–195
    radio, 172–175
    reset, 163
    Submit, as HTML buttons, 195–201

━━━ **C** ━━━

callback functions, 441–442, 479, 565
casts, 39, 87
cc headers, 418–421
ceil function, 43

CGI (Common Gateway Interface), 20
channel property, 438
characters, 320, 326
check boxes, 170–172
check_data function, 222, 235
chop function, 82
chr function, 82
chunk_split function, 82
__CLASS__ constant, 36
classes. *See also* static methods
    abstract, 294–297
    autoloading, 277–279
    constants, 306–308
    creating, 246–249
    inheritance
        base class methods, 267–271
        constructors and, 266–267
        overview, 262–264
        protected access, 264–266
    Reflectionfunction, 315
clauses, 363–364
CLI (command-line interpreter), 20
client-side data validation, 237–240
__clone method, 312
cloned objects, 312–315
closing files, 323–324
command line, 17, 20–24
command-line interpreter (CLI), 20
comments, 24–25
Common Gateway Interface (CGI), 20
compact function, 105
comparison operators, 59–60, 304–305
comparisons, array, 112
concatenation, 18
concurrent Ajax requests, 467–479
    JavaScript inner functions, 475–479
    multiple XMLHttpRequest objects,
        467–472
    XMLHttpRequest arrays, 472–475
conditional functions, 150–153
connectGoogleSuggest function, 486
connections
    database, 371–372, 376–377
    Google Suggest, 484–494
constants
    class, 306–308
    PHP, 36–37
constructors, 257–260, 266–267
context node, 553

continue statement, 78–79
control characters, 17
controls
　　hidden, 182–184
　　password, 179–182
conversion, string, 87–88, 106–107
convert_cyr_string function, 82
cookies, 395–402
　　deleting, 400–402
　　expiration time, 399–400
　　overview, 395
　　reading, 397–398
　　setting, 395–397
copy function, 343–344
copying, image, 535–536
cos function, 43
cosh function, 43
count function, 99, 105
count_chars function, 82
counters, loop, 71
crc32 function, 82
CREATE DATABASE command, 366
crypt function, 82
current function, 105
custom arrays, 215–218

━━ **D** ━━

data formats, 367
data types, 37–39
data validation, 221–223, 237–240
databases, 361–394
　　MySQL
　　　　accessing, 370–377
　　　　creating, 389–392
　　　　deleting records, 383–385
　　　　inserting data items, 380–382
　　　　overview, 364–367
　　　　sorting data, 393–394
　　　　storing data in, 368–370
　　　　tables, 367–368, 385–388
　　　　updating, 377–380
　　overview, 361–362
　　SQL, 362–364
DataHandler class, 301
DATETIME table data format, 367
dBase, 361
decbin function, 43

dechex function, 43
DECIMAL(totaldigits, decimalplaces) table
　　data format, 367
decoct function, 43
decrementing values, 48–50
default arguments, 132–133
DEFAULT_INCLUDE_PATH constant, 36
defaultHandler function, 568
define function, 35
deg2rad function, 43
deleting
　　cookies, 400–402
　　elements in arrays, 97–99
　　files, 345–346
　　with FTP, 411–413
　　MySQL records, 383–385
destructors, 260–261
development environment, 6–7
die function, 158
directories, 414–415
display function, 482
displays
　　image, 506–507
　　table data, 374–376
document elements, 456
'DOCUMENT_ROOT' server variable, 204
do...while loops, 74–76
downloading
　　with Ajax
　　　　callback functions, 441–445
　　　　images, 479–481
　　　　JavaScript, 481–484
　　with FTP, 406–408
drawing. *See* graphics
dumping form data, 212–215

━━ **E** ━━

each function, 103, 106
echo function, 82
echo statements, 14, 17–19
elements
　　adding with SimpleXML functions,
　　　　557–560
　　deleting in arrays, 97–99
　　document, 456
　　modifying with SimpleXML functions,
　　　　555–557
　　targetDiv, 444–445

ellipses, 513–514
else statement, 63–64
elseif statement, 65–66
e-mail, 416–425
 adding attachments, 421–425
 advanced, 418–421
 overview, 416–418
Empress, 361
end function, 106
endElement function, 571
equality operator, 59
errors, returning from functions, 158–160
executable script, 5
execution operator, 52–53
exp function, 43
expiration time, cookie, 399–400
explode function, 82, 107
expm1 function, 43
eXtended Markup Language (XML). *See* XML
extract function, 106–108
extraction, attribute, 550–552

━━ **F** ━━

fclose function, 323–324
feof function, 189, 322
fgetc function, 325–327
fgets function, 190, 322–323
fields, defined, 362
figures, filling in, 518–520
file function, 330–332
file handles, 189
file pointers, 343
File Transfer Protocol. *See* FTP
__FILE__ constant, 36
file_exists function, 332–334
file_get_contents function, 328–329
file_put_contents function, 355–356
FilePro, 361
files, 319–359
 appending to, 352–354
 binary, 348–352
 closing, 323–324
 copying, 343–344
 deleting, 345–346, 411–413
 downloading, 406–408
 file_exists function, 332–334
 images, 528–531
 include, 157–158

initialization, 339–341
locking, 357–359
looping over contents, 322
opening, 319–322
overview, 319
parsing, 338–341
reading
 into arrays, 330–332
 binary files, 335–337, 348–352
 character by character, 325–327
 entire contents of, 328–329
 text from, 322–323
setting pointer location, 343
size of, 334–335
stat function, 341–342
uploading, 187–191, 408–411
writing
 binary files, 348–352
 file_put_contents, 355–356
 strings to, 346–348
filesize function, 334–335
final keyword, 308–312
Firefox, 437, 439
flipping arrays, 120
float data type, 37
flock function, 357–359
floor function, 43
flow control, 63–80
 alternate syntax, 80
 do...while loops, 74–76
 else statement, 63–64
 elseif statement, 65–66
 for loops, 69–72
 foreach loop, 76–77
 if statement, 55–58
 overview, 41
 skipping iterations, 78–79
 switch statement, 67–69
 terminating loops early, 77–78
 while loops, 72–74
fmod function, 43
fopen function, 189, 319–322
for loops, 69–72, 99–100
foreach loops, 76–77, 101–103, 548–549
form data, 212–220
 custom arrays, 215–218
 dumping, 212–215
 handling on one page, 218–220

formatting strings, 88–91
fprintf function, 82
fread function, 335–337, 348–352
FrontBase, 361
fscanf function, 338–339
fseek function, 343
FTP (File Transfer Protocol), 402–415
    creating and removing directories,
        414–415
    deleting files, 411–413
    downloading files, 406–408
    overview, 402–405
    script permissions, 5
    uploading
        files, 408–411
        PHP pages with, 7
ftp_alloc function, 402
ftp_cdup function, 402
ftp_chdir function, 402
ftp_chmod function, 402
ftp_close function, 402
ftp_connect function, 402
ftp_delete function, 402
ftp_exec function, 402
ftp_fget function, 402
ftp_fput function, 402
ftp_get function, 402
ftp_get_option function, 402
ftp_login function, 402
ftp_mdtm function, 402
ftp_mkdir function, 402
ftp_nb_continue function, 402
ftp_nb_fget function, 403
ftp_nb_fput function, 403
ftp_nb_get function, 403
ftp_nb_put function, 403
ftp_nlist function, 403
ftp_put function, 403
ftp_pwd function, 403
ftp_quit function, 403
ftp_raw function, 403
ftp_rawlist function, 403
ftp_rename function, 403
ftp_rmdir function, 403
ftp_set_option function, 403
ftp_site function, 403
ftp_size function, 403
ftp_ssl_connect function, 403
ftp_systype function, 403

func_get_arg function, 134
func_get_args function, 134
func_num_args function, 134
__FUNCTION__ constant, 36
functions, 123–160. *See also individual functions
    by name*
    accessing global data, 145–147
    array, 104–106, 119–121
    conditional, 150–153
    copy, 343–344
    creating, 123–125
    defined, 8
    FTP, 402–403
    graphic, 303–306
    include files, 157–158
    inner, 475–479
    math, 43–44
    MySQL, 370–371
    nesting, 156–157
    overview, 123
    passing
        arguments to, 132–135
        arrays to, 127–130
        data to, 125–127
        by reference, 130–131
    returning
        arrays from, 137–139
        data from, 135–137
        errors from, 158–160
        lists from, 139–141
        references from, 141–143
    SimpleXML
        adding new attributes
            with, 557–560
        adding new elements
            with, 557–560
        extracting attributes
            with, 550–552
        modifying attributes
            with, 555–557
        modifying elements
            with, 555–557
        overview, 546–550
    static variables, 147–150
    string, 81–86
    variable, 153–155
    variable scope, 143–144
    XML Parser, 563–573
fwrite function, 346–348, 352–354

G

'GATEWAY_INTERFACE' server variable, 204
gd_info function, 501
GET method, 165–166, 451–454
get_html_translation_table function, 82
getAllResponseHeaders method, 438–439, 498
getData function, 436, 498
getElementsByTagName method, 460
getimagesize function, 501
getrandmax function, 43
getResponseHeader method, 438–439
global data, accessing, 145–147
Google Ajax application programming
    interface (API), 467
Google Suggest, 481, 484–494
graphics, 501–536
        arcs, 514–516
        copying images, 535–536
        creating images, 504–506
        creating text, 522–525
        displaying in HTML pages, 506–507
        ellipses, 513–514
        filling in figures, 518–520
        functions, 501–504
        lines, 507–511
        overview, 501
        pixels, 520–521
        polygons, 516–518
        rectangles, 511–513
        tiled images, 531–534
        vertical text, 525–528
        working with image files, 528–531
greater-than operator, 55
Gutmans, Andi, 2

H

HEAD method, 498
head requests, 497–500
headers, redirection, 211
hebrev function, 82
hebrevc function, 82
here documents, 19–20
hexdec function, 43
hidden controls, 182–184
hit counters, 429–431
HTML
        buttons, 195–201
        displaying images in, 506–507
    mixing PHP and, 10–13
    printing, 16–17
    tags, 241–243
html_entity_decode function, 82
htmlentities function, 82, 242
htmlspecialchars function, 82
HTTP headers, 205–206, 209–212
HTTP server variables, 205
'HTTP_ACCEPT' variable, 205
'HTTP_ACCEPT_CHARSET' variable, 205
'HTTP_ACCEPT_ENCODING' variable, 205
'HTTP_ACCEPT_LANGUAGE' variable, 205
'HTTP_CONNECTION' variable, 205
'HTTP_HOST' variable, 205
'HTTP_REFERER' variable, 205
'HTTP_USER_AGENT' variable, 205
Hyperwave Direct, 361
hypot function, 43

I

IBM DB2, 361
iDatabase interface, 297
identity operator, 304
IDEs (integrated development
    environments), 6–7
if statement, 55–58
image maps, 184–186
image_type_to_extension function, 501
image_type_to_mime_type function, 501
image2wbmp function, 501
imagealphablending function, 501
imageantialias function, 501
imagearc function, 501, 514–516
imagechar function, 501
imagecharup function, 501
imagecolorallocate function, 501, 505
imagecolorallocatealpha function, 501
imagecolorat function, 501
imagecolorclosest function, 501
imagecolorclosestalpha function, 501
imagecolorclosesthwb function, 502
imagecolordeallocate function, 502
imagecolorexact function, 502
imagecolorexactalpha function, 502
imagecolormatch function, 502
imagecolorresolve function, 502
imagecolorresolvealpha function, 502
imagecolorset function, 502

imagecolorsforindex function, 502
imagecolorstotal function, 502
imagecolortransparent function, 502
imageconvolution function, 502
imagecopy function, 502, 535
imagecopymergegray function, 502
imagecopyresampled function, 502
imagecopyresized function, 502
imagecreate function, 502, 504
imagecreatefromgd function, 502
imagecreatefromgd2 function, 502
imagecreatefromgd2part function, 502
imagecreatefromgif function, 502, 528
imagecreatefromjpeg function, 502, 528
imagecreatefrompng function, 502, 528
imagecreatefromstring function, 502
imagecreatefromwbmp function, 502, 528
imagecreatefromxbm function, 502, 528
imagecreatefromxpm function, 502, 528
imagecreatetruecolor function, 502, 531
image-creating functions, 505
imagedashedline function, 502
imagedestroy function, 502, 505
imageellipse function, 502, 513–514
imagefill function, 503
imagefilledarc function, 503, 518
imagefilledellipse function, 503, 518
imagefilledpolygon function, 503, 518
imagefilledrectangle function, 503, 518
imagefilltoborder function, 503
imagefilter function, 503
imagefontheight function, 503
imagefontwidth function, 503, 522
imageftbbox function, 503
imagefttext function, 503
imagegammacorrect function, 503
imagegd function, 503
imagegd2 function, 503
imagegif function, 503, 505
imageinterlace function, 503
imageistruecolor function, 503
imagejpeg function, 503, 505
imagelayereffect function, 503
imageline function, 503, 507–509
imageloadfont function, 503, 522
imagepalettecopy function, 503
imagepng function, 503, 505
imagepolygon function, 503, 516–518
imagepsbbox function, 503
imagepsencodefont function, 503

imagepsextendfont function, 503
imagepsfreefont function, 503
imagepsloadfont function, 503
imagepsslantfont function, 503
imagepstext function, 503
imagerectangle function, 503, 511–512, 529
imagerotate function, 503
images
    box, 506
    copying, 535–536
    displaying in HTML pages, 506–507
    downloading with Ajax, 479–481
    drawing, 504–506
    image files, 528–531
    tiling, 531–534
imagesavealpha function, 504
imagesetbrush function, 504
imagesetpixel function, 504
imagesetpixel method, 520
imagesetstyle function, 504
imagesetthickness function, 504, 510–511
imagesettile function, 504, 531
imagestring function, 504, 522
imagestringup function, 504, 525–526
imagesx function, 504
imagesy function, 504
imagetruecolortopalette function, 504
imagettfbbox function, 504
imagettftext function, 504
imagetypes function, 504
imagewbmp function, 504, 505
imagexbm function, 504
implode function, 82, 106–107
IN clause, 363
in_array function, 106
include files, 157–158
incrementing values, 48–50
Informix, 361
Ingres, 361
inheritance
    base class methods, 267–271
    constructors and, 266–267
    overview, 262–264
    protected access, 264–266
    static members and, 291–293
initialization (.ini) files, 339–341
inner functions, JavaScript, 475–479
input, database, 368–370
insertion, database items, 380–382
installation, PHP local, 5–6

INT table data format, 367
integer data type, 38
integrated development environments
    (IDEs), 6–7
InterBase, 361
interfaces
    CGI, 20
    Google Ajax API, 467
    iDatabase, 297
    OOP, 297–300
    PHP Iterator, 301
internal data types, 37–39
Internet Explorer, 437–438
Internet service providers (ISPs), 4–6
interpolation, string, 31–33
iptcembed function, 504
iptcparse function, 504
is_finite function, 43
is_infinite function, 43
is_nan function, 43
ISPs (Internet service providers), 4–6
iterating objects, 301–303
iterations, loop, 78–79
Iterator interface methods, 301

J

JavaScript. *See also* Ajax
    alert box, 239
    callback function, 479
    client-side validation, 237
    connectGoogleSuggest function, 486
    display function, 482
    downloading with Ajax, 481–484
    inner functions, 475–479
    push method, 472
    static Web pages, 3
    variables, 27
join function, 82
jpeg2wbmp function, 504

K

key function, 106
keywords
    clone, 312
    final, 308–312
    list of, 37
    static, 149
krsort function, 106, 110

L

lcg_value function, 43
Lerdorf, Rasmus, 1
less-than-or-equal-to operator, 59
levenshtein function, 82
__LINE__ constant, 36
line-ending characters, 320
lines, 507–511
list boxes, 175–179
list function, 103, 106, 108
lists, returning to functions, 139–141
loadXML method, 561–562
local installation, 5–6
localeconv function, 82
locking files, 357–359
log function, 44
log10 function, 44
log1p function, 44
logging in with Ajax, 495–497
logical operators, 61–62
logos, 12–13
loops, 69–80
    alternate syntax, 80
    do...while, 74–76
    for, 69–72
    foreach, 76–77, 548–549
    handling arrays with, 99–104
    multidimensional arrays in, 114–115
    overview, 41
    skipping iterations, 78–79
    terminating early, 77–78
    while, 72–74
ltrim function, 82

M

mail function, 416
math functions, 43–44
math operators, 41–46
max function, 44
md5 function, 82
md5_file function, 82
merging arrays, 117–119
metaphone function, 82
__METHOD__ constant, 36
methods
    abort, 438–439
    access, 253–257
    accessor, 252

methods (*cont.*)
   addAttribute, 559
   addChild, 558
   base class, 267–271
   class, 283
   GET, 165–166, 449–452
   getAllResponseHeaders, 438–439, 498
   getElementsByTagName, 459
   getResponseHeader, 438–439
   HEAD, 498
   imagesetpixel, 520
   Iterator interface, 301
   loadXML, 561–562
   open, 438
   openRequest, 439
   overloading, 273–277
   overrideMimeType, 439
   overriding, 271–273
   POST, 166, 452–456
   public function current( ), 301
   public function key( ), 301
   public function next( ), 301
   public function rewind( ), 301
   public function valid( ), 301
   push, 472
   send, 438
   static, 281–291
      creating, 283–285
      overview, 281–283
      passing data to, 285–286
      using properties in, 286–291
Microsoft WordPad, 6
MIME (Multipurpose Internet Mail
  Extension type), 421
min function, 44
Mini SQL (mSQL), 1, 361
modifications, with SimpleXML functions,
  555–557
modified data, arrays, 95–97
modifiers, access, 253
money_format function, 82
Mozilla, 439
mSQL (Mini SQL), 1, 361
MS-SQL, 361
mt_getrandmax function, 44
mt_rand function, 44
mt_srand function, 44
multidimensional arrays, 112–115
multiline comments, 24

multipart forms, 187, 422
multiple inheritance, 297
multiple select control, 176
multiple XMLHttpRequest objects, 467–472
Multipurpose Internet Mail Extension type
  (MIME), 421
MySQL databases
  accessing
      closing connection, 376–377
      connecting to database, 372
      connecting to server, 371–372
      displaying table data, 374–376
      overview, 370–371
      reading tables, 372–374
   creating, 389–392
   deleting records, 383–385
   inputting data, 368–370
   inserting new data items, 380–382
   overview, 364–367
   sorting data, 393–394
   tables, 367–368, 385–388
   updating, 377–380
mysql_affected_rows function, 370
mysql_change_user function, 370
mysql_client_encoding function, 370
mysql_close function, 370, 376
mysql_connect function, 370, 371
mysql_create_db function, 370
mysql_data_seek function, 370
mysql_db_name function, 370
mysql_db_query function, 370
mysql_drop_db function, 370
mysql_error function, 370
mysql_fetch_array function, 370, 375
mysql_fetch_assoc function, 370
mysql_fetch_row function, 371
mysql_field_len function, 371
mysql_field_name function, 371
mysql_field_seek function, 371
mysql_field_table function, 371
mysql_field_type function, 371
mysql_get_server_info function, 371
mysql_info function, 371
mysql_list_dbs function, 371
mysql_list_fields function, 371
mysql_list_tables function, 371
mysql_num_fields function, 371
mysql_num_rows function, 371
mysql_pconnect function, 371

mysql_query function, 363, 371, 372
mysql_result function, 371
mysql_select_db function, 371, 372
mysql_tablename function, 371

N

natcasesort function, 106
natsort function, 106, 110
navigating arrays, 116–117
Navigator, 437, 439
nested comments, 24
nested functions, 156–157
Netscape Navigator, 437, 439
newline characters, 326
next function, 106
nl_langinfo function, 82
nl2br function, 82
node types, XPath, 552
NOT clause, 364
NULL data type, 37
num_points parameter, 517
number_format function, 82, 91
numbers, required, 227–230

O

object data type, 37
object-oriented programming (OOP), 245–279,
   281–317
      classes
         abstract, 294–297
         autoloading, 277–279
         creating constants, 306–308
         creation of, 246–249
      cloning objects, 312–315
      comparing objects, 304–305
      constructors, 257–260, 266–267
      destructors, 260–261
      final keyword, 308–312
      inheritance
         base class methods, 267–271
         overview, 262–264
         protected access, 264–266
         static members and, 291–293
      interfaces, 297–300
      iteration, 301–303
      method access, 253–257
      objects, 250–253
      overloading methods, 273–277

overriding methods, 271–273
overview, 245–246, 281
property access, 253–257
reflection, 315–317
static methods, 281–291
   creating, 283–285
   overview, 281–283
   passing data to, 285–286
   using properties in, 286–291
objects. *See also* object-oriented programming
   (OOP)
      cloning, 312–315
      comparing, 304–305
      constructors, 257–260
      creating, 250–253
      destructors, 260–261
      initializing with constructors, 257–260
      iterating, 301–303
      XMLHttpRequest
         concurrent Ajax requests with
            multiple, 467–472
         creating, 436–440, 446–448
         opening, 440–441
octdec function, 44
ODBC, 361
onreadystatechange property, 438–439
OOP. *See* object-oriented programming
open method, 438
opening
   files, 319–322
   XMLHttpRequest objects, 440–441
openRequest method, 439
operators, 41–80. *See also* flow control
   array, 110–112
   assignment, 28, 46–48
   bitwise, 51–52
   comparison, 59–60, 304
   execution, 52–53
   identity, 304
   incrementing and decrementing
      values, 48–50
   logical, 61–62
   math, 41–46
   overview, 41
   precedence of, 53–55
   string, 50–51
   ternary, 66–67
OR clause, 364
"or" logical operators, 62

Oracle, 361
ord function, 82
overloading methods, 273–277
overrideMimeType method, 439
overriding methods, 271–273
Ovrimos, 361

■■■■ **P** ■■■■

pack function, 348–349
padding specifiers, 89
pages, PHP, 8–10
parent:: syntax, 270
parse_ini_file function, 339–341
parse_str function, 83
Parser functions, XML, 563–573
parsing files, 338–341
password controls, 179–182
'PATH_TRANSLATED' server variable, 204
persisting user data, 234–237
Personal Home Page (PHP), 1–39
    command-line, 20–24
    comments, 24–25
    constants, 36–37
    creating pages, 8–9
    development environment, 6–7
    echo statement, 17–19
    here documents, 19–20
    internal data types, 37–39
    ISP support, 4–6
    local installation, 5–6
    mixing HTML and, 10–13
    overview, 1–3
    printing
        HTML, 16–17
        text, 14–15
    running pages, 9–10
    variables, 26–35
        overview, 26–27
        storing data in, 27–30
        string interpolation, 31–33
        variable, 33–35
PHP. *See* Personal Home Page
'PHP_AUTH_PW' server variable, 204
'PHP_AUTH_USER' server variable, 204
PHP_OS constant, 36
'PHP_SELF' server variable, 204
PHP_VERSION constant, 36
phpinfo( ) function, 8
pi function, 44

pixels, 520–521
png2wbmp function, 504
points parameter, 517
polygons, 516–518
port parameters, 403
pos argument, 406, 409
pos function, 106
POST method, 166, 452–455
PostgreSQL, 361
pow function, 44
precedence, operator, 53–55
precision specifiers, 89
prev function, 106
print function, 83
print statements, 19
print_r function, 100–101
printf function, 83, 89
printing, 14–17
private access modifier, 253–257
properties, 245, 253–257, 286–291
protected access modifier, 253
public access modifier, 253–254
public function current( ) method, 301
public function key( ) method, 301
public function next( ) method, 301
public function rewind( ) method, 301
public function valid( ) method, 301
push method, 472

■■■■ **Q** ■■■■

'QUERY_STRING' server variable, 204
quoted_printable_decode function, 83
quotemeta function, 83

■■■■ **R** ■■■■

rad2deg function, 44
radio buttons, 172–175
rand function, 44
range function, 106
reading
    binary reads, 335–337
    cookies, 397–398
    files
        into arrays, 330–332
        binary, 348–352
        character by character, 325–327
        file_get_contents function, 328–329
        text from, 322–323
    tables, 372–374

readyState property, 438–439, 442
Really Simple Syndication (RSS), 540–544
records, 362, 383–385
rectangles, 511–513
redirecting browsers, 209–212
references, 130–131, 141–143
reflection, 315–317
Reflectionfunction class, 315
regular expressions, 231
'REMOTE_ADDR' server variable, 204
'REMOTE_HOST' server variable, 204
'REMOTE_PORT' server variable, 204
rename function, 344
'REQUEST_METHOD' server variable, 204
'REQUEST_URI' server variable, 204
requests, concurrent Ajax, 467–479
    JavaScript inner functions, 475–479
    multiple XMLHttpRequest objects,
       467–472
    XMLHttpRequest arrays, 472–475
required data, 223–234
    entered by user, 223–226
    numbers, 227–230
    text, 230–234
reset button, 163
reset function, 106
resource data type, 37
responseBody property, 438
responseStream property, 438
responseText property, 438–439
responseXML property, 438–439, 459
round function, 44
rsort function, 106
RSS (Really Simple Syndication), 540–544
rtrim function, 83

S

Safari, 437, 439
scoper function, 143
script
    executable, 5
    redirection, 211
'SCRIPT_FILENAME' server variable, 204
'SCRIPT_NAME' server variable, 204
script-level data, 145
SEEK_CUR constant, 343
SEEK_END constant, 343
SEEK_SET constant, 343
send method, 438

sending, e-mail, 416–421
sendRPCDone function, 491
server variables, 203–205
'SERVER_ADMIN' server variable, 204
'SERVER_NAME' server variable, 204
'SERVER_PORT' server variable, 204
'SERVER_PROTOCOL' server variable, 204
'SERVER_SIGNATURE' server variable, 204
'SERVER_SOFTWARE' server variable, 204
servers
    GET method, 449–452
    POST method, 452–455
sessions, 425–431
    overview, 395
    storing data in, 425–429
    writing hit counters using, 429–431
setcookie function, 395–396
setlocale function, 83
setproducts function, 458–459, 461
setRequestHeader method, 438
sha1 function, 83
sha1_file function, 83
shift operators, 52
SHOW DATABASES; command, 366
show_errors function, 225
show_welcome function, 235
shuffle function, 106
similar_text function, 83
SimpleXML functions
    extracting attributes, 550–552
    modifying attributes, 555–557
    modifying elements, 555–557
    new attributes, 557–560
    new elements, 557–560
    overview, 544–550
simplexml_import_dom function, 544
simplexml_load_file function, 544
simplexml_load_string function, 544
SimpleXMLElement->__construct( )
    function, 544
SimpleXMLElement->addAttribute( )
    function, 544
SimpleXMLElement->addChild( )
    function, 544
SimpleXMLElement->asXML( ) function, 544
SimpleXMLElement->attributes( ) function, 544
SimpleXMLElement->children( ) function, 544
SimpleXMLElement->getDocNamespaces( )
    function, 544

SimpleXMLElement->getName( ) function, 545
SimpleXMLElement->getNamespaces( )
    function, 545
SimpleXMLElement->registerXPathNamespace( )
    function, 545
SimpleXMLElement->xpath( ) function, 545
sin function, 44
single-line comments, 24–25
sinh function, 44
sizeof function, 106
skipped loop iterations, 78–79
Solid, 361
sort function, 106, 108
sorting
        arrays, 109–110
        data, 393–394
soundex function, 83
specifiers, 89
splitting arrays, 117–119
sprintf function, 83, 89
SQL (Structured Query Language), 362–364
SQL CREATE statement, 385
SQL INSERT statement, 381
sqrt function, 44
srand function, 44
sscanf function, 83
startElement handler function, 568
stat function, 341–342
statements
        alternate syntax, 80
        break, 68, 77
        continue, 78
        echo, 14, 17–19
        else, 63–64
        elseif, 65–66
        if, 55–58
        SQL CREATE, 385
        SQL INSERT, 381
        switch, 67–69
static keywords, 149
static members, 291–293
static methods
        creating, 283–285
        overview, 281–283
        passing data to, 285–286
        using properties in, 286–291
static text, 26
static variables, 147–150

status property, 438–439, 442
statusText property, 438–439
storing data, 27–30, 425–429
str_ireplace function, 83
str_pad function, 83
str_repeat function, 83
str_replace function, 83
str_rot13 function, 83
str_shuffle function, 83
str_split function, 83
str_word_count function, 83
strcasecmp function, 83
strchr function, 83
strcmp function, 83
strcoll function, 83
strcspn function, 83
string data type, 37
string operators, 50–51
strings, 81–91
        converting to and from, 87–88
        explode function, 107
        formatting, 88–91
        functions, 81–86
        implode function, 106–107
        interpolation, 31–33
        overview, 81
        writing to files, 346–348
strip_tags function, 83, 243
stripcslashes function, 83
stripos function, 83
stripslashes function, 83
stristr function, 83
strlen function, 83
strnatcasecmp function, 84
strnatcmp function, 84
strncasecmp function, 84
strncmp function, 84
strpos function, 84
strrchr function, 84
strrev function, 84
strripos function, 84
strrpos function, 84
strspn function, 84
strstr function, 84
strtok function, 84
strtolower function, 84
strtoupper function, 84
strtr function, 84

Structured Query Language (SQL), 362–364
Submit buttons, 195–201
substr function, 84
substr_compare function, 84
substr_count function, 84
substr_replace function, 84
Suggest, 481, 484–494
superglobal array, 203
Suraski, Zeev, 2
switch statement, 67–69
Sybase, 361
syntax, alternate, 80

T
't' flag, 320
tables
    creating, 367–368, 385–388
    displaying data, 374–376
    reading, 372–374
tan function, 44
tanh function, 44
targetDiv element, 444–445
termination, loop, 77–78
ternary operator, 66–67
text
    drawing, 522–525
    printing, 14–15
    required, 230–234
    vertical, 525–528
text areas, 167–170
text fields, 164–167
text strings. *See* strings
text-mode translation flag ('t'), 320
thickness, line, 510–511
tiled images, 531–534
timeout parameters, 403
timestamp, Unix, 399
trim function, 84
troubleshooting Web pages, 9–10
type specifiers, 89

U
uasort function, 106
ucfirst function, 84
ucwords function, 84
uksort function, 106
uncreation, variable, 30
Unicode, 4
Unix, 361, 399

unlink function, 345–346
unpack function, 349
updating, 377–380
uploading files, 187–191, 408–411
URL encoding, 450
usort function, 106
-v option, 4

V
VARCHAR(*length*) table data format, 367
vardump function, 58
variable numbers, argument, 133–135
variables, 26–35
    functions, 153–155
    overview, 26–27
    scope of, 143–144
    server, 203–205
    static, 147–150
    storing data in, 27–30
    string interpolation, 31–33
    variable, 33–35
Velocis, 361
vertical text, 525–528
vprintf function, 84
vsprintf function, 84

W
Web pages, 164–201
    check boxes, 170–172
    creating, 8–9
    file uploads, 187–191
    handling form data on, 218–220
    hidden controls, 182–184
    image maps, 184–186
    list boxes, 175–179
    overview, 164
    password controls, 179–182
    persistence of button data, 192–195
    radio buttons, 173–175
    running, 9–10
    setting up for PHP, 161–164
    Submit buttons as HTML buttons, 195–201
    text areas, 167–170
    text fields, 164–167
    troubleshooting, 9–10
Web site, PHP, 3
WHERE clause, 363
while loops, 72–74, 103–104

width specifiers, 89
WordPad, 6
wordwrap function, 84
writing
    Ajax, 435–436
    to files, 346–348
    files
        binary, 348–352
        file_put_contents, 355–356
        strings to, 346–348
    hit counters using sessions, 429–431

X

XML, 537–573
    creating, 537–539
    declarations, 564
    handling, 456–466
    interacting with other packages, 561–563
    overview, 537
    Parser functions, 563–573
    Really Simple Syndication, 540–544
    sending to browser, 560–561
    SimpleXML functions
        adding new elements and
            attributes, 557–560
        extracting attributes, 550–552
        modifying elements and attributes,
            555–557
        overview, 544–550
    XPath, 552–555
XML (eXtended Markup Language). *See* XML
xml_error_string function, 563
xml_get_current_byte_index function, 563
xml_get_current_column_number function, 563
xml_get_current_line_number function, 563, 567

xml_get_error_code function, 563
xml_parse function, 563, 567
xml_parse_into_struct function, 563
xml_parser_create function, 563
xml_parser_create_ns function, 563
xml_parser_free function, 563
xml_parser_get_option function, 563
xml_parser_set_option function, 563
xml_set_character_data_handler
    function, 563, 565
xml_set_default_handler function, 563
xml_set_element_handler function, 563, 565
xml_set_end_namespace_decl_handler
    function, 564
xml_set_external_entity_ref_handler
    function, 564
xml_set_notation_decl_handler function, 564
xml_set_object function, 564
xml_set_processing_instruction_handler
    function, 564
xml_set_start_namespace_decl_handler
    function, 564
xml_set_unparsed_entity_decl_handler
    function, 564
XMLHttpRequest
    arrays, 472–475
    concurrent Ajax requests and multiple
        objects, 467–472
    creating objects, 436–440, 446–448
    opening objects, 440–441
    send method, 445
XPath, 552–555

Z

zcontext, 319